BALANCING
ACTS

Essays by

EDWARD HOAGLAND

The Lyons Press

First published in hardcover in 1992 by Summit Books/Simon & Schuster Inc.

First Lyons Press edition—1999

Designed by Edith Fowler

Printed in the United States of America

10 9 8 7 6 5 4 3 2 1

Library of Congress Cataloging-in-Publication Data

Hoagland, Edward.
    Balancing acts: essays / by Edward Hoagland.
        p. cm.
    Originally published: New York: Summit Books/Simon & Schuster, 1992.
        ISBN 1-55821-743-6
        I. Title.
    [PS3558.0334B35   1999]
814'.54—dc21   98-31248
                                                              CIP

For Trudy;
and for Charles Simmons,
John Swan,
Brian Swann,
and Alfred Kazin

Contents

CONTENTS

Foreword

An essayist stands in for the rest of us, telling us what he feels and thinks and cares about, what he's seen and learned from childhood on, until finally he enters the country of the blind (as I did in 1991, in point of fact, whereupon two eye operations miraculously restored my vision), and perhaps even beyond. Mysticism, skepticism, a generous empathy, a supple zest and specificity, opinionated wit, informed comment—we expect an essayist to be rather abrasive and yet quite gentle, female and yet male, regretful, cool, exuberant, single-minded, paradoxical, quirky, balanced, passionate, and fair. He should be a sort of man for all seasons, in other words, loafing attentively, seizing risks, mastering data, summarizing what we'd nearly thought to say ourselves. He should know everything that two eyes can be expected to take in, yet make a virtue out of being a freelance observer, operating solo, not as a committee.

It's a tall order, and the twenty-five essays that follow—part memoir, part travel, occasionally controversial—may not fill the bill, but they were written with a good deal of fun and urgency, in the same spirit in which I started my first book in 1952: to write each day what I most wanted to work at, telling the tale or expounding the notion that pressed upon me hardest at the time. And though I remain proud of at least half my novels and hanker to do others, mainly it's more essays that catch me up: "On Snakes," "On Sexuality." These will be next, and on and on, I hope.

—Edward Hoagland
Summer 1998

West on the Zephyr

Bound for California, I recalled that my first memory is of a train—a wreck of the Great Northern's Empire Builder in North Dakota, to be precise, when the tracks slid apart in a rainstorm and our Pullman tipped over. A farmer with a hay wagon took Mother and me (age two and a half) and other "women and children" toward the distant kerosene lamps of a little station.

My parents and grandparents lived on opposite coasts, so I was privileged to have yearly round trips between New York and Seattle before World War II and, on the Chief or Super Chief, to Los Angeles afterward. In those upper berths I enjoyed my earliest privacy, when I zipped myself exultantly in behind the heavy green curtains; or I whiled away the long days watching for grain elevators, Indian reservations, cowhands, white horses, and other emblematic sights of the great prairie states leading into the storied Rockies. I got a penny apiece for those horses, if confirmed as being white and not gray, but wanted to skip nothing anyhow, and even amid the splendors of the dining car—starched tablecloths, sugary oatmeal, tasty ham, shining glassware, comfortable cocoa, and silver forks and spoons—I could gaze out. The Chief, the Empire Builder, the 20th Century Limited—traveling on these famous trains was inimitable.

I have also made the classic five-day sail to Southampton and Cherbourg, with its sudden, deep, hothouse friendships, broken off on the dock but no less perfervid for that, just as one never forgets the sea's blue pitch and sway. A train trip the same distance, three thousand miles, meant for me instead a constant zonal progression of scenery outdoors, the comprehensive change of milieu at the Midwest metropolis of Chicago and hourly stops at way stations where strangers of every character and condition might swing aboard. The startling or poignant confidences a seatmate can lay on you on a long-distance train do not have the same trajectory as shipboard infatuations, because you can't trust the other person even so far as to be there the following morning; he or she may simply vanish during the night. Nor is there the minimal point of reference of a passport vouching for an identity, or the financial letter of credit implied by one's being able to cross between continents. A raffish personality on a ship at least went by the appellation of "fortune hunter," had an international scope, and had purchased a hefty ticket in the first place. For these reasons, a midnight easing of the heart in a train's bar car might seem more chancy, though more comfy too, because to a regular fellow American, subject to American customs and laws.

My father fell into intense shipboard acquaintance with the likes of Jean Renoir and J. D. Salinger during his first-class days as an intercontinental lawyer, whereas when he was a scholarship student going from Kansas City to Yale he had had to work his way east on cattle trains, feeding and watering and shoveling their shit. Once, in middle Missouri, when he got off to relieve himself, he climbed the embankment of the roadbed again, to find the train gone, and walked miles to find a friendly section man, who put him onto a passing caboose. I've ridden in cabooses too, and when I was a child, staring out of the cross-country Vista-Dome, every time the train stopped I knew that a potential new life lay there in front of me: cows to milk, creeks to swim in . . . I had relatives in Ohio, Kansas, and Michigan, as well as in California and Washington, so the breadth of the journey wasn't intimidating. Every bump of the nation registered on me, which itself was a pleasure (we begin by bumping all over town in a womb), and the conversations adults deigned to direct my way hadn't the abrupt, fragmentary quality of talk on a plane. I could stroll about inside the car, stretch my legs in the fresh air on a platform, chug through a thundering storm, feeling the rain and the wind in my face, or be delayed at a nameless location en route by a breakdown, without tumbling out of the sky.

I love to fly. In the simultaneity of balsam firs, paper birches, prickly pears, and palmettos, you appear to bestride the world. Tortillas with salsa, Maine lobster, or Cajun cat-fish—who knows what you'll eat? In Detroit or Des Moines you can get each. It's dizzy, because where will it end? It's like talking into other people's answering machines and, for the efficiency, coming to prefer doing that. But also it's fun; and how nicely important you feel. However, moving between teaching jobs in March, I caught a train, the Lake Shore Limited, in Albany, New York, with a conveniently large col-lection of luggage, bound for Sacramento, another state cap-ital. It was 11:00 P.M., that cozy hour when one is ready for bed, and I had a bunk to look forward to. The platform was bustly with college kids going back after break. Girlfriends, boyfriends, uncles, and aunts make a railway station more festive than your average airport, or a bus station's desperate motif, with the halt and the lame, the homeless and on-the-lam.

"Hitting the lonesome trail?" my woman friend in Ver-mont had asked when I left, though I was coming back. And indeed, train travel is that, without the fast-forward thrust of a jet engine at the back of your seat, throwing your thoughts ahead to your destination. Instead you fussily settle in, the sweet-sour piquancy of your departure unmarred by emergency-escape rehearsals and the sensations of a sardine can being catapulted into the clouds.

In a deliciously intricate matrix of sounds and motions, squeaks, soft shrieks, and swaying vibrations, we gathered speed. I had a friend once, about twelve years ago, who, lying in bed, would say to me: "Welcome aboard!" The essence of life is to balance spontaneity with fidelity; and lickety-split, we began crossing upstate New York, as I sipped wine, re-clining, drowsy. The scent of marijuana filled my sleeping car till Sheila, the Amtrak hostess—small, kind, correct, with a black bob to her hair—announced on the intercom that you couldn't do that. The train rocked and clicketed, blared and rumbled, in a manner that only encouraged sleep. The twelve miles to Schenectady, running from the Hudson River to the Erie Canal above some waterfalls, was one of America's first pieces of track, dating to 1831, more than two decades before service was started from New York to Albany alongside the Hudson. The first U.S. railroad, the Baltimore & Ohio, had been chartered in 1827, though it didn't reach the Ohio River at Wheeling, West Virginia, until 1852. To begin with, of course, railroads functioned to connect saltwater ports like Baltimore and New York with barge traffic on interior waters.

I slept well but woke early, in Erie, Pennsylvania, a town that the Ringling Bros. and Barnum & Bailey circus train had carried me to in 1951, during another of the railroad-rich eras of my antique youth. We set up the big top next to the lake, as I remember, let the elephants bathe, and skinny-dipped ourselves, while some of the performers, as well as a crowd of towners, watched. Even we workhands became exhibitionists in such a daredevil atmosphere. The performers, including sideshow performers, traveled in roomettes like this one I was enjoying now, and my boss, the giraffe man (his neck wasn't elongated; he took care of the giraffes), who was the fat lady's lover, by virtue of that alliance bunked domestically with her. But the rest of us (I was the monkey boy or cat man, depending on which animals I took care of) traveled two to a wooden bed and with the beds stacked three high in the sleeping car, a space so very confined that if your bedmate was fat you needed to sleep with your arms over your head or sleep on your side; and the bunk above was immediately over your face.

Luxuriating in my Lake Shore Limited berth, I polished off last night's complimentary bottle of wine—this was, after all, a rest cure—while gazing at the reddish tinge of the budding trees in the chill rain outdoors. We were an hour late, which is not bad for Amtrak, and I walked through several rollicking coaches to the dining car for "Old Fashioned Railroad French Toast." Amtrak's magazine, *Express*, had nostalgic articles about the "Return of the Horse," "Return of the

14

Farmers' Markets," Thomas Hart Benton, and an "Indian Island" in Puget Sound. In 1869, when the Union Pacific, building from Omaha, met the Central Pacific, building from Sacramento, at Promontory, Utah, it became possible to go coast to coast by train. But not till that same year did the Lake Shore and Michigan Southern Railroad link Buffalo with Chicago, making possible this northeastern run.

Everybody at my table felt leisurely, reflective, and wry, full of their should-have-dones, which in these 1990s are quite likely to concern real estate that one should have bought or perhaps sold or maybe held on to. Two men and a woman, they wanted it known that they had disposable income, that loose-schedule traveling like this was a perk of having made good, but that they weren't *prosperous*. All of us were experienced sizers-up, from interviewing or hiring other people, used to the flux of hometowns that aren't exactly hometowns anymore, businesses that cut, switch, and fold; and so the risky, risqué quality that trains were thought to have in my parents' and grandparents' day—Sister Carrie's day—and in the Gilded Age, when riverboat gamblers, seducers, and swells moved onto trains, is gone. (I myself remember card sharks laying out an illicit blackjack or poker game in the men's lounge, next to the john, where the best conversations took place as well.)

Grifters, mashers, and stowaways—what innocence! The conductor was a fatherly cop, a fount of philosophy, an ace at categorizing humankind. You knew you were getting old when the conductors got younger than you. Trains were so extraterritorial that black men could work rather cheerfully on them—with their own union, incredibly enough, the Brotherhood of Sleeping Car Porters, established in 1925— joking with white people under a flag of truce, no lynch mob in the offing as long as they stayed on board. For a young woman like my mother, going back and forth between Vassar and Aberdeen, Washington, these waiters and porters were the only black people she ever spoke to. Even the woman who was hired to wash her hip-length hair every week, not to mention the cook back home, was white. Later on, after she had married my father, they employed black maids until he reached the conclusion that black people, even in a servant capacity, deflated the resale value of a house.

15

Boarding a train, you left property and propriety, sobriety, religion, and family, behind. "I got a brother from Virginia, and there's nothing about Virginia he likes," a guy drinking coffee in the bar car told me. All kinds of lawless thoughts. I said I was a teacher. "What do you teach *on?*" he said.

Near Cleveland we waited half an hour for a relief crew to reach us by taxi, lest ours surpass the mandated limit of twelve hours for operating the train. Like a slugabed, I slipped into my berth. The drizzle outside was wetter because of snowmelt, and the temperature felt thirtyish, like the tail of the winter, when I got off at Toledo, two hours later, to flex my calves. The Maumee River, where Johnny Appleseed paddled, looked brown with spring runoff.

West of Toledo, a sixty-eight-mile straightaway gave us a chance to strut our speed. Six thousand horsepower, two engines, the fields as brown as November, which March corresponds to. The Lake Shore Limited is fairly grubby, with "heritage" equipment, but the upbeat Sheila, and my car's porter, Berie, a bespectacled, schoolmasterly fellow with a sweet smile, proudly specified that they were "Chicago-based," not New York, and that it didn't always rain hard or seem like one ass-end of a town after another.

Chicago's Union Station, like New York's Grand Central Terminal, Union Station in Los Angeles, Union Station in Washington, and Union Station in Denver, still has grandeur. The California Zephyr, which would take me the rest of the way, pulled in on the next track just as we arrived, so I didn't have time for more sightseeing than a glimpse of the Sears Tower, "tallest in the world," as Sheila promised when we disembarked. I was feeling private, in any case, and wanted to remain in the cocoon of the trip.

The new cars, "superliners," were double-decker, most of the compartments being on top. You enter through a central sliding door and mount narrow circular stairs. My "economy bedroom," though statistically smaller than my "roomette" had been, felt larger because of its layout. The train had actual showers, which astounded me—trains come from the Saturday-night-is-bath-night era—and the toilets didn't immediately flush right down onto the tracks so that the local dogs could sniff our offal. The conductor and porter, both senior personalities assigned to this flagship train, were tactfully gauging everybody who entered for possible "whiners," muttering sagely as they consulted a printout. Cloyee, the porter, a brisk fireplug, originally a Burlington Northern man, had twenty-three years on the railroad. "But you want to get off those freight trains in the winter," he told me. It was Burlington Northern tracks that would carry us clear to Denver. And he, too, was Chicago-born.

The journey grew serious once we had left Chicago's extensive railroad yards and the badlands, wildlands, wastelands that surround them. Black-soil prairie began, with green farm machinery standing around every few miles. Unlike the Rust Belt, food is not an endeavor that goes into eclipse. On small farms or big farms, the mortgage may not get paid, but the sun beats down and food grows. We slow travelers unclenched our nerves a bit more and talked of sisters we had in Syracuse or Salt Lake, of being stationed fifteen years ago at an air base in Boulder or San Antonio, of "D.C." and Louisville, Lafayette, Louisiana, and Liberty, Iowa, crossing modest creek bottoms with curly cottonwoods between the vast soybean and corn fields all the while. The spaciousness out the window and the raucousness of the wheels loosened us, including cynics from the New York train accustomed to the notion that loose lips sink ships. With twenty-four hundred and sixteen miles ahead of us to San Francisco Bay, we couldn't help but relax.

A bulldozer factory at Aurora; pig farms at Princeton; the Spoon River at Kewanee. Popcorn was invented in Galesburg. Monmouth is where Wyatt Earp was born. Great-great-grandparents of mine spent the mid-nineteenth century in Bardolph, Illinois, as farm folks, and I, too, make much of my living from the out-of-doors in the sense that I write about it.

The younger crowd in the lounge car were chatting about their CDs, while in another area, oldsters enumerated *their* CDs, music versus bank balances. The dining-car waiters were vying with each other as to how wiped out they were, how little sleep they'd got, how many meals they'd missed during their six days off. "Love and work. That's what it boils down to," I said to ours, who combed his hair into the highest

Afro and was gentlest with elderly white people who needed his help. Now busted free from loved ones, he was enjoying the mustardy part of life for a traveling man: the departure. I remembered the same giddy pleasure after fights at home years ago, when my train cleared the Bronx's railyards for New England or my plane banked over the smoking buildings of Manhattan toward Anchorage.

The crew chief, Scott, was thirtyish, white, and a facilitator like Sheila, always up and about, organizing the intercom. I asked Cloyee what was done with drunks these days.

"Oh, drunks aren't a problem. You can put him off the train. Call ahead to the police. They take the problem away."

That was the coach passengers, but I pointed toward the bedroom suites, where he carried meals from the dining car.

"Money is everything in what you can do. With money you can just go your own way," he agreed quietly.

I told him my father had once got left behind by a train.

"When this train starts to move, get out of the way, because I'm going to get *on!* I'm always on!" It was still no joke for a black man to get left behind.

Grain elevators had marked our progress and measured the decline of the sun. We crossed the Mississippi at dusk in a mist at Burlington, Iowa. Both shores, with their froggy-looking marshes, and the couple of islands in view had a shaggy aspect, as if Huck Finn and Jim could have rafted through here on the sly among the drift logs without being spotted. Whether it's Mount Vesuvius, the Sphinx, or the Mississippi, whenever you look at an icon you receive a montage of the photos or more bookish imagery that you have absorbed ever since your teens; and like the Mississippi, railroads, losing three thousand miles of track every year, are becoming like that.

"Bob doesn't fly," said a compact blond Floridian who frequently smoked in the vestibule. "Bob is the man I'm with." Standing, swaying, she bent an ear to another Floridian, seventy-something, with a New Jersey accent, who would tell us about her household and financial arrangements with her son and daughter-in-law. In return, I volunteered the information that I earned about twenty dollars an hour from writing but that my surgeon had just earned a thousand dollars an hour for doing a job on me.

Speaking of surgeons, we had one on board, a gray-haired lady with a mystical quaver, frail and mentally shaky, it seemed, who said she had fled California a decade before, fearing earthquakes, and whose itinerary was complex indeed. We also had a world traveler, a woman of sturdy years with a canvas carryall, the proverbial expert on dodges and scams, who was therefore able to foil the plaint of another woman, humbler and sadder, who claimed to have been transplanting herself with a hundred-dollar bill as her sole sustenance and to have lost it. She kept repeating this in tones loud enough for a lot of people to hear, until finally somebody started to take up a collection. And this was when our world traveler stepped in, assured that it must be a scam—though who knows if she was right? Anyway, a sufficiency of good Samaritans contributed money that our unfortunate friend ate supper with us.

In the dining car, the splendid dim scenery swept by perpetually. Mount Pleasant. Ottumwa. Other isolated constellations of lights, cattle pens, grain bins, houses and shacks—"that vast obscurity beyond the city, where the dark fields of the republic rolled on under the night," as *The Great Gatsby* ends. The impetus for Melville's Ishmael's going to sea on a whaling ship (on land, of course, he would have boarded a train) was his impulse to pause before coffin warehouses, bring up the rear of funeral processions, and knock people's hats off in the street; and there were a number of passengers on our train—our total census was four hundred and seven (out of all the Americans crossing the country that day!)—who seemed grim about the mouth, whose cages had been rattled and who in fact were seething, underpaid, beat on by their bosses, with relatives in trouble, if you talked with them. And the money invested in our journey—was it going to be enough fun? asked one man.

Over baked halibut, I spoke with two New Yorkers who were leaving forever, uprooting in early middle age, a lesbian couple fleeing the megalopolis to find a new life. They were going to wander, loaf on their savings a few months, then settle near the older one's brother, who was equipped with a wife and children, a ranch house on a leafy street. She'd been a typist for nineteen years, a flying-fingers job with no retirement plan. The other woman was "in health care" and

19

didn't mention the furnace of AIDS but spoke of the home-less delirium in the streets above which they had been living for umpteen years. They wanted neighbors with children, two-car garages, and flower gardens, "the American dream," as the younger one, who intended to learn to drive and to trim a hedge, said.

The waiter's patter is half the production at these rail-road meals. The menu of beef, fish, or fowl is succinct, the vegetables are fresh, the dessert is sweet; but I waited for the summary justice that is dispensed, vivid in my memories of Empire Builder trips. Sure enough, when a family of four took the next table and the two small kids climbed into their chairs, one reached instantly for the tip and grabbed three coins. His sister didn't.

"*That* one's going to be a Rockefeller. But that girl's go-ing to wind up on welfare if she don't watch out. She don't pay no attention to money, does she? Don't want to pick it up."

My New York tablemates, getting up, asked the waiter if he would be certain to collect their tip or if the other man would.

"I'll break his fingers if he does."

Just so, fifty years ago, when I had misbehaved at the table and my mother asked the waiter what she ought to do—she generally appealed to the nearest witness for guid-ance, public humiliation being its own punishment—he picked up her steak knife and told me, "I'd cut your fingers off, young gentleman!"

When Harry Met Sally was shown on the lounge car's video. I have eye problems and couldn't see it and had missed more important things, but your mind's eye becomes your main eye anyhow. Oil storage tanks, milo fields, meat cattle in a pancake landscape, one-horse hamlets where a young boy walks against the flow of the train alongside the tracks "to feel like you're going five hundred miles an hour," as a friend of mine says. Osceola. Creston. The Iowa whistle-stops, as we raced through the dark, made me wistful, remembering two winters and springs when I lived in Iowa City very happily, in love with a gawkily willowy social worker who was intuitive, competent, much put-upon, as social workers do tend to be, who played the piano on Saturdays and Sundays, filled the house with flowers to last through the week, and took me out visiting Amish farmers and friends roundabout in that rolling lush country. The Amish with their joyful church services, great big workhorses, curried and effusive acreage, propane refrigerators, and splendiferous Sunday dinners—six vegetables, three meats, truly the Lord's work—had been an education for me. And when a plague of locusts descends, as happened during a drought in a later year when I visited, and your Amish hostess has just endured a mastectomy, you do sense in addition life's biblical scale.

With age, we become responsible for what's in our heads—the character of the memories there, the music we are familiar with, the storehouse of books we have read, the people we can phone, the scenery that we know and love. Our memories become our dreams, and when your eyes go bad you find out what's there. You either recognize a towhee's song or not, know an indigo bunting's or a mourning dove's, and the wild geese going overhead. Rediscovering your nose, you lift food toward your nostrils to smell as children do. I sometimes see what I want to see—an ice cream truck parked at the curb that isn't; the yellow bell of a jazz trumpet in a wheat field. In Iowa, though, I remembered my friend, now comfortably married to a psychiatrist. A decade before I knew her, I had crossed Iowa by train, going east in the company of a summertime love from Colorado, both of us agog in the Vista-Dome as we watched the last cowboys bump past in their pickup trucks and the Missouri River go under the tracks. She was twenty-one, I was thirty-four, so I thought the age difference might be too much. But quite swiftly, she won a Pulitzer Prize and married a man way past thirty-four and far more distinguished than I. We meet on the fringes of cultural events, she a patroness whose check perhaps indirectly pays me.

Before our Zephyr reached Omaha I fell asleep, lulled by the rock-a-bye wheels and the tick-a-tick tracks.

At breakfast, with McCook, in western Nebraska, slipping by outside the window, we were talking about roots and genealogy—the usual accidental collection of people. A courtly white-haired North Carolina man said his sister's hobby and duty as county historian was looking up deeds and the like, and it bothered her to have to read so often that "I bequeath my slave Hettie to my daughter Sarah." He glanced at the waiters congregated around the dumbwaiter, waiting for dishes and trays.

"To have and to hold," I said. I remembered my father's alarmed anecdotes about how hair-raising it was when his commuter train out of New York City occasionally would stall in the late evening on the tracks over Harlem on its way to suburbia and some hero would finally descend to the mean streets below to ask for police protection. The whole carful of bankers and lawyers and ad executives had begun to hallucinate about what would happen to them if the populace below figured out they were there.

Thursday was maids' day off, so that was one day when a scattering of black faces appeared on the train, but it was hard to imagine what those self-effacing, hard-scrubbing women we knew in our houses *did* in the dangerous and lurid environs of Harlem when they were "off." I suppose the idea of a social disease, as much as "property values," caused my father to ban them from the house. Later, I heard my mother ask him what it was about her and their marriage that he had appreciated most. "You were always a clean woman," he answered after considering awhile. Admittedly they were not getting on well, but he had come a long way from his Missouri days and working his passage to Europe on a cattle boat the first time. (My happiest-looking photo of him is from that boat.) When I was about ten, he did employ a black woman, named Arizona, to cook, but she was fired because she and I fell into the habit of giggling when I pulled on her apron strings, as though a flirtation had grown up. She also let slip, while feeding my infant sister Gerber's baby food, that she'd used to chew her own babies' food, since they didn't have Gerber's, instead of mincing it with a knife and fork as white folks presumably would do. It seemed too primitive—as startling as a glimpse out of Africa or some custom lurking from slavery—for her to stay. What else might there be?

We crossed the Nebraska-Colorado line in a snowstorm, with visibility a quarter mile. A lady who'd grown up on a milo and cattle farm in Kansas not far from here told me emphatically, "There's a reason why this is so empty!" She'd fled to Oregon years before; had been visiting her sick mother and caught the train to unwind on the way home. No, she insisted when I asked, she didn't even like *The Wizard of Oz,* not Kansas even in that peppy guise.

Soldiers, college kids, had their separate lingo. Leaning in the aisle—the coaches a war-zone scene of sprawled, sleeping bodies—they passed code words intended to mean I'm O.K., You're O.K. And a number of people wore Mona Lisa smiles, riding quietly encapsulated in thought. But other gray-haired souls had ventured east to see ailing parents or friends and were publicly pensive. The future lay in the West, a plastics salesman said. "Pain, pain," he muttered without going into particulars. We were running two and a half hours late because of brake troubles and our having been shunted behind a hundred-fifty-car freight, Cloyee said. The prairie looked ever more primal in the sleet storm. I peered outside, then into the washroom mirror because a police artist, interviewed in yesterday's Omaha paper, mentioned how people's ears fall, mouths droop, and necks jowl with age.

Sick parents were not as anxious a subject to talk about as troubles involving your children, however. I might hear in detail about arthritis or Alzheimer's disease, but no more than a wince in reference to how worried the same person was on a daughter's behalf. Yet we also had couples going to Las Vegas for a blow-off.

"It lets it all out," said a tool-and-die man. "You get successful, you become the victim of your own decisions. You learn to draw up a contract the hard way, because you got yourself sued. Human nature—partners—you learn about too."

Leaning forward, he told me he had been through the Vietnam War, but "that was just training for building a business up," keeping it afloat till his kids grew self-reliant enough so his wife could join him ("First as the receptionist!" she said) and he didn't feel like he was sinking alone. Both tall, athletic, with short-of-sleep faces, like people from a coffee ad—Sunday workers, not tennis players—they shook their heads.

We talked about airports. Did I remember when you could visit a client and get back to town to your children for supper—or piggyback calls on clients, if you stayed over? Airports were airports, you could get somewhere on a decent schedule; knowing your way around mattered. Congestion brings everybody down to the lowest common denominator. "The point is, when is it cheaper to charter a plane?" He had bought his installation crews mobile homes to travel in for trips of up to a thousand miles, which was both faster and cheaper than flying them there and putting them up at the Ramada Inn.

"We have a society where your customers sue you for maintenance mistakes their own employees make after the equipment changes hands—like they don't put *oil* in! Sometimes the most precious asset you have is just a handful of workers who use their heads and have an honest notion of what work is, and yet you can't really pay 'em what they're worth without being unbusinesslike. I'm the guy with the money, and I feel more akin to that guy that just has a paycheck than to my salaried man that wants his dues covered at the country club."

Jennie, his wife, with tously hair styled blond but a face just as skeptical, said Vegas was a dependable blast. Three days of it, and they'd fly home. "Three days does it, with the health club and all."

She told me they'd gone off to India to seal a deal, hoping to squeeze in some vacation time together. And the Indian businessman had put one of his sons, in a Jaguar, at their disposal. Barreling down a road, he had smashed into a cluster of five or six bicyclists, sending them flying through the air, and gunned the accelerator so he wouldn't be stopped. " 'It was of no matter,' he said, while I got sick in the car and sick afterwards. I'll never forget that."

"The good old U.S.A. I love it," said another woman. She was in business also. "I'm a builder," she told me, with a direct, pretty smile. "L.A.-based."

Softer-shouldered, small, she and the tool-and-die woman began chatting cozily about Himalayan cats versus Persian and Siamese, with the marvelous fluency women often have.

As we floated through Fort Morgan like a bubble located in the middle sky, we saw a coyote scouting the feedlots. This was "the season when farmers pull calves," said my Kansas-raised friend who disliked *The Wizard of Oz.*

At Denver we had a chance to stroll the spacious old

24

station. Tall benches, chalkboards, large ticket counters, a newspaper store, a coffee shop. There were some cheeky Indian physiognomies and bent cowpoke hats with seam-stitched visages underneath them, who, in the hollering bus-tle, joined us in swinging aboard. One cowboy was bound for the proud redneck town of Thompson, Utah, where loggers and dozer drivers have been beating up tree huggers lately in a dispute about land management. On the platform he stubbed out a "coffin nail" and tapped a toothpick out of a leather holder and set it into the cut of his mouth.

Being as this was Saturday, we also had trippers along for the five-hour ride up over the Rockies' Front Range to Glenwood Springs (not tree huggers; more the dental-floss-user type), there to soak in the mineral pools overnight and catch Amtrak back on Sunday. Dianne and Bill Robie, from Golden, have done this many times, for skiing outings too, and once in 1964, in what was their best courtship adventure, jumped on a freight-train flatcar at the top of the Continen-tal Divide, hid themselves, and rode through the six awesome miles of Moffat Tunnel, on down to Denver. She works for the chamber of commerce and he for Coors Beer. He proved an enthusiastic guide for me as the Zephyr coiled slowly up the two-percent grade, through lovely slots and intimate notches that unfolded a string of one-minute glimpses of piney, vertiginous, snowy, rock-framed scenery—the Roosevelt National Forest—in between an erratic succession of twenty-nine tunnels.

Dianne was quilting a pillow while Bill pointed out wooden mining flumes, old wagon tracks, and Mount Evans and James Peak, both of them over 13,000 feet high and partly hidden by the snow squalls that reduced visibility. In the middle of Moffat Tunnel, at 9,239 feet, I felt the grade change. We'd crossed the Divide and tilted downward. Ten minutes of darkness, then daylight, and the precarious ham-let of Fraser, "Icebox of America," composed of scattered cabins and prefabs, with a river of the same name, in its infancy, alongside. Loads of ducks winged and flittered. Many geese grazed in the sparse fields. Three eagles stood in the trees. We saw several bands of deer. Spring flocks of small birds in biblical numbers gleaned the thawed ground of bugs and seeds.

As we moved on, there were sudden, swift vistas of peaks and saddles, valleys like hammocks, passes like chutes, although at the towns of Granby and Kremmling, pleasing plateaus of high-up remoteness spread out into ranching country. Then came more private spells of wild terrain, narrow gulches, secret ravines, twisty, and stirring for me. Fraser Canyon. Byers Canyon. Gold rock or red rock whipsawed into pagoda shapes by the young Colorado River, with white rapids or roiling stretches often a molten green. Little river-bottom ranches relieved the tumultuous congruence of water and cliff occasionally. Gore Canyon extended twenty-two miles, with walls well over a thousand feet high, the water corkscrewing in shortcuts that we couldn't take or simply tripping lightly down its stairsteps, carving intense, enviable pockets of meadow beside purling pools I'd like to go back to and camp at for a week.

Out of Gore Canyon, we left the sweet companionship of trees. Sagebrush on yellow or red dry soil (though it was raining) took its place. Red Canyon is where the Colorado acquired its name, which means "red," and the vivid rocks were just as dramatic in shape. Glenwood Canyon, taller, browner, more bulky and gnarled, with precipitous walls and a swirling riverbed where you could drown, was scary if you cast your mind back to the early white men tiptoeing through here hoping not to meet Indians.

This sequence of canyons was the best part of my trip and the Zephyr's midpoint to San Francisco Bay. The sun came out for its sunset between Glenwood Springs and Grand Junction, amid open spaces everywhere except for the ridgeline of mountains. Baxter Mountain. The Parachute Mountains. Grand Mesa.

In the dining car, Scottish accents, German tourists. A union shop steward argued with a graduate student about how America had won the cold war. At my table we discovered that the headwaiter had seated three "QA people" together—Quality Assurance; a checker, an inspector, and a supervisor—with me. Quickly the hierarchy asserted itself. The checker, a modest, somewhat stooped woman, had not finished high school. Anne, the supervisor, by contrast, had won a master's degree in business administration, earned fifty thousand dollars a year, and oversaw nine inspectors and sixty-three checkers. She had a heady, push-ahead, gay sort of energy and, hearing that I was a teacher, told me with understandable resentment that she had been informed by an influential teacher in high school that she wasn't college material. I agreed teachers shouldn't play God.

Their pride in QA work was evident. It might be potato chips you were inspecting, but it was sure crucial. The problem, as Anne told me, was not that humans were more fallible than machines. "That's the cliché, but the machinery fails more often than the humans do. Except I have a hell of a time convincing my bosses of that."

The inspector said yes. She was an Indiana woman, of income, authority, and size midway between the slender checker and huskier Anne, and confided that she'd vowed to herself many years ago that she'd "see California before my sixtieth birthday." Good as her word, she was going to do so—arrive on precisely that day. Telling us about her family and family's families, she had a veritable root ball of attachments to account for the delay. Anne seemed much more alone in the world, as if maybe blowing her own horn to keep herself company. White-collar, blue-collar, "pink-collar": she'd witnessed it all. We chatted after supper, while James Bond's *License to Kill* blared from the video screen and Utah's Ruby Canyon, Green River Valley, Price River Canyon, and Spanish Fork Canyon swept by unseen in the dark of the night.

A hungry childhood; a mastery of computer flow charts and how to "network" at a conference—now Anne had a constituency of admirers and pals, so that her boss had become alarmed and, her secretary had told her that morning over the phone, was seizing upon her absence to go through her back file of faxes and, after demanding her computer codes, all of her disks, looking for anything he could nail her on.

"I don't *want* his job. I don't know if *mine's* worth it!" she told me.

She loved her job; yet was it displacing the truer values? The only child of an only child, she was traveling in a compartment with her mother, who, they had just found out, was terminally sick. Her lung had collapsed as she was being examined for a breathing ailment, and they were on this

27

train on doctor's orders lest the altitude shifts on a plane collapse the lung again. Who would take care of her? She lived three hours away from Anne, and what was the point of the fancy salary? You rack up a good performance chart as your mother dies? Shouldn't she throw over the super-charged job and move in with her? "There is a better way to live." This was a chicken-farm disease that cumulatively de-stroyed your lungs. "Ten hours a day walking through those chicken sheds breathing that dust, and never knew about it!" The ethics of business were not taught in school.

But she was buoyant also, full of curiosity and zest. We parted, and that night the train split, her five-car section veering from Salt Lake toward L.A., another five cars head-ing toward Oregon, and my seven going straight west.

By dawn, we were so late—about three hours—that Cloyee exclaimed that he scarcely remembered when he'd last seen the first town, Elko, Nevada, in daylight. "And on a sleeper you don't get much call for towns like him."

I'd been in Elko for *National Geographic* a couple of years before, and after hours one night the magazine's photogra-pher had taken me to drink in a whorehouse where a young lady had shown us the angel tattooed on one of her breasts. She told us she had never done this kind of thing until now. Her baby was lodged in his father's hands, and her lawyer wanted his money up front. She rode "the Hound" to San Francisco to visit the boy but didn't work there because "the police have no sense of humor, you know? It's better here, where it's legal."

I'd believed her, she was so vulnerable-looking and clear-skinned, but when I asked Cloyee if he would have, he shook his head.

No kids; but he has been married three years. Sleeps or rests through the first three of his six days off, even if friends drop in. Wakes at 5:30 A.M., goes out for the paper, and reads it until he can sleep again. Then in and out of slum-berland. Plum-colored, short, quick, with a quarter century of seniority, so that the railroad would have to buy him out if it folds, Cloyee—replete with turn-aside expertise in blunting white people's insults—is probably a hard man to wrong. During the summer he pulls rank and transfers himself to the Empire Builder, on the more placid northern route, which affords him a schedule of twelve days on, twelve days off.

In 1919 America had 265,000 miles of railroad track, lately cut to 150,000, and this flagship train runs on an anthology of famous lines: the Burlington Northern from Chicago to Denver; the Denver & Rio Grande Western on to Salt Lake; the Union Pacific from Salt Lake City to Winnemucca, Nevada; and the Southern Pacific from Winnemucca west. Our sleeping cars were new million-dollar jobs, but the lounge car dated to the Santa Fe era of the 1950s, when kids used to go to the Grand Canyon that way. In the summer of 1941 I went, and the complete experience—the all-day mule ride down the stunning South Wall, the red-rock tables and strata, the silence like nothing I'd ever heard, until we got to the roaring river at the bottom, in whose surge two deer were being whirled to their deaths—established a permanent awe and love for the West in me.

Also, when I went home, I wanted to be a trackwalker. The Pullman porter had pointed these people out to me, and back in suburban Connecticut, I discovered that our railroad spur off the New York–Boston line had a man whose job was to walk the roadbed regularly, looking for loose fishplates. Riding this "Toonerville Trolley," as we called it, I'd watch for him (my father did too, still having a vagrant streak). He would show up eventually, a skinny fellow in a shabby jacket, with a walking stick, whose face you would never see as the train passed because he was always looking down. His task was to see if the rails hopped. Perhaps I read into his attitude as well an impatience to have us be gone so that he could get back to his main job, which was to smell the lilacs and honeysuckle in people's backyards, look at their cats and chickens and dogs and the big old elms, watch for turtles laying eggs in a sandpile next to a pond, listen to the toads purring a song. I was outdoors a great deal too, scouting for ribbon snakes, milk snakes, spotted salamanders, screech owls, and had come to be known to the postman and other itinerants of our road as Nature Boy: as in "Hey, Nature Boy!" But scenery had more pull for everyone then. People commonly spent time outside and, without air-conditioning, knew what the weather was, and because their eardrums were in better shape, they heard more of the subtleties in the quiet air. The out-of-doors was a virtual newspaper that could be read at a glance by a great many people—limey soil or wet soil recognized by its flowers and plants, a skyline of trees identified by species and even board feet.

We had glided through the magical "emptiness" of Nebraska by night, and then Utah's majesty too, missing both because we couldn't see in the dark. But neither would have registered on our minds as landscape used to do before people flew. One's natural fear of the desert also evaporates. At Winnemucca (named for a Paiute chief) at breakfast time, we didn't even wolf down extra water as we gazed outside, though here began the ruggedest stretch for California-bound pioneers. My companions, over bran muffins, were a young man from Bakersfield who had been to visit his grandparents in Elko, his first expedition out of his native state, and who struck me as one of that twenty-four percent of Americans who can't find America on a world map; and a divorcée who looked scarcely older but was clever and savvy, possessed of a six-year-old daughter in Salt Lake, and was off to visit her boyfriend, a traveling accountant working in Reno. She was so personable, seemed so adjustable, I could see her remarried already.

The Cortez Mountains. The Shoshone Mountains. And Battle Mountain, a big, complicated, battlemented one with snow on top. We admired these. At the town of Lovelock, the Trinity Range lies to the northwest and the Humboldt Range to the southeast of the tracks. For three hundred miles we followed the Humboldt River valley, till its waters utterly petered out. In these "sinks," plants live on the dew at best and save strength even by their dim coloration.

Down in the vestibule with the hard-case smokers, I heard about divorce law and diabetes, bankruptcies and insurance-policy outrages, and points of love across this sloppy broad continent, where the individuals I was talking with could go to collapse or find the proverbial bosom to cry on. "Blood is thicker than water." I said I'd lost three hundred thousand dollars by my divorce—not to my poor wife, whom I bore no grudge, but because my father in his anger had disinherited me.

Bereft people confess to having Parkinson's or Lou Gehrig's disease, or children who refuse to communicate with them, lulled by the tranquil clacketing of the train and its fateful inevitability of arrival (unless—big deal, compared to a plane!—it went off the tracks). A small, smiling senior citizen told me how he'd robbed a bank in his salad days, during the 1930s, the Great Depression. "Never caught." The flesh that padded his cheeks had become an androgynous mask fissured occasionally by his grin, though retaining its teenage cast somehow, like an ancient habit that can't be lost. Another man told me about adulterous lunch-hour seductions in Central Park. What fun in your thirties, your forties. Mud smeared on your pant leg, your suit jacket drenched after a thunderstorm—you'll find inspiration to explain it, running back to Rockefeller Center. "Necessity is really the mother of invention." Highlights of your life, he said.

An hour east of Sparks, Nevada, we encountered the Truckee River, debouching onto the desert from the Sierra Nevadas with a delicious sparkle and birds sporting in it and even a Sunday fisherman. The sight of running water again was exhilarating. My eyes dashed like feet to go wading. The land lunged upward a little, beginning to build toward the big spine of mountains that stood between us and the Pacific. My feelings were different from when we had approached the Rockies. The Rockies are a kind of midriff for the nation; cross it, and you still have the desert ahead, a vast mileage. But the Sierras signify almost the end of the rainbow—goldfields, *Roughing It* stuff, or pristine, riverine forests and flowery bee meadows smelling like honey for a hundred miles, as John Muir described them, extending to redwood beaches lipped by the splendidly reiterative surf rimming the boundless Pacific. The pot o' gold. Letheland. Baghdad-by-the-Bay. Oranges for the picking. It's different, climbing toward California. Most of us have been happy as Cinderella there, at least if we cleared out before midnight.

At Sparks the Zephyr added an extra locomotive and changed engineers for the remaining eight hours to Oakland. Also three cars for the wiped-out losers in Reno, just ahead, who might be ready to go home earlier than they had expected. The "Fun Train" was parked on a siding for the regulars who would stay until late. Sparks is a railroad town, though the Nugget Hotel sticks up phallically in the middle of it. But Reno retains its wicked aura in my mind's eye, the divorce capital of my youth, where rich dames took their cheating husbands to the cleaners and cowboys earned drinking money at stud. Harrah's and Circus Circus are located near the train station, and Bally's is three miles east, self-contained, with its own hairdressers, gift shops, restaurants, if you want to avoid the panhandlers that two yuppie gamblers who boarded complained of.

However, surprising myself, I went off and wept awhile, as I sometimes do on a trip, drawing the curtains in my mini-bedroom. The same circumstances that seem like freedom one minute are loneliness personified the next. There is a reason why most good travel books are written on a shoestring. The superlative traveler is a whit down-at-heels, a trifle disreputable. His antecedents and his bona fides are questionable. Show him hospitality and if he doesn't plunder your silverware, he may smile like a villain while he is with you and then pillory you in his book. He is likely to be both smarter than and not as smart as he appears, or more weirdly dangerous, a devotee of voluntary poverty, an Eton boy like George Orwell down and out in London and Paris, certain to come up with lawless ideas. Or, as with Lawrence Durrell, Sir Richard Burton, T. E. Lawrence, his sexuality is faintly alarming. Why *is* he traveling? Besides the exuberance of going to far climes, there is usually a whiff of personal failure, opportunism, disloyalty, pecuniary embarrassment, the rat's scuttling off a sinking ship, or the misfit's eternal, compulsive restlessness. As with Marco Polo—who can believe him? Hasn't he just seen too much? One's fifties, my decade, are an age for grievance collecting anyway.

"It's a strange old world," said a codger in the bar car, where I went for a shot of comradeship. A railroad bar car is a pretty innocent site in this era of red-eye flights between tax havens halfway around the world and "mules" coming into the airport with their intestines loaded with heroin in condoms. It tends to be older people who believe we are responsible for our lives—old conductors, with that stern gaze: you either have your ticket or haven't. *Leave it behind* is the motto of so much travel, but in a train, at least you aren't skipping much in the way of bumps and grinds, not in the absurdist manner of a plane.

My great-grandfather Hoagland helped haul supplies by

mule and wagon for the construction of the Atchison, To-
peka & Santa Fe as it crossed Kansas to meet the Southern
Pacific at Deming, New Mexico, in 1881, for the second cross-
continental link. (The Canadian Pacific didn't cross Canada
till 1885.) And my grandfather Morley, on the other side,
had his own little railroad of sorts—three locomotives that
pulled virgin logs out of the old-growth forest to Gray's Harbor, Washington, where they were loaded onto Japanese
ships. My mother, too, was loaded onto a Japanese timber
boat, on the occasion of her falling in love with a man deemed
unsuitable because he'd been previously married. She was
twenty-two, and with her older brother, Dave, as a chaperon,
was sent on a tour of Japan, Beijing, and the Great Wall of
China, which, with the long bouts of seasickness coming and
going, were expected to expunge the cad from her mind.
(Thirty years later, however, and to my father's heartfelt
dismay, they found each other again.) My grandfather had
married a schoolteacher, and enjoyed the comradeship of a
schoolteacher mistress in downtown Aberdeen as well, during his years of roaring success. Not exactly a Babbitt, though
I knew him only later, when he had retired to apartment life
in Los Angeles and bungalow life in La Jolla and his Washington acreage had been logged off and the second growth
sold to Georgia Pacific and his sons had moved down to
Oregon with the proceeds and purchased virgin timber to
log in the Coast Range there.

My mother did social work in New York for a little
while—in the 1920s it was directed toward Italian families,
with then-scary customs in then-scary neighborhoods—and,
in Macy's personnel department, took part in a pioneering
industrial psychology project. After her marriage, she took
courses in flower arranging, had lunches and teas, went into
New York to concerts, was an active churchgoer, and during
the war taught first aid to air wardens, which intrigued her.
I remember her delight when the first dishwashers reached
the market, around 1950. My parents' marriage was about
average in its quotient of comity; a late marriage, but sexy. I
remember them wrestling on the couch when my father came
home from work when I was about three, and his name for
my mother's breasts, which was "the twins." Wear and tear
afflicted their relationship, as well as the later illusion of in-

fidelity—my father's with his buxom secretary from Minnesota (who *did* marry the boss who succeeded him and thereupon was exiled by the oil company that employed them to its offices in Saudi Arabia) and my mother's with her old flame, who turned up decades after that trip to Japan, chastened after a buffeting in his own business career. I don't know whether either of these was a carnal or a platonic affair, but platonic infidelities can have the same painful effect as the carnal kind, I think, from the evidence of my own and others' marriages. Anyway, a marriage from 1931 to 1967, when my father died, is no mean feat to maintain, and though he did not share her taste for church (she tended, too, to get crushes on the ministers, maybe because their salient virtues were different from a Wall Street lawyer's), they vigorously walked out of plays like *A Streetcar Named Desire* and *Who's Afraid of Virginia Woolf* together, and cut a two-week vacation in India to two days, once they'd got there and experienced "the dirt." They were an upwardly mobile pair, always hanging out with people with plummy accents—my father joined a fashionable cavalry squadron of the New York National Guard in the thirties and sang Gilbert and Sullivan in the Blue Hill Troupe—whereas I, like many of their friends' children and many writers, was downwardly mobile.

Sitting in the lounge car, I gave my tablemate, a board-game inventor from Big Sur, a précis of my monetary situation. He said he had lost a house in the settlement of *his* divorce but that he had just remarried: "a most amiable woman," with "a lap pool" behind her palisades house. She ran a decorating business, and after they had thrashed out the details of who would pay for what and what the deal was and were sitting poolside one morning over coffee, opening their mail as husband and wife, she'd handed him an envelope addressed to her.

" 'This will amuse you, dear,' she tells me," he said. "It was a check from a bank for close to a hundred thousand bucks. 'This will come four times a year from my trust, so we can live wherever we want and *do* whatever we want,' she tells me."

I chatted with a gold miner from Winnemucca who operates a computer that's as "simple as the buttons on an elevator." It administers cyanide, lime, and water in the correct proportions to reduce the ore to ninety-six percent gold, which is then shipped by highway to Salt Lake City. We joked about how those armored cars must be watched. Didn't they run decoys, empties?

"Yours sounds like a yuppie job," I suggested.

"It sure is that." He smiled, mellow.

We climbed slowly for an hour alongside the coils of the Truckee River (named for Winnemucca's father) from Reno to Truckee, in California, through foothills, saddles, and passes with a sweet range of views, more open and spacious than Colorado's had seemed. At five thousand feet there was smooth, shallow snow on the ground, though snow sheds projected over the tracks to fend off avalanches in a few places. In the winter some of this region gets thirty-five feet of snowfall, and forty-two members of the Donner Party, stranded near here, starved to death a hundred forty-five years ago.

Big Hole Tunnel, four minutes long, constituted the Sierras' divide, as Moffat Tunnel had in the Rockies. I lunched with a tech analyst from Santa Cruz and a phys ed teacher from Martinez—a volleyball spiker, as she confessed, when we asked. This two-hour passage from the resort hub of Truckee to Colfax, a tidier town of a thousand people, through the heart of the mountains was superbly scenic— Donner Pass and Emigrant Gap made easy. Castle Peak; Black Butte Mountain. Gold miners' flumes and slag piles, jumbo pine trees spreading over yellow sandy ground, and the astounding blue gorge, two thousand feet deep, of the North Fork of the American River, flowing down to Sacramento eventually.

Our end-of-the-journey, lip-of-the-continent cheeriness was enhanced by blue skies, balmy weather, clean-looking meadows and forests, spiring creeks and granite ravines, cerulean lakes and grassy valleys. However hard it must have been to build this stretch of railroad—and at "Cape Horn," Chinese laborers were lowered in baskets to hack at the cliff— the ride nowadays is benignly dreamy.

I lounged in the lounge with a San Francisco legal eagle of the female persuasion, whose career might be a paradigm for many Californians', though she was stubby, not tall, black-haired, not blond. Claire said she was helping fold banks into one another and sell credit-card operations, but she had grown up on the Arkansas River in a ramshackle house that got regularly flooded, across the street from a tavern known informally as the Bucket of Blood, where her mother worked as a barmaid. Her father, a war vet, had a metal plate in his head from a jeep accident, and she inhabited the same bed as two of her sisters, sitting up late reading under the overhead light while they slept. She chose only "the thickest books," because three was her monthly quota from the library bookmobile: *The Count of Monte Cristo,* or Dickens, or Sir Arthur Conan Doyle. Also, she collected bottles at two cents apiece to buy books with at the secondhand furniture store down the street.

Her mother swore like a trooper, her father tried to maintain discipline with his razor strop—this was the 1950s—but her obsessive study habits mostly exempted Claire from whippings. She was hungry a lot, however, because he drank and both parents' pride was such that they made the children come home from school at lunchtime if there wasn't a quarter for each of them to pay to eat, instead of applying for the program of free meals, though there might be nothing to eat at home either, and only beer nuts from the Bucket of Blood for supper.

When her father died, the man at the furniture store became her mother's protector and let her run it for him, having a wife and another store in the next town upriver. The store provided a place where the seven kids could receive phone messages, and the mother, alone, was not too proud to accept a turkey from the church at Thanksgiving. Claire, working three jobs, saved money for college, only to find that her mother had secretly spent it. Got through anyhow; took the civil service exam as an escape. Sought a posting to New York City with the IRS; did law school at night; saw the city courtesy of her fifty-year-old bachelor boss. Practiced there briefly; then drove west listening to tapes for the California bar exam.

"You get the picture?" she asked. "And what brings you here? Is your pen for hire? Is your heart torn?"

I said I'd hoped as a youngster to ride in a parlor car in state to Hollywood, having sold a big book to the movies, but instead I was just going to Sacramento to teach.

"What a shame! Maybe you should be riding buses. That's where the stories are."

"Are they?"

"*Were.* I should take pity on you and tell you my mother's story so you can go to Hollywood."

"You have a feel for the underdog," I said.

We looked at the opulent lowlands—eucalyptus, live oaks, almond and pear trees—inclining into the Central Valley, with its rice and tomatoes; then the Tiffany city of San Francisco, in a gemstone setting. She had come this way from Denver for fun and had watched me gleaning what I could from our fellow passengers.

"Why not?" she told me. "My mother was born in Chicago, and when she was twelve, she was shipped to L.A. to an aunt—said to be. Her parents couldn't take care of her, but in two or three years she said she realized she was being trained by her 'aunt' for a prostitute's role. 'Mother' and 'daughter' for a father-and-son combo. So she ran away. She borrowed and saved for a ticket home. But the bus driver she landed with, for a 'prank,' a cruel and misogynist trick, made a practice of stranding unattached girls at the Hoover Dam. It was under construction in 1931. He would tell them to get out and use the rest room, and drive away. So there she was, at the Arizona-Nevada borderline, without her suitcase, without any money. Fifteen years old. At the diner but couldn't even pay for her pie. Forced to choose which trailer house full of construction workers she should ask to spend the night in. My father was having coffee, and he told her she'd better trust him—he was better than the rest—and the rest just laughed. So what was she to do? He was 'a perfect gentleman. But one thing led to another,' she said."

We were passing McClellan Air Force Base. Claire was natty and neat, with a fin of a nose, small freckled hands, and an attorney's intentness, a nice but quick-vanishing smile.

"Make it a screenplay. There's your chance." She laughed.

We pulled into Sacramento, 1840s fur-trading hub, 1850s gold-hunting center, terminus of the Pony Express from Saint Joseph, Missouri, in 1860–61. Sacramento was founded, as Nueva Helvetia, by a former Swiss Army Captain named John Sutter, who died penniless in the East three decades after gold was discovered on some of his land. A big railroad museum, a good jazz festival, and much state politicking now mark the town.

Arrivals. Maybe it'll all come together in the Golden State, I thought, but the professor who was supposed to meet me wasn't on the platform. I wandered, pushing my luggage cart through the station, and finally sat down, fingering my packet of telephone numbers, which extends nationwide.

From Canada,
By Land

I'd been on a cruise from Nome, in northwestern Alaska, through the Aleutian chain of islands to the extreme southeastern part of the state; and it seemed a shame, after such a ceaselessly splendid parade of scenery, to hurry my return to what is called civilization. The obvious solution was to take the train, which three times a week, at nine-fifteen in the morning, leaves for points east from Prince Rupert, the small Canadian port, located near the Alaskan border, that is a terminus for Alaska's state ferries.

Canada is wider than the lower forty-eight states, so theoretically you can ride a full four thousand miles by rail before reaching the Atlantic Ocean at Halifax in Nova Scotia. I planned to get off in Montreal, a couple of hours' drive from my home in Vermont. I was eager—I'd traveled parts of this route in 1952 and again on three occasions during the 1960s—though perhaps it's even better to go westward by such a relatively slow means. The West has represented hope and change, and I've always thought it was a mistake to waste a potentially momentous transition from East to West by whizzing over the whole continent in just a few hours by plane. Or, to give a more concrete illustration: A friend of mine, leaving her marriage to a Boston psychiatrist, found it was just the ticket to catch the sleeper in Montreal and rock for four days in her berth till eventually she got to Prince Rupert, boarded a ferry, and got off in an Alaskan island village, where she found a job as cook on a fishing boat, rooming with the eighty-year-old, one-eyed Tlingit Indian captain, who hailed the gleam of her bare legs each morning when she swung down from her upper bunk to put coffee on, and otherwise was her good chum.

I love trains, despite the fact that my earliest memory is of derailing, and in later years I traveled the East and Midwest at night by circus train, with its rumble and natter and jiggle and sway absorbed in my dreams, a safe haven from the zany, more dangerous theatrics of the day.

Prince Rupert is a pulp-mill and salmon-canning city of sixteen thousand people at the mouth of the Skeena River, which is one of the wildest and most beautiful in all Canada. Once called "River of the Clouds" by the Indians, it flows for three hundred sixty miles from sources only recently surveyed. The modest brick station is an easy walk from where my ship docked, and with the sea's tilt still strong in my head and legs, I was soon rattling east.

A Pacific rain was falling, and the ocean bay that the Skeena empties into billowed with fog. Lovely shaggy cedars and hemlocks leaned over the bank. The river was split by numerous sandbars and drift piles and acre-long islands, and the low mountains were decked with clouds, as the train clumped along, never hurrying or varying its pace except for the syncopated jerks, clicks, and creaks that one could absorb soothingly without listening. There were two coaches and two sleeping cars. The stewardess for the latter told me she would be helping to cook the meals in the dining car, as well as doing her regular job, but that nevertheless she liked her work so much she wanted to stay on with the railroad until she wound up maybe as president.

The grayish-green Skeena coiled and swirled through strata-striped canyons, under ampler mountains beaded with waterfalls, or beside gravel beaches and heavy forests. I was glad to see that this valley, after a passage of twenty years, had remained undisturbed except for some patchy logging. Very few places one is fond of do not change in two decades' time, and I doubt that any scenery in America that can be enjoyed from a railway car is more sumptuous, even including the Alaska Railroad's run from Anchorage to Fairbanks. Past mountains like the Seven Sisters, which were still lavishly snow-spread in this first week in August, past Tsimshian Indian town sites like Kwinitsa and Kitselas, and Kitwanga and Kitseguecla, and past other stations, like Usk and Doreen, we saw the skies lift in this interior region. Big riverbank cottonwoods interspersed the spruce, and woods of birch and aspen replaced the rain forest. At Kitwanga, an Indian graveyard and several totem poles are in sight right from the train.

The Skeena poured and purled by our single track. Old-fashioned snake fencing graced the sparse clearings, with aging log cabins or sagging trailers. The train kabumped and harumphed, while the jade-green river turned milky gray wherever glacier meltwater joined it. Underneath Hagwilget Peak, its valley finally turned north toward its headwaters, as remote as any in British Columbia. We then paralleled by trestle and tunnel a narrower tributary, the Bulkley River. As I lunched with a couple from Düsseldorf, Germany, we admired the blue snout of a glacier on Hudson Bay Mountain, which lay suffering in the sun, the closest that glaciers ever come to a rail line in Canada. Though we were drinking British Columbian wine, I told them the local saying about country like this, when summer ends: "Good for Swedes and grizzly bears, but bad for horses and schoolteachers."

The engine wailed solemnly, but the sunshine was white on the aspens. Purple fireweed grew next to the track. After the town of Smithers, the mountains sank to a loaflike form, and there were hayfields between the black-spruce marshes and white-spruce forests. With Douglas fir and lodgepole pine, every dozen miles a sawmill was operating full blast. We entered a hundred miles of lake country, gazing out at a series of handsome fingery lakes with wooded turtlebacks or hogbacks and brushy streams between them, and sometimes a moose standing in the willows. A woman from Iowa spotted two bears. The train poked along, waiting in dinky stations for its schedule to catch up with it. It had crossed the Bulkley River about a dozen times. Now it crossed the Endako—a heavenly-looking river in the summer—eight times in only ten miles, and then connected with the Nechako River, plat-

41

terlike and silvery at dusk, following that one serenely for seventy-five miles. We were near the northern edge of the great Chilcotin cattle range, still as open as Montana's was sixty years ago, and we saw herds of Herefords as dark fell.

The train whistle's time-honored blare accentuated the lonesome appearance of lovelorn lights in tiny cabins. When we chugged around a long curve, the headlight in front of the engine made me remember not only riding a flatcar of the circus train across Minnesota when I was in my teens but also watching my little Lionel train rounding the endless circle of its track in the living room when I was seven. I went to sleep beside the Fraser River outside the city of Prince George—and woke up before 5:00 A.M. at Tête Jaune Cache in the Rocky Mountains (no station buildings at stops like this, just a dirt-road crossing), under Cinnamon Peak. The Fraser, in its infancy here, is eight hundred fifty miles long, one of Canada's great rivers, discovered in 1793 by Alexander Mackenzie during his epic walk to the Pacific (eleven years before Lewis and Clark's), where at tidewater he wrote on a rock the stirring boast: *Alexander Mackenzie from Canada by land.*

We soon saw the snowy reaches of Mount Robson, 13,000 feet high, though the usual disk of a cloud of its own making hid the top thousand feet. There was a cow moose in Moose Lake, under the Selwyn Range, standing with dripping water plants in her mouth. And a corridor of dozens of handsome mountains on either side led us grandly and energetically but much too swiftly through the Yellowhead Pass into Jasper, which is Canada's premier national park. The town of Jasper itself is ringed by panoramic peaks, notably Mount Edith Cavell, with its ice and snow and slanted, colorful strata. Then for an hour eastward, mountains, gray and saw-toothed, or brown-rocked and bulkier, promenaded alongside the train, while a muscular, new, green-glacial river, the marvelous Athabasca, rushed close by.

When we left the brief but momentous majesty of the Rockies, the Athabasca swung north and left us, as if impatient to head for the Arctic. I had lunch with a retired Alberta farmer and his wife. Both said they were happy to have gotten out of the business of farming before the wheat market collapsed. More than five hours' worth of Alberta passed by, much of it totally forested; then patches of farmland in the jack pine. At Evansburg a troop of Cub Scouts got off. Edmonton, Alberta's capital, and a boom city built by oil and wheat money, welcomed us through its back door, past junkyards and grain elevators. We changed trains, from the Via Skeena to the Via Supercontinental (Via being a government rail agency, like Amtrak in the U.S.), which had come east from Vancouver instead of from Prince Rupert and thus was larger and fancier, with a bubble-dome car and a less cheerful, less busy and versatile crew. I was pleased to notice, however, that even in the 1980s, as in the horse-and-carriage era, a man still walks beside the cars at divisional stops, shining a light underneath and tapping with a hammer. No hotboxes, but a steam pipe had broken; we waited an hour.

East of Edmonton, too, this northerly portion of Alberta remains thinly settled. I supper ed with a pink-faced New Brunswick man and an African-born Canadian and a Jamaican-born Canadian—a brown-skinned man who, because I was wearing a sport jacket, asked me with a laugh, "Are you for or against the establishment?"

"For *and* against."

He asked the black man where he had "originated from."

"Oh, that's getting into a can of worms, to answer that," said our tablemate. "I always say I was born in Churchill, Manitoba, because that makes people laugh: 'the polar bear capital of the world.' It was Ghana." He told stories of arriving in London and how a series of kindly landladies had fed him leg of lamb and lamb chops until "I always throw a stone at a sheep if I see one now."

The Jamaican-Canadian said *his* English landladies had had to light his gas heaters for him, after he had already dropped in several coins and filled the room with gas, and had singed both their hair and his own in the explosions that followed.

"Don't wash the dishes, because we're going to have to; we've got no money," he told the headwaiter. He ordered roast beef but specified, "No blood on the plate, please. I am a coward." He'd been a paratrooper for two years, but nowadays he didn't even care to fly. He said he'd spent four more

43

years as a military policeman in the American army. "And all that training went right out the window as soon as somebody fired a shot at me." He was trying to stop a barroom brawl and simply froze. "It was the waitress that saved my life. She dove at me and knocked me down before he shot at me again." He said that now he looks up the Red Cross in the phone book before he shaves in the morning; and we all laughed.

The headwaiter, a man for all seasons in the British style, pointed out the window at a beautifully trim little river valley and told us this was Sitting Bull's haven during his exile in Canada. If indeed that was so, it looked so cleanly pristine that it might have been still.

I woke up in Rivers, Manitoba—having slept through most of Saskatchewan—with the train running on Central Time and the scenery substantially greener and more cultivated than Alberta's, though not densely utilized. Plenty of intractable scrub where wildlife could hide stretched out between the wheat farms, the sparse towns and occasional isolated houses built idiosyncratically by hand.

At Winnipeg we changed trains again, to the Via Canadian, which was yet longer and more impersonal in its feel, having traveled east from Vancouver by the most direct, southerly route, through Banff and Calgary. It had separate bar and bubble cars for coach and sleeping-car passengers.

But there were really *green* fields here, from the increase in yearly rainfall, and new-mown hay lay spooled into barrelshaped bales. Leaning out the open window in the vestibule, I could feel the midsummer heat, see cattails in the ditches, and, when the train slowed, hear grasshoppers sing. An hour past Winnipeg, every acre was plowed for use except for some unimproved glades by the railroad tracks, where beehives were tucked away, and the houses began to have special amenities, such as round-crowned shade trees sheltering a comfortable yard. On feedlots, red-and-white beef cattle grazed. On dairy farms, the cows were Holsteins, black and white.

But then, in two more hours, we crossed the Ontario line and promptly entered a continuous coniferous forest, seeing muskeg again and frequent ledgy outcroppings of the Canadian Shield, which is some of the oldest rock in the world and "the nucleus of North America," as the *Columbia Encyclopedia* claims. The roadbed grew knucklier, as if to convey every bump of the continent. Hawks and ravens sailed by, past dozens of north-woods lakes in twisty, ingenious shapes, with white birch woods, dark tamarack swamps, and a varying succession of white and black spruce, balsam fir, and white pine. Empty grain cars were being pulled past us in lengthy strings, moving westward after having been unloaded at the Great Lakes ports, while our own train careened, swayed, and rocked at a much quicker pace than the ship I'd been on in the Bering Sea, though a speed that is, oddly enough, a good deal easier on the sense of balance of the inner ear than a nautical slow-and-steady motion is.

In the coaches, young kids were crawling over their mothers' laps in a hubbub of discontent, but in the sleeper passengers' bubble-dome car, two retired businessmen with drinks in their hands were talking about "sitting down and working things out" in South Africa, as if the crisis of apartheid were some kind of a union dispute. I had supper with a Swiss economics student who'd been honing his hockey skills at a camp in Brandon, Manitoba, and who in order to save money was limiting himself to one meal a day; and with two Quebec women who had been visiting one's forester son at the Lake of the Woods ("pickerel that melt in your mouth") and were trying not to worry about how his newlywed wife had been shouting at him because their trailer had no running water and electricity.

Strangers do talk on a train; the circumstances are at once venturesome and intimate; and when the drive shaft broke underneath the dining car and we came to a dead stop between towns, we joked about how our hearts would have stopped if an equivalent part had snapped between towns on a plane. For reading, I'd brought *The Portable Elizabethan Reader,* which was the sort of book to dive deeply into in case of an exasperating delay but not so topical it would tempt me away from my window as long as we kept on rolling. Yet stopping at nightfall almost anywhere was exciting. I'd get off the train for a minute and toy with my childish fear of straying too many steps away and being *left behind* if it started suddenly. The wheels and the springs under each car looked gigantic, as I strolled beside them, and the night lights from two shacks nearby had a faint but dubious hue, as though disreputable events were occurring inside.

After seeing the wheat-shipping town of Thunder Bay, on Lake Superior, I slept through eight hours of north-woods wilderness. One of the givens of long-distance travel by rail is that you're asleep for a third of the view, but when I awoke the sights were still so unpeopled it seemed remarkable to think that Ontario is Canada's most populous, prosperous province. After Sudbury, farms with silos, hay meadows, and large barns at last appeared, though there was soon plenty of forest again, less tough—more pines and less rock—and many, many of Ontario's recently dead lakes, still glittering in the sun but fishless and duckless because of acid rain.

Ottawa can make a fair show of pomp when you come in by daylight, but we arrived at ten o'clock on that fourth night, and it hadn't either the loft and the heft or the burly, kinetic magnificence of a major city, which can infuse even the darkest hours with a python presence.

Montreal lay a couple of hours farther east. And that was the high-hearted, complex old East I'd been traveling toward. Not just cosmopolitan, but bilingual, jostling itself with buildings taller than their physical height and with memories of dreams of development that had slammed clear across the continent in the nineteenth century with the torque of an earthquake. The brilliant sculptures of Joan Miró were on special display at the Montreal Museum of Fine Arts—his *Ladder of Escape* and sculptures of shoes often alchemized into birds.

So, from nature to art: from West to East. In North America, we go west with such hope and zest because we anticipate that nature will reinvigorate art and intelligence and patch up their inadequacies and failings. But we come east again, lonely for art, lonely in nature. For me the migration is perpetual: to nature, and then back to big cities filled with people.

Seeing Miró's shoes miraculously alchemized into birds was really an experience I had the next day. That night, it was midnight when we passengers struggled upstairs with our luggage from the station platform into the spacious old terminal building and immediately separated into two rather starkly divergent categories—the travelers who had people meeting them and the travelers who didn't. I was blessedly among the former. But everybody, if they were like me, felt the floor, and the very ground, swing underfoot under them for the next three or four days, and frequently peered out whatever window was near to "see where we are."

Up the Black
to Chalkyitsik

Wilderness has a good many
meanings. Bitter cold or uncommon danger can make of any
patch of the outdoors a "wilderness," but nothing precludes
balmy weather from the equation; nor are snakebite and
quicksand essential ingredients. My happiest experiences in
wilderness landscapes happen to have been in Alaska, and
my favorite town there is Fort Yukon, a dot of a place thrown
down near the junction of the Yukon and Porcupine rivers,
one mile north of the Arctic Circle, eight hundred seventy-
five river miles from the Yukon's Canadian headwaters, and
a thousand winding miles from its debouchment into the
Bering Sea. Canadian traders of the Hudson's Bay Company
established the fort in 1847, not so much to protect themselves from the Gwich'in Indians of the region as to fly the
flag and fend off the Russian traders operating from a station five hundred miles downstream. (Russians had discovered the mouth of the Yukon in 1834.)

This was the first English-language community in
Alaska, but after Alaska was sold by Russia to the United
States in 1867 for a price of $7.2 million, the Hudson's Bay
Company was forced to move its operations eastward to Brit-
ish territory. Fort Yukon continued to be a fur-buying center

under American auspices, however, and then it became a gold-rush way point for the riverboats headed for the Klondike frenzy near Dawson City at the turn of the century, and finally the site of a small radar base after World War II, as well as an administrative sub-hub for six or eight Indian villages in the surrounding fifty or sixty thousand square miles, a huge terrain, abutting the Brooks Range from the south, that is equivalent in size to two Irelands and includes the so-called Yukon Flats, which is an area of forty thousand lakes and one of the richest breeding grounds for waterfowl in the world.

Though the radar base has closed, Fort Yukon (pop. 650) is still fairly busy, a jumping-off point for winter trapping trips and summer jaunts up the Coleen, Chandalar, Christian, Porcupine, Sheenjek, and other pristine rivers that feed this portion of the Yukon. Thirty-year-old flying boxcars roar off the airstrip to bomb forest fires in the outback in July and August, till it sounds like a war zone. Surveyors for the Bureau of Land Management, or the Fish and Wildlife Service, federal and state social workers, construction crews, oil geologists, and health and sanitation experts bunk at the Sourdough Inn while they attempt to carry out various Sisyphean projects. Alaska is the land of the dubious contract, as one gradually discovers, and, besides the more drawn-out scams, is full of white people who are angry about whatever they were doing down in the Lower Forty-eight before they came up here, how long they kept doing it, and who they were doing it with. They lend a frenetic or malcontent air to a mainly Indian village like Fort Yuk (as they sometimes call Fort Yukon when they're in Fairbanks). Other whites, with better intentions, may feel they are being defeated as they struggle against intractable problems like fetal alcohol syndrome and a rising suicide rate and, like the first group, ask the perpetual questions, *"Shall* we stay in this crazy state?" and "Where are we going on vacation?"

Baja, Belize, Bangkok, or London over the Pole may be where they go, on the high salaries paid. Paris, New York, and Tokyo are about equidistant from Fairbanks by airplane, so one has the feeling one can go anywhere in a matter of hours—to the edge of the earth on the coastal plain of the Arctic Ocean, over the Brooks Range, where polar bears cross scent lines with grizzlies and wolverines, as maybe two hundred thousand caribou sift through; or to the Champs Élysées and Trafalgar Square.

This can be exhilarating but, if you've gone off the deep end over the long lightless winter, demoralizing too; freedom becomes vertigo. Of course, the complicated skies above Fort Yukon aren't really lightless even then. The sun flirts with the horizon, the moon rises, stars spangle the firmament, and the northern lights flicker, shoot up, and glow. You see what you look for—a collapsing conclave of "neo-Indians, salt-and-pepper Indians," as they were described to me by a flipped-out social worker, whose wretched and dangerous job was to take abused children away from violent mothers and drunken fathers; or a lively, self-reliant, age-old, resilient subsistence society still holding its own with at least some degree of élan beneath the drumfire of soap-opera television and do-gooding welfare programs, beer-hall bravura and bathos, and satellite-powered telephones. At the Sourdough Inn, one tilts back in a barber's chair at the pay phone to talk to New York. There's a daily mail plane and other amenities: the Alaska Commercial Company general store; the community hall, with shower baths and washing machines. The University of Alaska has put up a million-dollar log building for extension classes. The town has three churches; a Lions Club for bingo and Budweiser and a two-dollar cup of moose stew, if you're hungry; a new little historical museum established in the hope that tourists will come; a Wycliffe Society Bible translator, putting psalms into Gwich'in (though English has swamped Gwich'in by now); and Fort Yukon's federally funded psychologist, who estimates that a fourth of the citizenry shows up every year in her office, which is situated between the town-owned, tin-walled liquor store and the bootlegger's green plywood house, which opens for business when the liquor store closes.

The river itself, spraddled out with its islands to a width of three miles at this point, imparts importance to every settlement alongside, and its armies of salmon—kings, silvers, and chum—churn by invisibly from July through September, heading for Canada to spawn but at hand for the netting meanwhile. In the winter, frozen, it's a causeway for sled dogs, and during the summer, if you camp on its banks, you can lie at midnight watching a thousand swallows whirl in the wind, and the giddy sun loop like a rolling lasso along the rim of the forest, while the town's chained packs of dogs bay jubilantly at each other from several backyards. Although the Bureau of Indian Affairs has built rows of pastel prefab housing in a newer quarter, many residents prefer to live in the old log cabins close to the river and venture out in snowtime to run snare lines and trap lines. Six to ten thousand mink and two or three thousand marten skins are marketed through Fort Yukon's "A.C." store in the winter.

I fell in love in Alaska, with the person in charge of tracking tuberculosis all over the state, and therefore have visited Eskimo villages like Point Hope and Kotzebue and Crooked Creek, Indian villages like Angoon and Tanana and Sleetmute, Anglo towns like Dillingham and Tenakee Springs, while she tested and chatted with patients. I've seen the Copper River, the Susitna River, the Koyukuk River, and the Killik River, hundreds of miles apart, going from south to north. I've barged on the Yukon, summered in Fairbanks, wintered in Anchorage, and twice, when I've been in the north on other business, have dropped in by mail plane with a pack and a tent to walk Fort Yukon's dirt streets—streets refurbished with gravel after an ice jam during spring breakup in May 1982 floated six-foot bergs into town.

If I walk half a mile from the airstrip, I reach Fred Thomas's cabin, and he greets me with emphasis. (Everything he says is with emphasis.) And if it's lunchtime, Charlotte, his wife, will take out some beaver meat to feed us, knowing that, coming straight from the city, I will enjoy that. She is fifty-six, comely, husky, reddish-skinned, smooth-complexioned, aging gracefully, and, in the manner of Indian wives in these villages, does not talk to white strays such as me unless her husband is present, but has many visitors of her own sex and race, with whom she is warmly responsive.

Fred is sixty-four, compact and wiry, built smaller than Charlotte, with a beardless, keen, concentrated, round, predator's face, bristly short hair that is turning white, and a relaxed but peripatetic look. As a family man, he did maintenance work for seventeen years at the radar base in order to raise his six children well, and only trapped and hunted in his spare time, though still managing to average about fifty foxes and two or three wolves a year. But now he has re-sumed the calling of woodsmanship that he loves.

Fred's mother was a Gwich'in from a band that lived on the upper Porcupine (the Dagoo Gwich'in), and his father, Jacob Thomas, born around 1880 in Wisconsin, had worked on a Mississippi riverboat for a little while before joining the 1898 gold rush. He'd arrived late and mostly trapped mink and moose-hunted in the Klondike for meat to sell to the miners at a dollar a pound to keep things going while his partners dug holes. Nothing panned out for them, but as "Tommy the Mate," Fred's father worked on the Yukon boats for fifteen or twenty years, before settling down to have Fred and six more children and to carve out a life for himself far from other white men.

It was July 1919 in Fort Yukon when Fred's parents put him and most of their belongings in a boat and paddled twenty-five miles up the Porcupine River to the mouth of the Big Black River, and paddled, poled, and lined their labori-ous way up the midsummer shallows of the Black for two hundred more miles in the course of a month to its Grayling Fork, where they built a trapping camp, which has remained the heart of Fred's own family's activities ever since. They would stay out from August—when they already needed to begin laying in wild foods for the winter—till the following June, when the muskrats, last of the fur animals to lose the lush nap on their coats, finally did so, and the river was high and yet safe enough to travel upon with boats stuffed with furs, dogs, and youngsters.

Fred has a vaguely "Irish" look, which is darkened and blurred with the admixture of Athapascan Indian, so that he reminds me of several of the Cajun trappers I have traveled and camped with in southwestern Louisiana, and like them, he speaks the elided English of someone not so much bilin-gual as caught between two languages and master of neither. His two sons, however, live within yards of his house and trap and collaborate with him in the old-fashioned way (seen also in Cajun country, or any tribal region I've known) by which an older man becomes simply as strong as the number of his grown sons. And two of his brothers go out from Fort Yukon every fall to trap from cabins of their own on the upper Black. Flying in with the winter's supplies, they don't have to start as early as in the old days.

Fred spent so much time on the Black when he was a boy that he had only three years of schooling, but he is a sophisticated man, nevertheless, partly from watching hundreds of servicemen from all over the United States matriculate through a tour of duty at the little base at the edge of town, and partly because he contracted tuberculosis as a young man. After trying the local boneyard of a hospital and realizing he would die like the other Indians and métis there, he lived for three years alone in a tent to clear his lungs, never spending a night indoors. That, too, frighteningly, was of no avail, and so his father at last, pulling strings as only a white man—even a "squaw man"—could do, persuaded the government to send Fred to a sanatorium in Tucson, Arizona, to recover. So he's seen orange trees, though never an apple tree, he says.

His mother's father, Ab Shaefer, was also a white man, a whaler from Nova Scotia who had jumped ship in the Arctic with three other sailors about two decades prior to the gold rush by pretending to go on a caribou hunt. The ship's officers pursued them and shot one man, but the rest escaped and, it being summertime, passed safely through the Eskimo country of the Arctic Slope and crossed up over the British Mountains, which in the Yukon Territory correspond to the Brooks Range, and then were saved from the terrors of winter in the interior by the Indians at Crow Flats, the Vunta Gwich'in. Anyhow, on his way home from Tucson in 1945, Fred stopped off in Chicago to get acquainted with a few of his Shaefer relatives and saw a big city.

Ab Shaefer and one of his companions had married two sisters at Crow Flats village, near the head of the Porcupine. (The third of these surviving whalers floated down the Porcupine to Gwicha Gwich'in country at the village of Beaver on the Yukon River, thirty miles below Fort Yukon, and married a woman there.) And Shaefer, living at Crow Flats and Old Crow and trapping with his in-laws along the upper Porcupine's tributaries, like the Bell River and the Eagle River, sizable in their own right, which run to the Northwest Territories, went so happily native that he simply ignored the gold rush when it occurred, almost next door; did not participate. Fred has not many memories of Shaefer—except that he said, "Well, I'll be damned!" a lot—but remembers his own surprise, as a small boy visiting with his mother and father at his grandfather's winter camp on the Bell, where some of the vegetation was new to him, when he was sent out of the cabin to get dry firewood and chopped at a leafless tamarack, thinking it was a dead spruce, but found that because tamaracks drop their needles in the fall, it looked dead yet was alive. The other whaler who lived in Old Crow drowned in the currents of the Porcupine around that same year, and Fred last saw Shaefer in 1943, during his own scary siege with TB, when the old man came down the Porcupine on a riverboat to Fort Yukon to change boats and go up the Yukon to Dawson City (in this age before ubiquitous planes) to live in an old-age home.

Now it was Charlotte's father, a Tranji Gwich'in named Henry William, from Chalkyitsik, the one village that exists on the Big Black River, who, Fred told me, was sick. He suggested as we had lunch that we might make a trip of it and bring Henry William some fresh salmon. The Indian Health service doctors at the hospital in Fairbanks had discharged him after an operation for what they'd described as "an intestinal infection." Presumably, he had been sent home to die in familiar surroundings of bowel cancer. In Fairbanks, Henry had got sick of store meat—what he called "meat with no blood in it"—and the doctors and everyone felt that it was a shame he wasn't enjoying his meals these last weeks.

I said sure. A New Yorker born, I come to Alaska's high wilds like Alice diving down her rabbit's hole, and that great city, as I gaze back at it from the Northwest Orient Airlines Boeing, smokes like heartburn personified or a multiple smashup of racing cars. But in a dozen hours I can be smelling wood smoke, tending a supper fire in front of my tent, camped in Fred's yard, or with my friends Beri and Mary Morris (who manage the Alaska Commercial Company store), whose spare cabin lies close by, or else in the Anglican churchyard. Its veteran minister was on sabbatical on the occasion of this visit but had told me before to camp there, to cut down my chances of being robbed. Wilderness buffs sometimes raft or canoe for five or six hundred miles down the Yukon, surviving mazes of rapids and sloughs, though still less than halfway to the river's mouth, and then beach their craft on a sand spit within hooting distance of the Sourdough Inn, make camp on the beach with exultant relief, and rush to tuck in to a huge, candlelit, tablecloth meal and chat long-distance on the telephone, only to return to the spit and find everything gone.

Fort Yukon is full of violence—one of the worst posts to be a state trooper in the whole state—and stories abound of white people who commute to marriages elsewhere, while grinning meanwhile, come dusk, when an Indian mother on welfare shows up at the kitchen door wanting grocery money, beer money—a town of gunfire by night but considerable sweetness by day. I was camped, in fact, on the riverbank inside the fenced yard of another couple, the wife a retired schoolteacher here, the husband the man who installed satellite dishes and suchlike necessities. They may raise the northernmost tomatoes in the United States, and probably the northernmost honeybees. They were out, when I heard a knocking at their door and the voice of an English lady calling them. My tent was up, but my sleeping-bag zipper was stuck, so I went to introduce myself, tell her they were out, and try to persuade her to unstick it for me.

She did, although she exclaimed, "Oh, what an impossible nuisance you are! You're like my son when he goes on a trip with the Scouts. You've come all the way from New York, and you don't know how to zip your own sleeping bag? I suppose you're a world traveler too—we get those. How do you function?"

"There's always somebody to do it," I said.

In her forties, blond, younger than I, she turned out to be Fred's sister-in-law, Mrs. Johnnie Thomas.

For a novel that I was writing, I had become curious to learn more about Bigfoot, or "Brush Man," as the Gwich'in call the phenomenon, translating from their own word, *Naa-inn*, for Bigfoot. Sure, Bigfoot had lived in these river valleys, a number of people told me. Some had seen him or knew of circumstantial evidence of his existence. All had heard the stories, as well as others, about an odder, perhaps still more intriguing humanoid wild being: the Little People. These tiny, aggressive, quite talky inhabitants of the taiga and tundra had prodigious strength and cryptic personalities, living mostly underneath the earth and snow but contacting human beings more confidently than Bigfoot. They were self-sufficient, for one thing. They didn't need to steal food from a campsite, as Bigfoot would, and didn't hunger for the companionship of women either, like Bigfoot occasionally. They played quirky and raffish—or sinister and heartless—pranks, yet also were capable, when the spirit moved, of doing a good turn: saving a lone traveler's life or extricating him from great danger, if he pleaded with them. Whenever they proved troublesome, the only way to quiet them was to build bonfires over their burrows, boil pots of water, and threaten to pour that down their holes.

Bigfoot was a kind of howling fugitive, by comparison, an outcast figure apparently in need of fellowship with man at the same time as—glimpsed at the end of a trail or across a frozen lake—he fled from him. So I asked my new English friend, who had already heard about me from Fred, who I should seek out to talk about Bigfoot.

"And *Vanity Fair* magazine in New York City sent you to Fort Yukon to find this stuff out?" She laughed.

"No, *Vanity Fair* is sending me to Anchorage to find out about 'Alaska's Millionaires.' But that gets me to the state, and I come here. Or *House & Garden,* or another one, sends me."

Having fixed my zipper, she felt it improper to chat much longer, saying Fort Yukon wasn't Britain and she hardly ever missed Britain, much less went back. "I'm certain you'll manage. Ask on Front Street and ask Fred and Johnnie."

Front Street, a dirt track alongside the river, is where the row of old-timers' log cabins is—white prospectors', traders', and trappers' cabins at the turn of the century that now belong to their descendants, of mixed race but in solid-looking housing unmessed with by the Bureau of Indian Affairs. In no time, asking along, I met a middle-aged Indian woman, married here but originally from the village of Beaver, whose sister had been abducted by a Bigfoot, she said. All one summer her brother had tracked the two of them through the mountains, hearing the girl's cries receding in front of him wherever he followed, and had never caught up. A very sad thing. On the other hand, as kids they used to go out and shout down a Little People's hole that they knew about—not really afraid, as their parents would have been—for the fun of hearing words come back, she said.

"What words?"

"I forget. But you knew what they meant. Grouchy."

Getting interested, she led me into her house, which was a jumble of river and trapping equipment and furniture and cartons of food, with several kids, and two other women, who had dropped in. Her husband was heavy, paleish, drunk, sixtyish, reclining in the slatted sunlight in a broken easy chair, and unfriendly, assuming I worked for the government or a social agency.

"Why don't *you* go?" he told me, rousing slightly.

"He just wants to know about Brush Man," the lady explained.

"Brush Man!" he said, with a dim smile. "You're talking about olden days—my father's days, my days. My friend fed a Brush Man one time. Is that what you want to hear about?"

"Yes," I said.

"A whole family of them, three babies and the two big ones, came to his fire hungry, in the winter. He was a hundred miles from nowhere, camped in the snow. And he had half a moose left that he had shot, so he let them eat that. Just watched them eat, and they didn't say nuthin to him. Only he said you could tell what they thought without speaking. Why don't you go now?" he repeated.

Back at Fred Thomas's, I asked what *he* thought.

"Sometimes they're a downed airman," he said.

"A Bigfoot is?"

"I don't know. You see what you're looking for. It could be a pilot that's scared shitless, running around in the woods, gone off his rocker, after a crash."

"And how about before there were planes?"

"Well, then it might be an Eskimo," he said. "Or a family of Eskimos."

"Yes? How?"

Fred explained that before the whites arrived and instituted jails and asylums and so forth for crazy people and murderers, they were likely to be expelled from their settlements, or they ran away before they got killed. "And where would they go?" He pointed north toward the handful of Eskimo villages spotted along the Arctic Ocean and Arctic Slope north of the Brooks Range, six hundred miles or more above where we were. "They'd come down here, if they survived. All crazy and shaggy, mumbling Eskimo."

57

"There was a war on, anyway, with the Eskimos," Charlotte added.

"So he'd stay in the woods and be crazy there? Steal fish, steal food, look at the women from a hiding place?" I asked. This was an explanation, if not an answer.

Charlotte said when she was a girl she knew people who used to leave sugar, tea and salt for a Bigfoot at a certain rock on the riverbank, where he'd come down and pick the stuff up. And he learned to leave a few furs there, in return, for them to sell.

We went to check Fred's fishnet, which was set on a fifty-foot line, buoyed by empty ammonia bottles, out at the point of a midchannel sandbar two miles south of town and a mile from shore. The net seemed ludicrously short and small, in the scale of the vast yellow river, but three king salmon were tangled individually in its monofilament—a red forty-five-pound male, a reddish twenty-five-pound female, and a paler twenty-pound male. As Fred very carefully landed each of these, I sat holding the previous one under my feet in the little skiff to keep it from leaping back into the water. They filled the boat with their anxious and strangled despair, and if we had tipped over they could have lived, while we would have drowned very quickly, not just because of the water's hand-numbing temperature, but because its immense freighting of silt soon fills your clothes like a crushing weight and drags you down.

Yet such an easy catch of flesh exhilarated Fred and me, rather like a windfall of money. It suddenly made life seem more secure and, day after sun-swept midsummer day, is a commonplace coup on the Yukon. Besides providing for his father-in-law, Henry William, in Chalkyitsik (frontier Indians often chose two first names for their "white" name, because they would name themselves after several new friends, though sometimes an unscrupulous white man might "charge" them for his), Fred wanted to send a salmon or two on the mail plane to the Natsit Gwich'in of Arctic Village, on the Chandalar River, in the Brooks Range, the most remote and self-sufficient of these Gwich'in communities. In exchange, his friends there would mail him a caribou next winter. Even out in his bush camp, he seldom has a chance to eat caribou. Small bands of the Porcupine Herd straggle as far south as his Black River country only about once in every five years.

At home, Charlotte filleted the three fish, dropping the organs and roe into a jug to rot for trap bait and cutting the backbones into sections, which Fred would stick into punctured tin cans and hang close to his traps and snares. His practice is to set out literally hundreds of these in November and just leave them be until March. In his smokehouse, he also has strings of goose wings stored, which, when dipped in beaver castor, he will tie in low spruce branches to attract lynx. He laughed and told me he'd once caught thirteen two-hundred-fifty-dollar lynx in a single night, when they were moving through his trapping territory in one of their strange, periodic migrations, and how he had remembered then that his father, in hard Depression times, had wished he could catch even two thousand dollars' worth of fur in a season to feed his family of nine.

Charlotte showed me their photograph album, which, like other Fort Yukon photo albums, consisted, apart from its wedding and graduation memorabilia, of numerous pictures of dead bears and moose, *in toto,* then the same moose and bears being skinned; and of trap-line cabins and stilted caches on chutelike rivers, or trap-line catches pinned in a row on a clothesline rope in front of one of the cabins for the camera. The meat represented a winter's food and the line of wolf, fox, otter, mink, beaver, marten, and fisher skins a year's worth of money; so what else ought to be in an album of memories?

Jimmy Ward, the son of another old-time white settler, turned up for supper. We ate a snow goose, which Fred had shot last spring, and some pickled strips of dried salmon and left-over beaver, with store-bought spinach and rice. Jimmy Ward is a white-haired, black-bearded mischief-maker of whom it is no exaggeration to say that he is frequently drunk. He had been besieged in his cabin by gunfire one night a few months before and been carted away for a night in jail after the shoot-out, and while he was gone, his cabin had somehow caught fire and burned to a shell. Now the government had placed him and his Gwich'in wife in a ninety-cents-a-day government prefab for the rest of his life and, he announced cockily, he was sitting pretty.

"It was an active winter in Dodge City," he said. U.S. Representative Don Young's cabin—summer home to Alaska's perennial congressman—had also been set afire; and so had the Fish and Wildlife Service's cabin, from which the eight-and-a-half-million-acre Yukon Flats National Wildlife Refuge (itself as large as Massachusetts and Connecticut combined) is managed. So he didn't know whether to be insulted or flattered to be in such company. Tomorrow he and his wife were going out to camp in a favorite slough up the Yukon a couple of dozen miles and put out their fishnets and rabbit snares and lean back and enjoy themselves. After you'd split, smoked, and sun-dried a few hundred salmon, with those smells on the wind, you'd soon have a young black bear to cure too.

This is his summer camp, of course. In the winter Jimmy's trapping camp—like Fred's, it was his father's before him—is not on the Yukon but one hundred sixty miles up the Porcupine, between two of the Porcupine's principal tributaries, the Coleen and Sheenjek rivers, a less traveled territory, although as fall gets in the air in Fort Yukon, one hears people telling each other, "I'll see you on the Sheenjek," "I'll see you on the Coleen."

Jimmy said he wanted to die on his trap line, not shrink to skin and bones in a hospital bed, as several friends had. "I'd rather fall down in a rat tunnel and die."

Fred said that one spring he and his brothers had caught thirteen hundred muskrats on the Black. Last winter he and his sons had trapped about eighty lynx, forty marten, forty mink, fifteen red foxes, two wolverines, and seventy-five beavers. No wolves, but his brother Albert, who is based seven miles upstream from them, had got six.

Jimmy argued with him about how high a lynx snare should be set. But they agreed that the most fearsome creature in the bush is a "winter grizzly," a bear that is too hungry to hibernate and has woken up desperate and on the hunt for a quick meal. Jimmy mentioned, however, that he had once shot at a Brush Man. It had been standing on the ice of a lake, and he'd fired at it twice, but it wouldn't fall and didn't drop down on all fours to run from him either, as a bear would have done; instead it ran into the trees on its hind legs. So *he* ran, and was too scared to come back the next day to check on the tracks; instead had cleared out of that valley entirely.

I said Fred had said that Brush Man could be a downed airman instead of a Bigfoot, or else an Eskimo exiled from the North Slope villages, or maybe (I wondered) a Koyukon Indian, from the next tribal group, down toward Galena on the Yukon, where I'd also been visiting and where I'd seen snares set around a homestead cabin for Bigfoot—or Woods Man, as the Koyukon Indians called him, because their slightly milder climate on the Koyukuk River grows more woods, less brush.

"I don't see why you have to limit your options," Jimmy answered. "If you see a Brush Man, he could be a pilot that's crashed, or he could be an Eskimo that's lost his marbles, or he could be a Bigfoot. Couldn't he? When I first saw *you*, I thought you were James Watt, because you wore glasses and you asked too many questions and you smiled too much."

We laughed. It was not impossible that the horrendous secretary of the interior would turn up. Worse folks did. Later on that first trip, Jimmy had decided I was really a fur buyer who was scouting around from cabin to cabin to see everybody's catch by pretending to be a writer asking questions. At the end of my stay, he had swung around to believing my story about what I was, but then, just on my last day in town, I'd walked over to Fred's house and paid him two hundred fifty dollars for two little wolfskins. So Jimmy didn't know what to think. Gleefully, now, he informed me that I looked older. And he asked if I owned one of those tube-shaped tents and mummy-style sleeping bags that all of the river floaters and mountain climbers and trail hikers who passed through town had.

Because one of my annual pleasures is to be put down by Jimmy Ward, I said yes.

"You zip yourself inside that, and it's like a grocery sack for the old grizzly bear. You're all wrapped up for him. He can just drag you anywhere, and you'll never get to see who he even is. You'll be zipped inside, where he can hold you nice and still."

Fred said Jimmy shouldn't have shot at that figure on the lake if he didn't know what it was. When he was fourteen, he, Fred, had almost shot his own father. It wasn't a simple

61

case of buck fever, because he had killed his first moose three years earlier, but he was hunting moose and saw something brown through the brush across an opening, and because his father was supposed to be out overnight on the trap line, he took aim. But what had happened was that his father's lead dog had broken loose from the sled and gotten snagged in one of the traps. So his father was returning early to mend the dog's foot. Fred didn't fire, and within a few years he had his own nine-day trap line, with six overnight cabins on it.

Darkless summers are a jubilant time. I've been spoiled for some of my usual Vermont haunts by summering in Alaska, where, for instance, the daylight is continuous in Fort Yukon from May 13 through August 4. The sun's manic ball never dips below the edge of the sky. Instead it revolves incessantly, looping to different levels like the motorcyclist who rides around and around inside a giant barrel at a carnival, while the swallows dive after bugs and packs of sled dogs halloo to each other back and forth across town. Like the dogs, I found depression impossible. People, birds, bugs, dogs, didn't sleep much, and the sun, as if bleary from overwork, turned orange and red within the halo of its yellows.

That evening, before our departure for Chalkyitsik, I sat at the Sourdough Inn with some smoke jumpers from Montana, a fisheries expert from Anchorage, two mining men from Fairbanks, and a helicopter pilot from California, originally, by way of Vietnam. One of the "millionaires" I had interviewed in Anchorage for the magazine in New York in exchange for my air fare had made his money developing a shopping mall but had arrived in the state as a bulldozer driver. Had got off the plane drunk, he said, because of the breakup of his marriage; had rented a car and weaved toward the friend's house where he would be staying and immediately was impressed with Alaskan hospitality because the trooper who stopped him didn't arrest him, merely led him to his destination and wished him good luck. In the same spirit, he offered to introduce me to a woman friend of his and to take me sport fishing. But what was most special, he said, was that people here, whatever they did, were the best. Pipe fitter, electrician, dozer operator, geologist, bush pilot— they could work at thirty below or go round-the-clock in the summer and maintain quality. That trooper who had stopped him stood six foot five and "could have stopped the gunfight at the O.K. Corral."

I'd found the same thing. The pilot from New Jersey with whom you flew to lost little villages through snowstorms, fog, mountain ranges, either could cut it or pretty soon quit and went home—or died. The riverboat captain who ferried you to Yukon River settlements either could pick out the braiding of hundreds of channels that led him past hidden sandbars to his destination in the course of a week or grounded at a cost of ten thousand dollars. Mostly, I'd traveled with my tuberculosis supervisor, who flew to Eskimo and Indian villages, doing skin tests to discover latent cases of this antique disease, examining active or former patients, talking to the district nurse or a local health aide and occasionally speaking to the populace in the school gymnasium. We slept on the floor of the health clinic or a first-grade classroom or maybe the gym, staying a couple of days in a town of a hundred and twenty souls before moving on.

The district nurse, living in a center such as Bethel or Nome and flying out to a half-dozen individual villages, seventy or a hundred seventy miles away, which were under her own supervision, had life-and-death power. Not just in the sense that she quickly developed emergency-room skills; but there was no doctor on these scarce visits—a few days per village every six or eight weeks. She determined who got plastic surgery after a fire, or special prenatal care, or a timely cancer exam, or plentiful painkillers. With a limited budget, she authorized a mercy flight or a seat on the mail plane for somebody who wanted to see a doctor—or else she said no. I—whose eyelids froze shut in about five minutes in Arctic villages at forty below—had been much impressed by the stamina and panache of these women, sheltering humbly under their wings.

I napped on a cot in Fred's smokehouse for a few hours, till breakfast time, when we ate bacon and eggs. Fred's neighbor, a wide-cheeked, husky man who lives in a blue house across the road and takes phone calls for him, came over to help truck our gear to the riverbank. Fred had me store my valuables behind his daughter's picture on the mantel, which was the safest place there was, he said: his daughter who's working to be a lawyer in Massachusetts.

"There's no give-up in this guy. Good man for a trip,"

the neighbor told me. He drank a cup of Yukon-yellow river water. "Well, there's my coffee this morning."

Fred was zipped into a black windsuit, with a snazzy white life belt buckled to his hips. It was August 1, and as we got out on the water he remarked that it must be the first day of fall, because the thousands of bank swallows that nest in catacomb colonies in the river's cutbanks had begun vanishing, to get a good start on their flight to South America. So had the smaller flocks of white Arctic terns, which go nearly to Antarctica for another darkless summer at our antipode: true light-loving birds. Because Fort Yukon lies within the wide bowl of the Brooks Range and the more southerly White Mountains and Crazy Mountains, summer temperatures can go to one hundred degrees, but the first killing frost occurs around the third week of August. Our boat, flat-bottomed, square-bowed, thirty-two feet long, four feet wide, and powered by a forty-horse Evinrude, had been built for Fred by the local fur buyer to fit the chop of the Yukon's currents and the Porcupine's surge, plus for shallow-draft marsh running—a salmon boat, a muskrat boat.

In such a boat I'd crossed the Mississippi's mouth after muskrats and garfish, armored prehistoric-looking creatures as big as king salmon. On the Mississippi, dodging the high wakes of supertankers and containerships, our skiff had seemed like an anachronism. But on the Yukon, whose silent roar is bridged only once between Dawson City and salt water—a stretch equivalent to the Mississippi between Minneapolis and New Orleans—I felt natural.

After three breezy, down-slipping miles, we turned up into the Porcupine, which at its mouth looked to be about a third of a mile wide. The Porcupine is itself a major river, more than five hundred fifty miles long. Its waters are a rich shade of gray in the sunshine, not Yukon yellow, but just as cold and fast when you dip your hand into it. Less thickly silt-laden than the Yukon, it wouldn't cram sand into every interstice of your clothing if you found yourself unexpectedly swimming in it, but like any Arctic river, it has *gravitas*.

With the Porcupine's constant turns, and the sun's vagrant positioning over us, the water constantly changed color. It turned black and mirrored the sky, or shifted into a spectrum of handsome grays. Loons were flying determinedly every which way with breathless speed, propelling themselves in a goose's posture except that they held their heads lower. Snags in the current porpoised rhythmically, with their roots or stumps stuck down in the tangle of driftwood along the bottom, but their free ends poked out so much like whiskery heads that it remained a surprise to pass them and look back and notice that they really were stationary, and to watch gulls land on them even as they bobbed. Seals, farther toward the Yukon's great debouchment, do swim upriver for two hundred miles to feast on its salmon.

We slid by the mouth of the Sucker River, and then that of Eight Mile Slough, which looked just like the Sucker's mouth, though the Sucker in fact is a fairly intriguing river. Sloughlike in its sluggish currents, it is named for the bottom-feeding species of fish that thrives here, and it is a fine territory for beaver. A man used to live right here and make a good living from them (though he had to pay a price, with the nickname "Sucker"). Fred himself trapped along the Sucker River a good deal during the years when he was a wage slave for the air force because he could reach it easily from town—from foxes, he made a gold mine of the radar-base dump—and he had his two scariest experiences with grizzly bears here. Thousands of animals must have watched him from hiding places over the years, he says, but only twice has he realized it telepathically, and each time it was a grizzly, flattened down close to the ground, "with its nose going like crazy," along the Sucker, in springtime. He thinks an animal that large and formidable may be required to "register" on him; that the brain waves of slighter wildlife slip past. On each occasion, he made cautious haste to clear out, and then the grizzly cleared out. He is live-and-let-live with grizzlies, and he has prevented his sons, too, from shooting them when it was not necessary for self-protection and when the carcasses were too far out from home to be dragged back to feed to the dogs.

At Seventeen Mile (a location measured from Fort Yukon), the Porcupine looks about a hundred fifty yards wide, and there is one cabin left from what was once a small Indian settlement. Then we glided by the modest-looking outlet of the Grass River, where, as in the Sucker, whitefish can be netted in great numbers and the pike that congregate to devour them can be jigged for. The Grass River is a couple of hundred miles long, counting its tributary, the Little Black River, which curves in a parallel course through the same country that is drained by Fred's Big Black River. Only one trapper works the Little Black River nowadays, and as with all of the other rivers around, this relative emptiness of what is very familiar country to Fred, full of a hubbub of memories of dozens of families who worked the vast drainage of the Porcupine for furs, depresses him. It's not like the changes afflicting woodsmen in the Lower Forty-eight, where development is consuming everybody's old haunts. In much of Alaska, though perhaps temporarily, the land is emptier. Old-timers who went everywhere as a matter of course die off, and young people stay in their villages in the winter, drinking their government checks.

At Twenty-five Mile, chunks of ebony water appeared in the swift gray roil of the Porcupine. Then blocks of obsidian water. A sand spit split the river from the entrance of its tributary, the Big Black, on the right-hand side. We entered it. Two hundred miles up was where Fred's home was, but we were going only seventy-five, to Chalkyitsik, where Charlotte had come from. The Black, at first about sixty yards wide, narrowed to fifty, spread to seventy-five, shrunk again, and swelled, mirroring meanwhile the tiers of white clouds. The current was slower than the Porcupine's, with cherry-colored gravel visible on the shallow bottom and frequent grassy banks that were vividly green. Chattering kingfishers scolded us from both banks, darting between their roosting trees. Plentiful loons of three different species flew by in speedball haste, with giggles, and raffish large flappy ravens, croaking, and little mew gulls that nest on the tundra, and sizable herring seagulls. We saw five pintails and a family of goldeneyes, several mallards and a number of mergansers, or "sawbills," which dive and catch fish and therefore, like a fish-eating grizzly, are considered too "fishy" to be good eating.

At Steamboat Slough there used to be a cabin shaped like a steamboat—five-sided, and pointed at the bow end—which had been built by some cheechako prospectors after the gold rush for fun. "And then it fell down. And then it burnt up," Fred said.

Abundant dark-green spruce trees grew twenty to fifty

feet high for miles. But a few lightning burns are interspersed through this forest, with dead black spars remaining
that have refused to fall over, and alder thickets and willow
woods that are gradually growing up in place of the burned
spruce. Since these burns are of different ages, the new vegetation is accordingly lower or higher, but other patches have
burned in one wholesale sweep, except where the wind's
whimsy has spared odd vibrant clumps of waving spruce
trees.

Besides fire, permafrost is the other tyrant here—Fort
Yukon in winter is one of the coldest inhabited places on
earth—and creates what is called "the drunken forest."
Where lightning spares a stand of trees long enough for
them to begin to grow big, their roots meet the barrier of the
permafrost and are stymied until, top-heavy, they reel, they
slant like cartoon sailors, surviving for years at desperate
angles.

Mostly, though, the spruces and willow-poplar woods
alternated with a rhythmic pleasantry, often facing one another across the river, and on the mud flats in front of the
willows, moose, in feeding, had left their tracks. By the banks
where poplars grew, we saw beaver workings; and on the
grassy swales above the gravel beaches, bear paths. Black
bears were the best meat legally available now, so Fred kept
his .30-.06 at the ready. Moose weren't supposed to be hunted
for a few more weeks, but he was mentally noting each location where he saw tracks to tell his two sons and five brothers
about in Fort Yukon, as well as some of his in-laws in Chalkyitsik. He pointed out the signs of beaver to me with a more
detached, merely professional interest, because they were in
someone else's trapping territory.

"Goddamn, it's falltime! They're getting their food piles
ready already."

The Yukon Flats stretch for nearly three hundred miles
and host perhaps two million ducks during the summer. The
Wildlife Refuge proper, which we were within (and within
which trapping and hunting are permitted), is four times as
large as Yellowstone National Park, and it serves as a sort of
duck factory from the standpoint of the Fish and Wildlife
Service, producing, as the birds fan south over the continent
from California to Maryland, an estimated four hundred

thousand "hunter days" of recreation. Rounding the many bends, maneuvering between the frequent sandbars, we saw wigeons and scaup and canvasbacks and startled up a golden eagle, which had been eating a dead duck on a beach. As it flapped in a circle to gain altitude, the trees almost forced it to graze our heads. Both white-fronted and Canada geese appeared, and later a bald eagle; then an osprey's nest. And we saw a number of sandhill cranes, tall gawky birds who seem to shift and balance themselves as edgily on their legs as on their wings. And a great number of hectic loons, intent upon getting rapidly from one place to another and then back again, as if they knew they were already rare in the Lower Forty-eight.

The copses of willows and spruces changed sides too, from left bank to right bank, or right bank to left bank. The water was seldom deeper than three feet, and so clear that the salmon that run up the Big Black cannot be netted in any quantity because they can easily see the strands even during the summer's night. The cherry-colored pebbles on the bottom, and the clarity of the clouds reflected upside down ahead of us, and the black and silver riffles just ahead of them, were very beautiful, with the constant bending of the river's course revealing new vistas of trees, new beaches of sand or stones that we were coming to, or a little oxbow that had filled up with earth in the spring floods and grown up with grass, where animals came.

When I could hear him above the water's rush, Fred was telling me of trips like this up the river in falltime, with as many as thirty people transporting themselves to trapping camps above Chalkyitsik—camps at Red Bluff, Doghouse Slough, Salmon Fork, Grayling Fork, and the topmost tributaries of the Big Black—and how they'd sometimes get stranded in inadequate water and have to live on just the fish that they angled for and the ducks that they shot. The worst year, it was a month before a rain at last released them and they got off the river's "high bottom" in their slow, old, deep-draft inboard motorboats. And when they did, they poled around just three bends and saw two moose on the bank and shot them and camped right there and—between the thirty of them—ate all eight legs in a couple of days.

After four hours and maybe forty miles, we stopped at

Englishoe Bend for lunch. It's a campsite where Fred regularly stops, next to a muddy slough where nets for whitefish can be set, in grassy waters that are aswarm with pike, and opposite a long gravel bar where he said the women used to collect hundreds of tern eggs in June and then go back a week or two later to gather a hundred more, that the robbed parents had relaid. Board tables and butchering racks had been nailed between the poplar trees. We saw the fresh tracks of a three-year-old-size bear, which had wandered around in search of relict scraps, and heard the *chirp-chuk* of a ground squirrel, a delicious animal that Fred kept a watch for thereafter, to shoot for Henry William if he could, while we boiled salmon and potatoes for lunch and laid the salmon skins on a stump for the magpies to pick. *"Chuk, chuk, chuk."* With cupped hands, he tried to call the ground squirrel out of its den.

Only seven government staffers are assigned to care for these eight and a half million government acres, and they live and work in Fairbanks, more than an hour away by plane. So the original Gwich'in caretakers pretty much still have it, insofar as they go out, plus the fly-in white hunters and fishermen, who are not numerous enough to put undue pressure on the animals but can unnerve and infuriate an on-the-ground trapper by landing at his muskrat lake and making waves that throw both rats and sets out of kilter for a week, or by landing and shooting a particular moose that was slated for his winter larder. Only an average of six and a half inches of precipitation falls in a year—a desert's quota—but the fact that so much stays as snow for so long and is underlain by permafrost makes it a duck factory anyway.

Fred said the Indian families had acquired their "white" names when passing whites would bestow a first name such as William or John on a man and eventually his sons and daughters got another first name tacked on ahead of that one. Fred himself, being three fourths Caucasian, is another story, but he always chose the Athapascan life—and indeed, with the provisions of the 1971 Alaska Native Claims Settlement Act, passed under the gun of lawsuits by native groups that were holding up construction of the Alaskan oil pipeline, it became financially desirable to be classified as a "Native." In hindsight, he realizes that his own and other families probably could have, and certainly should have, founded their own statutory village on the upper Big Black River at its Salmon Fork, where there is an abandoned ancestral Gwich'in village site, at which his brother Harry still traps, fifty miles below Fred's cabin. If the proposal had worked, the government would have built them a school, brought in a generator, mail service, and other courtesies, and they could have set up a store, passed a restrictive liquor ordinance, and otherwise established a quiet place to live for themselves, with opportunities for going into business, if they wanted to. Chalkyitsik has survived into the post–World War II era because it's at the head of navigation on the Big Black. The little tug *Brainstorm,* pushing a barge with barrels of fuel oil, stacks of lumber, and heavy items of replacement machinery, still makes it that far up the Black once every year at high-water time in June. But some other villages are supplied solely by air.

With my friend Linda, I'd been to several of these, on the Kuskokwim River or the Chukchi Sea. It had become unusual for me to travel alone. I was spoiled, in fact; never in a tent without being in her arms; never in an isolated settlement without sleeping in the warmth of the health clinic, surrounded by the appurtenances of first-aid gear and medicines supplied to these places, or else in the womb of the school, in which all these communities focus their assets: the one sure oil furnace and hot-water heater; showers and laundry machines; and a communal kitchen stacked with cases of government-surplus peanut butter, canned peaches and peas, macaroni, and jack cheese. When I had insomnia, I'd wake in the middle of the night on a wrestling mat on the gym floor and shoot baskets—an ace at sinking three-point baskets at 3:00 A.M., being so utterly relaxed at that hour, my wrists loose as flippers, my fingers a pianist's, my eyes a dead-eye's. I don't believe a man should travel far without a woman's company; it's unnatural; and even when the war between the sexes comes to the fore, man is born of woman, spends nine months inside her, and depends upon her for long sustenance. Nor can I imagine dying with any degree of resignation, even of old age, anywhere but in a woman's arms. That women are taking over the Western world is no surprise; I've expected they would. They're awesome. The only protection from the power of women is a woman, and the best are the feminists, because they have all the virtues of men.

Fred tried to call the ground squirrel out of its burrow for Henry William's supper before we started again. *"Chuk, chuk, chuk."* But it wasn't fooled. The afternoon sky already looked cold, but autumn holds no terrors for a ground squirrel: as from Fred's rifle, it just goes underground. There were still plenty of dragonflies and many mosquitoes. "Where do they get all *their* food?" I asked. "There aren't that many of us around." Goldeneyes were running on the water, leaving patterns of footsteps like skipping stones as they took off, and we saw a mother merganser with twenty flightless though fast-swimming babies in tow. Four fledgling red-tailed hawks were awkwardly testing their wings between spar trees, and periodically we slid past a watchful, affronted owl.

The so-called mew gull, which mews, is a seacoast gull that nests along interior lakes and rivers and is so versatile that it feeds on swarms of flying insects like a swallow, but also upon bugs in a field, and on fish, crustaceans, and mollusks. It likes the gravel bars of the Black River to lay its three olive-colored eggs on. The babies, by now a month old and almost full-grown, still couldn't fly, but wore as camouflage a mottled brown, like the bars where they stood, ungainly, uneasy, as we went by.

More kingfishers agitatedly flew up and down between bankside sweepers—uprooted trees leaning over the current—and spar trees. At Agnes Bar (named for a local woman named Agnes Druck), Fred told of sneaking back here one time on a gaggle of honkers who thought they had seen the last of him and bagging nine of them with three shotgun shells. "This is my supermarket, this nice river."

On another occasion along through this stretch, during a spring flood just after breakup, he had lost control of his canoe and was swept violently under a sweeper and nearly flattened and swamped. "Whoa!" he'd yelled, forgetting he wasn't still behind his dog team—which had been part of his problem: he'd been sledding for so many months.

Then we spotted a moose in the water, which had been drinking. It wheeled and ran up out of the river and onto a high bank, where it stopped and stood surveying us, like a wild horse with horns, just the way that a hunter would want it to do.

"Lots of hamburger!" Fred laughed and said that it had "a three-year-old's palm." Shortly before freeze-up, he said, when he's hunting hard, he sometimes likes to sleep in his canoe, to be well placed at dusk and at dawn. But the warmest part of the day is also a good time to hunt, when moose and bears may wake from their noon naps and want a drink. Nowadays, when he hasn't strong arms for hard paddling, he hunts from this noisy skiff, but once he missed a shot at a moose when he'd just cut his motor and his own wake caught up with him and rocked his boat as he was firing.

We watched the riffles, watched for smooth but quick currents, following the cutbanks but avoiding disturbed water. Past bend after bend after bend, we watched the taiga and willow scenery unfold—the "drunken forest" of leaning spruces narrating where the permafrost rose momentarily underground; then placid tree lines again—until, three hours from Englishoe Bend, we rounded yet another bend in the river and suddenly sighted a bluff in front of us with several log buildings on top, a dozen beached skiffs at the base, and a sandy path leading up. Some kids were playing on the beach, and a couple of fishermen were flapping and tossing their short nets about to dry them in the wind. The Black River fishhooks around the bluff, past the mouth of a good fishing creek that faces the town, and so for both reasons Chalkyitsik is named Chalkyitsik, "Fishhook Town."

Walking up the path, we met John William, Fred's brother-in-law, a shambling but big-built, handsome, Indian-looking, young-looking forty-nine-year-old and born-again Christian, who promptly began lavishing elaborately scatological invective upon Fred, pausing only to introduce me as an honored visitor to the Reverend David Salmon, the Gwich'in minister of St. Timothy's Episcopal Church in town. It's said of the Yukon Athapascans that they're born into and die in the Episcopal Church but "shop around a lot in between." Just so, an evangelical family of fundamentalist preachers with Tennessee accents had dropped into town, and John enthusiastically let us know that he had fallen under their spell. Also, the state trooper whom I knew from Fort Yukon was here to deal with three teenage kids who had smashed up the town's pickup truck. Chalkyitsik, with only a little off-again, on-again general store, has a mere handful of teenagers and a single truck and perhaps one mile of road, which runs from the school to the dump. But they had snatched the keys and driven that far and come to grief on the way home.

"Sure feels like falltime. A few leaves turning yellow," John William said. He borrowed enough money from Fred to buy some sugar for our tea at the store, and he knocked on a friend's door and borrowed a small slab of moose meat to give us a good supper that evening.

"Going to make an Indian out of him yet. I already gave him some beaver meat and some snow goose and salmon, and he's only been here two days," Fred said.

John's house was as old as he was, John told me. The leaky sod roof was covered with plastic sheeting, and the walls were lined with flattened cardboard cartons for insulation. It stood next to the store and was hooked into the store's generator for electricity. He had a deep couch for me to sink into, two *Newsweeks* and a *Real West Yearbook* on the table, a wood stove fashioned from a steel barrel, and a Coleman white-gas burner for cooking. John took out his old violin and horsehair bow and played "Be Nobody's Darlin' but Mine," as Fred told me later he had been doing for visitors for thirty years. He'd been the storekeeper for a while and now was village council president. He had had eleven years of schooling, including stints at Bureau of Indian Affairs boarding schools in Sitka on Baranof Island, in southeast Alaska, and in Phoenix, Arizona, because he had impressed his teachers as being promising.

"But still it was just a glimpse," as he told me, of the immensity and complexity of the outside world and the wealth of cultivation beyond the watershed of the Yukon. Unlike a lot of the Indians and Eskimos I had been talking to around Alaska, who felt that they'd been unfitted for life in both worlds by the experience of being partially immersed in each, he wasn't sorry to have gone Outside. Liquor had been his weakness, he suggested, and *Newsweek,* he said, remained his link. In Alaska opinions tend to be strong and unambiguous, and many Eskimos and Indians are consumed by a rankling bitterness toward white rule, white society—and even a death threat whispered or yelled at a strolling white man who is transient in the community isn't uncommon, especially in Eskimo towns such as Barrow. But John wasn't angry. He had come back to Chalkyitsik to settle, not with the sort of ringing and emphatic choice of how he wanted to live that Fred had made. He was divided. He knew that there were other ways of living—with music, books, and bustle—that appealed to him. For Fred, the deeply drastic changes in Fort Yukon—like the "wine scramble" on the Fourth of July, when grown men scrabble in the middle of School Street to grab a bottle of wine; the crime wave, including a double fratricide last year; the rising rate of drownings and outright suicides all along the Yukon—were not cause for personal alarm but simply confirmed that the old life in the bush, with his brother Harry fifty miles below him and his brother Albert trapping seven miles above him on the Black River, was best.

There are many young men with a mocking bitterness toward everything they can identify as "white." They drink bottled beer, drive snowmobiles and "big-horse" outboards, and envy their fellows who fly off to be educated elsewhere, yet with a full dose of self-flagellation as well as a rancid, vituperative resentment of an outlander walking by. Then maybe, alas, you hear they've shot themselves while cleaning a rifle or have taken their boat out and rolled it over within sight of shore—a favorite sister possibly witnessing this in horror as the river effortlessly seized them and pulled them down. But it's not the fiftyish people who do this, or even share the fury, as a rule. Several times I met men or women of late middle age who said wistfully that the happiest years they'd ever known were when they'd left their native villages and gone and lived with a white friend in Seattle or Salt Lake City, removing themselves from Indian life altogether. It wasn't politically popular to say so, but sitting in an ancestral cabin isolated on a reach of riverbank no longer inhabited by others, they might confide.

Old people, however, had no such memories of a romance with a lonely Anglo schoolteacher, perhaps; no williwaw of doubts assailing them as they remembered a sojourn ten years before in Santa Cruz, where a summer lover had spirited them after a tryst on the Yukon and where they had worked on the amusement-park boardwalk, running a kiddie ride, until the lady in question—an anthropology professor on sabbatical, a social worker on furlough, a federal accountant, or whatever she was—after one drunken binge too many, bought them an Alaska Airlines ticket home. In these villages you may meet an Indian woman who at one point was carried off too—by a white barge worker, a store manager, a bush pilot, a firefighter, a hydrologist—and then gently sent home because, in Juneau or Los Angeles or Tulsa, she no longer looked so good. It was not that her hair was less black and lush or that the measurements of her bust had shrunk, but that she didn't know what to do; she had to be led by the hand everywhere. She became meek and confused, too easily bossed around and too tempted by liquor, or frightened of it, and couldn't pull down a healthy paycheck, and sat by the TV all day if left alone.

But the women somehow survive this kind of experience better. More flexible or philosophical, they go to work in the village post office and grocery store, or the village or tribal office, with enhanced skill. There seems to be a marked difference in how "Native" women bear up under the stress of demoralizing social change. They can remember the big-legged oil-field guy carrying them off to Houston when his contract expired and his wife, by letter, had informed him that he shouldn't expect to move back in the house. So instead he brings his Fort Yukon girlfriend to roost in a condo by the Ship Canal or Chocolate Bayou, and they lie in bed in a luscious X late every morning and drink shooters late into the night, living off his Prudhoe Bay earnings, while he phones divorce lawyers or tries to get through to his kids on the phone—him climbing her body half the night, in between bouts of snoring like a walrus—until one day he begins shaking his head and says, "Oh, no, no, it's no good. I'll drive you to the airport."

No, she protests, and he "kindly" gives her another chance. But he begins joking about "firewater" when they drink, and the fun goes out of so much of it. She feels foreign, inadequate, a dumbhead. She sneaks off to try to make it on her own in Houston, but finally her family sends her a little money, and a barmaid takes pity and deposits her on a plane for Minneapolis, where the stewardesses can steer her to the gate for Fairbanks—where the ancestral, rapacious cold itself is as steadying as a hand on her elbow.

"The hawk almost got you?" they say in the Arctic when you've just survived a close call.

But we didn't talk of these things in John William's log cabin in Chalkyitsik. Nor did I ask about his personal history. Instead John and Fred agreed that it was too bad the Englishoe Bend ground squirrel hadn't come out of its burrow, because John's rabbit snares were turning up empty and it was animals like these, cooked in their skins, that the old man found most palatable in his last illness. He was tired of eating pike, which were the easiest fish to catch in midsummer. Salmon swam by the town all the time but would not bite a hook, because when spawning they don't like to eat and the Black is as clear as glass in August anyway.

We went to look at John's new cabin, of which only the deck had been laid in quite some while.

"You better finish it," Fred said. "Your rafters look like deadfalls from lying there on the ground."

"I'm going to build a Log Cabin Syrup–type cabin," he said.

They talked more about wild foods. Fred said his mother used to bake hoot owls and that if you first boil and then bake a loon, it's pretty good too, though most people don't know that. We walked for a mile or two around John's snare line to see if Fred had any suggestions for improving it. Fred has been snaring rabbits in a serious way for half a century, in town and out of town, for a garnish for a meal or living off them when he had to, and never gets on a plane without a roll of picture wire in his pocket, in case the plane goes down and he has to set snares to survive—gave me some wire, for safety's sake, when I left him—and he said it was harder in the summer, without tracks in the snow to read like a newspaper.

John observed that a shot rabbit tastes better than a snared rabbit, because it hasn't strangled slowly in the snare, while its juices soured. He pulled an imaginary bowstring back close to his eye and sighted along his outstretched arm. But we weren't seeing rabbits that you could shoot at, either.

We went up on Marten Hill, where the old man was going to be buried and where Fred said he himself hoped to lie. Cranes were calling from the sky, and we also heard a ground squirrel's *chuk,* which made us all grin but was frustrating to the two men trying to tempt Henry William to eat. The view was low-lying but splendid—to the northeast, Frozen Calf Mountain; to the southwest, Bear Nose Mountain. Immediately beneath us lay Marten Lake, a modest dab of water that the "black ducks" (as they call white-winged scoters here) arrive at in legions on Memorial Day, even more concentrated than the mallards, which need less open water and arrive two weeks earlier. The Chalkyitsik hunters lie on this sunny cemetery hill and blast away as the exuberant, amorous scoters, which have wintered down the Pacific coast, swoop up again off the level of the water in wavering lines, sometimes without having landed, and skim up the slant of Marten Hill past them to have a look-see at the other lakes all around.

Fred talked bolt-action versus lever-action versus pump-action guns and showed me where they lay and how they fired. Probably more hunting fun is had here in this week or two, he said, than anywhere else around the village, so he'd like to have his grave dug where he can hear the guns and laughter and remember how it was. In their gleeful, flirtatious courtship activities on his own hunting ponds, farther up the Black, the ducks are so very unwary that, alone and paddling quietly after them, he can get close enough to shoot several, and then go home when they fly off, but come back and do the same thing again before dusk.

Before we returned to the village, he and John showed me two sites where arrowheads have recently been found that indicate raids that were staged upon these Chalkyitsik Gwich'in more than a hundred years ago by Indians of the Koyukon group, living hundreds of miles to the west, and by Gwich'in Athapascans from northeast on the Porcupine, who almost within living memory had attacked an outlying encampment by surprise one night, thinking it was the main one, with such force that they might have wiped out everybody if they'd got their target right. All these Athapascans, living south of the Brooks Range, also warred intermittently with the Eskimos, whose territory lay only two hundred fifty miles north of Fort Yukon. The animosity lingers in muted form at Native American rights conferences and the like, and

77

in Fairbanks bars. But Fred told me the story of the last Gwich'in who had died at Eskimo hands. He had come home very sick after a long hunting trip in the northern mountains and simply took to his bed, saying nothing about what might be the matter with him. He asked that he be buried with the regular ritual (which in those days meant being placed in a tree), except for one special stipulation: that nobody examine his body closely for three years, but then to do so. And when the period was finally up and his sons carried out these filial instructions, they discovered an Eskimo lance head—serrated like a harpoon head that holds sea animals—at the center of his bones. And they realized that by remaining silent, he had succeeded in bringing the long cycle of vengeance, countervengeance, and counter-countervengeance at last to an end.

Not just the local Indians and Eskimos tend to take a leery view of each other, but the whites who work with Native American Alaskans often choose sides. Alaskan Eskimos, if one can generalize, were more innocent until recently of whites' duplicity and brutality than the various Indian and Aleut bands. Because of the climate and remote locations in which they lived, they had been "discovered" later, and perhaps protected a bit better by the missionaries who interceded with the whalers, adventurers, and officials who visited their villages during the summer. The "Red Power" political movement and the rage accompanying it were slower to reach the Inupiat Eskimos of the North Slope than the Indians of southeast and central Alaska. Consequently, a traveler is more likely to be threatened with a beating or with getting shot in an Eskimo village nowadays—Indian activism having reached a more political, sophisticated stage. Thus traveling much there takes a bit more intrepidness (not counting the fact that my eyelids freeze shut). And I am a stutterer, and Eskimos will make fun of a handicap more readily. Their culture, pummeled by the exigencies of the Arctic, makes less allowance for handicaps; their religion itself seems simpler.

But with my nursing friend, I had an entrée and a protected status. Sometimes people even took me for a doctor at first, because I was accompanying a nurse. I would go with her as she visited patients: not just kids, but old men and women dying of liver cancer—to which Eskimos are particularly susceptible because they are subject to hepatitis B, a precursor disease. The bed would be by the window of the back room of the small, slapped-together, government-built house. The man lying there looking out would glance up, politics and Red rage being far from his mind, if indeed he didn't disagree with its premises from the different perspective of his own generation. Linda would feel his pulse, take his blood pressure, and do the mildly painful business of drawing blood, unless perhaps he was so close to terminal that she had the option of not doing so. She would ask if he was where he wanted to be—would he rather be in town at the hospital? No, no, he said, with his eyes fastened on the landscape again. Did he know that he could have a sedative or an anesthetic shot anytime he needed one—had the village health aide made that clear to him, and did he trust her to do it? Yes, he said. Linda explained with tenderness that she herself was from Anchorage and would not be back, but she would talk to the district nurse and that if he told her of any way she could help him from now on, she would. Resigned, his gaze outdoors, he smiled no.

At John's cabin, John showed me the moose shoulder blade he hunts with during rutting season in the early fall. The Gwich'in will gently brush a moose scapula across the bushes and branches as they walk through the woods or canoe a small creek, imitating the sound of a bull's antlers in order to provoke the approach of other bulls. At this time of year, a hunter doesn't necessarily try to walk softly. He may deliberately break a few sticks underfoot to mimic the noise of a bold bull that is looking for trouble. People who have hacking coughs, people chopping firewood—even drunks vomiting their breakfast at the edge of the village—have unwittingly attracted a rutting moose. Because moose don't eat much during their rut but drink lots of water, you hear the water slosh in their bellies as they come. A 1964 vocabulary listing gives eleven different Gwich'in words for "moose."

Fred and John talked about hunting in the old days, when if you met a cow and a bull, you shot the cow once, and then the bull once, and then the cow, and then the bull, swinging your rifle back and forth so that neither escaped, but husbanding your shots because each bullet ruined at least

79

a couple of pounds of decent meat. Fred's father apologized
if he needed more than two shots to immobilize a moose, but
then would patiently let it die in its own time. With moose,
you try for a heart shot—under the shoulder and from the
side—but in hitting a bear, you place your shots not so much
for a quick kill as to break the bear down so that it can't
charge, with shots into its shoulder bones and chest, or the
face and eyes. After a moose died, the Gwich'in immediately
cut off its ears, for reasons of piety which Fred has forgotten,
just as they would cut the muzzle off a wolf and tack it to a
tree, or put a piece of moose meat into the campfire at night
if wolves howled, to share their kill in this manner with them.
Bears, as they died and afterward, were treated with special
respect and gentle solemnity, befitting a manlike creature
whose spirit would go back into the pool of bear spirits and
help to determine how much luck the hunter would have at
hunting bears again. But except for putting meat on the fire
when wolves howled, Fred's riverboatman father didn't allow
"superstitious" practices in his household.

Fred and I ate moose for supper, while John preferred
to boil the heads of the two salmon we had brought. Henry
William, John's and Charlotte's father, came over to share a
bite and to meet me. Gaunt-chinned, pale, and crumpled
over, leaning on his cane even after he was sitting down,
Henry William wanted to tell me his story but was too tired to
say more than a very little.

With John's and Fred's assistance, he said that the first
time he had ever seen a white man was early in this century,
when his own father had taken their family cross-country
from the Big Black River to the Little Black River, and down
the Little Black to where it meets Big Creek to form what is
thereafter called the Grass River. But instead of continuing
down the Grass to the Porcupine and to Fort Yukon, they
went up Big Creek to its headwaters, at a rise that on its other
side overlooks the Yukon River opposite Circle City, which is
now the village of Circle, pop. 81. At the turn of the century
Circle City was a small trading metropolis, two hundred
ninety-two river miles below the larger hubbub of Dawson
City, and by sled, about a hundred sixty miles northeast of
Fairbanks. In fact, in 1896, just before the Klondike strike,
Circle City had boasted twelve hundred citizens, a million

dollars in gold extraction a year, two theaters, an opera house, twenty-eight saloons, eight dance halls, and the sobriquet, "The Paris of Alaska." The Klondike rush, much richer, had partly depopulated it, but even in 1906, fourteen years after the first Circle City strike, a quarter of a million dollars' worth of gold was taken out of there.

Although the William family was a bit late to see Circle City in its glory, the buildings did remain, and everything was new to them, he said—even flour. They bought some flour and stirred it into water with some newly acquired white sugar and poured this white white-man's gravy on their moose meat, not knowing any other use for it. After the meal, he, Henry, had carefully felt his face and looked at his hands to see whether he might not be turning white, too.

"Right down here in America we get a square deal," said Henry. "But in Canada, no. Shoot him! Shoot him! In 1919, natives scared of police. Grab a guy and smell his breath and maybe shoot him. Take a girl to the station and all screw her before they let her go."

After their initiation in Circle, the family had gone to Canada, but ended that unpleasant sojourn after World War I and came back to the Big Black River to set up a homesite at Doghouse Slough, upriver about twenty miles from Chalkyitsik. John, who consequently has some land rights at Doghouse, said he wants to open a "Doghouse Restaurant" when the tourists come, and that although he doesn't know how it used to be with those Canadian Gwich'in up the Porcupine and Yukon, now (on the grass-is-greener theory) "The girls are friendlier up there in Old Crow. They're more relaxed."

"But I'm sure glad that goddamn Seward bought this country from Russia," Henry told me—as if I, as a white American, could somehow share in the credit.

"Beautiful mornings, with the mallards and the laughing geese talking. On the Salmon Fork it's like Marlboro Country. Fast river. White mountains." John laughed, teasing Fred because it was Fred's brother Harry who actually trapped the Salmon Fork, whereas Fred's Grayling Fork, named for its grayling, a troutlike fish, was fifty miles farther up the Black, and "dark like a dungeon," and too shallow and slow-moving for salmon to choose to spawn. With no salmon holes, it had no salmon—"except for a few strays that missed the turn," as Fred himself admitted with a grin. Even the otters that wandered into his Grayling Fork got starved out by winter or else would put their feet into his mink traps simply "to get a scrap to eat."

Henry William let them kid each other without comment. Now that Belle Herbert had died—supposedly the oldest person in the United States, at 129—he was Chalkyitsik's senior citizen. Belle had lived so long that she outlived her family and dwelled alone, though comfortably, with a string that ran from her house to a bell in the next house, which she could ring if she had to.

Fred and I went back to the riverbank and put up separate tents, I with my air mattress to sleep on and Fred with a bearskin. We stood watching the river's ripples and fish surfacing and muskrats making V's as they swam about. Fred called the muskrats closer to us with squeaking sounds—saying his father "couldn't call a muskrat to save his life"—just as he does from his canoe when he is hunting them with a .22 after the ice goes off the lakes in the spring and they have so much freedom to swim anywhere that you can't trap them, but the fur's still good. Then the days have lengthened like mad, and the males think he's a male and the females also think he's a squeaking male, and both come for him. Between pursuing the muskrats and the gleeful ducks, it's such a happy time of year that he once tried to tape-record the sounds of May, to play back for himself in midwinter, but wound up mostly with his own voice cussing the recorder.

We built a smudge fire to fend off the mosquitoes, and John and Fred talked ducks, fish, and mosquitoes. But John said he was tired of fooling around alone in the woods. He wanted to get married now, "either to a white woman or to a red woman." Fred, being an old married man, said it wasn't so bad being alone. He regularly had only two lonely moments on the trap line, both in the early fall. The first was when his kids went back to go to school, and the other, right afterward, was when the geese went headlong overhead, which they did just as soon as their young ones had grown wings that could fly. Sometimes the geese's heading south seemed a little lonelier, maybe because his kids, but not the geese, were sorry to go.

A cousin of John's stopped by and, when I brought up the subject of Brush Man, said he thought he'd spotted one once but now doesn't believe it, because he was a kid. His father had told him they'd traveled overland from the Lower Forty-eight, just as the miners did, but, unlike the Klondikers, they couldn't go home again.

John said, "A guy here shot one a few years ago, but they paid him back—he blew his head off a little later." And expressing his impatience with white-style "proof," he added that "If they aren't still on the Yukon, they used to be, that's for sure. *Used* to be. Now you might have to go up north, up where the big bears are. They don't like the helicopters and all the stuff around Fort Yukon. Everybody's got a finger in the pie."

"But you mean they're in the mountains?" I asked him.

"And farther away than that. Way up north; what's that place called where it's so wild?"

"The Arctic National Wildlife Refuge?" I said.

"Empty place. Yes, that's it. You don't know what you'd find."

In broad daylight, we slept awhile, grateful that our tents were dark. Then we breakfasted at John's with the state trooper, Dan Hickman, whom I knew from Fort Yukon and whom John seemed quite interested in courting, both in the manner of a local politico and as someone who was fascinated by people who had found their niche in life. The trooper, in his turn, was curious to get to know Fred, because Fred had been the foreman on a local jury that recently acquitted a Fort Yukon Indian of the charge of threatening a policeman with his chain saw. A certain electricity flowed between them, therefore. Alaska has two varieties of trooper—the giant macho guys who look prepared for rifle duels, icy shootouts, treks by snowmobile, and bush-plane chases; and these more limber and amenable officers, who can tactfully adjudicate racial or domestic disputes. The tough troopers used to be sent to Native villages, but now that the Natives have organized and acquired collective wealth and clout, one meets the tougher troopers in the white cities and towns, whereas the skillful negotiators go out to Eskimo and Indian communities—men like Hickman, who say "Caucasian" instead of "white" and "Athapascan" for "Indian," even though the locals themselves happily use the informal terms. Our man, besides being less massively built than your stock-in-trade Alaskan trooper, was the son of a trooper and probably from birth had been free of the compulsion to vaunt his manhood.

We talked about a pending case where two trappers on the Black were said to have shot fourteen moose last winter to feed their sled dogs, instead of feeding them fish and rabbits the way everybody else does now that fly-in hunters from Fairbanks compete for moose. John kidded Hickman about the Mad Trapper of Rat River, a famous mystery figure who fifty years ago in Gwich'in country among the tributaries of the upper Porcupine River in the Yukon Territory led the Royal Canadian Mounted Police on a forty-eight-day midwinter steeplechase and shooting match. The Mad Trapper was a canny Swede named Albert Johnson, not a Gwich'in, and his stamina was superhuman, but even so, Alaskan troopers, as well as the Mounties, have to take some kidding in these Native villages about him, the trooper's job, meanwhile, being to cultivate contacts for solving a crime later on.

In the two weeks, altogether, that I spent around Fred, I never heard him speak of the bush as menacing or unmanageable. But from childhood on he has heard stories about berserk white men coming to grief in the drainage of the Yukon and the Porcupine: "Old Man Rice," for instance, a Southerner who did not like Indians because their skins were dark. He and a German immigrant, known on the Black River as Smitty, had had adjoining trapping territories along a rich beaver slough near the headwaters of the Salmon Fork. When Fred was young, they'd quarreled over who the slough belonged to, and shot each other one April. At least this was the theory. April is the season when trappers shoot beavers on the thawing ice, as their trap sets become less effective and the hungry animals emerge to forage through newly melted holes. Because the German's three dogs were discovered dead on their chain in front of his cabin later, the police, the Thomas family, and other neighbors drew the conclusion that Smitty had expected to come back. Apparently Old Man Rice was whipsawing lumber out on the ice for a boat he was building, when Smitty bushwhacked him. But presumably he played dead, when shot, to get his revenge. Then, at breakup, both bodies, as well as the boat, floated away. Neither individual had any friends—the one because of the language problem, the other because of his prejudices about Indians—so nobody cared very much, but it was the kind of insolubly enigmatic murder in the wilds-beyond that can provoke rumors of crazy-bad Injuns, or maybe a Bigfoot.

There is still a yearly toll of migrants into the Alaskan bush who come to a bad end. On a lovely, pristine river like the Coleen, a famished body will be found, twisted inside its muddy sleeping bag in a little tent that the rains have pounded askew, with its plaintive diary, the entries growing incredulous, frantic, pinched, sliding toward incoherence. The man may have made his way into the wilderness on his own, or been dropped off by a bush pilot who forgot about him, or else when the pilot did return, as scheduled, the wanderer was dead. No licensing procedures, no training requirements exist for people who wish to immerse themselves in frontier conditions. The plane, needless to say, just drops them off, and in an hour—as I've heard tell—the person may find himself wet to the waist in the spring thaw, with his pack soaked through, and no dry ground to stand on. The temperature is 33 degrees, and although he may not know the word for hypothermia, he is suffering from it. He has dry matches, he thinks, but where to build a fire? The expensive pilot has been told not to come back for three months.

Calamitous adventures are commonplace in Alaska. You can struggle for your very life for days in the muck and muskeg across Cook Inlet from Anchorage, within sight of its silvery skyscrapers. The same sort of dithery idealism that sends young people off to become hippies in Vermont and Oregon, or to demonstrate in front of a government building, propels them to risk their good health in a quick study of wilderness skills—a oneness with nature you can't back out of. The plane flies off and leaves you, and you build a hut, shoot meat and throw it up on the roof, and maybe learn enough about trapping to feed yourself that way too. You learn the intricacies of meats in balancing a diet; your woodpile is an object of high labor and devotion. But your candles run out; the night extends for eighteen, twenty, twenty-two hours. Will the pilot ever remember? One meets people in

Alaska who have literally frozen their buttocks off, wading for many miles through deep snow, though it may be that this ordeal began as a lark.

Pilots are heroes in the state, and one soon grows keenly fond of them—an unrequited fondness, as a rule, because once they have delivered you deep into the tortuous chaos of the Brooks Range, for example, they will drop you off and fly away to risk their lives alongside somebody else, dropping onto a dot-sized landing strip along another river, and then by day's end maybe five other parties as well. In the summer, pilots make lots of money and the sky doesn't darken to crimp their fun. Geologists, prospectors, surveyors, kayakers, hikers, mountain climbers, Native people visiting around (or pregnant, undergoing contractions, or schoolchildren going to a basketball game with a rival town), government experts of a dozen stripes with doctoral degrees or axes to grind or a sudden furlough—the complete cosmology of contemporary humankind in Alaska hops in and out of their aircraft. In many villages they are the sole reminder of the stopwatch tempo of the outside world, roaring in and out with insulin and bread and beer, housing specialists and sanitary engineers, wolf hunters, glaciologists, archaeologists, and behavioral scientists who intend to study bighorn sheep. The roar, the preliminary passage overhead to scout the runway, is followed by the abrupt, whooshing landing, a quick palaver, exchange of passengers and heaving of baggage onto the ground, possibly a cup of coffee, a ham sandwich, and up again, with that frenetic sangfroid.

A pilot is the one white man an angry Indian can't make fun of, because he covers ground, sees game, does good, carries the mail, and earns money putting his life in jeopardy. But the roar punctuates the static life of his sinking culture with news of its cruel eclipse. One of my social worker friends spoke of these Indian villages as becoming like "fox farms," which, during the boom of the twenties, when furs were in vogue, sprang up all over. People would pick a small island isolated enough so that foxes would drown if they tried to swim off, and breed and feed them till they overran the place, killing a crop when prices were right. But when the stock market fell and prices crashed, the people stopped bothering to catch and deliver fish to their fox-farm islands, just abandoned the places. The foxes turned into living skeletons, cannibalized one another or tried to survive for a little while on sea wrack and injured birds. And this, he thought, was about what would happen to these settlements, nurtured with hothouse oil-fed welfare programs, when the Prudhoe Bay fields run out.

The pilots, who teethed in Teterboro, New Jersey, or Huntsville, Arkansas, and who may go on to fly airliners someday pretty soon, are not overly interested in the deterioration of Indian culture and the morale of these villages, or in the private survival dramas of young hippies on a tiny quilt patch of ground sliding under the plane. Life was passing those guys by, too. You dropped them off and picked them up five months later, and they'd eaten some ducks and porcupines, masturbated to beat the band, fished a little, scratched in the riffles of their creekbed for signs of gold (of which they knew next to nothing anyhow), taken a fuzzy picture of a wolf that had surprised them by visiting, and gut-shot a moose that then got away. This is not really what life is all about. Of course, the white hippie may have originated in Teterboro himself and have his own perspective on things, but the pilot is a vivid reproach to younger Indians, who have no way of remembering how their society is supposed to work and see only its present decay, into which the plane plunges with groceries, hospital services, and so on; then darts off to cover ten other villages, carries native leaders to their lobbying meetings and kids to the dentist—living refutation of some Red Power arguments about the self-sufficiency of Native culture now. Old people, accustomed to living by the fishnet and snare and a few well-placed bullets a year, hardly care except when they look at their daughters and sons.

White sufferers, on the other hand, have come *from* home, are not *at* home, and are an entirely different breed. They can leave, if they want to, and go back where they came from, but in unusual cases, when they don't, they get into still steeper trouble, not just pulling a trigger on themselves or suddenly drowning, but a kinkier, lengthier unhappy ending. We have in America "The Big Two-Hearted River" tradition: taking your wounds to the wilderness for a cure, a conversion, a rest, or whatever. And as in the Hemingway

story, if your wounds aren't too bad, it works. But this isn't
Michigan (or Faulkner's Big Woods in Mississippi, for that
matter). This is Alaska. You get into trouble here and it's not
a cold spell, it's eight months of cold; whereupon if finally the
ice goes out on the river and you're on the wrong side, how
are you going to get back?—for days, floes splitting around
you. And Fred, though he recognized that people from my
world often went into the bush to get away from the ailments
of what they called civilization (so did he, partly, from Fort
Yukon's tensions), had no idea what a crazy constellation of
distresses these migrants sometimes brought with them. Nor,
in the serenity of his duck lakes and stick forests, did he quite
realize there were ills that might never be healed.

Alaskans take for granted, but then tend to conveniently
forget, the round of psychodramas of a good many migrants
and newcomers, who may arrive with the fervor of born-
agains, with furniture piled on the car, with infants in tow
and maybe a master's degree, riding their last dollar and
gallon of gasoline into Fairbanks to throw themselves on the
mercy of the first working-class family that smiles at them
and has a lawn to mow—a meal for a mow—but may not last
half the year. It's a tradition that you grubstake newcomers
and hope they work out. That's how the state grows. Nor
should anyone arrive too auspiciously. People who have managed their lives well elsewhere wouldn't be here.

In the towns of McCarthy and Manley Hot Springs, however, while I was living in the state, mad gunmen shot multiple sets of victims dead in fathomless rampages—the
McCarthy murderer a short-term resident in this white community reachable only by air, the individual in Manley Hot
Springs, a man who had driven as far west of Fairbanks as
you can go. And so drifters on the Yukon receive less of a
welcome than they used to, even from whites, and in the
towns at the end of the last road you can't be sure of a
grubstake now. Reversing the fundamentalists' old view of
the wilderness as satanic, people thought it was Eden for just
a while, and satanic souls may head straight for Eden if they
can, to see if their madness abates.

After the thick, frantic dramas of the gold rush, from
1885 through 1906—a hundred million dollars in gold; the
Northern Navigation Co. ran thirty-two stern-wheel river

steamers at once on the Yukon alone—veterans of World War I arrived, not simply for healing purposes but with the zest of the twenties too. What better place to roar? And in the Great Depression, hungry men came on a shoestring, needing grubstakes.

(These, mostly, were the pool of men whom I knew during my wanderings in the Stikine and Skeena and Cassiar and Omineca districts of British Columbia during the 1960s, men in their fifties and sixties by then but still able to get about pretty well if they needed to, though I met a few who had preceded them by twenty or thirty years, now going blind and lantern-jawed. When you walked to their cabins, usually by a river that they could fish in, a creek that they could pan in, if you wanted to stay over, the general etiquette was that you split wood for your helping of moose meat and a night's lodging, like in the thirties. Not just the supper's kindling and a summer night's firelight, but wood for the *pile*—"to remember you by when I'm all by my lonesome," as one guy said. He panned enough to buy his boat gas and groceries. Gold was hourly wages to him—so many hours put in: so many rice-sized grains or hangnail-sized flakes wound up in the bottle he kept. "There never comes a time when there's no gold in a place that has gold." That and his woodpile was all he needed. My book *Notes from the Century Before* was about such as him.)

Then World War II vets migrated to Alaska; then sixties hippies; then Vietnam vets: each group with its quota of nuts and hard cases. You read any old-timer's memoir of Alaska and you'll find some paranoid soul marching from the village of Dillingham, on the Bering Sea, over stupendous country to the village of Sleetmute, on the Kuskokwim River, in rags and burned black by the sun and the frosts. Or from the Kuskokwim, over another hump of the Alaska Range, to the Yukon River. Or from the Yukon over the Brooks Range to the Arctic Ocean, raving and muttering, mad as a hatter. These are the iron men, who survive. But others just go out and camp, get cold, wet, and hungry, shiver, and die.

In 1981, shortly before my first visit to Fort Yukon, a Texan starved to death near the Coleen River, only about thirty miles off the thoroughfare of the Porcupine River, and because his death needn't have happened and he kept a poi-

gnantly detailed, frightened diary, discovered by a newspaper reporter, it made headlines. But another such death,
in 1975, affected Fred more personally, because it was on his
own Big Black River. He and his son Jimmy may have been
the last people to see this man alive.

Fred was working at the Fort Yukon radar base during
those years and so on September 24 was on his way back
"downtown" with Jimmy after a vacation at his trapping camp
on Grayling Fork. The first night he stopped at his brother
Harry's cabin, fifty miles down the Black, at its Salmon Fork.
He could easily have made Chalkyitsik, seventy miles farther
down, by the next night but became curious, seeing a new
cabin going up on the bank at a bend halfway there, and
stopped to say hello. The fellow, who looked to be in his late
twenties, told Fred he had served in the Vietnam War and
"wanted to get away from people." Yet he was pleasant, and
although they were hurrying to get their skiff downriver
before freeze-up, Fred and Jimmy stopped to camp and get
acquainted with their new neighbor.

He'd made good workmanlike progress with his carpentry, but Fred remembers being surprised at how little exploring he'd done roundabout. He had paid a Chalkyitsik Indian
named Paul Ben to ferry him out there with six five-gallon
cans of gasoline (half of which had been burned on the trip),
five gallons of kerosene for his lamp, and a rubber raft, which
of course would be useless within a couple of days, when the
river froze up.

"He had no calendar or radio or watch, because he was
trying to get away from everything, and he had three or four
sacks of oatmeal—that was his long suit for food—but I didn't
see no rice or macaroni or stuff like that," Fred said. Fred's
brother Harry, on a visit, had given him a hunk of moose
meat to help him get started, and it was hanging in a tree
where the bears couldn't get at it. But the "camp robbers"
(gray jays) were pecking away at this at a great rate. He
claimed he didn't begrudge them what they could eat, but
didn't seem to realize that they would eat lots, just peck and
peck and peck and fly away to store what they got for a rainy
day. "They can do an awful job on your store of meat."

He had brought a fishnet, but it was lying on the beach,
not in the water, where it should have been right now during

the fall whitefish run, and he said he didn't know how to set it under the ice, a skill he would need in less than a week. Fred tried to tell him that freeze-up is the time to be working like hell laying in food for the winter while you still can. First whitefish and then the suckers are running past on their way back from their summer hangouts in ponds and creeks to deep holes in the river bottom, where they can get below where the ice will reach. Setting his nets in these few weeks, Fred fills a couple of washtubs with fish each day to throw up on top of his cache to freeze. And this is also the time when young rabbits born during the summer are foraging hungrily as the green things die off and the first snows begin hemming them in, before predators have caught large numbers of them. Before the fur bearers get prime, a trapper will devote days to stringing a regular maze of rabbit snares, laying up meat for himself and his dogs. Fred and his brothers caught sixteen hundred rabbits one very fine fall and threw them up onto the cache along with the whitefish. Their twenty dogs ate twelve pounds of cornmeal boiled with twelve pounds of these (or of moose fat) a day. By October it's a matter of grabbing all the flesh you possibly can, so, in the bitter weather, you can devote your energy to trapping.

Also, now that the willows alongside the river had lost their leaves, the moose would be leaving the valley for higher ground and wouldn't be back till the snows drove them down. So, quite apart from the legalities of the hunting season, it was crucial to bag one first. Yet it was easy for me to imagine this newcomer's sense of peace and relief. In the late summer he had built a sound cabin, and he felt that after surviving combat in Vietnam he could survive anything. He had a .30-06 for big game, but no .22 for rabbits and grouse. Rabbits, indeed, were all about, feeding on the tops of the trees he had cut for his house, but he said he'd seen enough killing; he was enjoying watching them.

"You talk about a man digging his own grave! He wouldn't let Jimmy shoot a few of them for him," Fred said. The ducks were already gone—Fred ordinarily goes into winter with forty ducks hanging in his cabin—but he'd had no shotgun to shoot them when they'd been around, and said he didn't know how to set snares for additional meat at the beaver house that Fred had seen half a bend upstream; nor

91

was he interested in learning. He seemed reluctant to kill anything. Two days before, he had watched a bull moose across the river but hadn't shot it, wanting, he said, to wait till it crossed to his side—he didn't realize the dark, hungry time was almost upon him and he should paddle like hell to get meat when he could. His few gallons of kerosene would quickly burn up. Fred uses nine-hour candles, thinly wicked, fat with wax—three of them set on spikes inside his cabin, so he can see while he skins, and one outside, sheltered in a punctured tin can hung by a wire under his snow roof to welcome him home from the trap line.

Paul Ben had gotten this poor fellow started, and undoubtedly Paul Ben would have looked in on him again to check on his progress after a while, or at least have come back to invite him down to the village for Christmastime. But what neither Paul Ben nor the man had anticipated was that Paul Ben would go to Fairbanks and get shot in a barroom brawl and not be in a position to take care of him again. Perhaps Fred is nagged by guilty regret that he himself, down in Fort Yukon, hadn't made inquiries. Paul Ben's Chalkyitsik friends may be too. Apparently the stranger, as Fred speculates, having watched the late-summer traffic of skiffs (such as Fred's) going by, was fooled into thinking there would always be people passing and had not been told that the winter trail the dog teams and snowmobiles used did not follow the Big Black River's endless windings, but cut cross-country considerably back in the bush from where he was. If he'd explored at all, he would have found it, and certainly would have discovered, too, that a Fort Yukon trapper named Harry Carroll, who winters in Chalkyitsik, had a trap-line cabin only two bends, or three river miles, down the Black from him. Harry Carroll didn't actually stop in more than once a week, but when the poor guy was starving in January he could have got his mitts on a whole stack of mink, marten, and lynx carcasses there to subsist on till the next time Harry came by. In fact, if he hadn't waited until his strength gave out, he could have hiked down the river to town in two hard days. Tracks showed that, late in the game, suffering hunger pangs, he had left his cabin in desperation and struck through the woods for a mile or two, but had missed both Harry Carroll's cabin and the winter trail.

The sad story, which in its particulars was like the dithering behavior of the man who had starved to death near the Coleen, except that this man was so close to help, puzzled Fred—unless you took it to be simply a story of suicide. He didn't think his having been in a war might have had much to do with it. The idea of people retreating here to lick their wounds, wool-gather, and recruit themselves seems odd to someone at home in the place, with a year-round raft of breadwinning skills, amid brutal extremes—Fort Yukon's recorded temperature range is −78 to +105. You can craft a snowhouse around willow boughs, or sleep on the boughs where coals have warmed the ground, with maybe a mooseskin propped up to cut the wind and a leeward fire—and on and on, if you know these things—but it's not the best site in the world for eremitic experiments or peace-love theatrics.

In Alaska you meet people who are still boiling mad at what they were doing before they got here, and it sticks in their craw that they have children growing up five thousand miles off, under another man's auspices, and their money from whatever project they failed at is gone. Children, money, time, love—what isn't lost? Such a honcho stands next to another in a bar (or next to an Eskimo who under different circumstances would be ranging behind a dogsled after caribou), and you may see the fur fly. The younger ones build nomad-type houses out of scrap wood, with cupolas and whatnot, and provisional marriages—one couple I knew "married" each other on a heart-shaped bed of purple fireweed—and hybrid careers. A bit of oil-rig wrestling at Prudhoe Bay, a bit of gold smuggling to Mexico City, or buying emeralds in Bangkok and hustling them back. "Gone to Goa," said a hand-lettered sign on the door of the jerry-built house of my fireweed friends, when I stopped in. Next time, Lethe-land; same people zonked out. Another man, a loner, has constructed bottle-shaped refuges dug into the ground in the deep bush that he can parachute to if he feels the need to, each with supplies and a plug.

Lassitude or pugnacity: if these are two of the stock reactions outsiders have to their awe or distress engendered in Alaska, I'm subject to lassitude. Fred was, I think, politely astonished, if not irritated, by how little advantage I took of my overnight stay in Chalkyitsik. He'd brought me so far in his boat, introduced me around, charged me a sum, and I had disappointed him by not venturing on my own into the cabins of older Indians who spoke English as a second language, at best, and might tell me Bigfoot or battle stories or lore even he didn't know. And of course he was right. He had watched me barge into old-timers' houses in Fort Yukon often enough, but here I sat engulfed in John William's broken-springed sofa, reading an out-of-date *Newsweek,* unless he led me out to meet people. Perhaps he wasn't reminded of the young veteran who'd got himself all the way to the upper Black River and then starved to death because he had ceased to exert himself, but I made the connection. My gush of energy in just getting to Chalkyitsik had exhausted me, which naturally puzzled Fred, for whom it was a boat trip between his and his wife's hometowns.

I'd first had to leave New York, entailing a fight with my wife—our marriage then being in its waning-fireball stage, her boyfriend calling her every day and spinning the dial on his phone to produce a Bronx cheer of clicks if I was the one who picked it up at our end. The flight to Seattle was an ordinary red-eye, with sleepy yuppies loosening their ties, the tempo of business breakfasts ahead. But the Alaska-bound passengers in the Seattle terminal are a breed apart. Headlong young men with grandfather beards and bristly mustaches; hectic but more ill-assorted souls, middling in age, who had fouled their nests and were banking on better luck in the "Last Frontier," hoping its rigors could swallow their bile. The profile airport clerks use to distinguish potential hijackers is presumably not applied to Alaska flights, or a third of the passengers would be pulled out of line to be questioned discreetly.

Then, on the Boeing, "Man Mountain," as he introduces himself, is your seatmate, an acidulous presence, obese as a bear, with a part interest in "the third creekbed down" in a nameless wing of the east Wrangell Range: that is to say, a Pleistocene creekbed, under another prehistoric creekbed, under one of the myriad present creekbeds in this almost roadless region of rock, ice, and snow. "The western end of this country has been ruined by the eastern end of this country," he says, with which I cannot entirely disagree.

Or the man next to you, in a "halibut jacket," with big hands, may be a Cessna pilot who earns up to twelve thousand dollars per long frenzied day during the brief herring season, spotting schools of fish for the boat he is contracted to, in highly hairy dogfight maneuvers over the ocean, competing with other spotter planes.

Or he owns a chain of California gas stations and has just opened a new one on the Glenn Highway for a tax loss and for fun and games, where he can let his hair down, hunt moose with an Uzi, hang out with mechanics who look like the Confederate general staff, and talk about "necktie parties" with them.

Alaska is also a place where people like big shaggy dogs. At the Anchorage end of the flight, with a bizarrely frozen musk-ox, mountain goat, and polar bear, all glass-encased, looking on, one sees them rassling a crate with a husky in it off the conveyor belt—"Going to count salmon!"—while kindred burly spirits with U-shaped beards yank at huge backpacks, at hundred-pound cardboard cartons wrapped in masking tape, and at reinforced trunks, as if aiming for a winter "assault" on Mount McKinley, as perhaps they are.

In Anchorage, there'd been my reunion, delicious but tense, with the friend who had taken me on TB investigations all over and who I had hoped would go to Fort Yukon too. She couldn't and so resented my going, and inevitably the division of allegiance and memories between New York and Anchorage caused stomachache, heartache, split-screen images of what was going on in one place at the same time that I was busy elsewhere. Infidelities are chickens to eggs, until it's hard to remember who started what; and my dark-haired Anchorage friend had turned me down when I wanted to transfer my home here, so the wrongs at issue had become a cat's cradle, indeed.

Some Alaskans like to call Anchorage "Los Anchorage" because of its temperate climate and nondescript sprawl, but the glass skyscrapers reflect a most muscular, lovely cloud action, as well as the big Chugach Range of grassy white mountains very closely crowding the city. You can hear wood frogs croak, see a pet caribou penned in a family's front yard directly across the street from the Atlantic Richfield oil company's headquarters, eat splendid king crab and other seafood that's fit for a king, and admire a couple of volcanoes across Cook Inlet, a glistening wide arm of the sea.

Fairbanks, more bleak and extreme in winter and summer, has a giddy, ad-libbed quality, being a long way from succor if the roof falls in. When I'm not exhilarated, I get lonely in Fairbanks; I get like a dog hearing thunder, after a while, and rush about seeking company, which in Fairbanks means people with breaking-up marriages as often as not. More hair of the dog.

I'd spent a couple of days there, visiting trailers, walking the tunnely corridors of the state university, huddled in an igloo of a hotel at a downtown crossroads where people have hunkered through a lot of tough winters. There's a great government store for buying maps in Fairbanks, and one or two riverfront restaurants overlooking the muddy Tanana River, and a bare-bones airport which is freight train, ambulance, and grocery store to that world.

Fort Yukon, where I had come next, is a more precarious place than Fairbanks by common standards: e.g., more gunfire, farther from a newspaper, a boiled shrimp, a Cat scan. In Fort Yukon the river is still primeval, and the stars, like the permafrost, hump close. The sky, where the weather god lives, is one story up. But as a consequence, if you don't panic, there's a dignity, even a gravity, to the spot; you could find worse spots to die.

Anyway, here I was in Chalkyitsik, on the roof of the world, irritating Fred Thomas by sitting on my ass on the morning of our departure reading month-old news of Manhattan in *Newsweek*. I should have gone to the camp meeting the night before. I'd liked Jerry Falwell in Anchorage, and this would have been better. The village was emotionally hung over, but as we undertook a final tour of his in-laws' cabins, something stronger seemed to be laced in their tea. Though Chalkyitsik had voted itself dry recently, the state trooper told me that, with a telescope at the end of Fort Yukon's runway, he had watched bootleg liquor being loaded for the flight here. I was finally feeling peppier, coming out of my shell and getting in shape for talking with people with dark skins, "Native"-looking faces, and heavy accents— which, alas, takes extra energy for me because, like most of us, I am a prisoner of my upbringing—but our time was up. John, who wanted to keep us around for another night, said the highbush cranberries were ripe and that the three of us should go pick a bunch. Or go fishing, maybe—wouldn't we like to stay? My middle name is Ambivalence, so much of my life, it seems, has been accidental, and I was willing to, but Fred got us into the boat about 4:00 P.M.

The bluff, with its tall view of swift water, is a congregating point for the villagers, who have rolled several logs there to sit on. Just watching the river makes you feel you are accomplishing something, and a clever eye can read news upstream and down from the wrack and the roil, the shadows of salmon, the impetus of quick birds, fat fish, inches of current. Two kids were poking a stick in a muskrat's hole, and we had half a dozen other people to wave us off.

A muskrat, too, would have been a treat for old Henry William. Fred's one regret was that we hadn't procured him any wild meat. Even I knew how good muskrat or squirrel can be. But it wasn't more than two or three bends down the river that I felt the boat rock silently, as Fred was wont to do to alert me. Looking a hundred yards in front of us, I saw two swimming heads close to the left bank.

"Bears," he snapped in a low voice, while reaching for his gun, because with only the tops of the heads showing, I didn't know. They turned, watching us, not sure what we were or what they ought to do. Fred revved the outboard motor so that they wouldn't reach shore soon enough to get away. Then he cut it and drifted down because of their reluctance to leave the shelter of the water. He didn't want to shoot one of them there and have to haul its carcass onto the beach. They were yearlings, he muttered, born the winter before last—he could tell from seeing only their heads, while their bodies were still underwater, as we waited for them to scramble up onto the mud. The mother had probably kept them with her until about a month before, when she would have driven them away in order to mate again, in accordance with her bearish two-year cycle. If we had not intercepted them, they would presumably have stuck together through another winter, hibernating as a pair and bolstering each other in the meantime.

At last we were so fearfully close, they did swim into the shallows, crouch for a hesitant moment, then dash out of the water in that adolescent spirit of *Oh, we've done it now! We better run!* As wilderness bears, they may never have seen a person before and did not really try to tear away until Fred's first bullet hit the smaller, plumper, blacker cub. Each weighed perhaps a hundred pounds, but one was larger, rangier, and browner.

Obviously they had never seen an animal shot. The black one stumbled, glanced at us, flopped down, got up. Fred fired four more times in slow succession, as our skiff drifted past, although he deliberately did not turn his gun on the brown cub as well, as it fled.

Shocked, seeming to sorrow like a human figure at what was happening, the black cub kept looking our way as it fell again and struggled up, swaying, gazing at its wounds and sniffing them, trying to absorb the separate calamity and mystery of each shot. Finally it fell and rolled up on one shoulder but could go no farther and began to kick reflexively, bled at the throat, began a wholesale jactitation, and died.

"Meat for the old man," Fred said.

We pulled ashore, checked that the little bear was dead, and recapitulated its story as told in the prints. Fred said that the two of them had just started out from this beach for a cooling swim, probably not intending to cross—had been eating highbush cranberries back in the brush but came to the river because the day was hot. Two sets of footprints entered the water, and two emerged. The larger bear had then paused at the first explosion of Fred's gun and its impact on his stumbling sister before bounding into the willows, where the mud became sand. The other set of prints meanwhile milled and bumbled about, were sometimes blotted by having been sat or fallen on, staggered slackly, and ended with the limp body of the bear herself. Fred, who is not afraid to make fun of himself, said he had aimed at the shoulder the first time, the way he does with bears—"to stop 'em, break 'em down"—but had hit her in the loin. He had then aimed at the shoulder again and had hit her there—he showed me—but too high. Next, he had aimed at the side of her head but had hit her jugular vein. Like tracks, the bullet holes were tactile evidence.

When I asked if he had spared the other yearling because of me, he shook his head. But the people back in Chalkyitsik (and later his wife, Charlotte) were so surprised at his restraint that I didn't quite believe him. He is known as a man who never shoots animals he can't eat, however, and as a conservative trapper who always leaves his trap lines with a breeding stock to repopulate them, even letting a creek valley "lie fallow" for a year, his fur buyer in Fort Yukon told me afterward.

After buzzing back to Chalkyitsik to tell John William about the meat, we returned to the mud bar, where Fred cut off the little bear's right shoulder and arm for his own family's use. The browner, humpier twin was poised on his hind legs, wraithlike, back in the willows, trying to figure out why his sister wasn't getting up. If John William really wanted him, all John had to do was hide on the far bank come evening, Fred said.

Sliding downriver, we saw horned owls and sparrow hawks crying *killy-killy-killy*. A couple of bald eagles swerved away from us in the air, sailing up a tributary. We saw many loons; many, many ducks. On flat stretches, the river meandered practically in 6's and 8's, marvelously slow going on a brightly cool day with the world afresh. A whole loop would bring you just about back where you'd started, and climbing the bank, you could see that the next loop would do almost the same. The geese feeding there would simply move over again.

We stopped at a Fort Yukon family's new cabin, chinked with sphagnum moss and overlaid with a sod roof; also boasting a seven-dog log doghouse. Tracks showed that both a mink and a fox had been foraging in the yard. "First sign of fur I've seen," Fred remarked happily.

Arriving at Englishoe Bend, we moored the boat and horsed two two-pound pike out of the slough by leaning over the stern and wiggling a trolling spoon past them on a broken fishing pole. They struck in five seconds. One spring, Fred caught fifty pike in two hours in the slough grass here. Another day, he shot a hundred thirty-nine muskrats on the ponds nearby. The point in a wilderness is that when you do this sort of thing, the slough or pond fills up quickly again with pike or muskrats from the virgin sloughs and ponds all around.

Pike are ferocious predators—eat baby waterfowl and muskrats as well as fish—and so their livers taste extremely rich, like the top of the food chain in these waters, which is what they are. We also fried a bear steak with bacon. Our bear had fed on salmon, leaves, and roots as well as berries, so she tasted complicated, munificent, protean, like the mistress of a larger realm, and Fred claimed that sometimes when you're eating a blueberry-fed bear you would swear she's had sugar sprinkled on her. One June, going upriver, he and four brothers lived on a bear cub the entire way, roasting it whole all during the first night, then boiling parts of it each successive night.

"Damn, sounds like springtime!" he said when the sandhill cranes started calling on the two river bars in front of our camp. *Garrrooo. Garrrooo.* Wide-winged, five feet tall, and yet small-headed, they seemed exuberant that their summer's householder duties were done. A wedge of what he called "laughing geese" (white-fronted geese) skimmed overhead, crying *Kla-ha! Kow-lyow! Ka-la-ha! Glee-glee!* And the various loons that we had heard before were howling up a storm, a regular hootenanny. The geese tootled. The cranes said *tuk-tuk.* The loons yodeled and wailed in falsetto.

Fred slung a mosquito net over four posts that were set in the ground and cut spruce boughs to serve as his mattress and laid them inside, with his bearskin on top, and his three-hundred-dollar Arctic sleeping bag and his .30-.06 rifle. He'd fed the magpies our scraps and put the remaining wrapped food on a bench twenty yards off, with some tin cans piled on top to give warning if a bear scrounged by. It was bait, so he made sure my tent was out of his field of fire.

In the lambent dusk we fed sticks to our supper fire, building it bigger than was proper for cooking, and watched the endless unfathomable tales the flames told. Fred talked about trap lines, which might be ten to thirty or forty miles long. Your main line followed a river, and "side lines" five to fifteen miles long would weave up each sizable creek. He talked strategy for catching marten, lynx, beaver, and mink, and about how he puts out hundreds of steel leg-hold traps and wire neck snares in November, leaving them in place into March, because "no matter how many animals come through the country, you can't catch them if you've got no traps out." Around now, he said, the ducks on the lakes are all moulting—when the young can swim well but can't yet fly. This is when the whole village of Chalkyitsik used to turn out and paddle slowly in a fleet of canoes down Ohtig Lake, which lies only about five miles behind town, driving the total year's crop of young and grownups into the narrow end, where nets were strung for them, and other people waited on shore with clubs, if they tried to climb out. That one lake could fill Chalkyitsik's needs, give up all its babies before they flew, yet be as good as new the next year, replenished by ducks from the dozens of undisturbed lakes round about.

He told me about the most recent gold rush in this area, during the 1940s, when small nuggets were found on the axle of a fish wheel twenty-four miles above Fort Yukon, on the Yukon, and a couple of thousand people poured in and put up a tent city. But it amounted to nothing more than that. If it wasn't somebody's hoax to bring in business, they figured that an old-time prospector coming downriver on a stern-wheeler must have lost his pokeful of gold overboard, or a Klondike barge had turned over.

He also told me about one fluke winter when a wing of the Porcupine Herd of caribou had migrated right through his Grayling Fork country and he'd shot ten of them. Fed a lot of people. Another year, however—this was before World War II—at around this same point during the summer, thirty people, including his dad's whole family, had started from Fort Yukon for their trapping camp at Grayling Fork, but the water in the Black was so low that they got stranded at about where we were now. For that month they couldn't budge, waiting for rain. They just jigged for pike and stalked ducks and shot small game in order to survive. Finally enough rain fell that they reached Salmon Village, at Harry's Salmon Fork, in about two more weeks of struggling. There at last somebody shot a moose.

"Everywhere you went, people had a pot on the fire and were offering you a piece." But then the skies rained so hard that the river went half over its banks and choked up with new driftwood that they had to dodge as they went on, hugging the banks.

He told me about a "magic" war between two shamans of rival villages, in which good old-fashioned poison, supplied by a miner, won the day.

And Fred said that in the Eskimo-Indian wars, which were fought across the valleys of the Brooks Range before the white men interfered, the Indians would try to wipe out the Eskimos, whereas the Eskimos would try to adopt any Indian children they captured—"because maybe Indians are smarter." He laughed.

He said the Eskimos hold more of a grudge against the Indians for the old feuds than vice versa; and that on the Kobuk and Noatak rivers, the inland Eskimos will still camp on islands overnight, instead of going up on the heights to sleep—which would be a better place for a hunter—because of the defensive habits they formed when they were scared of Indian attacks. (Of course, in Eskimo towns, you hear accounts of these campaigns that are quite the reverse.)

He said a moss-chinked house is the healthiest place to raise a baby, because the moss "breathes." And again he talked of hunting muskrats in his canoe with his .22 in May, his favorite time of year, quietly calling them to him one by one but paddling clear of the grizzly bears, down from their winter dens on the mountainside and hungrily digging out roots and muskrats from the edge of the pond.

On this short, bright night, the cranes and loons whooped, trumpeted, and hollered, above the river's continuous rustle: a party babble—hilarious voices—and young ones being schooled. I'm not accustomed to wildlife sounding loud when humans are around—short of Africa anyhow; and that, too, is being silenced. I told Fred that at home I was a person who would take in animals that were unwanted or had been "outgrown," such as South American parrots and African pythons, so that I ran a refugee center at times, sort of end-of-the-world or end-of-the-line. Hobbyists who went in for exotic animals in larger ways were willing to pay three times as much for a "liger" as for a lion. A "liger" is a cross between a tiger and lion. "And then what do they do with them? It's crazy," I said. "I took care of some circus elephants when I was younger, and now I take care of parrots, and I see that parrots use their beaks for the same purposes— reaching, pulling, prying, tasting—as elephants use their trunks. But they're both disappearing. It's like archaeology to know these things."

Fred smiled to show he understood, and we went to bed.

"Goddamn high bottom, I'll tell you!" he shouted next morning, as we traversed the river's numerous shallows. The river had fallen a few inches overnight and brought the bed closer. In the strong wind Fred steered for high waves instead of avoiding them, because where the waves were, the water would be deeper. At second sight, the river's course already seemed homey to me with its landmarks of gravel bars, winter-skinned knolls, and leaning trees. Bird heaven, just for the moment. Kingfishers, owls, diving ducks—the ducks gabblers and busybodies, the kingfishers florid, aggressive personalities, the owls buffaloed by the sunlight, though velvet-glove killers. Actually, we'd heard several owls whooping it up during the night, but the gleeful-sounding loons had been so vociferous or argumentative as to overshadow them. Owls put out a lot of noise when on their own turf and not maintaining hunting silence, but not like a loon. Loons have a fish-eating gaiety, like a barking seal's, versus the meat-eating reserve of an owl or a wolf. All of them howl and all of them bark, but the fish eaters seem to enjoy doing it more, as if with freer spirits—like the yelling that gulls often do versus the subdued mewing of hawks. Maybe it's because the earth is three fourths covered by water and their ancestral experience of food hunting has been so bountiful. The confidence of loons, seals, porpoises, and gulls reflects the amplitude and ubiquity of the sea. Our gulls of course were tracking the spawning salmon, skimming above their shapes underwater, certain that such a riot of fish would provide a feast.

Eventually the Porcupine's sea-green, sea-gray waves, triple-sized, swallowed the Black River's dark ropes of water, and in the wind there we had a deep-water chop, a new lilt and velocity. Then after twenty-five brisk, breezy miles of tangled low forest that seemed like a narrative I'd just come in on—it had started more than five hundred miles earlier, in the Mackenzie Mountains—the Porcupine's gray-green currents met the great yellow Yukon. This was no contest at all. Like motes among the forested islands, two other skiffs were busy on tiny errands, checking fishnets or carrying vegetables to families in fishing cabins downstream. We were scooped into the massive, monumental flow like a motorized wood chip wiggling upstream, and duly arrived in the sunny and slightly truculent town of Fort Yukon, where most of the kids were swimming in Joe Ward Slough, named for old Jimmy Ward's father, who was more of a public figure than

Fred's father, Jacob Thomas, though Jacob was maybe a better father than Joe Ward had been.

I went to the Sourdough Inn and sat in the swiveling barber chair next to the pay phone and placed some long-distance calls. A party of floaters who had rafted down the Porcupine from Old Crow were celebrating their safe arrival with a kitchen-cooked dinner in the dining room and joking about "catching the subway home." On the windowsill sat an ant the size of a cat, constructed of wires, facing a poster on the opposite wall, which showed a rat that seemed to be tunneling through, with the legend: *I gotta get outa this hotel!*

I ate mashed potatoes, beet-and-cottage-cheese salad, and chicken-fried steak with the floaters and joined them for a look at the town's new stockaded museum. We saw a Gwich'in awl made from a loon's bill; a moose's stomach displayed as a cooking utensil into which hot stones would be put; a three-pronged fishing spear; and a whistling swan's leg bone, such as Gwich'in girls had to drink through during their first menstrual spell. In the "white" graveyard next to the museum is a plaque:

> *In Memory of the People*
> *Of the Hudson's Bay Company*
> *Who Died Near Fort Yukon*
> *Between the Years 1840 and 1870*
> *Many of Them Being*
> *Pioneers and Discoverers and*
> *Explorers of Various Portions*
> *Of the Yukon and Alaska.*

I went back to Fred's in the bright dusk. He was still up and took me to see the log cache on stilts where he and his brother Albert store furs. By now everything was sold except miscellany, but he looked for a silver fox I wanted to see. Found a cross fox, instead, whose yellow, black, and red shadings were probably even prettier. In another gunnysack was a "bum lynx" Charlotte was going to sew a hat from, and a small wolf she wanted for parka ruffs.

"You never know what you'll find when you tip a sack upside down," he said. We discovered, indeed, six wolves in another bag, two of them black wolves seven feet tall.

I sat on a case of shotgun shells as we talked some more.

Flying boxcars were taking off to bomb a forest fire, and Fred remembered he'd wanted to give me a bottle of matches and a roll of No. 3 picture wire for rabbit snares for my flight south, in case the plane went down and I needed to live off the land. He showed me how to tie and set the loops, having just made two hundred forty beaver snares for the winter, and the same number for lynx. Dry and chatty, he said he goes to Fairbanks every couple of years for a medical checkup and doesn't mind the flight as long as he's prepared.

I put up my tent by the river and the next day heard of a grizzly bear that learned to mimic the bawl of a cow moose calling her calf, while lying in wait on the trail. And, again, of the man who had once fed a family of starving Brush Men who sat with him beside his campfire talking to him only by mental telepathy. Of how to set snares around one's cabin for a murderous Brush Man. And of the Little People, the trickster gnomes who live underground and are as strong as a dozen men—of the stealing but also the good turns they do. Probably the only way you can scare Little People into returning what they have stolen from you is by boiling pots of water and standing over their underground holes and threatening to pour. Brush Man you cannot speak to, but Little People will talk to you.

In Praise of
John Muir

We must go halfway with John Muir. He was more of an explorer than a writer, more confident of his abilities in botany and geology than of what he could do with the eagle-quill pens he liked to use (while encouraging a friend's year-old baby to clamber about the floor, lending liveliness to the tedium of a writer's room). He was a student of glaciers, cloud shapes, and skyscapes—a lover of Sitka spruce one hundred fifty feet tall, of big sequoias, tiny woods orchids, and great waterfalls. He put together his books late in life—he was fifty-six before *The Mountains of California*, his first book, was published—from magazine articles, most of which had themselves been reconstructed well after the events described, from notes jotted down in the field with wildfire enthusiasm but little thought of eventually publishing them. Though he was a wonderful talker, he was never entirely respectful of the written word and was surprised to find that there was an audience willing to read him, amazed he could earn a living by writing. Being one of those people "who give the freest and most buoyant portion of their lives to climbing and seeing for themselves," he doubtless wished that more of his readers preferred to hike on their own two feet into the fastnesses he had described.

Henry Thoreau lived to write, but Muir lived to hike. "I will touch naked God," he wrote once, while glacier climbing. And, on another jaunt, lunching on his customary dry crust of bread: "To dine with a glacier on a sunny day is a glorious thing and makes common feasts of meat and wine ridiculous. The glacier eats hills and sunbeams." Although he lacked the coherent artistic passion of a professional writer, he was Emersonianism personified. There is a time freeze, a time warp to a river of ice, as if God had been caught still alive, in the act and at work, and because Muir's passions were religious and political instead of artistic, Muir—unlike Thoreau, who in comfortable Concord only speculated that his Transcendental intuitions were right—put his life and his legs on the line in continual tests of faith in the arduous wilderness of the High Sierras. He believed that if his intuitions were wrong, he would fall, but he didn't ask himself many questions about what was happening, as Thoreau would have done, and didn't believe such exalted experiences could be conveyed to the page anyway.

Thoreau welded together one of the enduring prose styles of the nineteenth century. He may be America's paramount stylist and also established in his spare time a famously disobedient stance toward the institutionalized cruelties of the world, which later was to help Gandhi and, through Gandhi, Martin Luther King in formulating mass-movement nonviolent campaigns, before dying of TB at only forty-four, in 1862. Of course, Thoreau was in addition what we would call a conservationist, but not a militant, innovative one like Muir. Muir (1838–1914) was the founding president of the Sierra Club and the chief protector of Yosemite Park. Thoreau, on the other hand, anathematized American imperial conduct in the Mexican War and got still more exercised about slavery, angrily championing the early "terrorist" John Brown. Muir—who was all in all a more conventional soul in his politics—even after the end of the Civil War commented approvingly during a trek through Georgia that "the Negroes here have been well-trained and are extremely polite. When they come in sight of a white man on the road, off go their hats, even at a distance of forty or fifty yards, and they walk bare-headed until he is out of sight."

It's important to recognize that such contrasts were not merely due to the fact that Muir was born twenty-one years after Thoreau and thus lived through the ambiguities of Reconstruction. Thoreau sought out the company of Indians on his trips to Maine and respectfully studied their customs, whereas Muir generally disparaged the Indians of California as ignoramuses and children, dirty and cultureless wretches. Not until his adventurous travels to Alaska in middle age—he took three trips during his forties, three in his fifties, and one tour to the Bering Sea by steamer at sixty-one—did he admit a semblance of tolerance into his view of Indians. And though as a conservationist he was highly "advanced," a Vermonter named George Perkins Marsh, born back in 1801, proved to have sounded as modernist a tocsin as Muir's in a widely read book called *Man and Nature*, which came out in 1864. Thirty years before *The Mountains of California*, Marsh counterposed to the biblical theory that nature was a wilderness mankind should "subdue and rule" the idea that

> Man has too long forgotten that the earth was given to him for usufruct alone, not for consumption, still less for profligate waste. . . . We are, even now, breaking up the floor and wainscoting and doors and window frames of our dwelling. . . . The earth is fast becoming an unfit home for its noblest inhabitant, and another era of equal human crime and human improvidence . . . would reduce it to such a condition of impoverished productiveness . . . as to threaten the depravation, barbarism, and perhaps even extinction of the species.

Marsh was a complex personality, who served four terms in Congress and twenty years as U.S. ambassador to Italy, but he was a quiet visionary and public servant in the style of a New England Brahmin—not a public figure, not the man of mounting celebrity that Muir became. Muir as lecturer, as Westerner, as "John o' the Mountains," learned, like Walt Whitman and Longfellow, to wear a public sort of beard. Living to the ripe old age of seventy-six, he enjoyed three active decades that were denied to Thoreau and changed a good deal during the course of them. Although a far "wilder" naturalist, he had lived nearly as celibately as Thoreau for nearly as long. However, with no undue enthusiasm, he did marry, a week short of being forty-two. He then had two daughters—whom he deeply loved—and turned himself into a substantial, successful landowner and grape farmer as well as a well-known writer and a force to be reckoned with in Sacramento and occasionally in Washington, D.C. International lecture tours, friendship with Teddy Roosevelt, honorary degrees from Harvard and Yale—in these extra years he knew rewards that Thoreau had never aspired to, yet remained an adventurer to the end, traveling to Africa, South America, and Asia late in life. Only Jack London and John James Audubon among American artists come to mind as adventurers with a spirit to compare with his, and for both of them adventuring was more closely tied to ambition.

Thoreau, less and less a thinker and more and more a naturalist after he turned forty, was also changing in personality before he died. Supporting himself as a professional surveyor and by reorganizing his family's pencil business, he was making elaborate mathematical calculations in his journal and sending zoological specimens to Louis Agassiz. But though he didn't know it, he was already on the point of winning a considerable readership. Being in a small way a professional lecturer too, he might have capitalized on that development eventually, just as Muir did. In his last year he traveled to Minnesota to try to repair his health; and with the love that he felt for the big woods of Maine, Thoreau might well have given up his previous insistence that it was enough to have "traveled a good deal in Concord" if he'd lived on. Perhaps his best work was behind him, but there would have been some interesting darkening of the tints and rounding of the details if he had blossomed as a generalist and an essayist again.

It's doubtful, nevertheless, that Thoreau, given another thirty years, would have become as touching an individual as Muir. He was always a less personal man—less vulnerable, vociferous, strenuous, emotional. He would never have married; and not having gone through a childhood as miserable, a youth as risky and floundering as Muir's, he wouldn't have burgeoned in such an effusion of relief when fame and financial security blessed him.

Yet, really, no amount of worldly acclaim made Muir half as happy as being in remote places. Muir is touching just because he was so immensely gleeful in wild country—happier than Thoreau, Audubon, London, Whitman, Mark

Twain, James Fenimore Cooper, Francis Parkman, and other figures one thinks of as being happy out of doors. He was a genteel and ordinary man in most of his opinions, and his method of lobbying politically for his beloved Yosemite was to ally himself with rich men, such as the railroad magnate E. H. Harriman, who had the power to sway events their way if the whim seized them. He was no nay-sayer on social questions and never would have conceived of putting himself in jail overnight to register a protest, as Thoreau had done. He would have agreed with Thoreau's now famous phrase "In Wilderness is the preservation of the world," but Muir emphasized a wilderness of joy. And that, after all, is what the 1872 law creating Yellowstone—the first of the national parks—had stipulated: "The region is hereby . . . set aside as a public park and pleasuring ground for the enjoyment of the people. . . ."

Muir was not a hypocrite, and he once let Harriman hear of his saying to some scientist friends that he didn't regard Harriman as truly rich: "He has not as much money as I have. I have all I want and Mr. Harriman has not." Muir, indeed, devoted only seven years of his life to the primary aim of making money. ("The seven lost years," his wife called them, when he was managing full time the fruit ranch she inherited from her father.) But he valued money and respectability and held few views on any subject to alarm a "bully" president like Roosevelt or a tycoon like Harriman. Like Audubon, Muir was proud of being foreign-born. He nurtured the strong streak of business acumen, the religious if disputatious temperament, the Spartan understatement and resilience, and the excellent mechanical aptitudes that he considered to be part of his Scottish heritage. His mix of idealism and innocence with the hard-mannered Scotch burr—a familiar, respected accent in the immigrant stream of a hundred years ago—charmed at the same time as it reassured such men. ("Frenchiness" would not have been nearly as useful.)

Although Mr. Harriman's Southern Pacific Railroad had no stake in what happened to Yosemite Valley, he responded charitably and fancifully to Muir's pleas for help in 1905, when the valley's fate was being decided in the state senate, with a confidential telegram to his chief agent in San Francisco. The vote was whisker close, but to the astonishment of the logging and livestock industries, nine legislators that Southern Pacific "owned" suddenly swung their votes behind a bill to give this spectacular scenery to the federal government. The next year, Harriman wrote with the same potent effect to the Speaker of the U.S. House, and to Senate leaders, to have Yosemite included in a national park. And after Teddy Roosevelt's presidency had ended, Muir's odd appeal also worked upon William Howard Taft, a much tougher nut among presidents.

Muir as an advocate was a Johnny-one-note, but oh, that note! "When California was wild, it was one sweet bee-garden throughout its entire length," he wrote with yearning. "Wherever a bee might fly within the bounds of this virgin wilderness . . . throughout every belt and section of climate up to the timber line, bee-flowers bloomed in lavish abundance." Wistfully he proposed that all of the state might be developed into a single vast flower palace and honey hive to the continent, its principal industry the keeping, herding, and pasturing of bees.

When California was wild! Luckily he'd seen it then. He had arrived by ship seven years after Mark Twain appeared by stagecoach in Nevada, on the other side of the Sierras, to transcribe the experiences of *Roughing It.* Both Muir and Twain originally had harbored the hope of lighting out for the Amazon, but Twain got sidetracked into piloting Mississippi riverboats and Muir got seriously sick in Florida and Cuba en route to South America. Muir—who had reveled in one of the best adventures of his life in walking south from Louisville to Georgia—sailed to New York City to recuperate. However, disliking the city, he caught a packet immediately for San Francisco, landing in March of 1868, a month before his thirtieth birthday.

Unlike Twain, Muir hadn't gone west as a writer; not till he was thirty-seven did he resolve to be one. This was "the wild side of the continent," he said, which was reason enough. Yet he invariably soft-pedaled its dangers and hardships. Twain, quite the opposite, and quintessentially "American," celebrated the badmen and primitive conditions in marvelously exploitative tall tales, boasting of how his knees knocked. Twain used the mountains as a theatrical prop, having abandoned his career manqué as a silver miner as soon as he obtained a job as a newspaperman in Virginia City. The mountains themselves had small fascination for him, and he sought companionship with writerly acquisitiveness at every opportunity, whereas Muir at that time was grasping at solitude, avoiding "the tyrant of creation," as Audubon had once described mankind.

But the reason Muir so seldom speaks about the cold rains, the ice bite and exhaustion he met with in the mountains, the terror of an avalanche, of breaking through ice in crossing a waterway, or about the many deer he must have observed starving to skin and bones after a series of snows, is not simply Scottish diffidence and asceticism. He loved most of nature's violence—"the jubilee of waters," as he called one particular winter storm. In the earthquake of 1872, "disregarding the hard fist of fear in his stomach, he ran out into the moonlit meadows," according to Linnie Marsh Wolfe, his biographer. "Eagle Rock, high on the south wall of the valley, was toppling. . . . All fear forgotten, he bounded toward the descending mass," shouting exuberantly in the shower of dust and falling fragments, leaping among the new boulders before they had finished settling into their resting places on the valley floor.

Besides, when he got around to organizing the journals of his early wanderings, he had become sharply political. He had been jotting plant identifications and geological evidence of glaciation but now was gleaning memories from the same pages, meaning to write to save the wilderness from obliteration—and not just by the timber and mining companies. More pervasive a threat at the turn of the century was the injunction in Genesis that any wilderness was a wasteland until tilled, that man was made in the likeness of God and in opposition to wilderness and its multitudinous creatures, which were not. This seems a very old pronouncement; yet it had been the revolutionary edict of a new religion attacking established spiritual values—monotheism on the offensive against polytheism, which revered or at least incorporated the realities of the wilderness. Furthermore, later texts and preachers went beyond the objection that certain mountains, forests, springs, and animal races had been considered gods, to decry the wilderness as actually devil-ridden, inimical to the salvation of man.

Muir, like the eastern Transcendentalists, was not advocating polytheism. Nor was he secular. He believed that wilderness, like man, was an expression of one God; that man was part of nature; that nature, fount of the world, remained man's natural home, under one God. Like Emerson and Thoreau—and like Twain and Whitman and Melville and Hawthorne—Muir had found Christianity to be a stingy religion in matters vital to him. In his case, it wasn't the church's vapid response to the issue of slavery or to the mysterious ambiguities of evil or the imperatives of love that swung him toward the perilous experiment of inventing his own religion (for Twain, this became atheism). Polytheism was long dead, yet the wilderness was still perceived as inimical, and so Muir didn't want to increase by even a little the lore that had contributed to such a misreading.

His father had been a free-lance Presbyterian preacher, when not working on their Wisconsin farm—a hellfire Presbyterian, fierce with the one flock given into his care, who were his children. The family had immigrated to America when John was eleven, and from then on he worked like an adult, dawn to dusk in the summer, with many beatings. At fifteen, he was set the task of digging a well in sandstone by the light of a candle. Daily for months, except on Sundays, he was lowered alone in a bucket, and once, at the eighty-foot level, passed out from lack of oxygen. Though he was rescued only just in time, two mornings later his father punctually lowered him to the bottom all over again. Not till he was ninety feet down did he hit water.

This amok Presbyterianism helped to estrange Muir from Christianity, but not from religion, and paradoxically made him gentler toward everyone but himself. He had encountered kinder treatment from some of the neighbors and, despite his deficiencies in schooling, was welcomed to the University of Wisconsin in Madison, where a science professor and Emerson and Agassiz disciple named Ezra Carr, and especially Mrs. Carr, drew him into their household like a son. His education was so hard won that he seems to have gotten more out of his two and a half years at college in terms of friendships and influences than Thoreau did at Harvard, though both learned to keep an assiduous notebook and to insist that America had a great intellectual role to play in the world.

Muir was one of those people who believe in the rapture of life but who must struggle to find it. He wasn't always blissful in the woods. During the Civil War, when he was twenty-six, he fled to Canada, partly in order to evade the draft, and wandered the environs of the Great Lakes for eight months in intermittent torment. He had already aspired to be a doctor, then had leaned toward natural science, had exhibited a phenomenal knack for inventing machine tools and implements—the kind of talent that has founded family dynasties—and had won his independence from his father without bruising his mother and sisters and brothers unduly. He had had fine friends, had been in love; yet still he wanted to leave "the doleful chambers of civilization, the beaten charts," and search for "the Law that governs relations between human beings and Nature." There was one indispensable lesson he had gained from the brutal schedule of labors of his boyhood. When it was essential during the next couple of decades that he explore, laze, gaze, loaf, muse, listen, climb, and nose about, he was free of any puritan compulsion to "work." After the north-woods sojourn, he put in another two years as a millwright and inventor for wages (not drudgery, because he enjoyed it), before a frightening injury to his right eye in the carriage factory where he worked bore in upon him the realization that life was short.

Once, finding himself in the metropolis of Chicago, he had passed the five hours between trains by botanizing in vacant lots; and now, as he struck off like one of his heroes, Alexander von Humboldt, for the valley of the Amazon, he set a compass course directly through Louisville so as not to notice the city too much. Beginning this, his earliest journal extant, he signed himself, with ecstatic curlicues, "John Muir, Earth-planet, Universe." Later on, in California, he would set off into the radiant high country of "the Range of Light"—as he called the Sierra Nevadas—with his blanket roll and some bread and tea thrown into a sack tossed over his shoulder like "a squirrel's tail." He might scramble up a Douglas fir in spiked boots in a gale to cling to it and ride the wind "like a bobolink on a reed," smelling the flower fields far away and the salt of the sea. "Heaven bless you all," he exclaimed, in his first summer journal from the Sierras—meaning all California's citizenry, including its lizards, grasshoppers, ants, bighorn sheep, grizzly bears, bluebottle flies (who "make all dead flesh fly"): "our horizontal brothers," as he was apt to describe the animal kingdom.

On the giddy cliffs and knife edges he was not out to test his courage, like the ordinary outdoorsman, but was set upon proving the beneficence of God. More than Thoreau, though less than Emerson, he skewed the evidence. God was in the mountains, as he knew from his own sense of joy; and as he gradually discovered that his intuitions were tied in with compass directions, storms brewing, the migration of ice, and the movements of bears, he was preparing to preach the goodness of God to us as well as himself. In even the mildest Christian theology, nature was simply handed over in servitude to man, and the Transcendentalists were trying to bypass not only this destructive anthropocentrism, as they perceived it, but also the emphasis Christianity placed upon an afterlife at the expense of what seemed a proper reverence for life on earth. Such stress upon salvation appeared to isolate people from one another as well, because each person's fate was to be adjudicated separately. Transcendentalists believed in universal links and, while never denying the possibilities of an afterlife, chose to emphasize the miraculous character, the healing divinity, of life here and now.

Emerson admired and communed with Muir during a visit to Yosemite and afterward encouraged him by correspondence. Other intellectual doyens—Asa Gray, Agassiz, Joseph Le Conte—took up his banner, and he was offered professorships in science in California and Massachusetts, which he turned down. From the start he had seemed a marked man. Like his father's neighbors, his college instructors, and factory mentors, Muir's first employer in the Sierras, a sheep owner named Mr. Delaney, predicted that he was going to be famous and "facilitated and encouraged" his explorations, Muir said. Some of the Mormons, too, appear to have noticed him favorably when he descended from the Wasatch Range on one of his larks to hobnob a bit near Salt Lake City. Ardent, outspoken, eloquent in conversation, he wore his heart on his sleeve throughout his life, but although more driven, more energetic than Thoreau, he lacked Thoreau's extraordinary gift of self-containment and single-mindedness. He had more friendships—an intricacy of involvements—and was a "problem solver," as we say nowadays, a geyser of inventiveness. The trajectory of his career carried him finally to the winsome, wise figure leading day hikes for the Sierra Club, or posed on his ample front porch in vest and watch fob with his high-collared daughters and black-garbed wife; to the Muir quarreling publicly and condescendingly with the Hudson River naturalist John Burroughs, and Muir as a visiting fireman in London, or elected to the American Academy of Arts and Letters in 1909. Yet for all these amenities, and the freedom he won to do as he liked in the world, he never achieved anything like Thoreau's feeling of mastery over it—that easy-wheeling liberty to analyze, criticize, anatomize, and summarize society's failings with roosterly pleasure: "the mass of men lead lives of quiet desperation." Compared to Thoreau's spiky commentaries on his neighbors and other townsfolk, on politics, culture, labor, industry, civilization, "Boston," Muir's admonitory remarks sound aloof, stiff, and hostile, as if directed at targets with which he had no firsthand familiarity. For despite all his friendships, Muir sought the glory of God far from other people; and just as he had had to reinvent Transcendentalism for himself way out on a kind of rim of the world, he devised his own brand of glaciology to explain the landforms of Yosemite—notions at first ridiculed by the academic geologists, then vindicated, though Muir had taken no account of previous or contemporaneous studies, mainly because he was unacquainted with them. We need to remember that one reason he roamed so high and far was to measure living glaciers and inspect virgin evidence, but he was both too religious and too idiosyncratic to rightly pursue a scientific career, and so he moved on to become a rhapsodist, a polemicist, and a grandfather whitebeard.

He had seen the last of the Wisconsin, Appalachian, and California frontiers. Like twenty-two-year-old Francis Parkman on the Oregon Trail in 1846, like twenty-six-year-old Sam Clemens jolting into Fort Bridger in 1861, he had gone west for adventure. But he stayed in the West, stayed exhilarated, witnessing nature on a scale never presented on the Atlantic seaboard: volcanoes, landslides, calving glaciers, oceans of flowers, forests of devil's-club and Alaskan hemlock. He was thick-skinned to criticism, like Mark Twain, but more personally peaceable, as exuberant in Alaska as Jack London but indifferent to gold rushes and desperadoes. His favorite bird was the water ouzel—an agile, inoffensive creature living in mountain watercourses—not the golden eagle; and his favorite animals were squirrels.

> The Douglas squirrel is by far the most interesting and influential of the California *sciuridae*, surpassing every other species in force of character. . . . Though only a few inches long, so intense is his fiery vigor and restlessness, he stirs every grove with wild life, and makes himself more important than even the huge bears that shuffle through the tangled underbrush beneath him. Every wind is fretted by his voice, almost every bole and branch feels the sting of his sharp feet. How much the growth of the trees is stimulated by this means is not easy to learn, but . . . Nature has made him master forester and committed most of her coniferous crops to his paws. . . .

This is not the author of *White Fang* talking.

Like Audubon, Muir was often painfully lonely in wild places and was later pursued by rumors of romantic misconduct. With regard to sex, our nature writers tend to be damned if they do and damned if they don't. A special prurience attaches to inquiries as to whether Thoreau really fell in love with Emerson's wife, or why Audubon was abruptly exiled from Oakley Plantation in West Feliciana Parish, Louisiana, where he had been tutoring "my lovely Miss Pirrie," or whether poor Mrs. Hutchings, wife of Muir's sawmill employer in Yosemite Valley, left her husband as a result of her winter's companionship with Muir when her husband went east. Furthermore, *did* Muir sleep with the Honorable Mrs. Thérèse Yelverton, a divorcée celebrity who visited Yosemite in 1870 and made him the hero of a novel? Or Mrs. Jeanne Carr, his early benefactress at the University of Wisconsin? Still, it's true that most of our preeminent nature interpreters did not recognize that the nexus of the sexes could become a natural adjunct of what is lately called "the wilderness experience," and something faintly ludicrous attaches to their infirmity. They differed in this respect from he-men like London, from the internationally minded Audubon, and from certain British explorers, like Sir Richard Burton and Sir

Samuel Baker (not to mention innumerable mountainmen-squawmen).

As seems to be the case with many wounded hearts who make a decisive leap away from wherever they were wounded, joy eventually became Muir's strong suit. His joy in the bee meadows under sun-shot granite and ice, in the fir trees and river willows, the tiny water ouzels diving into cold rapids and running on the bottom after insects, ruddering themselves amid the currents with their half-open wings, was so tactile that he repeatedly experienced episodes of mental telepathy. He lived recklessly and efficiently enough to have done as much scrambling, ambling, trekking, and roaming as he sensibly could have, but at the age of seventy still had published just two books. His most delicious volumes—*A Thousand Mile Walk to the Gulf* and *My First Summer in the Sierra*—were reconstructed from his youthful journals only after that: journals by then forty years old. His true story of the brave loyal mongrel "Stickeen," which may be the best of all dog stories, took seventeen years to see print in a magazine after the night that they shared on a glacier. And he postponed work on what might have been his finest book, *Travels in Alaska,* until the last year of his life, when his energies were not up to the task. He died of pneumonia in a Los Angeles hospital with his Alaska notes beside his bed. A collaborator had to finish jiggling them into narrative form.

Although Muir helped to invent the conservation movement, he was a tender soul, not merely a battling activist, and lived with the conviction that God was in the sky. Yet the Transcendentalists, in revering the spark of life wherever it occurred, were groping toward a revolutionary concept of survival for Western man: that we must live together with the rest of nature or we will die together with the rest of nature. Centrist churchmen over the years had issued apologias for inquisitions, wars of racial and sectarian extermination, slavery, child labor, and so on, and their ethics were proving inadequate once again. And because Muir is such an endearing individual, to grow to care for him is all the sadder because the crusade failed. We lead a scorched-earth existence; so much of what he loved about the world is nearly gone. Naturalists themselves are turning into potted plants, and mankind is re-creating itself quite in the way of a born-again fundamentalist, who once went to school and learned some smattering of geology, biology, and human history, but who abruptly shuts all that out of his mind, transfixed instead by the idea that the earth is only six thousand years old, that practically every species that ever lived is right here with us now for our present service and entertainment. So it is with our preternatural assumption that the world was invented by Thomas Edison and Alexander Graham Bell.

Thoreau's optimism is out of fashion, but not Thoreauvian combativeness and iconoclasm. The whole theater of orchards, ponds, back fields, short woods, short walks in which *Walden* was staged remains accessible to anyone who wants to recapitulate the particulars of what Thoreau saw and did. Muir, however, is not the same. Less thoughtful, less balanced to begin with, he hooked himself to the wide world of wilderness for support, and now that that world is shattering all around, it's hard to imagine where he would tie his lifeline. Except as a tactician and a man of goodwill, he has no current solutions to offer us. More than Thoreau, in other words, he is a sort of historical embodiment, like some knight of chivalry, or a leader of the Wobblies from 1919. Frank Norris employed him as the mystic Vanamee in his 1901 novel, *The Octopus*, opposed to unbridled industrial power.

"Instinct with deity" was how Muir described the elements of nobility that he recognized among the Tlingits of southeastern Alaska, who were the only Indians he ever took to. His own "instinct with deity" was gushier, vaguer, more isolated in character, being linked to no central traditions, no hereditary culture, no creation myths or great-grandfather tales. Muir, not born to it, blundering and fumbling as he sought to create a religion in reaction to his savage foe from childhood, Presbyterianism, left out a lot that the Indians put in. There were no carrion smells beneath his landslides, no half-eaten elk in his glacial basins, no parched nestlings fallen from his spruce trees and aspens. More than Thoreau, he let his philosophy dictate which observations he wrote down. But though his embrace of nature is not to be confused with the more intimate and inherent conjugality that animist tribal peoples on all continents have had, his was sufficiently headlong that we would find it almost impossible to duplicate now.

We have disacknowledged our animalness. Not just American Indians spoke affectionately to turtles, ravens, eagles, and bears as "Uncle" and "Grandfather," but our ancestors as well. The instant cousinhood our children feel for animals, the way they go toward them directly, with all-out curiosity, is a holdover from this. Even now, to visit the Tlingit villages on Admiralty, Chichagof, and other islands of the Alexander Archipelago, where Muir kayaked and boated, is to meet with a thicket of animal life—whales in the channels, bears ashore—from which the native clans trace their origins and which therefore were seldom hunted. Bears still have territorial spheres of influence on these islands, which are accepted, and the roofs in the villages belong to the ravens as much as the streets do to the people, while eagles bank as closely as seagulls overhead.

In looking on my bookshelves for a contemporary writer who has the same earthy empathy and easy knowledgeability for what is going on out of doors as Muir did, the nearest kindred spirits I could find were the Craighead brothers, Frank and John, who are old hawk, owl, and grizzly experts, and the coauthors of a field guide to Rocky Mountain wildflowers, which was first published thirty years ago. It's too unorthodox and informal a book to be particularly popular now, but I love thumbing through it. The fact that brothers wrote it is appealing. Like the Murie brothers, Olaus and Adolph, who ten years earlier had studied elk and wolves, waterfowl and wildlife tracking, the Craigheads possess an old-fashioned air of blood alliance and clannish loyalty. And writing about the Rockies, whose climatic zones vary too much for ecological cycles to be described simply by dates on a calendar, they say that wild violets come into bloom when wood ducks are building nests and crows are brooding their eggs; that vetch vines flower at the same time that moose are having calves; that chokecherries blossom when prairie falcons are about to fledge, fireweed when bald eagles are making their first flights from the nest, and primroses when young goshawks leave for good. Coyote pups depart from their dens at about the time blueberry plants have fully bloomed. Bearberries start to flower when tree swallows return from the south, are in full blossom when Canada goose eggs begin to hatch, and the berries themselves, although still green, have formed by the time young chipmunks are to be seen scampering about. The life schedules of wild licorice and lodgepole lupine are linked to the flight lessons of ruffed grouse; meadowsweet to long-eared owls; balsamroot and serviceberries to bighorn ewes; harebells and silverweed to mallard ducklings; long-plumed avens to bison calves and Swainson's hawks.

On and on these virtuosos go. Since the book is about flowers, they are limited to events of the spring and summer, but we know that this inventory of lore could spin around the larger cycle of the year as no ecologist of a younger generation would conceive of trying to do. The Craigheads and the Muries did not age into crusaders on the order of John Muir, and they were too late to enjoy Muir's faith in God. But in their various modest books the same joy is there—and the feeling of an encyclopedic synthesis of experience and observation on a scope and scale Muir had and few outdoorsmen will ever be permitted again.

Holy Fools

My English friend Aaron Judah, raised in a mercantile family in Bombay, didn't mind my occasionally teasing him with the name "Jude the Obscure," because we were all pretty obscure. His first novel, *Clown of Bombay*, was about to come out. My second, *The Circle Home*, had just been published and had crashed in flames, as I liked to say, though total invisibility would have been a better word for it. With a few other struggling artists—a Maori painter named Ralph Hotere, an Oregon novelist named Don Berry—we were comfortably couched under the protection of the beautiful Countess Catherine Károlyi in her little art colony in the village of Vence in the Alpes Maritimes in the south of France. When not at work, we would visit the Matisse Chapel or hike up an augerlike river canyon, past deep caves which underground springs gushed out of, and past otter pools, dizzy cliffs, swimming holes, waterfalls—my wife, Amy, and Ralph's wife, Betty, enlivening the crew. I was living on the Lower East Side of New York otherwise, on $2,500 a year, as was commonly the case among writers thirty years ago, before big book contracts and university writing programs had been invented to boost their incomes. Not just the Beat spirit Seymour Krim but Philip Roth lived on East Tenth Street too.

The countess was the widow of the Hungarian patriot Mihály Károlyi, whose brief presidency in 1919 had been a beacon of democratic enlightenment between authoritarian regimes. She was vibrant, passionate, the friend or lover of Bertrand Russell, Gordon Craig, and other flamboyant intellectual figures of prewar days, and now in her sixties was beloved by her large German shepherd. She lived with a middle-aged Englishwoman in this declining epoch but had such zest that, hearing of the giddy canyons we had discovered, she galvanized herself to accompany us. And as a colony founded by a generous patroness to nurture the arts, hers was the very type of several I stayed at later, on Ossabaw Island, off Georgia, in Sweet Briar, Virginia, and at Saratoga Springs, up the Hudson River. Paying six dollars a week for a room in 1955, fifty dollars a month for a room in 1958, a hundred dollars a month for an apartment in the early sixties, I was a "low-rent" writer, in Tom Wolfe's phrase— "downwardly mobile," as Gay Talese used to kid me at publication parties—and needed a break.

But then my friend "Jude the Obscure" startled us all by fainting from hunger. He was cut from that rare category of person whom I think of as "holy fools" and whom I like to draw very close friends from. But he was a gloomier personality than my own quite standard brand of New Englander's transcendentalism, or Don Berry's Oregon frontier go-do-it energy, for that matter. He had been gloomy in India, in England, and in Israel, and had skipped too many meals for the sake of completing his work. Now he was starving. Ralph and Betty found him lying on his bed, unconscious.

Countess Károlyi of course soon put a stop to the hunger, and her companion, his countrywoman, I think may have succored him just as directly. She had offered to succor me also, but, being married, I had refused. Later, unmarried, I visited her in Paris and was startled all over again to discover her studio apartment decorated with paper skulls and cut-out skeletons to remind her of "how bizarrely little time I have left." Her doctor had told her that she was terminally ill.

"Succor your starving artists while ye may" might be a good motto. I never saw my hunger artist again, and I'm writing of an ancient era when artists were mostly male. People knew the sculptor Mary Frank not as *Mary Frank* but as the photographer Robert Frank's wife, Mary; and the theatrical innovator JoAnne Akalaitis not as *JoAnne Akalaitis* but as the composer Philip Glass's wife, JoAnne. Yet I've known women who comforted an array of men, ranging from Donald Barthelme to Marlon Brando, Edward Abbey to John Berryman, and never regretted it. Abbey and Berryman, red-eyed and coughing, used to look in on me on their trips to the city and speak gratefully of bosoms opened to them, though, as always, such flings could be complicated. An old pal might throw a shoe at them too. I knew a kind-natured Playboy Playmate who owned a whole shelf of presentation copies and bore no writer a grudge (at least in that heyday). On the other hand, a wealthy woman who made a practice of taking in lorn famous writers like Berryman told me she fed them according to their income level. Rich ones got steak; poor ones spaghetti. It was her pleasure, as well, when she bought a painting, to make love with the artist on the floor under it after the gallery had closed. Sadism was surely part of her thrill, and as with housing a doomed gladiator, the sense in his ardor that *We who are about to die salute you.*

This must still go on, but the milieu has changed. A youngish writer recently asked me to recommend him for a stay at the MacDowell Colony on the strength of a $300,000 advance against royalties he had received. He'd not previously published a book but, wanting to do a travel volume, had announced to various publishing houses that he would set forth only if he received a $200,000 advance. Now, having done quite a bit better, he was seeking quarters for the winter while he wrote up his notes.

I didn't know how to reply. Great travelers, from Wilfred Thesiger to Colin Thubron, tend to operate on a shoestring, but there is a feeling of entitlement among many new writers: budding novelists who want lifetime job tenure at a college somewhere and a Volvo in the garage. The particular angst, anguish, poverty, or precarious circumstances they describe in their fiction should never be visited upon them. People quote Samuel Johnson's celebrated line that "No man but a blockhead ever wrote except for money," though Johnson's own career refuted the idea, like his affection for the ragged genius Christopher Smart. The low-rent life of William Blake or Dostoyevsky would seem absurd.

It wasn't like that as we struggled in those years—Richard Yates, Ivan Gold, Joe Flaherty, Joel Oppenheimer, Marge Piercy, Hayden Carruth, Frederick Exley, Galway Kinnell. During my apprenticeship in shoe leather, as I called it, which I served for the first twenty years after I got out of the army in 1957, I reached my largest audience with an essay called "The Courage of Turtles," for which I received thirty-five dollars. I was glad to, because it was a newsprint audience, in *The Village Voice,* bigger than I'd had. My third novel had also crashed in invisible flames—"A Typical Example of Fictional Blight" was the *Times*'s headline—sales of nine hundred copies after five years' work. For my next novel I shifted from ballpoint pens to using a typewriter, but that one took twenty years to do.

Meanwhile, however, I hit the ground running with a travel journal from British Columbia and a fluent exuberance that greased my wheels: in effect, my first essay, a form I discovered I had been made for. As with my previous books, I could recite the entire thing by heart when I was through, and like the first, I slept with it under my pillow the night the first copy arrived in the mail. But I let my hopes scud too high. When *Notes from the Century Before* scarcely received any notice at all in the *Times,* sold two thousand copies, and got good but scanty reviews elsewhere, what I did was go to the country to lick my wounds. They were bloody, and after licking them for a week or two, I vomited, vomited blood.

For me it ranked as an equivalent crisis to when my poor avatar, Jude the Obscure, had fainted from hunger. He'd looked for changes to institute in his life, and so did I. I'd begun teaching, for three hundred dollars per semester, at the New School for Social Research; and for fifty dollars did book reviews for the *Herald Tribune.* My rent by 1970 had risen to two hundred dollars. I'd grown up in an expensive suburb of New York, going on to prep school and Harvard—but a writer's life is leveling. My father had tried to discourage me from embarking on my career, then had asked that if I must write I use a pen name, and then he had contacted Houghton Mifflin's attorney to ask that the publication of my first novel be stopped, arguing that it was "obscene." So when I published stories in the *Paris Review,* the *Transatlantic Review,* the *New American Review,* it was important to me. My policy was that once they were finished, they were never allowed to spend a night at home. If they bounced back from the *Atlantic Monthly* in the morning, out they went to *Harper's* that same afternoon. Even so, the boost of seeing them in print might take eighteen submissions. The very first, called "Cowboys," wound up at Saul Bellow's magazine, *The Noble Savage* (five issues, 1960–62; with Bellovian generosity, he wired me when he accepted it), which I suspect he had started in the aftermath of his anger at *The New Yorker*'s rejection of his short masterpiece *Seize the Day*, which had then appeared in *Partisan Review.*

Antaeus, Witness, Pequod, New England Review, like alternative publishers such as North Point Press and *The Hungry Mind Review,* have counted for me, just as their counterparts did for so many writers I knew—Kenneth Rexroth, Gary Snyder, Craig Nova, Hilma Wolitzer, Tobias Schneebaum, John Haines, Gilbert Sorrentino, Jonathan Raban, Hortense Calisher, Wendell Berry, George Dennison. Raymond Carver was homeless, broke, "belly-up," as he said, when I met him, adrift, shortly before his first success, on his way to El Paso from Iowa City. Those of my friends who felt that inspiration lay partly in gin and cigarette ends (and they may have been right) didn't live quite as long, but their hardships were all of a piece with the rest of us: buildings where the furnace broke or caught fire or the boiler blew up, where leaks developed in the ceiling that were not fixed for endless weeks, where tenants suffering a nervous breakdown ran through the hallway wielding a knife.

Does one still meet "starving" artists? Yes: a poet off an ore boat who has driven to the East Village and is being "eaten alive" by New York, he says. And regularly there are brand-name writers who need help in getting a cancer operation; regularly, young strugglers coming up—Fae Myenne Ng, Elizabeth Tallent, Sara Vogan, Annie Prouxl, Molly Gloss, Clarence Major, Charlie Smith, Howard Mosher. But whether they think of their work as being improvised like a jazz riff or plotted like a piano sonata, whether they ramble through wilderness country or case the Big Apple, choose their subject matter from what they love, like John McPhee, or what they hate, like Joe McGinniss, "go Hollywood," lobby for a position on a magazine's masthead, or chair an English department, writers do tend to turn bitter. In fact, I can't recall ever meeting a middle-aged writer who wasn't somewhat bitter. Greeting-card and comic-book writers, thriller writers, sci-fi or sitcom writers, American Academy of Arts and Letters writers, front page of the *New York Times Book Review* writers, sports-page or cookbook or mule-train writers—in forty years in the trade I've known hundreds. The big divide seems to be between the free spirits who sit down every morning to speak their minds without first calculating the market for it, and staff writers in what I call mule trains—well fed, nicely harnessed, with bits in their mouths and bottoms upraised for the whip of an editor—who write cover stories for *Time* or dance attendance upon the mind-set of *Vanity Fair* on retainer, perhaps.

There are talented people of my generation who devoted the meat of their careers to anticipating the tastes of *The New Yorker*'s legendary William Shawn, with his three-year inventory of profiles and stories, all bought and paid for (oh, *would* he use yours!). The crotchets of Mr. Shawn, like those of his predecessor, Harold Ross, recounted with an anxious edge to the voice, were fodder for thousands of cocktail parties. I went to the Sudan and to Maine for Mr. Shawn ("You won't be political, will you?" he asked) and to Alaska for *Vanity Fair*'s Tina Brown (whose interest was limited to its millionaires), but in each case my attention strayed to politics and to the mountains.

The price of independence is occasional despair, however. You see it in Melville, Dreiser, Hemingway, Faulkner—whoever. Bernard Malamud, among recent writers, elaborated best upon the uses to which despair can be put, like a kind of elixir at last. I remember lunches with Donald Barthelme in Greenwich Village and suppers with Hayden Carruth in Johnson, Vermont, fifteen or twenty years ago, in which each writer—separately, and at the height of his powers—expressed the belief that he was played out and about to die: like Raymond Carver, "belly up" at about the same time, and Philip Roth, virtually paralyzed with despondency, as he has described.

Stubborn, foolhardy, profitless writing may free one to say something new. John Updike, E. L. Doctorow, William Gaddis, Grace Paley, Paul Theroux, and Bellow have also marked me with lessons I've tried to learn—about modesty, fecundity, self-preservation, stamina, gaiety, and ingenuity. The core of writing well is to tell your tale at your own pace, just as you wish, taking your chances. From the Bible to *Peter Rabbit*, that's how it's been done. We all want to strike the perfect pitch that will win us an hour's ease and aplomb, heart to heart with a million readers, fathoming their fears and their funny bones, with our own loneliness only a fortifying toxin, or sort of like how heavy hitters swing two or three bats before going to work. If the middle-aged writers I speak of had been simply bitter, they would have got nothing done. An ebullient openheartedness and mischief-making has enlivened even the most choleric ones, like John O'Hara and Edward Dahlberg.

O'Hara relished money and Dahlberg pined for it, but surely money has never meant more to authors than it does now. The smiley buzz and slippery hustle of agents, auctions, talk tours, mall blitzes, "pencil" editors versus "belly" editors (who "just do lunch"), and young writers standing around at soirees like brat-pack bond salesmen comparing "scores," are a far cry from my fond hunger artist, Jude the Obscure. But greed and integrity do their dance down through the ages and in each of us. For every Kafka-pure anorexic following his or her inner compass, you could cite a couple of geniuses of the fat strutting stripe of Dickens or Twain, in whom the two drives intertwined fruitfully also.

I don't see any Kafkas, Dickenses, or Twains around, but who knows? Among the bohemians camped in voluntary or involuntary squalor (and they inhabited crevices of even the eighties too), there may be a boomingly, lusciously talented soul, neurotic, fretful, and bereft of hope, but churning out radiant prose. Too many writing courses are being offered, too many aspiring novelists stoop over word screens, for the number of earnest readers at large. It seems as if writing has become a therapy for loneliness, or part of the new search for solitude, like "meditation" or jogging, like Walkmans, Jacuzzis—a societal symptom instead of an individual aptitude too pressing to ignore.

Writers are prickly, blithe, callous, and manipulative, the top of the food chain when it comes to processing other people's experiences, eavesdropping upon them, milking them of their bewilderment, happiness, or grief. Tell me your story and I'll make it mine. It's a higher gossip, a Mixmaster process, but once in a blue moon—in Becky Sharp, Ebenezer Scrooge—the tale becomes *ours*. All the posturing, the ego swagger, the pinched nerves that go with having writers around appear to be worth it. We willingly succor them. I've never known one who was worth reading who didn't require the mercy of patience and tact, of sympathy and a breast to cry on. And usually, he or she found it.

Maximize

The American branch of PEN, the sixty-two-nation writers' organization, which was founded in 1921, is a yeomanly group that holds contests for first novelists and prison inmates and protests the incarceration of writers who are prisoners of conscience abroad.* But this week, for the first time since 1966, it hosts the annual congress of its parent body, a rare occasion when American writers in any numbers take notice of the existence of a world beyond our own borders.

Writers, like other affluent citizens here, do make the rounds of the countries that were regularly visited by Henry James. They know London, Venice, Geneva, as vacationers. But I would guess that five times as many have been to Tuscany as anywhere on the whole continent of Africa; that more have visited Barcelona than all of South America. We have no tradition of travel writing (Washington Irving and Lafcadio Hearn are isolated figures in our literature), except in

*I should gratefully mention that in 1991, five years after this piece was published, the Freedom-to-Write Committee of PEN rode to my own rescue after I'd temporarily lost a teaching job for political incorrectness. Any essayist who is always "politically correct" should have his head examined; and PEN's Robert Stone realized that.

connection with the exploration of our own continent, or else when we go, like Mark Twain, as "innocents abroad." In no other Western country, I suspect, has the intellectual community remained so unfamiliar with and uninterested in the changing postwar world, and much of the extraordinary ignorance of most Americans about what has been happening elsewhere on the globe since the 1940s is due to the fact that our eyes and ears—our writers—have stayed home. Exceptions exist, like Philip Roth's championing of Eastern European authors, John Updike's brilliant African novel, *The Coup*, Paul Theroux's Asian travels; and various writers have followed our troops to Vietnam, and into the Salvador-Nicaragua imbroglio. But nothing has occurred among American literati in the past forty years that corresponds to the opening outward here of writers in the decade or two that followed the First World War. They went to live in Europe, which then seemed as venturesome as going with serious purpose to Brazil or South Asia might be nowadays, and they came back—Hemingway, Fitzgerald, and the rest—with books that were new to their time and place, a mini–golden age of literature.

We are a continental country with, locally, much to explore. We are also a nation of immigrants. For many writers, America itself has had the qualities of a foreign land, pre-empting their curiosity and energy as they recapitulated the discoveries of generations that had come before. And we are an entrepreneurial society that thrusts upon its better-known authors a special style of celebrity—self-important, self-celebratory. Many successful novelists turn into pouter pigeons, addicted to a constant deference, and probably wouldn't be much good at travel writing anyway, no matter where they went, because the genre requires a certain modesty and self-effacement, an openness to unexpected sights, to timid or argumentative voices, or even to silence.

But let's leave out these pouter pigeons. Imagine if some of our young writers who do "minimalist" short stories traveled to quarters of the world where life no longer seemed minimal to them. Our fiction has become ingrown, repetitive, and tired, and without advocating that Americans start writing novels about Lagos or São Paulo, I am suggesting that breathing a little foreign air might infuse vigor into it—as plainly did really happen sixty years ago. They might return possessed by a salubrious anger, or perhaps a despair that no longer seemed facile, or even a belief in God.

And suppose a dozen of our neoconservative theorists were to get off the Washington-London-Bonn axis and travel through an equatorial continent for a few months, instead of merely jeering sight unseen at the three fourths of the human race that lives in the third world. Western intellectuals had an obvious agenda to address after the end of the Second World War. They needed, first, to sort out and attempt to record the unspeakable enormities of the Nazi war; second, to begin to consider what the world might be coming to, with new forms of totalitarianism and nuclear weaponry; and, third, to try to explore the new societies and nations arising nearly worldwide in an age like none before. But among Americans, only the first of these imperatives has been gone into thoroughly. The dead have been memorialized, but the living in their myriad millions have been neglected by American intellectuals to the point of bankruptcy in numerous magazines of opinion here, while many of our fiction writers—who should have needed no "agenda" apart from the promptings of the heart—have allowed their temperaments to shrink to miniaturist provincialism and minimalist response.

Balancing Act

There are writers like Evelyn Waugh, Graham Greene, and V. S. Naipaul who seem to go looking for bad journeys, for various reasons—political rage, an edgy personality, an appetite for satire or disaster—to our profit, indeed. But there are others who can be counted upon to make no ado at all about a bad trip—Marco Polo, John Muir, T. E. Lawrence—because their agenda and their virtues are different.

My own questing instinct tends toward a fairly tolerant, patient, almost trusting viewpoint, and I don't find people suspect or dislikable by clan or race. I've experienced racism as a white man in Africa and religious prejudice as a Christian in Israel and Yemen, and of course I have recognized such vices within myself also. But I find that the balancing act by which I make my way among personalities and groups at home is not so unlike getting along with strangers abroad.

Arriving in Dar es Salaam or Cairo at night without reservations a decade ago—or when stranded on the wrong end of Kodiak Island during a perpetual rain—I've had some bad times. I've been lonely in Vienna and London too; have worried about possible gunfights between militia bands along the Red Sea; and have felt panicky or stranded in blizzards north of the Arctic Circle. Yet all these interludes worked out pretty well eventually, as my optimism beforehand had expected them to. Though, in shaky planes flying out of Fairbanks, or in Land-Rovers crossing desiccated patches of the Sahel, I was not such a fool as to think no mishap might befall the particular aircraft or vehicle carrying me, none did. And although I'm a lifelong New Yorker, I've never been mugged—or assaulted elsewhere in the world—and the tumors that doctors have discovered in me have thus far been benign, not malign, knock on wood.

This, perhaps, is my luck. In Mexico and the southern Sudan I've seen whimpering hunger. In Casablanca and Chicago I've seen people viciously clubbed. I know that life is an abyss, among other things, and like other travel writers, I enjoy wire walking a bit, courting, in a sense, a catastrophe. Yet otherwise I believe in a deity—not one that will choose to protect me in a crunch, but one that makes the story of life, when grasped as a whole, a rhapsody. Nor would my dying slowly in the broken fuselage of a bush plane someday refute this idea, really.

But to come back to Dar es Salaam and a story: An Englishwoman, whom I had met in Nairobi, and I, after a certain amount of fuss, located a place to eat and sleep after our night arrival by bus and much rushing about the black streets afoot, shouldering our baggage. Then for several days we contented ourselves with the pleasures of the small port and capital city. My friend had been raped on a beach on Lamu, an island off Kenya, shortly before joining forces with me. She had not otherwise been physically injured, however, and had waded into the surf in the aftermath to wash herself. But now she wanted to go swimming at an isolated beach south of "Dar," which we had heard was dangerous. I said it was a foolish notion and wouldn't, but she went alone and, in this old slaving center, again was raped by a leggy, vigorous, Swahili-speaking man—nearly the first who noticed her lying on her beach towel—who, like the other rapist, wanted to penetrate but not use his knife on her. So, again, she was free to wade into the Indian Ocean and douche afterward and return to the hubbub of Tanzanian bus stations, market bazaars, and expatriate Greek restaurants, alive.

Why, oh, why, I asked her, when her flood of tears had

partly subsided. She said, in effect, that she had wanted to trust Tanzanians, as she had wanted to trust Kenyans, not behave like the British who didn't. I was massaging her neck and scalp as we talked, to comfort her, and there discovered an astounding dent under her hair, in the top of her head, for which she had no explanation that she could remember. She said only, with hesitance, that her mother had told her that her father had clobbered her with a frying pan when she was little—an incident absent from all recollection, which she now discounted as a subsequent influence.

As a matter of fact, this new misadventure, too, she managed to throw off, and we went on to have a good further tour of the country. But suppose she hadn't been able to throw it off? Would her Bad Trip, versus my Good Trip, be the result of having a horrendous father? John Muir's father almost killed him also; yet Muir was a Good Trip man. I'm scarred with a stutter from my childhood's contretemps that is a much more visible mark than her dent, but my travels are quite devoid of nightmares—are comparatively mundane but as cheerful as Marco Polo's. And ought one to conclude that T. E. Lawrence was a happier man than V. S. Naipaul because his travels sound nicer?

What *makes* a trip bad, in other words? Well, crashing on the tundra just as dusk fell might do it. Or breaking down in the desert without enough water. But Felix Krull and I: we do O.K. in third class rail travel. And I'll sleep in a station with my feet on my luggage in reasonably good humor for lots of hours. In feverish delirium, I'll doze in my hotel room instead of telephoning the U.S. ambassador; in my mind's eye, I haven't become an important personage. Within the limits of my present experience, a bad trip is likely to be an organized trip with officious organizers, not a trip where reality intrudes its snaky head. I like both snakes and reality. And that she did too, ultimately, was why we were fast friends.

The Circus
of Dr. Lao

Just as, in a menagerie, some people will pause to marvel before the cage of an exotic creature from another hemisphere while others haul their children past, scarcely permitting them a glimpse, so, at the circus, some of us gasp at the trapezists' and the tumblers' feats, and other paying customers move restlessly in their seats and check their fingernails. In a circus we see mostly what we are ready to see. There is no script but chance and hope and spontaneity, and thus it is appropriate that this masterpiece of circus literature describes an imaginary circus, not a real one. No circus ought to be too "real."

Dr. Lao's stupendous show, which arrives abruptly in the Depression town of Abalone, Arizona, one hot August morning, introduces us to a hermaphrodite sphinx, a 2,300-year-old satyr, a lion-lizard-eagle dragon, and a gentle green hound, "less carnal than a tiger lily," with chlorophyll in its veins and a plait of ferns for a tail. Also, an angry sea serpent eighty feet long, whose one soft spot is for the circus mermaid; an ancient, intellectual magician who can bring men back from the dead; and a beautiful medusa who with a glance kills them.

Dr. Lao, the Chinese proprietor, travels with only three

wagons and no roustabouts. Yet his numerous tents, black and glossy, stand about like darkened hard-boiled eggs on end. For such miraculous transformations he is indebted to his indispensable thaumaturge, Apollonius, who walks about "drowned in thought." Dr. Lao himself is energetic, impulsive, irascible, and resourceful—an impresario who, according to the emergencies of the moment, switches from the language of a poet-professor to the stock-comedy dialect of a Chinese laundryman "washing the smells out of shirttails," as two college boys, Slick Bromiezchski and Paul Conrad Gordon, put it to him.

The good doctor does have his troubles. The men in the crowd complain because the werewolf has turned into a woman three hundred years old, not the hot young dish they claim they were promised. A scientist who has examined his fearsome, enigmatic, phlegmatic medusa only wanted to identify the several species of snakes that constitute her hair (for which separate diets must be gathered). Circuses carry "a taint of evil or hysteria," Dr. Lao admits with regret. "Life sings a song of sex. Sex is the scream of life. . . . Breed, breed, breed. . . . Tumescence and ejaculation." One cause of his friend Apollonius's melancholy exhaustion is that things on the circus lot are forever getting out of hand—between the sea serpent and the dragon; between Satan and the witches who appear in the finale, some of them airsick from their flight to perform; between the bear (or is it a "Russian"?) and the mermaid it carries around the hippodrome; and between the satyr and Miss Agnes Birdsong, a high-school English teacher who has come early in order to see the "Pan" that she observed driving a wagon during the opening parade through town.

Apollonius of Tyana, who is so old that he was born contemporary with Christ, remains a bit of a perfectionist. He is disappointed when a live turtle that he conjures from a handful of soil for a small boy turns out to have two heads. "These aren't tricks, madam," he tells the boy's mother, after calling up "a big brute" of a flower. "Tricks are things that fool people . . . tricks are lies. But these are real flowers, and that was real wine, and that was a real pig. . . . I create; I transpose."

With enough exertion, and occasionally the aid of a

Christian cross, there is nothing he can't accomplish. On his command, Satan stops fornicating with the witches, and the satyr obediently pricks balloons with his horns. Out pops Beelzebub from a boar's ear. The witches dance to a chorus of frogs around a fire burning on the carapace of a huge tortoise, who feeds the flames with mouthfuls of dripping peat ripped from the floor of a magical swamp.

Yet what is the point, when the upshot of almost every mythological spectacle endlessly repeats itself in concupiscence and greed; when, in fact, most miracles have an everyday version that attracts no special attention whatsoever?—viz., a tadpole's metamorphosis into a frog. No press agent's hyperbole really equals what goes on at a circus, and no circus extravaganza equals the fish-into-person miracle of a human being.

Furthermore, what's the point for poor Apollonius? The little shriveled dead man whom he brings back to life as a sideshow stunt at Dr. Lao's suggestion has on "overalls, old worn army shoes with leather laces in them, a blue hickory shirt, and an old worn-out cowboy hat. In the leather sweatband of the hat were the initials 'R.K.' floridly delineated in indelible pencil." One of his leather shoestrings has been broken and retied in several places, the knots looking as if they had been done by a seafaring man, as the author continues to explain with irrepressible exactitude. And Apollonius begins to pray a low, thick prayer. "His eyeballs turned dead green; thin, hazy stuff floated out of his ears" from the terrific effort of doing so. Finally the man sits up, coughs, asks where he is. "Well, lemme outa here. I got business to attend to," he mutters, and rushes off, unaffected by both his own death and his resurrection.

Charles G. Finney, our cheerful author, was only thirty in 1935, when his *Circus* was published, so that his reactions are not the same as those of Apollonius, or even the "old-like, wealthy-looking party in golf pants" who represents Abalone's solidest citizens. At the time, Mr. Finney, great-grandson of a famous Congregational divine who founded Oberlin College, was the veteran of a Missouri country boyhood, a year at the University of Missouri, and three years of garrison duty with Company E, Fifteenth U.S. Infantry Division, in Tientsin, China. An autodidact and intellectual rebel, he counted as his favorite twentieth-century writers Conrad, Kipling, Joyce, Proust, and Anatole France (but included no Americans). He had started the manuscript there in the army barracks in the American compound, writing in longhand, then laid it aside till he got home, because it had turned too lecturey. Later, he dedicated the book to a soldier buddy in Tientsin, whom he never crossed paths with again.

China had opened young Finney's eyes to the breadth of the world, the overpopulation of human beings, the random character of death, the relativity of morality and religion. Still alive in 1983—suffering from Parkinson's disease but, after half a century, still living in Tucson—he said in the course of several interviews with me over the telephone that *lao* means "old" in Mandarin and Cantonese, so Dr. Lao is "Dr. Old"; that his particular source for the fussy, commonsensical, yet incendiary personality of Dr. Lao was Lao Tehr, the proprietor of a shop that purveyed live Chinese crickets and grasshoppers in straw cages, who had befriended him; that he had discovered Apollonius of Tyana as a mythic figure in Flaubert's *La Tentation de Saint Antoine;* that he never traveled after his trip to China except to go to New York in 1936, when his book achieved a third printing and won the "Most Original Novel" award of the American Booksellers Association; and that he had been a "Truman type" of show-me Democrat, who voted against Franklin D. Roosevelt all four times. He said his indifference to his literary compatriots extended even to Nathanael West, an almost exact contemporary, whom he resembles as a writer.

However, the book is marked by a brutality more than "Chinese" (as it would have seemed in the United States in 1935). In slapstick anecdotes, people are 'dobe-walled by Pancho Villa, and a child is killed by a ricocheting bullet meant for a deserter. A lady is turned to stone ("carnelian chalcedony") for looking at the medusa. Circuses are brusque and brutal by nature anyway—much as they are above national considerations of patriotism or politics. And this is a young man's tale, full of cynicism and whimsy, carefree prurience, elegant language, and gratuitous learning. Where surreal scenes of violence may be shocking in a Hollywood novel like West's *Day of the Locust,* which to some degree speaks to the dilemmas of America as a whole, a circus lends its air of utter license to any extravagance of the imagination. Besides, Mr. Finney, after disposing of the subjects of justice, life, death, and comparative religion so handily, from what seems to have been sheer exuberance, felt a young man's delight and pride in being absolutely specific, which is what has kept his writing fresh. Few 1930s books begin more in the modern manner than his first paragraph, for instance:

> In the *Abalone* (Arizona) *Morning Tribune* for August third there appeared on page five an advertisement eight columns wide and twenty-one inches long. In type faces grading from small pica to ninety-six point the advertisement told of a circus to be held in Abalone that day, the tents to be spread upon a vacant field on the banks of the Santa Ana River, a bald spot in the city's growth surrounded by all manner of houses and habitations.

But somehow Finney's failure to travel again, seeking new fields for his imagination—when travel had proved so invaluable to him in the 1920s—signaled, as well, a failure of ambition. So did the withering of his interest in other writers of his century. Having no foreknowledge that although he would publish an army memoir and three other novels during the next fifty years, while writing headlines and editing the stock market page at the (Tucson) *Arizona Daily Star,* he would remain essentially a one-book novelist, he announced happily on this, his first dust jacket, that he had been able to find no other job after returning to his homeland than that of a part-time proofreader—which is what "Mr. Etaoin," the sanest witness in Abalone, is.

"Etaoin," another of Mr. Finney's word games, is part of a phrase by which linotype operators signaled themselves that they had made an error in a given line. We learn no more of Mr. Etaoin. Just as would be the case in an earthly circus, each character does a "turn"; no character is presented with finality or thoroughness. Not Dr. Lao, who says his preference for luncheon leans more toward sharks' fins than Chinese noodles; not the unicorn, whinnying like a bugle and "flinging its icicle horn skyward"; nor the satyr, wearing a gold ring in his nose, his torso as lean as a marathon runner's, who eats only vegetables but refuses garlic and onions. (And how bewildered he'd been, retreating in the early centuries of the A.D. era from the onslaught of Christian celibacy, to China, where the foot-bound maidens could not dance to his piping!)

The dragon eats rattlesnakes, spitting out the rattles, and asphyxiates the desert gnats, snorting smoke and ashes instead of moving its bowels. Only its love of the moon enabled the doctor to capture it, by means of a mirror on a mountaintop. The mermaid's sleek-scaled, sea-green fish tail has a fanlike fin on the end, as pink as a trout's. Bits of water foam cling to her hair. But the water nymphs have horsey hips and the stomachs of washerwomen.

The seething, glistering sea serpent, with a scarlet throat and a long yellow naked nerve of a tongue the size of a man's arm, vibrates his tail so that "a whirring arose like a woodsaw's song." "Why?" asks young Etaoin, in a duel-like dialogue they engage in in the privacy of the serpent's tent. "It is my fondest atavism," the beast replies. He adds that he needs to masturbate nowadays, though he had used to smell his mate all the way across the world and swim to her, stopping at islands along his route to gulp down a coffee-colored boy or girl, "much as you would swallow an oyster and with every bit as much right, if you will pardon an ethical intrusion." He mocks the proofreader for wearing glasses, although supposedly a member of the earth's master race, and later strikes across the big top to seize hold of the doctor during the main performance, only relinquishing him when Apollonius invokes a winter frost to freeze his coils.

Bats "like wavering, restless flakes of soot"; minks that "loosened the drawstrings of their scent sacs"; scorpions, worms, Gila monsters, salamanders in a muddy pig wallow— seldom since Christopher Smart has a writer so celebrated the dukes and troopers of the animal kingdom, as well as its fishiness, pigginess, snakiness. A gigantic roc's egg hatches. "Silly pinfeathers, big as ostrich plumes, adorned its grey skin, and the yellow at the corners of its mouth was as yellow as butter. . . . The roc chick stood weeping in the litter of eggshell. It opened its mouth and wailed with horrible hunger."

This verisimilitude to the misery of birth is too strong for the customers, however. And one father had told his kids that the egg was a fake, so after watching it hatch, they have to leave. The mermaid, with whom Dr. Lao himself is in love, provokes only the question, "What do you feed her, doc?" When a local widow, Mrs. Howard T. Cassan, in her thin brown dress and low shoes, comes to consult Apollonius as fortune-teller, he speaks for our impatient author:

"Tomorrow will be like today. . . . You will think no new thoughts. You will experience no new passions. Older you will become but not wiser. Stiffer but not more dignified. Childless you are, and childless you shall remain. Of that suppleness . . . that strange simplicity which once attracted a few men to you, neither endures. . . . Must I tell you how many more times you will become annoyed at the weather . . . shall I compute the pounds of pennies you will save shopping at bargain centers?" he asks harshly—throwing in the terrible thought that she has a voice in government and that enough people voting the way she does could change the face of the world. But her only response is to ask Apollonius to move in with her.

Mr. Finney's sympathy for humdrum people and ordinary lives had a short fuse. Perhaps partly as a result, his book ran out of steam after ninety pages or so. When the delight and spontaneity begin to wane, we know the performance is almost over—not because of some inner novelistic logic but because, just as at a circus, the acts that he has brought to town have now all appeared, and it is simply *over*. In fact, the book's shortness probably explains why it is not better known, compared to bulkier underground classics, and why it needs reviving.

At the end, "a thin wispy rain came weeping." Also at the end is the funniest section, and Mr. Finney's own favorite, the Catalogue, where he sums up everything and everyone who has pranced by. There are ticks, camels, polar bears, crustaceans, frigate birds, geologists, and silly men's sillier wives.

Wonders were what interested Finney—"real honest-to-goodness freaks that had been born of hysterical brains rather than diseased wombs," "the sports, the offthrows of the lust of the spheres," foaled from the earth, suggests the good doctor, the way the Surinam toad bears its offspring, through the skin of its back. Dr. Lao's perpetual, exasperated dither, the lassitude and boredom of Apollonius, and the pell-mell terror of much of the show are the price of having a performance at all—which, for reasons unstated, of course must go on.

Always the point is indicated that the natural wonders next door—a child's somersault, the birth of a kitten—are equal to what is seen here. A circus works its marvels by parading in front of us what we could see anyhow if we were more alert and less prejudiced, more curious and devout, and opened our eyes.

For, *"This is the circus of Dr. Lao"* (as that personage explains, banging a gong) . . .

> *Oh, we've spared no pains and we've spared no dough;*
> *And we've dug at the secrets of long ago;*
> *And we've risen to Heaven and plunged Below,*
> *For we wanted to make it one hell of a show . . .*
> *Long past the time when the winter snow*
> *Has frozen the summer's furbelow.*

Replicas

Having worked in the circus forty years ago, I went to the splendiferous auction of circus memorabilia held at the Seventh Regiment Armory on Park Avenue in New York City to see the exact replicas, in one-inch scale, of the cookhouse tents I used to eat in and the supply wagons I slept under. Also, about ninety horses with snakepit manes and flaring nostrils, gaping mouths and out-kicked hooves, which had been cannibalized or left over from dismantled carousels. The gorilla Gargantua II, whom I knew in his childhood, sold for $20,350, stuffed, with a fine true-to-life, benign expression, and his tremendous fingers brought up to drum on his gigantic chest.

Carved dioramas re-created circus history from Barnum's elephant Jumbo's arrival in America, in 1882, and from the day when Albert Ringling set off from Baraboo, Wisconsin, with his four brothers two years later, balancing a plow on his chin to show the world what he could do. An honest-to-goodness mud scene of the 1930s depicted twenty horses trying to budge a pole wagon that had got mired to the axles, with an elephant dutifully shoving it from behind as well. And in a miniature menagerie, yaks stood shouldering water buffaloes and musk oxen, from an era when Americans still lived close to and were intensely intrigued by animals.

A bunch of Felix Adler's clown costumes were auctioned off—dummy heads and bizarrely broad bare feet, wild zany wigs and rubber noses, pneumatic suits, dog masks, and a Siamese-twin monkey outfit. Adler (1897–1960) was a "grotesque white-face," in circus parlance, which means he painted his features to exaggerate them. He called himself the King of the Clowns, sometimes sporting a gold crown, which irritated several colleagues. He stuck beach balls into the seat of his capacious pants to make his rear end swell, and on the bulb of his nose he wore a red light, which occasionally shorted out when he went backstage between acts and put on his wire-rimmed reading spectacles. His trademark was the succession of little pigs he trained to follow him around the hippodrome track (and fed a secret diet of baking soda to keep them small for as long as he could). But he had many other ring-wise wiles, and, carrying his six-inch umbrella on a five-foot handle, he performed at the White House, first for Calvin Coolidge and then for Franklin Roosevelt. A part Sioux from Clinton, Iowa, he had appeared under a big top at the age of ten with a dog-and-pony show but claimed that he preferred pigs because, "like clowns, they have sad, suspicious eyes and yet always look as if they're smiling." He didn't marry until he was fifty, meeting his wife, Amelia, in a department store in Richmond, Virginia, where he was performing during the off-season. His pig had got loose and run under her desk in the credit office. He died in New York City in February, while waiting for spring in another off-season, and his obituaries ought to have mentioned that he was regarded as probably the most generous-spirited clown to have inhabited a circus tent in living memory.

At the armory, too, I noticed and was touched by an old scalloped, medallion-shaped, yellow-and-beige sign that was being auctioned:

AGNES

Although native to Africa, "Agnes," a reticulated giraffe, was born eight years ago on a Ringling Bros. and Barnum & Bailey circus train passing through

Pittsburgh. She measures 22 feet tall and weighs over 2,000 lbs. Her favorite food is fresh, alfalfa hay.

I might have liked the sign anyway for that last comma, but what reverberated for me was the memory of how Agnes used to bend her limber stalklike neck deeply down on a hot afternoon to lick my sweaty cheeks, and how on cold or stormy nights I often took shelter in her wagon.

I bid; then dropped out when the price grew silly (two-foot model bandwagons were bringing as much as a new Ford costs), although sure it was an artifact from that marvelous year when I was eighteen and traveled from Connecticut to Nebraska with Ringling Brothers for wages of fourteen dollars a week, plus my keep. The next morning, however, I woke up with the knowledge that the giraffe I had lived with was not Agnes at all, but Edith, Agnes's mother. Agnes had been a young squirt of an adolescent when I had thrown half-bales of hay up into the racks of their cages and hung the water pails as high as I could lift them. "Edith!" I would call, and watch her bow her lofty neck way down, unsheathe her purple tongue, and I would feel it tickle my whiskers as she licked my face for salt to help her (as I learned later in biology class) with the important task of digesting that hay.

The stock market has been booming lately, so among the folk-art collectors and antique dealers were numerous financially cheerful people looking for a merry-go-round horse for a picture window or a parade wagon for an end table. There were shopping-mall developers in search of a drawing card and investors after a tax shelter. Hustlers with a Ferris wheel to sell, or an entire steeplechase of wooden horses, circulated in the rich brew of that cavernous drill room, alongside present-day circus performers with exotic, dashing sorts of faces who were on a busman's holiday, and one rueful gentleman who mentioned having bought a fifty-two-horse carousel for $4,100 in the late 1950s, which he'd quite promptly resold. The horses might be worth $4,100 apiece nowadays, to judge from the prices we were witnessing.

Mostly, women were buying the carousel horses (or husbands in their fifties were buying for women in their thirties), and men were buying the various circus relics—men whose still-boyish faces were concealed behind forbidding beards or business bifocals or the physiognomy of a poker player. I spoke to a few circus veterans who had given their lives to show business, not simply a matter of months like me, and we were philosophical about being no match for this company. We had our memories, and no more needed a scale model of the circus than carvings of the Main Street buildings of our hometowns.

Oddly enough, a real circus wagon, one of the full-sized green supply wagons I had used to sleep under, was auctioned too, and it brought only one hundred dollars. It wasn't in the armory; a photograph of it, down in Orlando, was flashed on a screen. I was asleep at the switch, after so many failures, and let it go by, but the man sitting next to me, a hobbyist from a Main Line suburb outside Philadelphia, did purchase it. He was a chubby individual, who appeared to be enjoying life on an inherited income, and said I'd be surprised at all the things he had on his place. His wife never knew what he was going to bring home next.

New York Blues

Most of us realized early on that we are not our "brother's keeper." Yet perhaps we also came to recognize that "there but for the grace of God go I." If the jitters we experience on a particularly awful afternoon were extended and became prolonged until we couldn't shake them off, after a few drastic months we might end up sleeping on the sidewalk too. Character is fate, we like to say: hard work and fidelity (or call it regularity) will carry the day. And this is just true enough to believe. But chemistry is also fate: the chemistry of our tissues and the chemistry of our brains. We know that just as some people among us get cancer at a pitiably young age, others go haywire through no fault of their ethics, pluck, or upbringing.

Still, what do most of us do when we notice a hungry, disoriented person slumped on the street in obvious despair? Why, we pass quickly by, averting our eyes toward an advertisement, the stream of taxis, a shop's window dressing. Part of the excitement of a great metropolis is how it juxtaposes starvelings blowing on their fingers in front of Bergdorf Goodman, Saks, and Lord & Taylor; urchins shilling for a three-card monte pitchman alongside a string of smoked-glass limousines; old people coughing, freezing, next to a restaurant where young professionals are licking sherbet from their spoons to clear their palates after enjoying the entree. Already in the eighteenth century Tom Paine wrote that in New York City "the contrast of affluence and wretchedness is like dead and living bodies chained together." Or as is said nowadays: Takes all kinds.

Those hungry people apparently didn't start a Keogh plan or get themselves enrolled in some corporation's pension program thirty years ago and stick to the job. They didn't "get a degree" when they were young; they were uncertain in direction, indecisive about money; they plotted their course badly or slipped out of gear somewhere along the line. Or they may merely be "defective," in Hitler's sense of the term—a bit retarded, a trifle nuts. So they are not being maintained at the requisite room temperature that society provides for the rest of us year round. They are standing in the cold wind, hat in hand, as the saying goes, or lined up docilely, forlornly, in front of a convent for a baloney sandwich at 11:00 A.M.

It's not as if we had the leisure or quietude to worry overmuch about the souls whom we are well acquainted with who, in reasonably comfortable, well-stocked apartments, may nonetheless be drinking themselves to death. And what could we *do* about those on the street? Empty our wallets and rush to a money machine for more cash to give out? Run for public office on a philanthropic platform? Become social workers? Set an example in the manner of Mahatma Gandhi? Move to the country and forget it all? I'm of a generation of Americans that tended to ignore the magnetic model of Gandhi in favor of his beguiling contemporary Freud, who explained or micromanaged individual psyches in a subtly satisfying, amusing way. Our living writers of choice were the genius nay-sayers, starting with T. S. Eliot and Jean-Paul Sartre, through Samuel Beckett, who befitted the nuclear age and gave no more guidance than Freud for remedying a social collapse. Social collapse, or Kafkaesque mirror tricks in the name of totalitarianism, were to be presumed. We knew that Gandhi would not have fared well against Hitler or Stalin, and so he was considered irrelevant. Though not foreseeing the appearance of an American Gandhi, Martin Luther King, in the 1960s, we would have thought his assassination, like Gandhi's, no surprise. (Besides, for activism, our intellectuals were enamored of Karl Marx, even as a god that failed.)

I went against the grain of much of this. Nature redeems mankind in many writers who mattered to me, and nature had no place among these postwar intellectuals. April was "the cruellest month," not a genuine rebirth. Life seemed richer, too, to me with an admixture of social ideals, but Surrealism, Black Humor, the Theater of the Absurd, Existentialism, and lately Minimalism have all assumed the impossibility of holding viable ideals. Our mass escape from both a nuclear holocaust and *1984* were not in their cards. Nor did the cadre of French authors reigning in the 1950s, and Kafka, Eliot, and Beckett, picture life in any light that has squared with my experience of school (rebel though I was), and of the army, the open road, marriage and divorce, career success and catastrophe, fatherhood, love affairs, suicidal spells, political unpopularity, blindness in the form of cataracts, and religious revelation in the years since, or the elementary buoyancy with which I wake up every morning. They were waiting for Godot, and, impatient with realism, they may have missed reality, which was more complicated than their perspective allowed.

On the other hand, they were writing from a background of war, whereas we're afraid that we are witnessing a more peaceable delirium of social collapse. Nature, the redeemer, has not survived; and families, finance, and traditional faith are not doing a lot better at the moment. "New York is getting unlivable," people say. Among the privileged, an adage is that "you can't live on less than $150,000" (a year). But if this isn't swinishness talking, what is really meant is that it costs that much *not* to be in the city—to be elevated above the fracases, dolor, and grief of the streets, with sufficient "doorman" protection to shield you from the dangers, to exclude anyone with a lesser income, and to conceal from you the fact that cities *are* their streets. A city is its museums too, but in New York, Goya is in the streets.

Our ancestral wish as predators is that somebody be worse off than we are—that we see subordinates or surplus prey or rivals hungering, to assure us we're prospering. Rather in the same way that we dash sauces on our meat

(Worcestershire, horseradish, A.1., or béarnaise) to restore a tartness approximating the taint of spoilage that wild meat attains, we want a city with a certain soupçon of visible misfortune, with people garishly on the skids, scouting in the gutter for a butt and needing to be "moved on" (the policeman's billy club banging on their shoes if they fall asleep on a bench). In a metropolis, in other words, there should be store detectives collaring shoplifters while we finger our credit cards, white-haired men being bullied by midlevel executives younger than them or forced to hustle around the subway system as messengers, occasional young women selling themselves, and suffering exhibitionists publicly going mad. That quick-footed, old-eyed gentleman with the wife in a lynx coat, grabbing a cab on Sixth Avenue to go uptown after a gala evening, leaves behind a Purple Heart soldier with his broken leg in a cast, scrambling for a tip, who, at sixty, may sleep on a grating tonight in the icy cold. *You're sick? You have no co-op to go to? No T-bills, mutual funds? Where've you been?*

A city is supposed to be a little bit cruel. What's the point of "making it" at all if the servants in hotels and restaurants aren't required to behave like automatons and if plenty of people at your own place of business don't have to bootlick and brownnose? A city with its honking traffic jams, stifling air, and brutal cliffs of glass and stone is supposed to watch you enigmatically, whether you are living on veal *médaillons* and poached salmon or begged coins and hot dogs. But stumble badly, and it will masticate you. Sing a song and exhibit your sores on the subway, and it will nickel-and-dime you as you gradually starve.

All this Dickensian tough stuff, however, has often verged on the playful in American myth, because in the past it has been tied in with rags-to-riches stories. The ragamuffin enshrouded in burlap, sleeping underneath a bush at the edge of the park, might be a new immigrant who in another seven years would grab his first million in the garment trade. He had links to the Statue of Liberty, to put it bluntly, so don't be a glib fool and dismiss him. Ben Franklin entered Philadelphia that first time to make his name with one "Dutch dollar" to live on.

Or he might be a hobo, riding the rods for freedom and

fun, a hero of folk songs and such, whose worst sin was stealing Mom's apple pie as it cooled on the kitchen porch and a chicken from the dooryard for his "jungle" stew. He might be a labor organizer traveling on the qt. Or if the figure asleep in the park was female, she might be Little Orphan Annie, soon to charm Daddy Warbucks and be spruced up by him. Fallen women (versus ladies in distress) did exist, but not bag ladies and mad people wandering loose in superabundance. And in hard, bad times like the Depression, the Arkie and Okie families hitting the open road for a chance at a better life—one of the most hallowed American rites—were white. For many urbanites, what makes the heart pound at being surrounded by street people is that a preponderance of them are black, and sometimes very black, by no coincidence, because their color has been a disadvantage to them from the word go. Also, when those disheartened farmers from the dust bowl indulged in what is lately called "substance abuse," hey, they were just winos, drunks. We all knew what getting three sheets to the wind, and the hangover, was like. There was nothing arcanely, explosively mindblitzing about liquor, even during prohibition. Hillbillies (or "Legs" Diamond) smuggled it into town, not "Colombian drug lords." Besides, during the Great Depression as many as a fourth of U.S. workers were unemployed; we were all in a mess together.

Then we pulled together to fight World War II. And the veterans came back, as from previous wars, and had to start over. Even ten years after 1945 it remained easy for a white man to hitchhike anywhere—just stick out your thumb. People kept a rabbit's foot in their pocket for good luck. The random nature of death, like the Depression, had reminded everybody that success is partly a matter of luck, and may be a question of cowardice. Just as cowards come back from wartime alive, so they may get rich and sleek and influential. Yet you'll remember the happy slogan "The best things in life are free." This might be said tongue in cheek, but seldom cynically. Religious belief, for example, was surely free; so were sunshine and open spaces (though people might leave them to come to the city). Children were free, falling in love was the next thing to free, and friendship was not necessarily "networking." Movie idols played happy-go-lucky roles, with the good guys often the poor guys. Every middle-class person in the city wasn't stitched into the disciplines of a telephone-answering machine, an exercise club, and psychotherapy. People let the phone ring, let a call slip by once in a while, and walked between business appointments when they could. They weren't keyed nearly to computer tempo, fax speed.

What has also happened in New York is that we no longer assume we like most people—assume that strangers are not a cause for alarm and may be worth a second glance or tarrying over. In the old neighborhoods of mixed incomes, one's tribal affiliation was not just mercenary. All kinds of factors operated in layers to populate the place—religious, ethnic, style, and taste—and the residents didn't invariably appear as if they could raise (or not raise) a loan of a certain sum. The stores too, when rents weren't sky-high, could be handed down from father to son, acquiring a mystery or no-cash-flow look. The almighty dollar, where spoken of irreverently, was not.

But now when we take note of people on the sidewalk, we flee on past them, dodging by as if the human shape had become adversarial. And along with the dusty shops and greasy spoons and rent-stabilized buildings with a quirky variety of tenants in them has gone the idea that the smattering of bums one used to see were familiar characters, a part of the regular world. There on the corner by the subway steps stood "Buffalo Bill" or "Grover Cleveland," "Golda Meir" or "V. I. Lenin" or "Yogi Berra" to contribute to—not an encampment of war-zone refugees fighting for space on a steam vent, under a scrap of carpeting, or in a sofa carton. Statistically, New York was less violent when it was more crowded. People merely had homes.

The discovery that you could build dwellings taller and taller or sell air rights above a building was like when the Indians discovered that they could sell land: and then it was gone. Sunlight, like falling in love and raising children conscientiously, has become expensive, and with the money pressure unrelenting even in flush periods ("We have no *downtime*," as a friend who is doing O.K. expresses it), the flippant malevolence of racism increases, as well as a general sense of malaise and deterioration or imminent menace. A man with his head bandaged says at a party: "I was on my way to work, and half the world seemed to be standing around on the platform, including a Guardian Angel, while those creeps were beating me, but for a minute I had this ludicrous feeling that I was about to die."

Some days the ills of the city seem miasmally mental, a bedlam of drugs and dysfunctions, a souring in the gut like dysentery. The creeds or the oratory that ought to invigorate us seem exhausted, whether derived from Marx, Freud, or capitalism (newly perverse). Nationalism as idealism reached its nadir with the Axis powers and has not carried our own country far since Korea. Judaism has bent itself awry in the conflicted Middle East; Christianity hasn't been tried in years. "Tell it to the marines!" one of the elder statesmen of finance or marketing striding to lunch might want to tell the sad-sack young blacks wanting a coin on Fifty-first Street, but they may have already *been* in the marines. The fact that the city's former economic base of muscular industries like transport and manufacturing has been supplanted by an employment pattern of money-processing and "information" jobs—electronic paper-pushing—has made it a city of myriad key-punchers, legal assistants, commercial pulse takers: the suddenly rich, the high-skimming strivers who live by their wits, and their countless clerks, and a piggishness to suit. The leavening of physical work that was present before brought more good humor, loosened the effect of so many people whose bread and butter is their nerves.

I remember trolley cars, and business deals clinched with a handshake, New Yorkers who knew the night sky's constellations, and how easy it was to raise a thumb, catch a ride, and reach Arizona on ten bucks. I can't claim this made it a golden age or even that the city's faces were much happier then. Needless to say, I see lovers now, and business people alive to their work, and immigrants thick in speech but alight with hopes. High is handsome, and fast is fun, not just brutal. No other world city has had quite such a bounce; has been dreamed about from so very far off. A "mecca," "on the edge," and still a fine hotbed in which to be young. And that it has curdled doesn't mean it hasn't remained so rich that you could choke.

"But they're so ruthless," several of my middle-aged

friends suggest, speaking of the new professionals sprinting as they start. I don't know. Planes are more ruthless than cars, but more gleeful as well, as long as they don't burn up travel itself. I love planes, arriving out of the heavens at strange locations and picking up instant friendships, easy come, easy go. Or call them battlefield alliances, if you prefer. Anyway, that's the style of the day. Look at your watch, pat your passport, and expand upon conversations you had last evening in a different country, a different climate, a different time zone, with somebody these people won't ever know.

We New Yorkers, rushing to keep up with our calendars yet pausing to open a fast-food package, and finding the plastic wrapper resists our fingers, immediately, unthinkingly, move it to our teeth. Wild we still are, but possessed by velocities too quick to stay abreast of ourselves, and strewing empathy and social responsibility behind us as we go. In losing contact with what used to be whole rafts of blood relatives and the complex, affectionate sense of diverse "walks of life" that families had—a barber uncle, an actress aunt, pig farmers, anesthesiologists, linoleum salesmen, typesetters, shoemakers—we have fractured into interest groups. Our variety is our national strength and should help to sustain the web of democracy, but without the tolerance that down-home, firsthand familiarity (even if left behind in a home-town) brings, professional insularity is added to racial prejudice as a national handicap. And airplanes and computers don't cure that.

The American dream wasn't only money. "There but for the grace of God go I" was a metaphor to mitigate the clashing claims of equality and meritocracy. It was different from the European concept of noblesse oblige, but, like the Statue of Liberty, to be useful it didn't need to be literally believed. Dog-eat-dog laissez-faire, or cradle-to-grave security—which version was our democracy meant to be? A good many of the stockbrokers and financial lawyers who commuted daily with my father on the subway from Grand Central Terminal to Wall Street during the 1950s saw their children grow up to be hippie carpenters and plumbers a decade later, just as some of the electricians and carpenters who sat across from them on that subway ride watched *their* kids become lawyers and brokers. That's been the genius of New York and America: the two-way street.

Whether as kith and kin, or else in church, or on the subway, people have somehow got to sit together for democracy to work. And now, when guns have legs on them and wander everywhere, when poverty is more anonymous than perhaps ever before and homelessness amounts to a continental phenomenon, when cousinhood and neighborhoods are disappearing, common sense has little play, and the most fundamental decencies must be enforced by litigation or legislation, it seems. There hadn't been endemic starvation in America since before Franklin D. Roosevelt's New Deal set into place an elementary safety net of programs such as Social Security in the 1930s. But now it's likely that, without them, there would be. People "on the wrong side of the tracks," as poverty used to be, were close enough to become known quite personally, not ghettoized thirty miles from a plush suburb, where it can be said, as during the 1980s by federal officials, that ketchup in a school lunch program "is a vegetable."

Money has engendered mean spirits since seashells were currency, and time has not reduced our tribalism. But we are sinking underneath the impersonality of disasters flashed in by satellite from Yugoslavia, Cambodia, Nicaragua, or wherever (Timor, Liberia, Somalia . . . Kurds, Afghans, Eritreans, Tutsis), which overflood the homegrown, street-corner miseries that we can witness in person, and blur them. Catastrophes worldwide are recapitulated. The city, any city, meanwhile surrenders its gloss, as, in a casual hour, we can visit Sydney, Hong Kong, Amsterdam, Miami, just by being couch potatoes. Bangkok, Geneva, Cape Town, Edinburgh, Kuala Lumpur: just watching the commercials. Florence, St. Petersburg, Rio . . . without truly seeing them.

About H. D. Thoreau

I t is a pleasure to sink into the
personality of a masterpiece and enjoy its company at one's
own pace. And like *Robinson Crusoe* or *Oliver Twist, Huckleberry Finn* or *Moby Dick,* Thoreau's *Walden* has a succinct motif that, along with its personality, has helped to carry it down
through the decades since its publication in 1854. Not a castaway or a waif, not a raftsman or a whale fisherman, Thoreau (1817–1862) was a Harvard graduate, the son of a
mildly successful pencil manufacturer in Concord, Massachusetts, who, after floundering a bit, at the age of twenty-
seven built himself a ten-by-fifteen-foot cabin of pine logs
and secondhand boards beside Walden Pond and lived there
alone for twenty-six months, raising much of his own food.
This was not then a cliché, though twentieth-century back-
to-the-landers have sometimes threatened to make it seem
so. Like George Orwell, the great English essayist, a hundred
years later—an Eton boy who chose an urban form of self-
denial while "down and out in Paris and London"—Thoreau
was seeking special insight from a stripped-down existence.
Both men were radicals, but Thoreau was after rapture, not
social realism. Both were essayists, but Thoreau in his rash
and roosterly optimism is quintessentially American.

Walden is not fiction, yet, during the seven-year period when he drafted and revised it, Thoreau shaped his experiences for careful effect, almost as if he were composing a novel. He compressed two years' events into one, for example, and left out many elements of his life which didn't fit his purpose, such as the grief that he still felt for his brother, John, who had died in his arms of lockjaw in 1842, or his guilt at having accidentally set fire to three hundred acres of Concord's woods, for a loss of more than two thousand dollars, in 1844. (Here was a nature lover who entitled his first chapter "Economy" and boasted of having spent only twenty-eight dollars in building his house.) He left out his past failures in love and at the profession of schoolteaching too, as well as scarcely mentioning the night he voluntarily spent in jail in 1846, at about the midpoint of his sojourn at the pond, by which he fostered the concept of civil disobedience for later figures like Gandhi and Martin Luther King. He was protesting the government's continuing tolerance of slavery and America's invasion of Mexico that year, which he considered imperialistic. What he did for his brother, of course, was to write a separate book about a boating trip the two of them had taken on the Concord and Merrimack rivers, and then he wrote a separate essay, called "Resistance to Civil Government" (later, "Civil Disobedience").

A book on serenity is necessarily also about its absence, and Thoreau starts *Walden* in quite a feisty tone, ridiculing the notion of private property—young men "whose misfortune it is to have inherited farms, houses, barns . . . Why should they begin digging their graves as soon as they are born?" The mass of men lead lives of quiet desperation. Six weeks of work in a year should suffice, he says. By sauntering, "hooking" apples, watering the red huckleberry, living "like a dolphin," he gets more genuine profit from Concord's farms than the owners do. "What my neighbors call good I believe in my soul to be bad, and if I repent of anything, it is very likely to be my good behavior," he says. "There are nowadays professors of philosophy, but not philosophers."

He turned his face to the woods to transact some private business with the fewest obstacles, he adds. He was a man of impulse, excursions, independence, nonconformity, who roamed the woodlots several hours a day. Walkers should be a sort of "fourth estate," outside of Church or Governmei or the People. True walking "of which I speak has nothing i it akin to taking exercise," he writes in another essay, and, i *Walden*, "men of ideas instead of legs" are intellectual cent pedes. He ended up keeping a two-million-word journa from which he stitched his books, including two fine trave meditations, *Cape Cod* and *The Maine Woods*, edited by hi sister Sophia and a close friend, Ellery Channing, and pub lished posthumously.

Thoreau had good friends, was never bereft of support ers, but Nathaniel Hawthorne, who, like Ralph Waldo Em erson, Thoreau's principal mentor, also lived in Concord probably spoke for many of his acquaintances when he de· scribed Thoreau as "a young man with much of wild origina nature still remaining in him. . . . He is as ugly as sin, long-nosed, queer-mouthed, and with uncouth and somewhat rus-tic, although courteous manners. . . . He has repudiated all regular modes of getting a living, and seems inclined to lead a sort of Indian life among civilized men." Even Emerson, though more sympathetic—it was Emerson who bought and then loaned Thoreau the land on which he built his hut—was occasionally alarmed by his extremism. When he spent the night in jail protesting slavery, Emerson complained to a friend that it was a "mean and skulking" act "and in bad taste," and wrote in his journal: "Don't run amuck against the world. . . . The prison is one step to suicide." But Emerson housed and nurtured Thoreau during his shaky periods as a young man, eulogized him after his death from tuberculosis (Orwell, too, died of TB in his forties), and lent Thoreau books and ideas during his gradual progression from blun-dering nature lover to visionary, rhapsodist, and social critic ripe with the most supple specificity. He recognized that his protégé was the "American Scholar" he had called for in a famous essay that was delivered first, coincidentally, as an address at Thoreau's graduation—a writer who rubbed shoulders with Irish ice cutters and French-Canadian wood-choppers, an inspector of snowstorms, a man who studied bean fields and breadmaking as well as the *Bhagavad Gita*, Ovid, Milton, and Homer.

In winter, the whooping ice was Thoreau's bedfellow, and a red squirrel was his alarm clock, "as if sent out of the woods for this purpose." "A man is rich in proportion to the number of things which he can afford to let alone," he wrote. And, "I would rather sit on a pumpkin and have it all to myself, than be crowded on a velvet cushion." As for the railroad that ran by the pond and embodied industrialization: "We do not ride on the railroad; it rides upon us." (He also thinks humorously of the fish feeling its rumble.)

Some sounds of the town—church bells and roosters—he enjoys in the woods, however. Sauntering is what he does—from *à la Sainte Terre*, "to the Holy Land," as he says elsewhere—and his genius, he brags, "is a very crooked one." He never knew "a worse man than myself." What he means is not some form of depravity, but complexity and paradox. Emerson, in his essay "Self-Reliance," had written the clarion adage "A foolish consistency is the hobgoblin of little minds." And Walt Whitman, Thoreau's contemporary, whose *Leaves of Grass* first came out a year after *Walden* ("I loafe and invite my soul,/I lean and loafe at my ease . . . I think I could turn and live with animals, they are so placid and self-contain'd"), wrote in the same vein. "Do I contradict myself?/Very well then I contradict myself/ (I am large, I contain multitudes.)" Thoreau's way of saying the same thing was "I love a broad margin to my life."

The first summer he preferred hoeing beans even to reading, except for those mornings when he sat in his doorway from sunrise till noon, "rapt in revery, amidst the pines and hickories and sumachs, in undisturbed solitude and stillness." He had planted a couple of acres of beans but allowed the woodchucks to eat part of the patch, stopped cultivating much of the rest, and exchanged some of the twelve bushels that he harvested for rice, which he preferred. The second year he planted just a third of an acre, not wishing to be indentured to his crops, as he suggested that dairymen are to their herds. Considering the importance of a man's soul, he believed "that that was doing better than any farmer in Concord." Life is a long haul for many people, but Thoreau was "anxious to improve the nick of time . . . to stand on the meeting of two eternities, the past and future." Fishing for horned pout in the moonlight on the pond, he thinks of casting his line upward into the air for ideas and thus catching "two fishes as it were with one hook." And with amusement, at other times, he strikes his paddle on the side of his boat, eliciting an echoing growl from the woods. The pickerel are gold and emerald, fabulous, as "foreign as Arabia to our Concord life." He even bends over with his head between his legs to capture an upside-down glimpse of his beloved Walden ("earth's eye") and its skimming swallows; or sounds and maps its 61½ acres, 102 feet deep; or creeps out onto its thin black ice, prone "like a skater insect," to study the bottom shallows, giving a disquisition upon bubbles. The thawing sand in a railroad cut looks like leopards' paws, birds' feet, coral. An outlandish spotted salamander reminds him of the Nile, though he had never been to the Old World.

Transcendent is the word. Transcendentalism for these New England enthusiasts was a borrowed garment, from German or English figures such as Kant, Goethe, Coleridge, Carlyle, and Wordsworth. But the idea that intuition has divine authority, that there is an "Over-Soul," in Emerson's term, within which every person's particular being is subsumed, was especially suited to an optimistic new country experimenting with democracy. "No man ever followed his genius till it misled him," Thoreau says. Flattered for a moment that he thinks we *have* genius, we nearly believe this unfashionable idea. The most vivid expression of Transcendentalism ever written is *Walden*'s "Conclusion," ending with the sentences "Only that day dawns to which we are awake. There is more day to dawn. The sun is but a morning star." We can still thrill to it, but after two world wars and the twin juggernauts of Marxism and Capitalism, we wouldn't pay attention to such upbeat faith if Thoreau hadn't more to him.

"I love the wild not less than the good," he says. And elsewhere, in his essay on walking, "In Wilderness is the preservation of the World." About the Flints (or "skin-flints," as he calls them), who own the shores of a neighboring pond, he suggests that they "loved better the reflecting surface of a dollar, or a bright cent," than the miraculous water. To farm right there is to raise potatoes in a churchyard. Farmers were then burghers, not an endangered species, and, like other people of a certain wealth, weren't so much an offense against philanthropy, in Thoreau's individualistic view, as slaves to their own avarice. He was a revolutionary.

We Americans tend to forget that our country was born in sedition, subversion, and violent dissent. Protest, if not Protestantism, was our founding creed and helped foment revolutions around the world. For every immigrant who sailed here to get rich quick, another may have come to get away from money grubbing, tenant grinding, and flag waving. Thoreau speaks of the distended "vast abdomens" of imperial nations. "Patriotism is a maggot in their heads," he says of people whose loyalty is all external. Explore thyself; the defeated and deserters from *this* battle go to war, he says. The only conflict he's ever watched was between ants, and the martial fuss of July 4 wafting on the breeze gives him "a vague sense all the day of some sort of itching and disease in the horizon. . . . But sometimes it was a really noble and inspiring strain. . . . I felt as if I could spit a Mexican with a good relish . . . and looked round for a woodchuck or a skunk to exercise my chivalry upon."

Rebelliousness is appealing and keeps Thoreau fresh for younger readers, generation by generation. But it's also an American note, common to Walt Whitman, Herman Melville, Mark Twain—the yawp of the New World—sounded by Abraham Lincoln as well, in a speech to the U.S. House of Representatives in 1848, protesting the conduct of the Mexican War, while Thoreau, his fellow protester, was working on *Walden*. "Any people anywhere . . . have the *right* to rise up, and shake off the existing government, and form a new one that suits them better. This is a most valuable,—a most sacred right—a right, which we hope and believe, is to liberate the world," said Lincoln. It's the line of thinking of the revolutionist Thomas Jefferson, too, in 1776, in the Declaration of Independence. "We hold these Truths to be self-evident . . .," wrote Jefferson, beginning his explanation to the rest of the world for the American Revolution. It's what you'd sort of better say when you are saying something new. All men are created equal, endowed by their creator with certain inalienable rights, among them life, liberty, and the pursuit of happiness. With aplomb, with serenity, Jefferson announced that these ideas are "truths" and are "self-evident!" *Where?* a conservative with a law library might have asked.

This aplomb in announcing impious, outrageous ideas is

notable in *Walden,* in Whitman's *Leaves of Grass* ("I celebrate myself . . .,/And what I assume you shall assume,/For every atom belonging to me as good belongs to you," it commences. *Really?* a Tory would have asked), as well as in Melville's *Moby-Dick*—each of which was composed during the nation's anguished and tumultuous buildup to the Civil War.

But we don't read Thoreau simply for his pronouncement that the mass of men lead lives of quiet desperation, or as a protoconservationist either, or as an eremitical Tom Paine. It is his glee that wins us over. Glee is rarer than outrage, at least in books, and whether he is house building, boiling hasty pudding, going a-chestnuting, a-berrying, a-fishing, or looking into a partridge chick's intelligent eye ("coeval with the sky"), his happiness is catching. "I rejoice that there are owls," he tells us—and otters, bullfrogs, whippoorwills on his ridgepole, moles in his cellar, and a nighthawk wheeling like a mote in the eye of the sky. "This is a delicious evening." A friend leaves him a note penciled on a walnut leaf. But mystery is never far. On the bottom of White Pond are sunken logs like huge water snakes perpetually in motion.

In *Walden* Thoreau doesn't write about a dachshund or a tabby cat, the way so many modern essayists do who take up the subject of nature. But it's important to remember that nothing he did is beyond our means. During a summer in New England I regularly see deer, moose, bear, and wild turkeys—animals that were no longer part of Concord's woods and that Thoreau mourned for, though they are on an upsurge now. He felt the woods diminished by this loss; yet he didn't head for the Rocky Mountains, where there were grizzlies, buffalo, and all. He made his masterpiece out of modest materials, deliberately choosing a setting where the issue was to subdue and cultivate not a wilderness but "a few cubic feet of flesh" instead. (And his serenity would be less interesting if we did not also sense his edginess.)

Walden's shore was "as much Asia or Africa as New England. I have, as it were, my own sun and moon and stars." Advance confidently toward your dreams, and the world will accommodate you, he said. As you simplify your circumstances, your surroundings will appear less tangled, "and solitude will not be solitude, nor poverty poverty, nor weakness

weakness." What faith!—and to imagine, when you have so far won an audience of nil, that you can speak to the ages and catch "the broad, flapping American ear" is as extravagant. Almost by definition, essayists are teachers, reformers, gadflies, and contrarians who look against the grain of prevailing attitudes to point out paradoxes, follies. The farmer plowing behind his ox tells Thoreau he can't believe in vegetarianism because it's got "nothing to make bones with"—the ox's vegetarian bones meanwhile are jerking both plow and farmer along. But in Thoreau, besides the New England ag'iner, there is the lilt of advocacy. "I wish to speak a word for Nature, for absolute freedom and wildness," he says in an essay on walking. "I wish to make an extreme statement." Sounds like great fun: except extremism cuts both ways. In *Walden* he argues that "all sensuality is one." Not even a singing kettle stands between him and nature. Sex, wine, luxurious food, "sensual" sleeping, go by the boards. The spring water from Brister's Hill, or raisins in his bread, were enough of a treat for him. His senses are so clarified that he can sniff the pipe smoke of a passerby at better than three hundred yards.

He was a critic of society but not antisocial, and wanted "so to love wisdom as to live . . . a life of simplicity, independence, magnanimity, and trust." This is not mere iconoclasm, and his book does become gentler, fonder, more good-humored, less adversarial, as it goes on, detailing the struggling lives of freed slaves who had lived in squatters' cabins near Walden Pond, welcoming a more heterogeneous set of visitors to his own lodging than the "poets" who had come before—even an occasional farmer, whom once he might have said knew "Nature but as a robber." Nature after all extends from "the quiet parlor of the fishes" underneath the ice "even into the plains of the ether." Nature after dark does sometimes discomfit him with what he calls "questions," which he then tries to discount by suggesting that nature isn't really nature until the morning.

He says he left the woods for as good a reason as he went there. He had other lives to lead. But he doesn't tell us whether he became lonelier or exasperated or assailed by doubts; whether he burned the midnight oil and paced his tiny cabin in his long johns talking to himself and suffering insomnia and sexual fantasies. Like Henry Adams, that other saliently American memoirist—whose *Education* never mentions the suicide of his wife, Marian Adams—Thoreau didn't think a reader ought to know the author's messy personalia. Excavations a century later revealed that he had bent and spoiled hundreds of nails with his bad aim in putting up his hut, not a frustration that he ever mentions, incidentally. But who knows what berserk streak a more precipitous excavation might have uncovered: Emerson's hint of a leaning toward "suicide," for instance? Thoreau required considerable nurturing from his friends, boarding with the Emersons for months on end, and more than once suffered a nervous collapse, in particular after his brother's death and after the hanging of John Brown, the abolitionist, whom he revered.

The Transcendental idea that people are innately good until tainted by civilization is out of fashion, as is Thoreau's personal asceticism and literary discretion. But we don't need confessions from every author. ("Every generation laughs at the old fashions, but follows religiously the new," he says.) His skepticism about regimentation, industrialism, and materialism, the liberties he took with public authority, his anguish over the skinning of the land, all ring a popular chord. Like his contemporary Karl Marx, he wanted to stop Capitalism in its tracks, but from an opposite angle. He also wanted to lure a generation of hothouse intellectuals outdoors, to lend them courage and confidence in their own surroundings, and to wean them a little more, as Emerson and Whitman were doing, from Europe and the superstition of European superiority. By his middle thirties he had written his best work and become more of a natural scientist than a moral philosopher. He was a radical in politics but a social conservative, like so many of the conservationists who have succeeded him, and he died unmarried but in the bosom of his family, muttering the words "moose" and "Indian," still true to his youthful enthusiasms, and a minority of one.

"I did not wish to take a cabin passage, but rather to go before the mast and on the deck of the world" to see the moonlight on the mountains, he wrote in *Walden*. And, "We should come home from far, from adventures, and perils, and discoveries every day," and not breathe our own breath over and over. For such visions we read him, and for his playful exactitude: the horsehair rabbit snares he finds, tended by "some cow-boy," the pines that under the snow's weight sharpen their silhouettes until they look like firs, and the squirrels whose motions "imply spectators as much as those of a dancing girl."

In closing, Thoreau claims with splendid extravagance that "a tide rises and falls behind every man which can float the British Empire like a chip," if it were ever summoned. How charming a rhetorical flight of fancy, his scanty band of admirers must have thought (and what humbug, to his detractors). Who, in the mid-nineteenth century, could have supposed that this quaint man, whose books at the time of his death were either out of print or not yet published, would easily outlive the British Empire? And, beyond that, who could have imagined that by helping to inspire Gandhi, Thoreau would prove to be in on certain pivotal events of that very feat of flotation a hundred years later?

That Which I Saw

One reason literary minimalism had only a short run of being in fashion recently is that life itself is maximal. Even in Kafka, who by main strength in his books exerted a python's effort at constriction, we may find that we are turning into a dung beetle, not just serving a life's term in lockstep. And Hemingway, in brilliant furtherance of the notion that life is overblown, stripped his style to minimalist marblings that, as much as Faulkner's sunburst profusion, emphasized how strongly colored life is. Eventually we *die*, for heaven's sake. Poof!—like that; and then abruptly putrefy. How gaudy of us. From Laurence Sterne or Herman Melville to Günter Grass, Isaac Bashevis Singer, Gabriel García Márquez, literary realism of a genius caliber often strives toward reality through "magic."

I mention this to introduce myself as a reviewer, believing, too, that classic writers tend to carom off each other, Louis-Ferdinand Céline and Singer contributing to a reading of either, regardless of how the two of them—Céline anti-Semitic and Singer writing in Yiddish—might have loathed each other if they had been thrown together personally. To take a different example, I think the great chroniclers of European imperialism, like Rudyard Kipling and Bernal Díaz del Castillo, will become monuments of "third" as well as "first" world literature, national treasures to the countries they first strode as conquerors. Homeric feats of heroism are everybody's, not just the Trojans' or the Greeks'. (And Igor Stravinsky and W. H. Auden fled World War II's bombardments for a safe haven in the United States, whereas Dmitri Shostakovich and T. S. Eliot did not. Once, to patriots, this seemed to matter, but who cares now?) Indeed, I hope that feminists soon come to realize that at least the best of the writing some of them have been dismissing as "macho" celebrates humanity, not merely men, and can enliven existence for everyone.

Kipling, prolific and popular, has been championed by better advocates than me. But Bernal Díaz (1492?–1584) started as a common foot soldier and wrote his only book, *The True History of the Conquest of New Spain,* in old age. Though as immortal as books get, it needs a bit of trumpeting to an English-language readership occasionally.

Díaz had left Castile to seek his fortune on the Spanish Main in 1514, landing in Panama, then called Terra Firma, though it was in a state of anarchy. He went to Cuba, where he dawdled for about three years before embarking from that base of occupation as arrow fodder in two bloody reconnaissances of the Yucatán peninsula. He set out again with the expedition of Hernando Cortez (508 soldiers and 16 horses at their first muster on Cozumel island) in early 1519, and himself participated in 119 battles or skirmishes of the invasion and conquest of Mexico, which besieged and toppled the seat of Aztec rule, Tenochtitlán, now Mexico City, by August 1521.

Empire against empire, the Spaniards were riding the tide of victories already achieved by their fathers' generation over the Moors—Granada had finally fallen to Catholicism in 1492—and were profoundly aided by several of the Aztecs' angry subject tribes, like the Tlaxcalans, as well as by a scourge of smallpox and Montezuma's indecision. Confusing Cortez with the god Quetzalcoatl, he delivered just the wrong gifts to him, such as a cartwheel-sized disk of gold, and foolishly reined in his warlords at crucial junctures. Yet the taking of Mexico City, with possibly a million inhabitants, was a coup almost biblically stunning, and Díaz—not in the end a war-lover, and no racist—is among the finest on-the-ground historians ever.

Wily Captain General Cortez had destroyed his ships after arriving so no one could desert, and even the sailors had to join him. He utilized the Sacajawea-like talents of an Indian princess named Doña Marina, who loved him; led on or played off numerous Indian chieftains; defeated a larger Spanish armed party sent out by Cuba's governor to arrest him for insubordination (the conquest was unauthorized), and, adding them to his force also, skillfully maintained a kind of military democracy; yet rallied the survivors and new fighters after a lieutenant's misjudgment had caused 850 of his 1,310 men in the first seizure of the capital to be killed.

As a memoirist, Díaz is admiring but not unctuous about Cortez, and he excels at honest, nutshell characterizations of his comrades; at fair, respectful estimations of Indian enemies and allies; and at vivid, resplendent descriptions of the civilization that was being destroyed: the great city's glorious gardens and granaries, aviaries and markets, temples and palaces, pyramids and plazas, its notables in feather garments, jesters, priests, and stilt dancers—the entire spectacle married to bloodthirsty religious rituals, and from a distance seeming to float like a dream of a second Venice upon shallow lakes crossed by three causeways. Apart from George Catlin, three hundred years later, it is hard to conceive of a North American diarist who could have done as well at serving as history's own witness, and Catlin would not have survived.

Like Cervantes and Henry Fielding, Díaz was spurred on by exasperation with earlier writers' efforts, who spoke the truth "neither in the beginning, nor the middle, nor the end," he said. He proffered his *True History* to Spain's Philip II and the world with what may be the most winning preface in literature, but his book was not published till long afterward, in 1632, and then only in a version that was vetted by an officious friar of the Order of Mercy. It was first translated into English in 1800; once again in 1844; and again around the turn of this century; and, best, in an obvious labor of love, by Albert Idell in 1956. The only translation available at the moment in the United States is a Penguin paperback (J. M. Cohen, 1963), which is slightly inferior to Idell's, I think, but managed to sell 4,500 copies last year.

W. H. Prescott drew on Díaz as a principal source for his own famous *History* (1843), but never surpassed him. I needn't plead for this masterpiece, however. Let Bernal Díaz speak:

I have observed how the very famous chroniclers, before they begin to write their histories, first do a prologue and preamble with the argument expressed in high-flown rhetoric so that the curious reader may partake of their harmony and flavor. But as I am no Latin scholar, I dare not attempt to. . . .

That which I myself saw and met with during the fighting I will write down, with the help of God, like a good eyewitness, very plainly, without twisting events one way or another. I am an old man of eighty-four and have lost my sight and hearing. It is my fortune to have no other wealth to leave my children and descendants except this, my true story, and they will see what a wonderful one it is.

Wowlas and Coral

In Belize you will meet deter-
mined birders, working on their "life lists," trying to sight a
jabiru stork. You'll meet a roofer from Milwaukee taking the
winter off; a junk bond salesman who has lost his job for
"liquoring the Indians" (selling to bankrupt savings and
loans' execs); a cashiered chef from Santa Monica; an adver-
tising person jettisoned in an agency shake-up. I, too, had
lost my job, as a college professor, for political incorrectness,
and was looking for a rain forest respite, coral sand beaches,
Mayan ruins, preferring a mainland landfall to an island
destination because of the resonance of continents—jaguars
and mountain lions, whole Indian nations, and the knowledge that I could walk from these mangrove swamps and
limestone plains clear to Alaska or Argentina, should I so
choose.

What I did was get myself to Miami and on board a TAN
SAHSA jet for Belize City. TAN SAHSA is Honduras's airline,
and en route to Tegucigalpa, after crossing the aquamarine
Caribbean to Quintana Roo and paralleling the heel of the
Yucatán—and after the stewardesses had served rock cornish
hen (you could do worse than TAN SAHSA)—it dropped me
off in Belize, an English-speaking democracy formerly

known as British Honduras. The country achieved independence from Great Britain in 1981 but, being coveted by Guatemala, still keeps two thousand of Her Majesty's troops on its soil to thwart these designs. About the same size as El Salvador, which has six million people, and Vermont, which has six hundred thousand, Belize is only a third as populous as Vermont. It boasts seven hundred species of trees, as many as in the entire continental United States, and fifty-four kinds of snakes, six opossums, ninety bats, twenty-three flycatchers (ocher-bellied, sulfur-rumped), and five kinds of wildcats. Though regarded as a political anomaly by Honduras and Mexico too, it won admission to the Organization of American States in 1991, partly by denying U.S. forces landing rights during the invasion of Panama. The British are said to have coached the Belizeans on this.

As an oasis of tranquillity, far less populous than when a million Mayans lived here a thousand years ago, Belize has lately received some spurts of anxious refugees from civil wars in El Salvador, Honduras, Guatemala, and Mexico. And from the seventeenth century it was a hideout for the so-called Baymen, Scottish and English privateers who hid in the river mouths that indent the mangrove swamps and robbed Spanish shipping. The world's second-largest barrier reef further sheltered them from retaliation, and one buccaneer in particular, Peter Wallace, who is said to have arrived with eighty companions at the mouth of the area's most navigable river in 1638, may have given that river and the country his name (Wallace; Willis; Belis). On the other hand, a Mayan word for "muddy" is *beliz*.

Jamaica's governor, the nearest British authority, intermittently put the kibosh on such freebooting, whereupon the Baymen would buy slaves and cut logwood, a small, locally abundant tree whose heartwood provided red and purple dyes for Europe's woolen industry. When new technology eclipsed this livelihood, they shipped mahogany, Spanish cedar, pine, oaklike Santa Maria trees, and splendid sacred Mayan ceiba or "silk-cotton" trees (for their fluff), at the lofty top of which godlings once dwelt. Slavery among off-duty pirates in the woods became more of a meritocracy, a looser, more rascally, rum-punch, miscegenatic operation than regimented plantation slavery, and white supremacy was hard to

maintain. Kidnapped Mayans and escaped slaves from elsewhere were added to the Creole brew; and Carib Indians
began arriving about 1802, after surviving tribal annihilation
on some of the Lesser Antilles islands, which they in turn had
conquered from the Arawaks. (*Carib* meant "cannibal" in
Arawak, and thus the Caribbean vacationlands have an am-
biguous semantic ring.) Later additions included Sepoy mu-
tineers deported from India, Chinese coolie wanderers,
Mosquito Indians from Nicaragua, Mexican mestizos fleeing
the Caste War in the Yucatán, and disgruntled U.S. Confed-
erates deserting the ruined South after the War Between the
States.

In 1798 the Baymen had secured their hold on the territory by beating off a fourteen-vessel Spanish fleet at Saint
George's Cay, near Belize City; and by 1871 the uncharac-
teristically reluctant Crown was persuaded to formalize its
relationship with the colony. Bananas, citrus fruits, cacao
beans, sugar, molasses, coconuts, and tortoiseshell in dribs
and drabs were not exports to make a merchant banker's
mouth water, and the market for mahogany petered out:
thirteen million board feet exported in 1846, three million in
1900. Chicle tapped from sapodilla trees as a base for chewing gum then replaced mahogany, just as mahogany had
replaced logwood as a forestry and economic base early in
the nineteenth century, but after a boom of thirty years or so,
synthetics were invented, which by World War II had ren-
dered chicle superfluous too. Sugar and citrus are the main
crops now, and—in the forests—ecotourism and marijuana.
Ecotourism, indeed, may have supplanted marijuana. You
meet rapscallions aiming to run ecotours who seem not altogether unlike eighteenth-century logwood buccaneers.

Hard-drug courier planes drop off enough white pow-
der when refueling for the flight north that Belize City has a
cocaine problem, however. It has become Footpad City,
which is a shame because otherwise it has a flavor like Mom-
basa's a couple of decades ago, a peaceable, planetary hum
that can transport you out of the Americas for a very cheap
airfare. Stay awhile, but seek security.

From the airport go to the Fort Street Guesthouse, if you
are midscale. (To Mom's, on Handyside Street, if you are
traveling light.) In a wicker chair on the Fort Street veranda,

with a margarita and a glass of iced rainwater and a lovely bouillabaisse in front of me, I found my cover pierced immediately. A British naval officer seconded to Belize's navy paused in flirting with my traveling companion to say, "You look like a college professor who's just been sacked. That special seediness."

"You're right. You should work for the CIA," I told him.

"Don't think they haven't tried to bribe me," he remarked, amused that an American diplomat was approaching, with his mother, to have supper.

There on the veranda I also met a local beer brewer, and an elderly butterfly hunter who was rumored to have been fired from his job in London only four months short of when his pension should have kicked in; and then Sharon Matola, who is the soul of conservation in Belize. She is a thirtyish woman who ran away from Baltimore with a Romanian lion trainer and toured with a circus in Mexico, before coming to Belize as a jaguar trainer in a movie company. She cajoles party ministers to set aside swaths of rain forest in reserves, and British soldiers to help her build the Belize zoo. And there was a Yorkshireman who flies Puma helicopters for the Royal Air Force. He told me about the fun of lowering a snake scientist into the jungle to capture boas, imitating the man's herculean rassle with a thirteen-footer, until the shy herpetologist himself showed up for supper. A diminutive person, he confided that he had recorded thirty-three species, including a frog new to knowledge.

Belize City has sixty thousand people. Hurricanes flattened much of it in 1931 and again in 1961, so the seat of government has been moved to a village called Belmopan, fifty miles inland, though no one who had a choice moved. At the Swing Bridge over Haulover Creek you are in the center of town. Putt-putts and pitpans (river craft), lobster boats, sailing sloops, and little lighters tie up here, or you can get on a dive boat and rent scuba gear. Banks, the post office, police station, Lebanese stores, Hong Kong restaurants, the green Catholic church, the president's green frame house, and the People's United Party's blue headquarters are close at hand. You can buy papayas and Bombay cloth, see Ibo and Ashanti faces speaking the Jamaican patois which is street English, overhear lots of Spanish, and visit the Mennonite furniture mart nearby. Pale, burly, blond, in straw hats and bib overalls, Belize's six thousand Mennonites came from Manitoba by way of Chihuahua in Mexico in search of clean living. They raise Belize's chickens, breakfast eggs, and green vegetables, converse in a sixteenth-century Swiss Anabaptist Low German, and look at you aware that you are going to hell. Some are such fine mechanics that they are called Mechanites. Others use a horse and buggy and have been departing for Bolivia or Paraguay to start the gargantuan drama of pioneering primeval jungle all over again.

Colorado surfers, Gurkha artillerymen, Boston remittance men pass slowly by, as the muggers with shoeshine kits circle them. I'd heard of Belize on the Yukon River, where some of the young placer miners operating in solo couples spoke of winters in Placentia like a luscious secret, ducking down when the creeks froze up and paying in nuggets. ("What do you make in a year?" I'd ask, and they laughed, aghast at my gullibility. "No placer miner makes anything; they break even.") It was twice as expensive as the rest of Central America yet half as expensive as North America, and no need to feel sorry for anyone: just sun, swim out to wrecks, eat fish, smoke dope. Red parrots, blue grottoes, Indian pyramids. Buy in dollars, not quetzals, cordobas, lempiras, balboas.

Haulover Creek is lined with slapped-together shacks of misfitted boards in cheap landsmen's pastels or deeper, sea-savaged mariners' colors, some built of salvagers' booty off the teeth of the reef, some out of junkyard crating and hurricane damage. Nothing to make you weep unduly if it blew down again, but handy and homey, set up on stilts; people run for the concrete schools in a flattening storm. The gardens are hedged with conch shells, sharks' heads, turtle skeletons, crocodiles' skulls. Then on Albert Street and Regent Street you've got more substantial white clapboard two-story houses, in the modestly porticoed, gingerbread-and-iron-railing style of superseded British colonial ports worldwide, as you walk south of the Swing Bridge to the handsome brick Anglican cathedral, the first in Central America, constructed in 1812–26 from a Christopher Wren parish-church design—three Mosquito Coast kings were crowned here by the British—and Government House, a ramblingly graceful white wooden mansion of the same era.

On Orange Street live the Zabone family of woodcarvers. And the Swing Bridge is worth half an hour any time. But after a day or two you may want to head for the bus station, or go to a gray house on stilts at the corner of Euphrates Avenue and Orange Street and talk to George Young, an ambulance driver who also runs a couple of ramshackle station wagons and may be pleased to drop everything and take you on a chartered tour of the country. My travel mate, Trudy, a college psychologist, and I spent four good days with him. George is fiftyish, a black Creole, the son of a sailor who would sometimes come home from the seven seas and ship out the same night when George was small, and who had an "outside family" to keep up with too. But George has paid school fees for six kids, maintains close-knit relations with them, and got to know his father fondly and his half-brothers also, before the old man's death from pneumonia at fifty-five. His mother and three brothers live in the United States, but George chose what he calls "the slow lane," staying here as a family man and taxiing occasional tourists around. He's visited them, but gets enough taste of the United States when he catches a bus to Houston for an auto dealer and chauffeurs vehicles down. After the blistering racial climate in Texas, his adventure continues through Mexico with cold mountain deserts and fogs, and the gauntlet of officials asking for bribes, wanting to ticket him if he stops to eat and gives them a chance. But the worst risk is bandits, if he doesn't stop, but drives through the night. At gunpoint a new car was hijacked from him. He wasn't shot, and begged his way back, persuading the local taxi association to take up a collection for him. In Guatemala you can have bandits and guerrillas, and the police don't just arrest you for money, like in Mexico. "They are savage. They want to hurt you. Throw you in jail and watch you suffer." Being black in Belize is never as dicey, though the two parliamentary parties, the People's United Party and the United Democratic Party, do tend to divide along racial lines, with Hispanics in the latter.

George drove us north to Crooked Tree, Guinea Grass, Orange Walk, Sarteneja, and the ruins at Altun Ha, two excavated ceremonial plazas with pyramids, temples, ball courts, and palaces, covered with irrepressible greenery and imbued with a marvelous seabed smell. In the ball-game plaza would-be kings competed in life-and-death matches.

Crooked Tree, a placid agricultural village bordering a waterfowl sanctuary on a lagoon, grows cashews and mangoes. Guinea Grass is Wild Westville, by contrast, druggy and closed-mouthed; and you can see a fortified, floodlit villa gleaming white behind razor wire. You can also rent a skiff for the twelve-mile trip up the New River, braided through mazy lambent sloughs, to the ridge and ruins at Lamanai, or "Submerged Crocodile," some of which are twenty-five hundred years old. As recently as 1867 Mayans fought the British here (five million people in Mesoamerica still speak Mayan dialects), but with the huge, vine-hung, moss-strewn, orchid-stippled trees, the vivid river, the lakelike lagoon, and the sun on the marshlands beyond, a quietude prevails. The two-square-mile center of Lamanai seems scarcely excavated, though more than seven hundred building sites have been identified and there are three temple-pyramids, one a hundred feet high, that you can climb, decorated with jaguar and crocodile and sun-god masks. It was here in the sixties that archaeologists found the largest piece of carved jade in Central America: a nine-pound head of the sun god, Kinich Ahau. Palms, ferns, and philodendrons swarm nearly everywhere, fountaining vegetation at each cleared spot, and spider monkeys gab and amble in the canopy overhead. In the limey, lichen-covered rubble you can find sea fossils, inches from the honey smell of brilliant flowers. Lichens, limestone, fossils, and flowers blend the scents of soil and sea, and nature here is veined with history. We tasted custard apples, like warm ice cream, and soursop fruit, admiring the clouds reflected on the water, and the sailing trees. Mayan civilization is thought to have collapsed a thousand years ago in the general region of Belize with a revolution of the peasantry against the nobles.

On the pearly, black and blue river, kids in pirogues were collecting firewood and catching fish for supper, and we saw several Mennonite farmers, who widely populate the banks of the New River, as we skimmed out.

Sarteneja, east of the mouth of the New River, is an isolated fishing village a couple of hours' drive from Guinea Grass through large sugarcane plantations, the marl road strewn with cane leaves where the big trucks have passed.

Wages are ten or twenty dollars (U.S.) a day, though illegals from El Salvador may work for only three, which is about the price of a pack of Independence cigarettes and a bottle of Belikin beer. George talked about how many cane cutters get bitten by "tommygoffs," or fer-de-lances. "Wowlas" are boas. The king vulture is called "King John Crow"; the screech owl, the "monkey bird"; the osprey, the "billy hawk"; the toucan, the "bill bird"; the blue heron, the "full pot," because it's so big its meat fills a pot. The otter is the "water dog." The kinkajou is "nightwalker." The tapir is the "mountain cow." Howler monkeys are "baboons." Pumas are "red tigers." Tayras (a weasel) are "bush dogs." We saw cornfields and beehives, and little *milpas* growing yams and plantains. "Lots of sweets in this soil," George said.

This is Spanish country, the heartland of the United Democratic Party, whose colors are red and white, and party officials' houses were sometimes painted that. George's Creole party, the People's United Party, uses blue and white. "But your feet be lifted off the ground here if you make much noise about that," George said. "You might wind up in a well. They's a lot of wells around. You can't ax them about politics. Very distressful if you did."

Sarteneja is a beach town of sixteen hundred souls on Chetumal Bay. It's got blue water; a row of coconut palms and almond trees; a new mooring dock; some fishing sloops from which people go out in dories to dive for lobsters (called "crawfish") and conch or to angle for red snapper, bluefish, shark, and mullet; and two dirt streets of tin-roofed, cement-block houses, some hungry dogs, a nondescript one-story hotel, and several vacation huts going up. Egrets, ibises, anhingas, roseate spoonbills, and wood storks fly about, because of the lagoons and swamps, and there are frigate birds and cormorants, pelicans and agile terns stunting over the salt water, and Mayan ruins to investigate ashore. The gringos who've discovered this place—schoolteachers, diner owners—are mostly from upstate New York, though I met a stone-broke Quebecois whose single asset seemed to be a sailboat he had built; he was awaiting a buyer. In countries like Belize, no particular relationship exists between a gringo's income and how imaginatively he travels.

I'd come to meet Jan and Tineke Meerman, a string-bean fortyish couple from Holland who manage the twenty-two-thousand-acre Sarteneja Reserve surrounding the Shipstern Lagoon. It's owned by a group of Swiss butterfly fanciers, and Jan raises and mails out the pupae of perhaps thirty of the reserve's two hundred species to commercial butterfly farms in Europe (Britain alone has forty of these), where visitors enjoy the relaxing ambience of greenhouses full of tropical plants, waterfalls, and exotic birds. He can also, of course, cater to the bottomless market for dead butterflies, which are collected like stamps worldwide. But what has happened to Jan and Tineke—very tall, he wears a U-shaped beard; very precise, she clips her hair short; and they live by kerosene lamp in a former oil-drilling camp—corresponds to Sharon Matola's transformation from jaguar trainer to conservationist. Sharon dreamed of taming lions, back in Baltimore, and now is a front-line ecologist. Jan, a carpenter's son from Zeeland, the Netherlands, arrived in Belize as an amateur lepidopterist with some brief experience of wildlife work in Yemen and Tanzania. But in the process of going into the forest and marsh after butterflies (catching thirty quick species in any morning), and then to identify and dig up for his screened pens the food plants the larvae of each species eat, he, too, became a committed ecologist. He speaks of reintroducing howler monkeys to the eight thousand acres of gallery forest within the reserve, and of the necessary education program, which would involve the villages around. His recreation used to be collecting lucrative butterflies for the carriage trade—with a graceful tweaking motion he catches them by the wings between his fore- and middle fingers. Now it's sleeping on jaguar and puma trails in the rainy season, when the tracks show up well, listening to the cats roar or scream, and studying the habits of several individuals he knows.

Married nine years, Tineke and Jan are a good team and have a "night" dog and a "day" dog to perform different duties outdoors (bite and wag). They have a pet wowla, a small croc, some turtles, and a collared peccary. A Royal Air Force jeep stopped by with a Kew Gardens biochemist, who was studying how toxic butterflies build up their protective toxicity and how the plant that the Mayans ate to fight diabetes achieved its effect. We had a shrimp-and-grouper dinner, and his military driver let me peruse a British Forces map. Then he solemnly took it back. "You have just read this map. Now I must kill you."

We talked about Belize's three coral snakes and four tommygoffs, and why hot countries have a slow pace, and how Mennonite apostates, as George put it, "try to get bad," going to bars, flirting clumsily.

We slept in the bunkhouse and in the morning walked the nature trail that Jan maintains, labeled with dozens of trees. Trumpet tree, bullet tree, mimosa, waterwood, poison-wood, strangler fig, chicle tree, cotton tree, gumbolimbo, mother-of-cocoa, royal palm, finger palm. Tiger heron, tri-colored heron, Amazon kingfisher, pygmy kingfisher, curas-sow . . . the roll of birds we saw went on. Then we wound down the old Northern Highway, through a pleasant back-water of cane fields, little cattle ranches, shallow wetlands, and second-growth woods, back to Belize City, where a cab-driver excitedly hailed George to tell him that another driver, using George's other station wagon, had been arrested for running drugs. "He want you to bail him," he said. It seems that George's own good reputation had prevented the car from being impounded, however, and George was disin-clined to extract the man from jail right away. The trouble was, George suggested, that jail was too soft. Imprisoned British soldiers are still forced to dig graves for a coffin full of stones and dig it up again, or to build a mountain of sand and run up and down with their packs on. *That* is jail, he said.

At the airport, Mennonites in severe frocks and blocky shoes were meeting new pilgrims from Canada, who looked as raptly distracted by God as they—while Trudy and I ren-dezvoused with our new guide, Neil Rogers. Neil, a rolling stone and Englishman with years of tourist herding in India under his narrow belt, seemed as symmetrical a type to my own as were the resident and visiting Mennonites. Sex in Belize City was "a melee, a free-for-all, bad for relationships," but he'd fallen in love with the co-owner of the Fort Street Guesthouse, he said. Life here was lived "on the knife edge," going either beautifully or awfully, which was how he pre-ferred it. And I, too, am a professional traveler and only hope to die respectably of old age in my bed, not a suicide or the victim of a scary virus or a plane crash. Just as I like to eavesdrop to get an inkling of what is in store, Neil was eavesdropping upon us slinkily from behind a door as we approached, before introducing himself. He, too, had arrived "at loose ends" in this spot where reef divers "bubble around" and the sky seems so big and the world so small.

The ceiling fans, slotted blinds, the Doberman pinscher on guard against thieves, the tattooed Cockney paratroopers with pink rum punches on Fort Street, all are organized by Rita and Rachel from Colorado, who are known informally as "R. and R." Neil was lovesick (I, too, fall in love in foreign climes to anchor myself), so I went to see Alexander Featherstone at the U.S. Embassy, who told me the U.S.A. spends six and a half million dollars a year on Belize.

Travelers aim for salient sights and memorable days that slice through a cross-section of a new country. In the Pyrenees they want to spend a sunny hour with a goatherd who has been hiking these same meadows for a half a century; or they will barge in on a glassblower on the island of Murano who's been doing that since before they were born. Spanish laceworkers who have gone blind making tablecloths in the service of m'lady; fisherfolk in the Bay of Fundy whose ancestors were riding the tides when King George squabbled with George Washington. Old wines, tapestries, porcelains, and cathedrals: continuity and devotion are what tourists are after, because they're gone at home. Ah, the peasants in the fields, *they* still believe!

Of course, the rain forest is so old it's where snakes chose to lose their legs. They were originally lizards who found that wriggling on their bellies through the tumbled vegetation was faster to begin with. Animism, pythonic religion, a faith older than Christ or Moses, is what we look for in the jungle. Otherwise we want to chop it down.

Neil, in his Land-Rover, sped us west from Belize City toward the Guatemalan border, an eighty-mile trip that till the 1930s could take two weeks of poling up the Belize River, with landings at Double Head Cabbage and More Tomorrow, at Burrel Boom, Dancing School Eddy, and Never Delay, at Black Man Eddy and Bullet Tree Falls. In the Valley of Peace, Salvadoran refugees grow peanuts. Neil spoke of the virginal spelunking in the mountains to the south, and maybe ten days' wilderness walking either north or south.

His boss, Mick Fleming, at the Chaa Creek Lodge, where we were headed, had recently been on an expedition to a precipitous twist of the Raspaculo Branch of the Macal River, where no human beings may have set foot for a millennium.

Short of the Hawkesworth suspension bridge over the Macal River at San Ignacio, the British have their Holdfast Camp, with a few tanks and Harrier jump jets to foil a Guatemalan invasion. San Ignacio is a friendly Hispanic town surrounded by scenery, including Xunantunich, a Mayan ruin on the international border, and Mountain Pine Ridge, a large reach of high ground. Chaa (for Chocolate) Creek is an African-style lodge with round whitewashed thatched-roofed cottages, a raised patio for having drinks on, breadnut trees spreading overhead, with parrots and keel-billed toucans feeding in them, and the river flowing by in front. (Needs only a couple of hippos.) Mick left Uganda a few steps ahead of Idi Amin. He's English, and Lucy, his wife, is from New Jersey, and at supper, two of the guests, from Great Neck, Long Island, discussed whether their son should be sent to Yale or Princeton, while a retired British Signals light colonel with white mustaches told tales of India and Malaysia. "At my age I've got one foot on the bus stop and one foot in the grave," he said.

Next day, a retired British tank sergeant named Dick Strand, from Bath, took a group of us bumping by Land-Rover to admire the thousand-foot Hidden Valley Falls on the Rio On, and then a sumptuous, arched-mouthed cave that the Rio Frío slips through, sandy-bottomed and radiant, tranquil in February, with leafy green backlighting at both ends, while the silent high ceiling seethed with black-and-white reflections of sun shafts glancing off the moving water. Strand took us up on the pine ridge to watch British cannon fire and see where survival teams live off iguanas, armadillos, and coatimundis. He has done this, and has five tours of duty in Northern Ireland to reflect on, plus better stints in Germany and Cyprus. But he came back, married a Belizean, fathered two daughters, and bought a comfortable house on which his property tax is twenty-seven dollars a year.

Next door to Chaa Creek Lodge, a herbalist from Chicago named Rosita Arvigo will give you a massage and an infusion of tonics learned from a genuine Mayan shaman

182

near Xunantunich named Eligio Panti, who has been assist-
ing the National Cancer Institute of the U.S. in collecting
wild drugs. She has cleared out a "nature trail" in the bush,
where you can examine rubber and allspice trees, mahogany
and bay cedar, fiddlewood and custard apple, and the give-
and-take tree, a handsome palm whose spines can deliver
painful wounds that its own bark will cure. She's a tously,
somewhat offish woman who lived for years with a tribe of
Indians in Guerrero, Mexico, before moving here.

Neil then piled Trudy and me into a car and took us
upriver till the track petered out on a fertile plain, by the
Macal (which is named for the edible *macal*, or taro, plant),
probably the site of the Mayan capital of Tipu, which was not
decisively overrun by a Spanish expeditionary force until
1707. Previous campaigns had penetrated to Tipu in 1544,
1567, and 1608, but the Mayans succeeded in revolting in the
1630s. The classic-period sites of Tikal and Caracol, as well
as Xunantunich, are not far off.

A young man, William Morales, met our jeep with his
mule at a modest melon-and-squash farm, strapped our bags
on the beast, and led us up a limestone gorge. The river
sashayed, smiling, through tawny pools, past amber, white,
and gray rock facings and forest patches, great sacred cotton
"world trees," bullhoof trees (named for the shape of the
leaves), tall palms, rosewood, fig, and Santa Maria trees,
which were my favorites because the trunks are like oaks.
Palmettos and ferns were underfoot, and vines draped everywhere, over tapir, deer, tayra, and agouti tracks. The river
ran like puppies, leaping down rock ledges, with tarpon and
snook in the quiet parts. "Gibnut" (agouti, a big rodent) is the
national meat for Sunday "boil-ups," when everything goes
in the pot—cassava, kidney beans, chilies, geese, rice, hog
plums—and old-timers drink cashew wine, William said.

Most days, he rides seven miles at dawn to chain-saw a
piece of the jungle for a hydroelectric project, hearing howler
monkeys holler as he goes and comes; but his lungs were
bothering him. We climbed a bluff to his parents' pretty farm
at the lip of a waterfall on top. Antonio and Leah Morales
had tried to raise cattle, but the jaguars kept killing their
stock; now they were trying coffee. By candlelight we dined
on homegrown corn, beans, peppers, chicken, pineapple,

and coffee, and Antonio told how, when he and his brothers built watch fires to protect their cows, the biggest jaguar just sat down by one of them and warmed his back—then splashed vigorously through the stream when he saw a gun, his colors gorgeous in the firelight, and loped away. Even hunting opossums and white-lipped peccaries ("warree") for the pot is an adventure, because the men go barefoot at night on paths where tommygoffs are also hunting and will suddenly rise up—the proverbial "two-hour snake." Tommygoffs can give birth to as many as seventy young, and Antonio has seen one strike a gibnut just as he himself had drawn a bead.

Antonio is Belizean, born of Mexican and Guatemalan parents. Leah is Salvadoran, and she and her parents had to flee Honduras, too, during the so-called Soccer War in 1969, when twenty thousand Salvadorans and Hondurans died after a series of disputed games. The starlight and the silence, except for gouts of water going off the waterfall, set her story of being a refugee in relief.

In the morning's green-pink sunrise, with a hundred birds sounding like tin whistles and all the world a stage for them, Antonio led us through the woods—monkey bushes, ink plants, medicine trees, negrito trees—to a cave he'd found while gathering roof thatching and tie-tie vines. Head high once we'd crawled inside, it wound down for maybe two hundred yards, with stone shelving providing niches for occasional polychrome pots painted with monkeylike or humanoid figures, and even a few grains of corn remaining in them. There were a couple of low-ceilinged side chambers that you could scramble up into, marked by ceremonial fire rings (these caves were underworld religious sites, never places where Mayans slept), and behind an impressive stalactite an offshoot passage sloped into an ultimate cul-de-sac, which had an altar in it.

I'm crepuscular by nature and feel at peace in caves, and Antonio likes the night. He told about how as a child he'd led mule trains through the dark forest to the *chicleros'* camps, with just a bell mare to help him, the big cats never attacking. Starlight can belong to people too.

Soon we walked down the footpath to the canyon floor, with palm fronds clacking gently overhead, the pell-mell river swooshing by. A "Jesus Christ lizard" poised beside an eddy. (They run on their hind legs across a strip of water.) Neil was sitting hidden by the trail to eavesdrop upon us and, finding we were happy, put us in a Land-Rover with a driver named Ricky Monzameros, who had grown up in Bullet Tree Falls, for the four-hour, fifty-mile drive to Tikal the next morning.

Ricky spoke English fluently, like a policeman, which he had been for five years. "Five years in the police and never arrested anybody. So nobody's mad," he said. He'd been stationed at Benque Viejo del Carmen, where Guatemala starts, so our entry was smooth.

Immediately the colorful poverty—the begging children in prismatic cottons—of Mesoamerica began. In Guatemala, wages can be a dollar or two a day, money is color coded because of illiteracy, and high-school graduates teach other children through the sixth grade. Teenage soldiers, green-clad, manned a roadblock, and a college student whom we picked up said that "if you stick your head up above the crowd, you'll just be another grave." Her father had been beaten to death by the police and then stuffed in the wreck of his car, which mysteriously went off the road.

A girl carried a string of fish in her hand; another, a cluster of bananas on her head; others balanced plastic water jugs. There were bicyclists, horsemen, donkeys toting sacks of corn. Very little vehicular traffic, though we saw a Ferris wheel set up alongside a general store, and brightly pink and chartreuse fundamentalist *iglesias*, for the ride to heaven, in between a long series of hand-to-mouth farms. Red shirts, red skirts. Insects sang. We jolted over the bulldozed road, and the Mopan River (which becomes the Belize) snaked slowly across swampland alongside, with waterbirds and waders all over, dashing ducks and solemn storks. Red-vented woodpeckers and white-collared seedeaters perched in the trees. We saw chestnut-bellied herons, green and red trogons, masked red tityras, yellow-lored parrots, and colonies of oropendola birds' stocking-looking nests, and an iguana in an *agate* tree. A truck full of cheese chips and pork rinds had tipped over in the soft dirt, and we saw a hunter with an old gun on his shoulder and a mongrel on a string.

Ricky's father was a hunter and a *chiclero* and taught him

to find warree, gibnut, and "mountain cows" for the pot, and reptiles for their skins. At thirteen, Ricky was taught to climb and bleed a chicle tree by the traditional method—his father lit a fire under him, so he had to keep climbing. After the market for it died, they made their own gum by boiling chicle sap and pouring in a purple dye and Colgate toothpaste, for taste.

Of a philosophical turn of mind, he asked me, "In the world, Ted, are there more eyes or are there more leaves?"

"That's a good question, if you're counting insects' eyes," I said.

His tourists run to people who may be vacationing on Easter Island next Christmas, or Christmas Island next Easter, and talk to him of Machu Picchu and Botswana and Hyderabad, of real estate consortiums being reorganized, of rock stars dumping their managers. It being Sunday, we watched a mass baptism of adults on a scenic beach at Lake Petén. The young minister possessed a deeply cut, charismatic face, and the enthusiastic singing of his parishioners was gleeful, as baptisms ought to be.

Tikal was a major capital for a thousand years. In six square miles, three thousand remnant structures have been mapped. A million potsherds, a hundred thousand tools and other objects, have been unearthed. I climbed Temple IV and Temple I (a gray fox came out immediately to smell where I'd sat), saw the bronzy ocellated turkeys, the brachiating monkeys, the scarlet macaws, the floral extravaganza all about. "Undiscovered" until 1848, it seems as arbitrary a choice of site as, say, Manhattan. To try to think about the politics and commerce, astronomy and superstition, art, gardening, bombast, and war that had been concentrated in these blackened, seashell-smelling ruins would be fruit for years, and I was on a jaunt. I roamed the jungle, mused, and met a rare, white-and-black anteater, a magical sort of pandalike creature, gazed at the plazas, acropolises, and temples—a jaguar had recently borne a litter of young in one of them—and enjoyed the huge trees.

Back at Chaa Creek two days later, the supple Neil Rogers put Trudy and me into the hands of a driver named Elmo Richards, thirty-one, a friend of Ricky Monzameros's, who

186

had grown up in a hamlet called Las Vegas, near Bullet Tree Falls. His father, too, had been a hunter, selling crocodile hides at three-fifty per foot, fer-de-lances for twelve dollars, boas for five dollars, puma skins for fifty dollars, and one-hole jaguars for seventy-five dollars. (Now a good woodsman is more likely to grow "Belize Breeze" in an off-road patch.) Whereas Ricky had escaped from his twig-fire village by joining the police, Elmo's way was more free-lance. He worked at first with his father in a slaughterhouse in San Ignacio (a hundred lambs a week for the British military), until, restless, he went to Los Angeles to visit a cousin. Like George Young—like so many Belizeans—he found the U.S. alarming, although watched relatives make a go of it. When he went outdoors, young toughs would home in on him, reaching for his beer money, his pizza money, asking, with death in their voices, whether he was a Crip or a Blood. Life was so cheap, and there seemed so little space for him to squeeze into, that he was relieved when his cousin simply gave him a secondhand truck to take back to San Ignacio. At the slaughterhouse, he would load it with meat and drive southeast to the coastal town of Dangriga, selling wholesale at every crossroads shop. In Dangriga he'd pick up a load of fish and start the return, a twelve-hour round trip. Because his sister had married a Dangriga politician, he was well rooted at either end.

Elmo, like Ricky, sympathized with the U.D.P. party, opposing George Young's P.U.P. party, which had recently won reelection after two years out of office. But as with George, politics made both of them uneasy. They didn't speak of possible violence, the way he did, but rather of bureaucratic retaliation in matters like a building permit, a tax reassessment. "They watch to see if you vote, because they know how you'll vote," Elmo said. When I asked him about the British, he told me they were O.K. when sober, but that in 1982 some of them had danced naked on a bar with some San Ignacio girls and had set off an all-night brawl in which four thousand people fought.

From the nondescript capital, Belmopan, a barracks village, we turned onto the so-called Hummingbird Highway, which is so rich in hummingbirds, orioles, laughing falcons, blue-crowned motmots, and swallow-tailed kites, the name seems not a hype. The gravel road swings past a dozen quick amber creeks, pocket valleys, mini-jungles, past grapefruit and lime groves and sweet-potato *milpas*. Good Living Camp. The Sibun River. Over-the-Top Camp. Alta Vista. We saw a drug czar's *finca*, a Hershey chocolate farm, a Nestlé orange-juice factory. The Maya Mountains to the west lent the scenery a panache, and finally we turned toward them and drove into the Cockscomb Basin Wildlife Sanctuary, 103,000 acres, named for the country's highest mountain (3,700 feet), whose profile is like a rooster's comb. Elmo, pleased with us, invited us to his family's next boil-up—his father dumped in pigs' tails, peppers, palm oil, chocolate, possums, bananas.

There were three cabins at the reserve, one for the wardens, one for us, and one for the three soldiers guarding us from bandits. Walking out, we swam idyllically in South Stann Creek under a spreading bri-bri tree and smelled the droves of warrees that had been eating palm nuts underneath the cohune trees. Elmo showed us tree rat, gibnut, gopher, bush dog, and ring-tailed cat tracks, plus a bullhoof root, such as he chews for a toothache, and "jackass bitters," a plant whose leaves when brewed relieve fevers. Soapseed, pimento trees, bay-leaf palm, laurel tree, Boy Job tree, My Lady tree.

The soldiers (Belize remains a democracy partly because it has only a six-hundred-man army) included a Creole corporal, tall, black, and street-smart, from Belize City; a slim, straight-shooting mestizo from Orange Walk, or "Rambo Town," as George Young had called it because of its drugs; and a Mayan from the Punta Gorda district. Kekchi and Mopan Mayans live here in the south. The four wardens were small-framed, muscular, round-faced Mopan Mayans, with the bark of woodsmanship on them, an air of watchful stillness, a less obtrusive body language, a different tempo of ears-eyes-nose observation. These canebrakes and "tumble" forests (called so because the hurricanes bowl them down) were their home, and like good wardens, they had hunted jaguars before the preserve was established, using a large gourd with buckskin drawn across its mouth, which grunted like a rutting *tigre* when you scratched your nails across the top. The Creole corporal, to my untutored eye, could have been Tanzanian; the mestizo could have been from Tijuana;

and the Mayan serviceman had been assimilated to the point where he looked generically Amerindian—could have been in Arizona or South Dakota—but not these guys. Ignacio Pop, the head warden, was hide hunting a two days' walk from his village when a tommygoff bit him. Luckily, he says, he was not alone. His two friends packed him out to a logging road in the course of eleven hours and got him to a snake doctor, who cured him in about a week.

After a balmy night of insect songs and bat activity under the panoply of stars, and some more walking in the morning, Elmo drove us to Dangriga (a Garifuna word meaning "Standing Water"), whose population is climbing toward nine thousand. Sun-soaked in February, the reddish streets were a promenade for ladies carrying black umbrellas to block the heat. (The men we saw were mostly drunk.) We ate lunch in the Starlight Café, a Chinese restaurant with Christmas lights around the bar, next to the Local Motion disco and the Tropical Hotel. At night, Elmo said, some drugs or sex may be peddled, but in a more good-humored spirit than in Belize City. We heard that a local *obeah* man rises from the image of a coiled snake if you go to consult him in his cabin, that the boas grow venomous fangs at nightfall, and that a Welshwoman has been living alone in the mangrove swamps for two decades. Also an American lawyer. The Chinese fled here from the Japanese in World War II, and now a second wave is leaving Hong Kong in fear of the Communist takeover. Lebanese own many of the citrus farms. They arrived as storekeepers but have lately sold their businesses to "Hindoos" (East Indians), to become landowners. You see them less often, Elmo said, but everybody eats Chinese.

The Garifuna, or "Black Caribs," as the English called them, arrived on this coast in the early nineteenth century. They were seafarers, dugout paddlers, island raiders, cannibal warriors, whose name in the language of the Arawaks, the "Caribbean" tribe they preyed on, is where our word "cannibal" came from. Interestingly enough, only the men spoke Carib; the women, many of whom were captured Arawaks, spoke Arawak, until the languages blended. At the time of the European conquest, the Caribs, paddling from South America, had swept the Arawaks from the Lesser Antilles and were perhaps prepared to move on Haiti and Cuba.

Instead they were decimated and temporarily given Saint Vincent's Island as a designated "Indian Territory," though scalawag French and English, and blacks from a slave ship that wrecked just off the island in 1675, joined the brew. The "Yellow Caribs," those with white blood, were permitted to stay, after the British reassumed control, but the Black Caribs were deported in 1797 to Roatán, an island off Honduras, and some wandered here to the mouth of Stann Creek, a former trading post set up by English Puritans from Nassau, whom the Spanish had evicted. The Mayans still seem metaphorically stunned at their self-inflicted decline as a civilization, which began five hundred years before Columbus, but the Garifuna, whose "Carib" conquest of the Caribbean was arrested at full tilt by the English, French, and Spanish, have energy to spare. They go to sea, or colonize Brooklyn (which has more Garifuna than Belize), or become schoolteachers, merchants, government clerks.

In Belize we are thrust into the climate in which we were born—body temperature, like the womb, like Olduvai Gorge. And the pyramids have such basic forces inscribed on them as the Sun, Maize, the Tiger, the Croc. Friends whom I met in Belize City like to swim nude every morning near the mouth of the brawny Belize River, five fathoms deep, where it enters the sea and dolphins and sharks and whatnot show up, fast mountain currents joining the punch of the tide.

Stann Creek and Dangriga are gentler. We hired a boat from Ringo Usher, the son of the local dentist, and headed twelve miles out to Tobacco Cay, a seven-acre island where those seventeenth-century Puritans grew tobacco and where Garifuna turtlers later settled, with a church and a school. Ringo and his father are building tourist cottages in Dangriga, and Ringo has found a dozen mangrove trees growing on a patch of reef unclaimed by anybody and, by placing drift logs in such a way as to trap coral sand washed into these shoals, is constructing a beach for more cabins. He showed us, en route. All up and down this coast, old seasnake and saltwater-crocodile islets are being converted to money, though we did see one that has been preserved for the boobies and frigate birds to nest on. Hundreds wheeled over it; landed to roost; flew up. At one end was a special tree, where, Ringo said, the birds went to sit when they were sick and preparing to die.

The frigate birds steal fish from the boobies by "beating on them till they spit it up," as Ringo said, and we saw other avian or piscine dramas. Ospreys diving. Herons. Water birds, from limpkins to soras, from loons to grebes to whistling swans, have celebrative cries, saluting the dawn or the rising moon as if God were alive in the world. But we—lizards that we are—tend to hoard the sun, gaze out with a basilisk's impassive stare from our beach towel, when we are by the water, bathing in a kind of fugue of memories while feeding heat to our cold bones. And the breaking surf eases our hearts. *Thump. Thump.* Its failure to accomplish anything except in a cosmic time frame is comforting, yet the energy soothes and reassures us.

Tobacco Cay sits right atop Columbus Reef, so swimming from the beach, you can dive a few fathoms down the splendidly awesome wall of that, or else paddle about in the extensive shallows on top. Or you can do what I did, which was to step from Ringo's skiff straight into the hammock that Winnie and Nolan Jackson, his grandparents, have rigged on their dock and stay there awhile. The surf thundered hard, the wind blew boisterously, the sun skidded off the tossing waves. With a bit of thatch shading me, I was in heaven, though Nolan grumped that if the wind always blew like this, "We would go crazy."

It was suppertime, and going off to collect two lobsters from one of his traps for Trudy and me to eat, Nolan remarked over his shoulder, "It's a shame these poor lobsters have to die for you," a sentiment I've often shared, watching diners stuff themselves in restaurants on Cape Cod. Because Nolan didn't know us from Adam, his grouchiness seemed refreshing. People come to his hammock and little hotel for their honeymoons or divorces or a cancer recuperation or to celebrate a cash bonus, dressing in beachcombers' "sweats" as if they were pleasantly indigent. Winnie said she'd moved out here for her asthma, but demurred when we complimented the view. "It's just pretty; it's not beautiful," she said.

She baked johnnycake, fried plantains, and boiled rice and beans to go with the lobsters, while the wind blew pelagically, the thatch over us rattled, and the Atlantic crashed against the rim of the reef a short distance away. You could see why these Belizeans didn't need to be pirates at heart to find plenty of wrecks to pick over and drowned bodies to strip and dump back for the sharks. The Black Caribs who had fought subjugation on Saint Vincent's Island, the rebel Mayans who had revolted and fled to Belize from defeats in Quintana Roo, and the Jolly Roger crew of Englishmen raiding Spanish shipping from the mouths of Belize's rivers must have blended in the mind's eye of their contemporaries remarkably.

Nolan grew up on an island on Glover's Reef, which is eighteen miles farther out, an island he says his brother has now "thrown away to an American for seventy-five thousand dollars." Nolan himself shipped out on Liberty ships in 1945 with Panamanian papers to see the world. Making friends, he soon acquired a dead American's papers, too, and worked on American ships as "Josnik Kowalski," pretending his accent and darkish skin were Polish in origin, at twice the money. For seven years he traveled to Europe and the Far East, a deckhand in the summer, a fireman in the warm engine room when the weather turned cold, and stayed at the Seamen's Church Institute in New York, taking astronomy courses and studying for a mate's license between jobs. It was a fine spell, but so many regular navy men were demobilized that ships became hard to find. He remembers the brutal glitter of New York with a certain startled pleasure—the "rum shops" selling beer "for a shilling" (twenty-five cents) and "people getting drinks off you," the museums, the social possibilities, the excitement of the uptown streets, the breakneck competition—but marginal folk like him felt crowded out.

He came back to Glover's Reef and fished for red snapper, grouper, and tuna, till he lost his boat off the beach one night in 1978 when a north wind blew and he couldn't afford to buy another. Tobacco Cay, where he and Winnie started over, had been Winnie's grandparents' home, though "if you lived here you were nothing," she says. "If you lived in town you were something." Back when tortoiseshell was worth ten dollars a pound, the village sent two big schooners down the Mosquito Coast to Nicaragua, after hawksbill turtles, and it still harbors a few fishing smacks. Though small and closely inhabited, built up with holiday houses, Tobacco Cay has a

nesting pair of ospreys, sixty feet up in a coconut palm, and
catbirds, tanagers, grackles, turnstones, pelicans, herons—
and almond trees, papayas, sea grapes, under the sloping
palms. The houses have solar panels for electricity, and tub-
ing to carry rainwater from the roofs to cisterns for storage.
In these overfished waters, "sometimes nothing is left but
your tan," Nolan says, but he remembers the bums sleeping
in Central Park in December, their legs cased in newspapers
that turned hard like plaster by morning because of the
body's frozen moisture; they had to "break out."

I roamed the island, ringed with bleached conch shells,
admiring the palm trees' idiosyncratic, windblown slant, and
imagined drifting ashore here as a castaway, famished with
thirst, and trying to crack open a coconut for water to survive, then hoping that another would fall before I collapsed.
I swam, lazed in the hammock, and met Elwood and Sandra
Fairweather, Belizeans who, like Nolan Jackson, made me a
bit homesick. Elwood, in a foundered leather easy chair next
to his beach shack, said in a gravelly, impenitent voice:
"Twenty-eight years in New York." He and Sandra, a pretty
woman with a red ribbon in her hair, had been married
fifteen years and had just had a baby daughter. Sandra
laughed at how long they'd delayed, and showed me some
charcoal drawings she'd made, and a jaguar cub skin. Elwood
has three grown kids from his first marriage, to an Italian
woman in Brooklyn; he'd worked in a bookstore for eight
years and then as a typographer, until computers made him
redundant.

I sat in a broken wooden chair seat next to him and met
his chums who wandered by: a dugout lobster fisherman, a
diving guide, a buffaloed Texan, who had sailed down here
from Galveston and had just lost the motor off his boat. It
had dropped off the stern into three fathoms, and he had a
charter arriving, a woman from Minneapolis—what would
she think? Would she advance him money? Elwood dispensed a fatalistic calm. In New York he'd haunted Greenwich Village, he said, "and generally was a beatnik." Bleecker
Street, the New School, Saint Mark's Place, Washington
Square—we found we'd shared some city sites and obsessions
of the sixties; and like Nolan, he didn't seem to have returned to Dangriga by fervent choice.

193

Raw rubber, Scotch, and lumber used to be scavenged from wartime wrecks on the reef when he was a child, and now drug boats are sometimes scuttled there for insurance money; people scavenge furnishings from them. Elwood's ancestors fought the Spanish at Saint George's Cay in 1798. Later another, as treasurer, signed British Honduras's paper money. His father is a distinguished Anglican minister, who worked in New York for many years and whom I visited at the cathedral in Belize City. But with that lineage also goes the proud tradition of "going for a stick"—a cotton tree—for a dugout canoe, precursor of the Garifunas' seamanship, as well as the *obeah* stories. Even in New York, Elwood told me, an *obeah* woman can retain her powers—walk down the street with a gold chain on, and no snatcher will grab it lest it turn into a poisonous serpent in his hands. (He'll drop it in horror, and she'll stoop down and pick it up and it will be gold once again.) One *obeah* man, however, got his comeuppance, despite his supernatural powers. He liked to sleep with married women, after first slipping out of his skin so they didn't know who he really was. But he ran afoul of a clever husband who discovered where the *obeah* man had hidden his skin, and sprinkled salt on it, so that it shrunk. The poor lover snuck back from his dalliance and couldn't put it on. It didn't fit! *Skinnee, Skinnee, Skinnee, don't you know me?* he cried—a song still sung by schoolkids.

Sandra, who is a dancer and a Belize City Creole, not a Garifuna, draws some wicked-looking nudes, and there are Garifuna stories of young girls propitiatorily fed to crocodiles. These perhaps balance the apparent likelihood that Garifuna men who captured Arawak women for wives in pre-Columbian times first ate the Arawak husbands, thus adding a certain vividness to life and making the victory memorable. Though not much more than do the gastronomical rituals of success and failure in New York.

We tourists wear bifocals. Pious about the survival of the sixty species of coral in the Caribbean, we nonetheless want a strobe-light vacation, both light and dark. "Ecotourism," and yet malice aforethought for when we get back and begin scrambling for money and status again. Eat well, dress well, and strip the earth to pay for it—and not just for lucre, but for the endless OJ and burgers grown in the tropics on bulldozed rain forest, the gas guzzling, shrimp guzzling, resort rambling. Tourists come from consuming countries, and once they pass Passport Control and get home again, they are Central America's problem, not yet its solution.

Africa
Brought Home

For Joseph Conrad, too, ours is a world where absolute power corrupts absolutely, where drumbeats only mimic heartbeats, and the white unexplored patches on a map that a boy dreams over are "darkened" for him as he grows up and explores them. Conrad's savage tribes can be exceedingly savage—anthropology has not yet catalogued and explicated their customs—but not more so than the frenetic Europeans, greedy or demented, who show up among them with alarming regularity and soon degenerate into tin-pot tyrants or, in the case of his famous enigma, Mr. Kurtz of "Heart of Darkness," an ivory dealer on the fictionalized Congo River, into what nowadays we would call a recreational or serial murderer.

Conrad did not romanticize England. Industrial London was an ominous dynamo (and Brussels sepulchral); the very Thames had probably been sort of a Congo to its Roman discoverers, as he reminded his readers. But Mr. Kurtz could not have turned from an eloquent Schweitzerian idealist into a capricious taskmaster whom even white friends and African allies had to approach at a crawl—who countenanced human sacrifice and posted the heads of "rebels" on the poles of the stockade surrounding his house—in London. To flower fully, the evil in him needed the license of a wilderness; and the Congo (three thousand miles long) surpassed the Nile (four thousand miles) and the Amazon (four thousand miles) in the barbarous images it conjured up in Europe at the turn of the century, because unlike the Nile, the Congo had no storied, ornate civilization such as Egypt's at its mouth, and its natives were black, not reddish brown like the Indians of the Amazon. Indeed, Conrad, wanting to introduce a sexual strain in Kurtz's precipitate slide into depravity but not wishing to overdo his portrait, quite arbitrarily made the queen who adores him, and whose male subjects assist him in his raids and atrocities, tawny and bronze. A black-skinned mistress would have been too dark.

Conrad of course was taking an advanced, enlightened view in bringing distilled evil to Africa in the person of this apostle of European culture, whereas today, in the brilliant revisionism of V. S. Naipaul, white men and women in Africa (*A Bend in the River*) are likely to be presented as abused, foolish innocents, and blacks as the villains. Conrad wrote a less passionate, perfervid, more relaxed, ironic variation on his theme in his other African masterpiece, "An Outpost of Progress." He did believe in the notion of wilderness Edens, but these were not in Africa—they were in the South Seas, on wild virginal islands whose light-skinned inhabitants he rather romanticized, although no more than other distinguished literary witnesses, like Herman Melville and Robert Louis Stevenson. White men self-marooned in the Pacific islands could suffer the same poisonous drift in fundamental values, but it was far from being the fault of the natives or the beautiful setting; nor did the natives much participate. And in any case, a boyish dreaminess persisted in such a place for a white man like Lord Jim, even to the brink of his own destruction. He felt no foreboding that this was the White Man's Grave.

Conrad's novels of intrigue and politics like *The Secret Agent* are unsentimental and contemporary in feeling, and his sea is a slam-bang sea, the most sumptuous and comprehensive in all literature—this perhaps because he spent longer following the sea than Melville did, for instance (something like nineteen years to Melville's three and a half), and set down his vast store of memories with a bracing exactitude, in sailors such as Singleton, captains like MacWhirr, ports like Bangkok, pirates like Gentleman Brown, ships like the extravagant *Narcissus* and the unsinkable *Nan-Shan* and the sweet, doomed *"Judea,* London. Do or Die."

Youth is youth in Conrad, captains are captains, a man's ship is his one sure friend, and his character is his fate. The austerities of circumstance are dependably stern—only character isn't—and because it has lately become part of the privilege of wealth (or a privation of poverty), beyond the means of most middle-class people, to discover at some point in one's life whether one is a physical coward or not (one must own a ketch or a plane, it seems, or travel extensively in the Arctic or through a tropical continent), this antique question is often exhilarating.

Conrad loved the sea as few authors love their subjects, loved our actual planet, which few people now know intimately. But he did need to come ashore, alas, and rivers were another matter for this seaborne enthusiast. They narrowed and twisted claustrophobically, closing into confines where the stage was set for treachery and tragedy. With "the patient forest" all around, issues of conduct and craftsmanship were not straightforward but bewildering, and death came not in the midst of a violent storm but by dreadful, draining, silent fevers—"the playful paw-strokes of the wilderness." "Men who come out here should have no entrails," says Kurtz's boss, the manager of trade on the river, in "Heart of Darkness." Besides his dysentery, Kurtz has also suddenly gone bald. "The wilderness had patted him on the head, and, behold, it was like a ball—an ivory ball; it had caressed him, and—lo!—he had withered," says Marlow, the narrator.

Marlow, telling the desperate story to four complacently office-bound shipping company executives in London, explodes with the exasperation that Conrad himself must have felt, like most travelers to rough places, returning to colleagues in a great commercial center and its comfortable suburbs: "Here you all are, each moored with two good addresses, like a hulk with two anchors, a butcher round one corner, a policeman round another, excellent appetites, and temperature normal—you hear—normal from year's end to year's end." His bafflement at the stay-at-home's ignorance of the risks and fragility of life is familiar not just to travelers who have returned from intemperate latitudes but to anyone who has had a close brush with death.

Yet no ocean voyage ever frightened Conrad like his trip up the true Congo River in 1890, which nearly broke his health. This was the era of Henry Stanley's *Through the Dark Continent* and *In Darkest Africa*, but writers such as Naipaul and Alberto Moravia still find the journey forbidding. Africa is different. Faddists in the West don't dabble in its religions, as they do in Zen Buddhism, Sufism, and Bahaism. Westerners don't regard it as an enormous social experiment like India or China, or go to it as to the Himalayas for romantic derring-do. It isn't recognized as a kind of sister continent, like South America, rich in European and New World traditions, with a new and formidably inspired literature.

On our own continent, rivers have generally wound back to a simpler existence—to virgin hunting territory or gold country, to bountiful fishing, crisp forests, mountain scenery, each turn of the valley perhaps revealing a deer or moose standing on the riverbank waiting to be shot, a waterfall leading to a sandy creek with nuggets in it, or a village of comradely Indian squaws to "marry" for a season. But the Congo for many white men meant mysterious pestilences like fungal meningitis and blackwater fever, resulting in delirium and death (and the local women suffered from yaws and onchocerciasis). For distant readers it called up the immensely complicating factor of slavery: these black barbarous tribesmen did not just stay on their continent like American Indians, to be massacred by force of arms or annihilated by European diseases, but instead were captured in large numbers to be brought across the ocean under circumstances past even discussing, to live and be abused and bred for sale in the most intimate proximity to many readers' ancestors.

Most recently, it is African famine, not African slavery, that unnerves us—maybe thirty million people at risk. The figures vary, but a human catastrophe is building, unprecedented in scale, in peacetime at least, since the Black Death of the fourteenth century. Like the untreatable, incalculable diseases or like slavery, famine is horrifying partly because of its anonymity—children with fly-sucked eyes, bloated bellies, and geriatric faces, in as much pain as if they'd just swallowed a stick, and with what is called the tail of hunger, six inches of intestine, protruding from their backsides. If one is equipped with a passport and credit card, one can fly from New York to such a scene in a day or so, witness agony and elephantiasis, and promptly vanish again, via Swissair or Lufthansa, physically unscathed. This is a phenomenon as new to civilization as the idea that the human species can be extinguished practically in a flash, and it has revived a kind of solipsistic tribalism: who is starving and who is not. Certainly for the duration of this famine Africa will remain as grotesque and enigmatic in our mind's eye as it was to a Polish-British mate named Korzeniowski on the riverboat *Roi des Belges* on the Congo in the summer of 1890.

But *upriver* is no more—neither the notion of an Eden's innocence waiting to be exploited and despoiled nor a spot where an extraordinary evil will effloresce from any tarnished soul who happens to be at hand. Upriver has become the same as downriver as regards such things, and the gulf between the true traveler and the tidy stay-at-home has diminished because there are fewer of each. AIDS didn't stay in Africa, but stepped on a plane and flew here. From "heart" to "darkness," definitions have blurred, as has the ideal of fidelity, which was Conrad's watchword. We still yearn for the absolute, however, just as we yearn for a slam-bang sea. Conrad's literary longevity is assured by his love and his loyalties. And who's to deny that we'll come to believe in honor, decency, and austerity again, that the truth lies with absolutism—that we yearn for it only because it is real?

Arabia Felix

Ma'rib was the Queen of Sheba's capital nearly three thousand years ago—a burgeoning garden spot and trading center on the spice, myrrh, and frankincense caravan route that wound north from the Gulf of Aden through Mecca and eventually to Gaza on the Mediterranean. It was the largest city in Old South Arabia, or Arabia Felix, "Happy Arabia," as the region later came to be called (versus Arabia Petrea, "Stony Arabia," the Romans' idea of Saudi Arabia). The magnificently engineered dam six hundred yards long that had captured "seventy rivulets" flowing out of the mountains and had irrigated the four thousand acres of orchards and fields of this breadbasket city didn't break once and for all until around A.D. 570. Now the broken ruins atop Ma'rib's citadel are all that remain to be seen of a city otherwise under sand dunes at the edge of the vast Saudi Arabian Empty Quarter. And this whole major archaeological site is virtually unexcavated—the first and last team to make a real start managed to flee by a ruse from threatening Murad tribesmen forty years ago—and is a rarity for that, though oil was discovered nearby by the Hunt Oil Company of Texas in 1984.

Ma'rib is a pleasant four-hour drive on a road built by

Swedes through the mountains east of San'a, the capital of the present-day Yemen Arab Republic, better known as North Yemen. San'a itself is a most ancient town, founded, according to legend, by Noah's son Shem, who must have hiked down from Mount Arafat in Turkey, where the Ark landed, to accomplish the feat. The name means, appropriately, "Fortified City," but since the revolution in 1962, which overthrew the absolute rule of the last of the Zaydi imams, it has been expanding way past its walls in low gray cement-block constructions, with the din of Toyotas, Suzukis, Mitsubishis, Datsuns, Nissans, Daihatsus, Hyundais, and Mazdas tooting along raw new roads. In the old quarters, the best-kept houses are chocolate brown, with whitewashed trim, built of rows of mud brick above striped layered limestone or igneous foundations, on a narrow yet feudally lofty impulse, and painted like six-story palaces, with high-up, monastic, filigreed windows of stained glass and alabaster, and sometimes a garden hidden behind. Gardens with vegetables thickly growing in them and apricot, almond, or walnut trees still seem to abound in San'a, which was built to withstand a siege. The latest, in the winter of 1967–68, lasted for seventy days before the republicans inside succeeded in breaking the renascent royalist lines; but in 1905, when the imam Yahya besieged a Turkish occupying force, half the populace died. (He then besieged it again in 1911, and after he was assassinated, in 1948, his son, the new imam, Ahmad, sacked the city arbitrarily on general principles.)

San'a, with its dagger markets and raisin markets, its cramped, medieval mud skyscrapers that look like cliff dwellings, its steam baths heated by human dung, its blindfolded camels underground turning oilseed grindstones, its hundred mosques with muezzins crying out over every neighborhood at dawn, noon, and bedtime, blending their voices with a passion appropriate for a land converted to Islam within the Prophet's own life span (indeed, San'a's inaccessible Great Mosque is rumored to be the only one outside Mecca that has a kaaba), lies at seventy-five hundred feet, surrounded by mountains more than four thousand feet higher, and thus catches both the tail end of the Mediterranean's spring rains and the late-summer rainfall from India's monsoon. Highland Yemen traditionally could feed itself with rain-grown sorghum raised on the plateaus, as well as a gamut of vegetables and fruits planted on the intricacy of terraces that whorl down every slope not too sheer to hold soil, and used to export its world-famous mocha coffee and some cotton from the port of Al Mukha also. But this is true no more. Yemen has a remittance economy based on payments sent home by the million Yemeni men who work in the Arab oil-field countries and the billion dollars a year of direct foreign aid funneled in by Saudi Arabia, which frets about every untoward event in this alarmingly martial Nebraska-sized nation on its southern border, which has a population (seven million) about the size of its own in one tenth as much space.

San'a, established perhaps by Sabaeans (Saba-Sheba) and then invaded by Himyaris, Abyssinians, Persians, Egyptian Mamelukes, and Ottoman Turks—sending its merchants as far afield as India, Indonesia, and Moorish Spain, although not itself propelled into modernism until Gamal Abdel Nasser galvanized the imagination of the Middle East—now blares with construction and vehicular noise. But Ma'rib's citadel, caving and peeling, sand-blown and silent except for a few shepherd squatters and their flocks of sheep, comes further unstrung with each seasonal splatter of monsoon rain. Close by, several columns of Sheba's own putative temple remain, along with another, dedicated to the moon god Almaqah. Islam is a sister religion to Christianity and Judaism, and most Christians and Jews are familiar with fundamentalist votaries of their own faiths who quite correspond to the range of Muslim practice and belief. But how does one go back in the mind's eye to an astral religion?

Well, there are ways, in fact, and the astral religion of Old South Arabia was similar to Babylon's, from which our astrology derives. However, in the midday heat, Martha, Bjorn, and I weren't really attempting to do this, except for appreciating why the moon rather than the pummeling sun was the Sabaeans' main deity. Martha, a slim, black-haired Californian with an innocent air and a freckled face, whose physiognomy indicated her Boston ancestry, was celebrating her thirtieth birthday in Yemen. Bjorn, a tall, shambly Norwegian, was several years older than that, with a fluffy mustache, kind, inquisitive eyes, and hair that winged out above his ears. He'd trained as an architect and had worked at betterment projects here for eight years, so he was doing the translating for us. Ali, from the town of Wadi Dhar, near the capital, was our driver, and because the car was actually his, a man of property as well, with seven children and a coolly hopeful mien, always trying to get us, and maybe principally his car, past the incessant dramas of travel in this balkanized region.

We had just picked up the "Director of Antiquities" at Ma'rib, a bumptious, nattily white-robed, callow, clerkly young man named Mohammad, who told us in Arabic that no, he had never attended a university, but nevertheless he clearly did play a supervisory role among the half-dozen soldiers who were posted there to see that no stones were taken away—though the fabled seventeen original temples and other structures of the site have already been picked apart by local villagers through the ages, to the point where you will notice old houses in neighboring hamlets with friezes of ibises flying set into them as building blocks, upside down.

"I'll spray you if you grab anything," Mohammad joked to Bjorn, waving his assault rifle. Like practically every man in northern Yemen, he wore a curved foot-long dagger belted in front of his belly, as well as a Russian AK-47 slung on one shoulder, with ammunition clips at his waist and a pistol peeping out from under his shirttails. Yet he didn't seem a warlike fellow—more like a grown-up mama's boy whose father was influential and had found him his job. He took us to the ruins of the dam, which is still an eloquent presence in its dry corkscrew ravine, and later, inside the moon-temple compound, where again for us it was a matter of attempting to stretch the mind back to imagine the mystery and power of this kingdom (circa 1000–115 B.C.), from which not only the known world's incense and spices were thought to originate but also tiger skins, ostrich eggs, peacock feathers, Chinese silks, Indian textiles, ebony, ivory, pearls and gold, dexterous monkeys and fanciful slaves. The Red Sea was dangerous to navigate, and so goods from India, Punt (now Somalia), and Ethiopia traveled north by this same camel route, commingled with valuables from Arabia Felix itself, paralleling but safe from the sea.

The outlines of Ma'rib's plantations remain too, although as much veldt as desert once surrounded them. Lions and giraffes roamed Arabia then, and giraffe horns still make the most favored dagger handles in Yemen, costing even more than rhino horn. Rhinos have been driven to the brink of extinction in Africa to fill this market, but the average man will buy cow horn (and a poor man, goat). When the Sabaeans built their twenty-story palace in San'a, with each side crafted of different-colored stone, they put bronze lions at the four corners of the roof, aimed outward in such a way that at least one would roar, whichever direction the wind blew.

The featureless, monochromatic heat made pondering these ecological and cultural complexities so difficult that we went to a little restaurant and enjoyed a sumptuous lunch of sorghum dough and sheeps' vertebrae dipped in a foamy green fenugreek broth. Also rice and stir-fried tomatoes and eggs and fava beans boiled in fat, with chilies on the side and flat bread to dip the dishes up with, plus lots of the good bottled Shamlan water, from a well outside San'a, that middle-class Yemenis drink. The restaurant was crowded and loud. Lunch is the main meal and, with liquor forbidden, is imbued with the sort of festivity that elsewhere accompanies a six-pack of beer. Husky Mercedes trucks with eyes painted on their hoods were parked outside, powerful vehicles that for many years have proven ideal on the smugglers' run across the roadless Empty Quarter from Oman to here. The drivers were celebrating what has lately become the end of the working day, and like them, we went to the market square after eating to buy a lapful of qat.

Qat probably came to the Arabian peninsula from the Horn of Africa during the fifteenth century, and although it is either forbidden or not popular in other Arab countries, it is more pervasive than ever in Yemen. If Saudi Arabia sometimes seems God-struck—all else subsumed in religion—Yemen is qat-struck. Qat is a woody shrub five or ten feet high with birchy-looking leaves that contain an ephedrinelike addictive drug with effects like a mild amphetamine—excitement, insomnia, loss of appetite, constipation—though if you swallow them you'll get a bellyache. But you don't swallow them. You hold a freshly cut branch and slowly pluck off the tenderest leaves, as you chat with your friends and smoke a water pipe, or hubble-bubble, and sip from a glass of water, while gradually wadding the leaves into one cheek, which at the end of an hour will bulge as if you had a toothache or a chaw of tobacco there. Taking care not to shift the wad, lest bits of leaf fall into your throat, you squeeze, suck, and swallow the juice. Nibbling these leaves makes even the solemnest citizen appear somewhat goatlike, and the juice's astringence causes a continual thirst, so that Bedouin who might otherwise get by even in the hottest weather on a few cups of water a day are drinking and spitting, drinking and spitting, incongruous-looking in their desert robes and head cloths, cradling more twigs on their knees.

The stalls in the souk were thronged with bargainers fingering the separate batches of qat, which were closely wrapped in banana leaves. A rifle hung muzzle-down from each man's shoulder like a third arm. Bjorn, who is a connoisseur and had been missing the drug during the past two years, which he had spent in Cairo, was exceptional in that he was looking specifically for insect tracks on the plants to show that they hadn't been doused with insecticide. The rarest type of qat tastes like licorice, but we settled for something less expensive that had the flavor of spearmint and cost about six dollars per portion, or about half the nation's median daily wage. (The use of qat, therefore, has become a major cause of malnutrition among children in North Yemen.) Yemenis seldom haggle much over price. Nor do they practice the more general Arab custom of extending special courtesies to foreigners. North Yemen, which has never been occupied by a Western power, feels no awe or deference toward Western technological and cultural achievements and tends to consider Americans who operate within the country as agents of Saudi Arabian foreign policy, not vice versa. It would no more look to Europe and America for inspiration in solving its problems than Americans might look to it. (Indeed, even in South Yemen, which was heavily British-influenced for a century beforehand, the sultan of Lahej, just outside the port of Aden, as recently as 1934 had publicly crucified three of his slaves in the marketplace on Christmas Day.)

But both the Sunni and Shiite branches of Islam are moderate in tenor in their Yemeni form, invoking neither "fanatical" excesses of hospitality to strangers nor religiously sanctioned assassination and martyrdom. Rather, in this Afghan-like cockpit of undiluted tribalism, daggers are drawn, shots are fired, and hostages are taken in kinship quarrels. Hostage holding was a tool of governance during North Yemen's lengthy imamate. In 1939 Yahya had around four thousand immured in various castles after a "unifying campaign"—the boys were said to be in "boarding school." And Ahmad, as late as the 1950s, held two thousand, some of whom he even carried off with him when he went to Rome for medical treatment. Yahya fathered more than forty children, who brought him much sadness. He had ruled for nearly two decades before he saw the sea, but confronted the Turks and Saudis and British fearlessly, warring with the Saudis along the coast; then when the British cut off his kerosene during World War II because he'd been negotiating with the Italians in Ethiopia, he cut off Aden's qat. Ahmad was more mercurial—sadistic at beheadings and so suspicious that he liked to have the treasury's gold transferred among a series of hiding places by slaves who afterward were killed. When Ahmad's palace doctor succeeded in evoking an erection in him with hormonal shots after eighteen months of impotency, he is said to have called his whole household together to witness the phenomenon.

In Ma'rib's souk there were veiled Arab women, among whom I glanced in vain to catch a glimpse of Sheba's countenance, masked but perhaps still extant after all these years. Also, bold-faced, black-skinned women of the street-cleaner caste who had traveled inland from the Red Sea coast and gazed unveiled, with smoldering eyes, at any white man who might be persuaded to give them money. Such people have their own tribes or clans and may be descendants of African slaves. Or, on the other hand, they may have had as antecedents the conquering army of Christian Ethiopians who invaded South Arabia in A.D. 525 at the instance of Emperor Justinian of Constantinople and overthrew the Jewish convert king, Dhu Nuwas (who, apart from an eighth century A.D. king of the Khazars of Crimea, was the only Jewish king ever to reign outside Israel), after Dhu Nuwas's massacre of some of the area's Christians. Tubba (King) Dhu (Lord) Nuwas (of the Forelock)—called Joseph by the Jews—is said to have spurred his horse straight into the Red Sea after his defeat and was never seen again. Whereupon, after suffering Christian rule for a while, the Jews who were left called in the Persians to defeat these Christian Ethiopians. Whereupon, after another fifty years, in A.D. 628, the last Persian satrap in Yemen embraced the newborn religion of Islam.

Yemen's history coils gaudily from dynasty to dynasty— Ya'furis, Ziyadīs, Rasuli sultans, Rassī Zaydis, an abortive Roman invasion, Tahirīs, Qu'aitis, Fatamid caliphs, Ayyubīs, Wahabis, and the Ottoman Empire. The apostle Thomas probably passed through on his way to India (cathedral ruins underlie part of San'a's Great Mosque); and so did Mohammad during his early career as a trader. Before the Sabaeans' ascendancy, Yemen had been the home of the Minaeans, a people now shadowed by more than three thousand years of wind and sand, and after the fall of the Sabaeans, the Himyarī tribe was dominant until Dhu Nuwas was beaten.

Our Mohammad, director of Ma'rib's antiquities, offered to take us to another pre-Islamic ruin, called Baraqish, which was presently off-limits to visitors but had been a district capital of the Himyarīs from perhaps the time of Christ. First, we needed to get through a roadblock, but this was not an unusual procedure. On any trip outside San'a we carried Xeroxes of our travel permit, to leave with the security men at each station, but here the soldier decided he didn't want one because our trip was unauthorized except by the antiquities director; he simply moved the barricade. We had thought this sector of the province might be closed off because of military camps or maneuvers, not realizing that instead it was still a zone of "insolence." For much of the period after the 1962 revolution, the entire stretch of the country north and northeast of San'a, extending to the Saudi border, had been known as the Zone of Insolence, and in the fevered tribalism of Yemen, Bjorn had often had to cross the lines to visit his girlfriend, an Algerian aid worker who lived in former royalist territory—where cars then bore no license plates and bootleg gasoline was sold from tanker trucks beside the road—using no pass at all except for the insouciant bulge of qat leaves in his cheek and the clutter of qat twigs next to him on the front seat.

After fifty miles, we picked up a hitchhiker at a tiny store and turned down a dry streambed, or wadi. Martha and I, being cautious in our consumption of the drug, were still suffused with the soothing initial effects qat has, but Bjorn, Mohammad, and the hitchhiker began gabbing happily at a pitch of intensity, as if they'd each just drunk six cups of coffee—swigging bottled water, too, and lighting one cigarette from another, as qat chewers do when they have no hubble-bubble. We remembered that our new friend had been skulking inside the store, not hustling for a ride out front, where he might have been better able to flag down a car, when he told Bjorn in Arabic that although he worked on the coast at the port of Hudaydah, he was rushing home to his village near this wadi "to help with the killing." His village and the next one were at war, and his uncle had been shot. He apologized to all of us for having only a hand grenade with him. People living in Hudaydah or traveling through San'a were not allowed to carry a rifle. But with Mohammad's two guns and his grenade, we could put up a brief fight if his village's enemies should corner us.

Poor Ali's four-wheel-drive Toyota was taking a beating, because we couldn't even follow the main wadi track; we'd now had to dodge off onto rougher paths, more suitable for camels, where a truck patrol from the other village would be less likely to catch us. Our hitchhiker pointed up at two promontories on the rock ridges above us, where enemy outposts faced each other, and, laughing, lifted the grenade from his coat pocket, saying he hoped it wouldn't go off accidentally from this jouncing. Though he was glad to be with foreigners, whose presence might help to protect him, he was scared. Qat often kites people into a red-eyed daze, as peyote does, after the first storm of conversation, but not under these circumstances.

Anyhow, we reached the gallant-looking, crumbling, red, wild ramparts of Baraqish, which was set between the rival villages, within sight of each, and scrambled up over a caved-in portion of the wall to climb inside. We discovered that a space possibly equivalent to two football fields had been enclosed, with several shells of old buildings still visible, including two temples, beautifully proportioned, that had been dedicated first to a stellar religion and later to Islam but were now deeply smothered in sand. The windy silence was exhilarating, like the height of the rude battlements and the sense of the abyss of history here. Near the center of this little fort was a wide-mouthed well, out of the depths of which a flock of blue desert doves came laboriously beating. We would have examined every building, three fourths covered in sand (though the friezes on the porticoes of the temples showed), if the sun hadn't been low and Ali hadn't begun anxiously honking his horn for us to return to the car almost as soon as we'd left it. The local villagers themselves guarded this site as a matter of pride, and the only reason they hadn't already come out to interrogate us was that during the current hostilities it lay in no-man's-land; they were scared of being trapped by their adversaries.

We dropped our friend safely within gun range of his relatives, and he invited us to spend the night, telling us that they would slaughter a sheep for us and throwing pinches of dust on us, a traditional gesture by which a reluctant guest may be persuaded that he should come with you into your house to wash and stay over. Nevertheless, we took off, now able to follow the main wadi bed directly (though a pickup truck full of young men pulled close to scout us), and struck the paved road just at dark. Mohammad rode on into San'a with us, checking his rifle, as required, at the army roadblock on the city's outskirts, and argued with Bjorn so long and vociferously for an outlandish guiding fee at the door of his dark caravansary that the high pitch of good fellowship they had shared on the strength of the qat was totally dissolved.

"So you're here to promote tourism?" our Lebanese landlady in San'a asked me when she heard that Yemenia Airways had given me a ticket and was providing the services of Ali and his Land Cruiser for free. "I hope the Yemenis don't kill the tourists if they come," she added with her sharp Beirut laugh. In a hostile town north of San'a, she and her American husband had been waved away at gunpoint when they'd stopped for coffee. At her villa, specializing in American scholars, we were guarded unobtrusively by two or three plainclothes government security agents, who watched over us from a van parked not far from the gate or while loitering in the butcher shop across the street, whose proprietor sat in the doorway in a cloud of flies most of the day, spraying bug dope on the meats that he had on display. This newer sector of the city was sparsely but convivially lit by thin neon signs after the sun set in the dusty sky, and there was a continual din of high-pitched horns. Streams of pedestrians swung quickly along, surefooted as people who'd walked everywhere until a dozen years ago. We were near a big Health Department facility called the Blood Bank, which I could ask for when lost. San'a has the complexity of a capital city, and I had astonishing difficulty in mastering its riddle of antique fiefdoms and hasty alleys. Half the citizens sported a foot-length *jambia* (dagger) like a rampant penis poking up from under their belts, while the other half were swathed from head to foot in robes and capes and veils. (Somehow the *jambia* in its sheath is regarded as no more dangerous than a woman's face: unholster either, and somebody's life will be altered forever.) No street in the old city ran straight enough for one to see ahead more than a couple of blocks. Each just curved in among its brothers and sisters till suddenly blocked, and there were no street signs and few billboards to catch one's eye as landmarks.

In Yemen one meets a good many expatriates who have been displaced by the Lebanese fighting, including surviving *bons vivants* of the Beirut "Dangerous Diners Club," who had managed to quit the city before they got blown up or kidnapped from a restaurant. The Palestine Liberation Organization, too, has used North Yemen as a kind of rest camp, designating the country its military headquarters after fourteen thousand of its fighters were evacuated from Beirut with American help at the time of the Israeli invasion—Tunis became its political headquarters. Their tents are located in a small valley on the road running south from San'a, where they have "made the desert bloom" not far from a campsite previously occupied by Yemeni refugees from the Vietnam War. Palestinian militias of more radical factions have bases in South Yemen, whose 1967 Marxist revolution from British rule was partly godfathered in its preliminary stages by the Palestinian leftist George Habash.

Yemen's highlands, because of the twenty or thirty inches of rainfall they catch in a year, were abundantly populated from early on and spun off many wanderers and traders, who had all of East Africa and the Indian subcontinent to sail to, or beyond, though they usually wished to return home toward the end of their lives. They still come back—also from the Arab neighborhoods near the Ford factory in Dearborn, Michigan—often to the lush, scenic hills and mild climate around the city of Ibb, among the Sunni Shafiis who constitute most of the nation's bureaucrats, merchants, truck farmers, and scholars, and to a culture that does not look askance at a man in his sixties with a pension from overseas who marries a girl in her teens and starts over. Indeed, with an infant mortality rate of fifty percent (as we were told at hospitals in two different regions) and virtually no opportunity for a woman to do more than raise children, it's not such a bad idea for her to marry an avuncular man who can provide her family with plenty of food and clean bottled water and an education.

Eight hundred years ago, Ibb was the seat of power of perhaps Yemen's pleasantest dynasty: Queen Arwa's. An Ismaeli, a member of a Shiite splinter group more recently followers of a holy man who lives in Surat, India, she was a woman of legendary beauty, masterly at "stratagems," who devoted her peaceable reign mainly to road building and other graceful good works. We stayed overnight in the lovely medieval hill town of Jibla, with a ninth-century mosque where Ismaeli dignitaries are buried, in a jagged, auger-twist valley where twenty years ago a farmer strangled the last local leopard with his bare hands. The streets were lightless, cobbled with boulders, and only the width of the ribs of a donkey. When I went walking alone, two black-garbed women with bell-like voices asked me through the mask of their veils if I had any chocolate.

We celebrated Martha's milestone thirtieth birthday that evening with a dinner of beans, red tea, and bread in the town's café, talking with Jibla's gloomy druggist, who had studied in Alexandria, in what had been for him a happier period, and gazing out at the modest yellow gleam of kerosene lamps in the huts across the wide gap of the wadi. We were cheerful, Martha teasing me that after reading one of my books she had decided it would be better if she didn't sleep with me. I said she would keep her girlish freckles forever, then; that she was our official "adventuress," being the in-house representative of Sobek Expeditions of Angels

Camp, California, which was feeding and housing me in exchange for mention of their services. Sobek is a company of trek guides and river runners, who have named themselves after a Nile crocodile god, and I said she herself, being the one unveiled woman in Jibla, was a river god. She said I was the proverbial toad, whom no princess had ever kissed, and might remain so. She was cooking raisin oatmeal for me in the mornings, however, and since she wasn't sleeping with the younger, handsomer Bjorn either, our jigsaw bedroom arrangements in these little *funduqs* (inns) were painless.

Beyond Ibb, the American-cut, German-paved highway that connects San'a with Ta'izz, North Yemen's principal southerly city, climbs a pass and descends by sumptuous switchbacks—each with a peddler sitting beside baskets of tomatoes, carrots, onions, potatoes, or corn—to this *Aruzat al Yemen*, "Bride of Yemen," as Ta'izz is sometimes called. Only seven hundred years old, it has an ease and tolerance, a vibrancy and buoyancy. People spice their qat with betel nuts occasionally, or sauce their tea with opium. The market is full of unveiled businesswomen from Jebel Sabor selling wheelbarrowloads of dates, oranges, papayas, and mangoes, barrels of millet, wheat, barley, and lentils, sacks of saffron, turmeric, cardamom, and caraway seeds, and especially qat. What with the old university and theological centers like Dhamar, Zabid, and Bayt al Faqih having slid into decay (Yemenis claim that Zabid is where algebra and logarithms were invented), it was in Ta'izz that one could imagine poetry being argued over and politics of a less violent stripe being plotted. The Shafiis of this part of Yemen were tribal mostly in theory—long-sedentary taxpayers who were warlike only when they needed to protect themselves from the Zaydis of the north. They're the scribblers and traders, the modernists of Yemen.

Bjorn was full of an architect's zeal, and we were soon climbing to the heights of the city to inspect a six-hundred-fifty-year-old mosque whose painted interior had been whitewashed or cemented over during the bad days of some benighted conquest, when the mosque had been turned into a tannery. Now it was being restored wherever the cement hadn't damaged the decorations irretrievably. The confident, well-knit, old, short-bodied, white-haired master mason who was in charge told Bjorn he was working for free and said gaily in Arabic, "Ever since I was sixteen, I've walked so straight in life that I could walk on the ocean now if I wanted to." He led us up the circular staircase inside the fat minaret to gaze over the rolling, ocher-colored, mostly four-storied little city cupped in the curve of a mountain; at its broken outer walls, its domed baths, its squat, square tenements, and its tan and white towering religious edifices. Way overhead was the former Turkish citadel on a knife-edge spur above us.

We stayed at Al Ganad Hotel, a fine foursquare downtown villa that, although inexpensive, boasted bougainvilleas in the garden and servants, "British-trained," who had fled the Communist takeover in Aden. (Newly constructed tourist hotels are on "Baboon Hill," where, until some of the firepower incidental to Yemen's civil war was brought to bear upon them, baboons used to live.) At dawn, a muezzin on a minaret coughed into his microphone briefly to clear his throat and then roused the whole city with a voice like a ram's horn:

> God is greater.
> I bear witness, there is no god but God.
> I bear witness, Mohammad is the messenger of God.
> Come to prayer.
> Come to salvation.

It sounded so stirring that all Ta'izz's dogs, roosters, and donkeys chimed in. Even Haile Selassie's gift of a pride of lions, which are caged at the gate of Imam Ahmad's former summer palace on a breezy elevated point of the city, sent forth a volley of roars.

The gates of the imam's winter palace, which was lower down, are bracketed not by lion cages but by the dungeons in which languished those of his prisoners whom he wanted closest to hand. Though he was a Zaydi Shii (like all the imams: "caliph" was the term for an equivalent figure among the Sunnis), maintained in power by the Zaydis' force of arms, he chose to locate his capital in this tractable Sunni city of Shafiis. Only once, in 1957, when he was sixty-eight and nearing the end of his turbulent, tyrannical reign, did he hold a press conference, which the British journalist David Holden, in *Farewell to Arabia,* describes thus:

His voice came in rapid, hoarse gasps, as if he was in pain . . . his hands tugged at his black-dyed beard, and his eyes—starting from his head as if with goitre and the effort of speech—rolled like white marbles only tenuously anchored to his sallow flesh. At a glance one might have thought him literally staring mad. But if he was he remained uncannily alert. Nothing in the room escaped him: his eyes could be riveted in the instant upon the slightest movement, and he listened to every questioner with an intensity so fierce and so impatient that he seemed at times about to leap up, crying "Off with his head!"

—meanwhile indulgently patting two of his small sons, who were playing like puppies about his feet, but sharing a fearful, mocking smile with the newspapermen as he did—

These flashes of grim, ingratiating humor, when the full lips were drawn back over broken teeth and the dark brows were lowered over popping eyes, gave an extraordinary humanity to what might otherwise have seemed a mere, broken monster. One grasped not only the power, cruelty and suspicion of a total despot, not only the weaknesses of pain, sickness and age with which his will seemed to be in open, tigerish conflict, but also the sense of a man fearfully alone.

Ta'izz is close to South Yemen's border and to its capital, Aden, which the British ruled as part of India for a hundred years, then as a separate crown colony for thirty more. Aden became known as "the Eye of Yemen," because it was the Yemenis' sole opening to the Western world, or as "the Coal Hole of the East," because ships sailing to India and the Orient were fueled and serviced in the harbor—six thousand a year by 1964. Only London, Liverpool, and New York surpassed it as a bunkering port, and tens of thousands of tourists shopped there duty-free and explored the volcanic crater that holds the old city, while glancing northward, perhaps, toward the sealed-off, mysterious mountains of Yemen itself. Ta'izz received a trickle of goods from all this saltwater commerce, and injections of novel ideas, but South Yemen got such a flood of foreign entrepreneurs and ideologies that, with independence, it very soon wound up as the only Arab nation in the Marxist camp, and it is still administered with tough severity against some of the ulema as well as the kin of former emirs, sultans, and sheikhs.

Ta'izz, however, has the pep of a city just tasting new ideas, not swamped by them. We ate *kibda*—tidbits of liver sautéed with tomatoes and peppers—in cubbyholes off the street, and drank *gishr*, the Yemeni version of coffee, made from the husks after the precious coffee beans themselves have been sold for export. And we kept going back to the souk, bargaining for jewelry with an unveiled, fierce-faced sheikhly widow who casually but baffingly juggled our money between us to shortchange us, then placated us, when we complained, with an ancient-looking copper coin apiece. Many Yemeni families, in response to the oil boom, have traded in their traditional silver pieces of jewelry for cookie-cutter gold stuff that looks like a walking bank account. So she had handsome antique bracelets, rings, necklaces, snuff-boxes, and breastplates. Other booths offered brocaded belts and dagger sheaths, Persian pearls, Siamese fans, and long-barreled, scrimshawed guerrilla rifles from forgotten mountain fights in the Ottoman wars. Or simply pots and pans, Indian fabrics, gowns and scarves, vests and shirts, sandals, turbans, pillbox hats. In the morning it was a watchful place, the men sitting cross-legged and unsmiling in their pleated kilts (except that several gave me a thumbs-up sign when I walked back a ways to give a few rials to a beggar), as in the days when the motto of the markets had been "Chop one hand off: save a hundred." But in the afternoon, after the qat had taken effect, you could pass half a dozen stalls being watched over by the same men's young daughters or by boys under the age of ten; the stall owners were out of sight.

We were teasing Martha about how little she'd been eating of our millet porridges and sorghum pancakes, our spicy meats and fiery stews and yogurt gruels. She had vegetarian tendencies, which I suggested might be the death of her in Yemen, where the best food was meat, and she had also brought with her from California the notion that eggs contain harmful amounts of cholesterol, when of course it seemed to me that we needed to burn all the cholesterol we could in order to keep going. But if Martha needed encouragement in eating, I was having trouble walking, having been weakened by a six-week bout with flu in the United States. She was protecting me from Bjorn's accesses of enthusiasm. His passion for Yemen was indefatigable and had even resulted in his designing buildings to be built of mud brick, like the historic quarters of the cities, and losing some prospective architectural business from the impatient technocrats at the government ministry in San'a.

Bjorn was a touching man. Although flexible, reflective, and gentle, he struck me as growing rather puzzled now in his late thirties by the ways of the world. Even Yemen had more citizens than Norway, and America more Norwegians, so he appeared to think that being Norwegian was in itself a precarious proposition. He had left there, returned, left, and returned again. Norwegians are travelers, and he had spent part of his childhood on the Arctic island of Spitzbergen, where his mother had worked as a nurse and where the summer tourists had gawked at him and her, he said. Later he had served as a steward on cruise ships carrying American tourists through the Pacific, which had probably reinforced the underdog spin that his perceptions already had; he spoke a bit bitterly of the rich "Love Boat" Americans who allowed him to burn his hands holding hot teakettles for them and who seemed to enjoy prolonging the torment. He wore his architecture school class ring, but after living in San'a and Cairo for a decade he hadn't had very much chance to practice his profession, and from living abroad he was losing his own language, he said. He thought as well as spoke in English more often than in Norwegian, but in English, as in Arabic, his vocabulary was limited, so that the free flow of his ideas was constricted; and meanwhile his Norwegian vocabulary had shrunk or rusted alarmingly. He was a man of ebullience and intuition, but he was wondering what to do. Indeed, on most adventure treks—of which in a professional capacity I've made too many—one finds that the guides, though quite big-brotherly in their role and manner, are people who aren't practicing whatever kind of work they had trained for and are wondering what they ought to begin doing almost as soon as the trip ends. The customers, on the other hand, tend to have been maneuvering in a sleekly turned-out profession for decades, maybe too skillfully.

•

South Yemen invaded the North as recently as 1979, almost cutting the road halfway between San'a and Ta'izz, with Russian military advisers facing each other on either side of the battle until the signals were switched and a pull-back arranged. So because in each town we had rambled into we'd enjoyed having a special errand to pursue, and because Ta'izz had been a cold war "listening post" since the British lost Aden, we tried to figure out who the Americans' spy-master was, now that the American consulate—where one or two of the CIA's crack young Arabists had trained—is closed. We popped into the Danish consulate, close to our hotel, for want of an alternative, and asked who was "running agents into South Yemen for the West nowadays." The consul (it's an honorary position) seemed to be an ordinary bustly Yemeni importer trying to keep track of a pile of inventory, and he was nonplussed.

The most numerous, effective foreign agents in Yemen have been Egyptians, however. Nasserites helped plan and arm the overthrow of Ahmad's son, the more liberal sixty-sixth imam, Mohammad al Badhr, within a week of his accession, in September 1962. Then the Egyptian army, during a grinding, dreary, five-year war, which was regarded afterward as "Nasser's folly" and "Egypt's Vietnam," repeatedly beat back tenacious Saudi-financed royalist tribesmen in their counterstrikes upon the republicans, amazing them sometimes with air power. Tribal warriors equipped with Mausers, whose favorite tactic had been to loll on a crag and pick off an enemy toiling below, with the gunstock kissing one cheek and the muzzle cradled between two outstretched toes—and who'd been taught as boys that airplanes and even trucks were really *djinns*—watched in utter frustration as Migs made bombing runs over their walled villages.

Thus Egypt, more than any direct Western influence, effected radical changes upon North Yemen; and South Yemen's revolt against Britain, culminating in independence at about the same time that Egyptian troops were forced to withdraw from the North after the debacle of the Six Day War with Israel, drew confidence and inspiration from these. But Egypt's thinking altered after the Six Day War. Since Nasser's death, in 1970, the cadre of thirty thousand Egyptian schoolteachers remaining in North Yemen have gradually become a far more conservative factor, together with their many Sudanese colleagues, who generally (like the Sudan with Egypt) follow their lead. They are the backbone of Yemen's Muslim Brotherhood. The Brotherhood is an international, fundamentalist, youthful but reactionary force in Arab societies whose governments are working for a secular future (whether socialist or Westernized), and a Puritan element in the oil-boom nations with a new-minted devotion to worldly goods: in other words, in a whole range of countries from Saudi Arabia to Syria and Egypt itself, where the Brotherhood was founded in 1928. Although they do engage in violent acts, the Brothers are typically of a more hortatory or intellectual bent and find plenty to disapprove of anywhere, being determined that an unvarnished form of Islam stay paramount throughout the Middle East.

At the embassies in San'a, people talked to me "deep-background," for which they rather apologized but which, not being a newspaperman, I quite enjoy. Newspapermen need somebody to quote, whereas a free-lance larcenous soul like me may be content to appropriate any ideas he is told anonymously. In fact, the Western embassies approved of what was going on in North Yemen politically. They did believe that the economics of allowing the fabulous thousand-year-old agricultural terraces to wash away down every mountainside, while the populace chewed up amounts of homegrown qat equal in cash value to the foreign food aid that has to be shipped in, was absurd and disastrous. (South Yemen permits qat chewing only on weekends; Saudi Arabia will jail a chewer for five years.) But "Yemen (San'a)," as the country is known among diplomats, has a competent president, Ali Abdallah Salih, who, though not a charismatic speaker, has succeeded in balancing Zaydi and Shafii, as well as Saudi and South Yemeni, interests.* He is a former sergeant and tribal fighter who sports a pistol low-slung on one hip and looks like a Mexican movie star in the still photographs that are posted up all over, or on the nightly news, when the camera pans endlessly across an auditorium full of delegates, candidates, or graduates, while a Sousa sound track is played and the announcer repeats the hopeful phrase "the Homeland" in Arabic. His predecessor was killed when

* *Since my visit, he has managed to unite North and South Yemen.*

a briefcase chained to the wrist of an envoy from Aden blew up; and the president before *that* was poisoned, along with his brother and two French prostitutes, with whom they had been foolishly dallying, all four bodies then being dragged into the same room and shot up together to make for a scandalous scene. Revolutionists from the National Democratic Front, who prefer South Yemen's model of governance, are a threat, but there is a religious sanction among the conservative Zaydis, too, that if a leader has committed substantial sins, others more appropriate for his position rise up and kill him.

The two most powerful and martial tribes in Yemen, the Hashid and Bakil—once known as "the wings of the imamate"—inhabit villages in a quilted pattern across the northern mountains. They dominated the Shafiis for centuries but are so rivalrous that they have had to establish "confederations" to keep from flying at one another's throats. Salients of each tribe sold their talents to the highest bidder and then sometimes switched sides during the civil war. But both would generally have been thorough royalists if Imam Ahmad in one of his temper tantrums had not had the head of the Hashid's paramount chieftain chopped off (also his son's) during a supposed safe-conduct parley that the imam had arranged with them in order to settle a money dispute. Both maintain private armies and, to oppose Marxism, with Saudi kibitzing, have set up an Islamic Front that would be a formidable countervailing element in case of a new insurrection from South Yemen by the National Democratic Front, or a leftist putsch by officers of the army or security forces.

To hear anecdotes of political killings in the two Yemens—the machine-gunning of practically the whole cabinet in Aden in January 1986, as well as various smaller traps that have been set and sprung—is to imagine anarchy. But Ali Abdallah Salih has survived in office since 1978 by conciliation and negotiation, allowing two earlier presidents to return from exile and permitting a smattering of Yemeni Muslim Brothers to enter government service alongside the conventional Shafiis and Zaydis, some Islamic Front people, and even, at the opposite pole, a few representatives of the National Democratic Front. The ten-thousand-man, black-bereted security force keeps a watch on the red-bereted, thirty-thousand-man army, and the tiny air force wheels its several F-5 fighter planes over the middle of the country, as yet another factor, once a day.

From Ta'izz, we rolled down a spacious, loop-the-loop highway toward the Red Sea coast, past millet, tobacco, and tomato fields, oxen plowing, banana plantations, hobbled camels browsing on the thorn trees, mangoes and oranges growing, and the rich-soiled bottomland to which the stick-plow sharecroppers and small landowners on the mountain-sides used to descend after a rainstorm to carry back the soil that had washed down. We saw black goats, white sheep, brown dogs, and women herders striding serenely, garbed also in black. One girl walked toward a well with a pail on her head that she was rapping rhythmically.

Once we left the mountains, the desert created mirages that gave camels eight legs, and Ali used his headlights instead of his horn to warn approaching cars. Our immediate mission was to buy some bootleg whiskey for Bjorn's expatriate friends in San'a. The former coffee port of Al Mukha has silted in so much that sizable ships seldom use it, but it's still suitable for smugglers' shallow-drawing craft that dart across the strait of Bab al Mandab from the French protectorate of Djibouti in Africa. Founded by Himyarite traders, its fortunes peaked under the Ottomans during the seventeenth century, when it is said to have boasted three hundred mosques. It was the Turks' port in Yemen until the old Sabaeans' port of Aden, expanded by the British, eclipsed it.

Johnnie Walker Red Label and Carlsbad beer cost less than they would have in New York City but had to be bought surreptitiously even by foreigners. We gave our order at a crossroads gas station to a slim, predatory-looking young man as swift and boneless in his movements as a snake, with a slave trader's deeply cruel and amused face—I was suddenly reminded that Al Mukha had been a slaving port, too, until rather recently. Our savvy party refused to receive the booze at the gas station but instead pulled down the road out of sight, where we lifted the hood of the car as if we had broken down. By and by, along came the young man on his motorbike with a box strapped on the back, his face muddy-colored but aquilinely Arab, and that expression as though he were laughing at a slave girl's thirst on a march across the desert after he had decided that her thirst was not going to hurt her.

Al Mukha is now a huddle of decrepit gray buildings covering a tenth of the historic city. But the Red Sea was a fresh jade green, whipped silvery by the wind, with the eternal sand blowing hard in our faces, or spindrift when it shifted. We drove north on truck tracks that paralleled the water closely, through date palm plantations, past salt evaporation pits and little settlements of round grass huts with conical thatched roofs, surrounded by wattle fences, just as in Africa. Among them walked a taller, chocolate-black, veilless people, and sometimes we saw small rowboats or rudimentary rafts on the beach, and the fishermen's throw nets drying. Short bogs alternated with stretches of outright desert or dry scrubland or, again, a carefully irrigated patch of date palms growing fifty feet high, and a water pump thumping. We'd see some huts built of grass and palm leaves, with a couple of children playing beside the rope beds set outside, three or four dogs asleep, and a goat wandering loose.

"These are just blacks," Ali said in Arabic with a laugh, driving hard to keep out of sand traps. Sometimes our path completely disappeared, and he would need to swerve and speed up or grind down into first gear in order to keep going. Or else it ran straight into the surf, so that we had to backtrack. Deep sand gave way to miles of saltbush or lumpy, irrigated soil planted with sorghum. We found a derelict mosque whose oven-shaped domes were inhabited by swallows and bats, with animist amulets set into niches on the wall in the back; but later we saw another mosque, in a further huddle of huts, neatly swept, beautifully cared for, and gracefully structured, with a deep, cool, clean, blue-painted cistern where people could perform their ablutions before they prayed.

Ali did pray, with open fervor—the first time we had seen him do this—prostrating himself with his arms outstretched in the Sunni manner. (Shiis keep their arms by their sides as they bend forward repeatedly from a kneeling position.) Praying five times a day with strenuous obeisances is good exercise, and it is said of the older Yemeni men that although chewing qat makes them impotent at a fairly early age, they keep fit otherwise by an austere regimen of prayer and mastering their mountainous terrain.

But we weren't in the mountains. We were by the wild sea, with spray hitting our noses, on a precarious track the high tide threatened as it thundered, or that could become completely obscured by a ten-minute sandstorm. We'd stop dead and sit as if night had fallen and, when that let up, would discover that the furrows we had been following had nearly filled in. Ali had to drive fast to keep from stalling, but to go fast was to risk flipping over or shooting off into a sinkhole or winding up in the sea.

Inshore, the sea was a lighter green than out beyond the reef. Whenever the sky cleared, which it did abruptly, the sight was stunning—those splendid nuances of green, the curve of the waves and the froth on them, the conflicting angles that they ran from, and the white band of narrow beach they splashed against. Often the beachside grass grew head-high, so when we came upon a hut and *shamba* it was a surprise for the people who lived there. The women in their brightly patterned cotton wraparounds, carrying thatch or firewood or household goods on their heads between compounds, seemed refreshingly personable because we could look at their faces as we passed. But whereas most Arab women would have made a show of ignoring us, not acknowledging the faintest possibility that they might ever be accosted by a stranger, these women acted agitated, if not actually frightened, as we approached. Especially if one of them was some little distance from her house, she was likely to break into a run in front of our van, glancing back over her shoulder, almost as though slavers still prowled the area and she might be scooped up and carted off. It was so startling to see a pretty woman scampering like a fearful deer in front of us that predatory impulses were aroused in me; and I doubt I was the only person to want for just a second to grab her. Even in San'a, when Bjorn, Martha, and I had sat chewing qat in a businessman's *mafraj* (chewing room), our host had jarred the otherwise placid proceedings by telling Martha in Arabic several times with a salacious grin that if Bjorn and I forgot about her and left her behind, "I'll lock you up in that closet under the stairs and sell you in the souk tomorrow."

Another sandstorm cut our visibility and threshed the surf vigorously. We ate dates, driving through the date groves, feeling that funny sensation of icing on our teeth, and finally camped close to Al Khawkhah, a fishing village with a fleet of old-fashioned longboats, each now equipped with a Yamaha outboard, beached on blocks for the night. Kids on bikes and men on motorbikes showed up to question us, while several camels stalked slowly by like elk. Overhead sailed a medley of black crows and brown hawks, blue doves, high vultures, and fast kites.

"Why should I go to school? I can work on the sea," said a boy with a face like a pirate's, in Arabic, when Bjorn challenged him as he liked to do with the children who surrounded us in every village begging for ballpoint pens—"Qolam, qolam"—even when they had pens in their hands. He would ask them to show some pride, ask interesting questions, at least, and to think before they spoke, to be individuals instead of a mob, and to remember their geography when he told them he was from Norway, not assume Norway was part of America, like Martha's California and my New York.

These were dark-skinned Arabs, the men with mussed hair and miscellaneous features like movie buccaneers, not kindly-looking, not people whose shores a castaway would want to wash up on. But the boy we'd talked to led over his Sudanese schoolteacher from the village, who walked with a stately posture in a spotless long white gown and asked for a book published in English so that he could practice reading in the evening. He added, however, that he and two compatriots were working "night and day" with class preparations, teaching one hundred sixty kids in all the grammar-school grades, double-shifting them to fit everyone in.

"Only one or two are smart," he explained, with his big, even, benign-looking, Sudanese smile, though a discomfort fluttered just under the surface of it. "They're terrible to us, but also sometimes kind." He was a prepossessing, detribalized man from the Gezira cotton-growing region south of Khartoum, and he was working like an exile here in the punishing heat to save money to be married. We were sweating in February, but the summer's heat on Yemen's coastline has the reputation of hounding even British aid officials stark, raving mad. When I asked, he said it was indeed worse than Khartoum's, and by his generous, philosophic manner made me homesick for that gentler city. But he left us with a hint of disapproval when Bjorn hauled out our dilettantish sack of qat.

All that moonlit night, low foaming rollers dashed toward the beach. It was a cocoon of sound, but I woke up with an ache in the sinuses above my cheeks and my mouth still mildly stinging from qat. The fishermen were back to launch their boats, sitting in raucous yet ceremonious groups while each crew of six or eight established their plans and good cheer and rapport for the day. They gave a kind of yell in unison at the end, like football players before running onto the field, because theirs could quickly become a life-and-death venture if a storm blew up, and was a hand-to-mouth existence at best.

We stopped in Zabid, a Koranic university town, which was at its height in the thirteenth and fourteenth centuries. It has a ramshackle but imposing citadel and a big shell of a mosque where Yemen's Sunnis still bring their thorniest religious disputes, as well as a pleasant park full of birds, furnished with hammocks instead of benches, where I displayed the parts of my Swiss Army knife to a crowd of children.

Farther along, at Bayt al Faqih, pickup-truckloads of sweltering sheep waited to be sold, and twenty camels knelt in a circle, each tethered to a stake by a thong through one nostril. Mainly, the vast market offered coffee husks in bags, boll cotton, leaf tobacco, walnuts, peaches, apricots, a motorcycle mart, and bales of Indian clothing and madras cloth. Old tribal costumes that looked like museum pieces were being proffered for a song, for want of foreign tourists to buy them. The market women wore straw hats wound around with bright scarves, and red, black, and green dresses with low décolletage. Disdaining a face covering, they bargained with panache, while furloughed burros roamed the alleys, eating garbage with the dogs. Burros haven't the significance of camels in Yemenis' minds, and all over the country one sees them simply manumitted from labor by the arrival of Toyota cars and trucks.

From Al Hudaydah, the new port modernized by the Russians, we left the baking coast and drove into the mountains through a beautiful series of valleys planted with papaya trees, tamarisks, and banana plants, with the remarkable sight of water sparkling in some of the wadis, and egrets flying up and down. Although the agricultural terraces spreading up the mountain slopes out of view were not being maintained anymore, the kids we saw playing hopscotch still "terraced" the boundaries of their game instead of drawing lines on the ground. A shepherd was blowing his flute; firewood was stacked for sale next to the road; and corn was drying on the stone roofs nearby—though after all the invasions of Yemen's highlands that have been launched along this route, most of the rock-built houses we passed were wedged precipitously onto cliffsides as far back, up, and away from the road as the ancestors of the present occupants had been able to jimmy them. Some you would have needed a rope to climb to and might have lost a dozen men in capturing the residents; an army of conquest hurrying toward San'a would have just gone by. All had gun-slit windows, but several of the more cheerful ones were whitewashed and painted with jubilant-looking airplanes, like a child's drawings, in celebration of the safe return of somebody in the family from a *hajj*.

The reason that these valleys didn't appear entirely like a fairy tale is that they contained so many little castles, not just one in each. We slept in the chewing room atop a vertiginous *funduq* in the formerly much persecuted Ismaeli town of Manakhah, seven thousand feet up—the "Gibraltar of Yemen," its houses themselves pinnacles—which we reached by many switchbacks, and which the Turks, early in this century, had held through many "risings." The view was giddy in the moonlight, and in the morning we breakfasted on puffy disks of pita bread laden with honey. Haggara, even higher, on an adjoining spur of Jebel Haraz, had fifteen hundred people living in seven-story houses painted with what resembled M's and X's and images of eagles, the latticed windows filigreed with gypsum. The children, as always, chased after us asking for *suras* and *qolams*, photos and pens, as if the very act of shaking hands with three large heathen was an adventure.

A woman carrying a pail on her head asked in Arabic what nationality we were; then joked, "I'm German." But after Bjorn started talking to her she soon spoke of "the time of the Old Ones," when people were wise. There is of course considerable poignancy to a country that has been propelled from feudalism into the late twentieth century in two and a half decades, and few of the older Yemenis we talked to were in love with progress, except for the money they could earn by leaving home to pump oil. The unreconstructed royalists, in particular, resent the thousands of little pickups penetrating every cranny of the country, hauling splintered trees out for a quick sale, hauling building cement in, or joyriding all over as if God were no longer alive. Even republicans will often end up parked for a while at a turn in the road at a height of land, feasting their eyes like the mountain people that they are. They'll bring a picnic to eat, sitting on the rocks at the top of a pass, and may improve the time by changing their oil. Whole families turn out, with a man to handle the wheel, but often more women and children, because so many men are away earning foreign exchange. (Middle-class young men in San'a sometimes become part-time taxi drivers for the chance to talk to women unchaperoned; their girlfriends at the university will arrange to "call a cab.") The revolution brought pants to Yemen, and a man's politics were sometimes judged by whether he adopted pants or stuck to the traditional skirt, but plenty of men who put on pants to go to work still wear a skirt on their days off, up here in the clean air, the paterfamilias draining the carburetor while enjoying the language of the rocks and birds.

All scenic highway edges are stained with motor oil and shoe-deep in plastic litter and tin cans. Plastic was never envisioned in the customs of tribal Yemen: that any kind of waste could be invented the goats and donkeys would not eat or that the day might come when goats and donkeys would seem to be in short supply. The blind leap of this small country toward hustly homogeneity with the rest of the world is poignant, and yet the reason that one's heart doesn't go out to the local people is that their previous existence was so far from a state of innocence. With slavery, serfdom, the bushwhacking of travelers and kidnapping of hostages, with the infinitely variable autocracies that sultans, sheikhs, and emirs (each with his prisoners and his harem) exercised over its patchwork of ranges and valleys, medieval Yemen was a knotty place. The dozens of walled towns that we caught sight of in the course of our tour, with their picturesque earth-colored battlements and tenementlike houses, bore the same message as scars—being the mark of sieges suffered and frequent or incessant war. To capture such a community, bashing down its log gates, sweeping over its mud fortifications, pulverizing its simple defenses, cracking it like an egg and biting it like an apple, before bringing into play the proverbial slave headsman, must have increased the slaughter and rapine. After the revolution, an army machine gunner replaced the imam's famous grinning executioner, whose sword was publicly broken. Instead, crowds witnessing the event would line an alleyway just wide enough for the volley of bullets to hit the doomed man without killing them.

Our road from Manakhah curved past Yemen's highest mountain and down again onto San'a's lofty plateau, where Egyptian and Chinese monuments commemorate the breaching of the final royalist siege only twenty-five years ago, when the Chinese road-construction crew outside the city took up arms to help the Yemenis and Egyptians inside break through the Bakils' lines.

Spring rains arrived the night of our return to San'a, the city's first wetting in five months, and dawn erupted with bird song. The people were equally happy, marveling at the deep mudholes over clogged drains at the crossroads. Taxicabs knew how to negotiate high water without stalling, but ordinary car-owning Yemenis driving to work were likely to steer right into the middle of a standing pool in a panicky fashion, lose their nerve, and stop, while the pedestrians hollered. One thoroughfare is the riverbed, dry most of the year. Kids were splashing in it, throwing stones.

A butcher led a flock of sheep through the twisting streets with only the bait of a fresh green bough cradled in his arms. A good deal of a city is its food, and women walking to work were nibbling breakfast bread by slipping pieces of it underneath their veils, using the hand that wasn't carrying a briefcase. They are employed as bank tellers and secretaries and at other jobs requiring dexterous attentiveness, though as a matter of propriety they will still generally do their shopping after work with a young son along to speak to and convey their decisions to the storekeeper. And with their slim forms, straight postures, and forthright, even peremptory air, their skirts drifting, their mantles blowing, their veils continually needing readjustment, the women's presence was very noticeable, at least for a foreigner unaccustomed to such scenes. Every woman looked extraordinarily "feminine," with her face left to the imagination while her hands manipulated the folds and billows of her unbelted clothing, as if somewhere under one of those gauzy veils and black, red and white tie-dyed *marmoukhs* that appeared to have been painted with huge ox eyes were the face and figure of Queen Arwa or Sheba's queen. They were probably closer to being chattel than queens, but several older women we encountered in back lanes were using their veils merely as scarves, so it was possible to see that they looked not unlike Greek or Italian women of sixty and, as they joked with us, that they had not been cowed by going around veiled from the age of nine.

San'a's Revolution Square holds the tank that first fired on the palace of the imamate, and lots of concrete laid out in a lopsided triangle, with an ad for an orange drink on a rooftop at one end. It's ugly as such places go but is an opening to fix on in the otherwise bewildering hive of passageways, cul-de-sacs, and souks. Like Florence, Alexandria, or Zanzibar, San'a is not a city where one can ever expect to see more happening than has occurred before. Yet like many great architectural sites of the distant past, it does not merely reach the pre-Christian or pre-Muslim sources in us but goes back perhaps to neolithic experiences that can lend an intermittent, subterranean terror to perceiving oneself as an interloper here. And of course generations of Christian leeriness of Islam, with the bugaboos of current bigotry, leave a mark.

San'a has a population of four hundred thousand, and the two walled old quarters intersect like the halves of a figure eight at what used to be a natural choke point for snuffing out a rebellion. The dirt or cobblestone streets loop like footpaths, and the fanciful and teetery mini-castles and idiosyncratically tall mud tenements with gun-slit windows that only begin four stories up are like cliff dwellings. But then you see a friendly and straightforward face, a market scene, or children playing, and the illusion that this is a glimpse of prehistory is banished. People say one reason the houses are built of mud is that "mud swallows bullets," as stones do not; a bullet will ricochet off stonework and strike again somewhere else. On the other hand, a cannon shell that will knock down a stone house may pass right through a mud one. Yemenis most resemble the Omanis, another spiky, rigorously fractured mountain people, who live along the opposite side of the Empty Quarter, warring sporadically with central authority—in their case, a sultan assisted by British mercenaries. And in San'a, as in Muscat, one sees faces from the edge of India and East Africa, Zanzibaris, Mombasans, and so on.

Most Yemenis are cold-climate Arabs, with a faster idea of pacing and less patience for haggling than some hot-land peoples. A tick-tock rush of activity—white-turbaned laborers, black-turbaned craftsmen—prevails in San'a, as in other proud cities. Stalls selling bread or lettuce, stalls selling betrothal baubles. Blacksmiths, silversmiths, brass workers. By wandering we even found a hospice for donkeys with broken legs, fourteen animals hobbling about, nibbling clover, the remarkable charity of an old locksmith who looked like any average fellow in that central "Souk of the Cows," as the market area is called, but who was the object of hoots and catcalls from other stall owners when we located him; he got mad and wouldn't talk to us. Yemenis don't kill domestic creatures if they can help it, but often treat them inhumanely. A dog is considered good luck as a scapegoat—the family's bad luck may fasten upon him, particularly if his ears have been cropped—but his saliva is ritually defiling; while a cat is respected as cleaner in the Prophet's eyes, and more generally for mousing. Yet both may be allowed to starve.

Yemenis, and Yemeni Shiis in particular, are not very public in their religious observance; one doesn't notice them touching their foreheads to the pavement the way a good many people do even in Cairo, for instance. This, and the vigor of commerce in the morning, might give rise to an impression that cultural relativism holds sway; that jet-setters might soon be flying in to this zanily picture-book city to buy hideaways, as on the cozy island of Zamalik in the Nile, or in Tuscany's quaint hill towns. But Yemenis are not like Cairenes or Italians. Drunkenness, bawdy noise, late-night visitors, unclad females glimpsed through an apartment window, can provoke an anguish of concern, and in San'a the neighbors are not likely to let the matter drag. Nor is their means of bringing their grievance to a head easy to ignore. The European offender may first hear of it by the sound of bawling in the street and, looking out, discover that a leggy bull calf is being hauled unwillingly to his doorstep. There, the splash of blood as it is slaughtered signifies that an important parley must take place.

Besides the six-story houses, painted fantastically, with windows of stained glass and alabaster, there were plenty of hovels, but the massive, roan-red Bab al Yemen, "Gate of Yemen," with its fountain, the southern portal to the city, and the Gate of Constantinople, on the north, seemed mesmerizing, as though processions were still arriving from Dar es Salaam.

We drove north from San'a for five hours toward the walled district capital of Sad'ah, close to the Saudi border, through twisty, bouldery, bandity little valleys where every house was provisionally a fortress—though glyphed with gypsum and whitewashed at the windows—and across a series of short plateaus planted to sorghum. Sometimes when the road curved we would see a small cairn memorializing the spot where a child or a goatherd had been run over and killed. The pavement would be interrupted where angry relatives had tried to manufacture bumps to slow the traffic down. Yet we met vehicles only every five minutes or so, most of them ragtag cars making the once-a-year-or-two trek back from Saudi Arabia piled to double their natural height with brand-new tables, chairs, bureaus, refrigerators, mattresses, bedding, baled goods, television sets, and other appliances in packing boxes roped to the roof. Half a million Yemenis work in Saudi Arabia, earning thirty or forty dollars a day, which is three times the typical wage at home, so it's no wonder the road occasionally has bandits on it. Since the war, every man carries a Kalashnikov as a matter of custom and needs only to slump one shoulder to let the magazine slide into his hand.

We paused to watch a crowd of vultures and carrion eagles feeding on a goat at the bottom of a cliff. The towns

have boxy, earthen-colored dwellings with a staccato high
row of window slits, the relative width of which, as well as
their distance from the ground, provides a quick estimate of
the relative friendliness of the residents to strangers and how
much gunfire they and their ancestors have had to withstand.
In some of the fields thousand-year-old stone watchtowers
still mark the points at which grain was threshed, dried, and
stored. The houses are built upon the ruins of older houses
at each defendable squeeze in the valley's walls, with cave-
house remnants higher up, and maybe an Ottoman citadel or
an older redoubt on the crags of a saw-edge ridgeline, where
Turkish soldiers holed up between tax-collecting expeditions, until Arabia's revolt and their country's defeat in the
First World War ended their empire.

In these self-sustaining villages one can see sights startling to a Westerner, such as a man wearing leg irons in lieu
of serving a term in jail (with a string in his hand to lift the
chain when he wants to walk somewhere), or a madwoman
caged into a tiny store where she can sell candy, soap, and
sundries instead of being carted off to a harsher fate. Another woman might be walking around in a swarm of flies,
with the odor of vaginal fistulas that cause her to leak urine
continually. Tuberculosis is commonplace among the women
of some of the villages, cooped up indoors, and bilharzia
among the men. Cholera has been conquered, but typhoid
can be renewed with the spring rains.

A bride's price averages seven thousand dollars in Yemen (blood money paid to a victim's family after a wrongful
death, Bjorn said, will be about twelve thousand dollars), and
she comes with no dowry, only her skills, but the money is
refundable if either partner complains that the marriage cannot be consummated. There is the usual ceremony of the
sheets being exhibited after the wedding night, but on the
rare occasions when a match-up doesn't work out—the blood
displayed need not be human blood, if the two parties agree
to pretend that it is—in this clannish culture, the whole community is likely to feel collectively responsible. The ordeal is
shared, not such a subject of derision as it might be in a more
worldly setting.

Sons and mothers do get tied closely together in a society
where women do not ordinarily have the chance to choose

their husbands and afterward are cloistered from contact with the opposite sex—it makes for a certain predilection to nervous breakdowns among the young men. The one Bjorn remembered best had occurred when a boy's father insisted upon divorcing his mother in order to marry a fifth wife; Sharia law of course provided that he could have only four at once. Yet in this same region Sheikh Abdallah ibn Husayn al Ahmar is said to be able to field an army of twenty thousand men in a matter of days if a woman of his Hashid tribe is insulted by a Bakil tribesman. Bjorn's girlfriend had been working here on various water projects for an international agency when she fell afoul of the national security service and was abruptly incarcerated in San'a's Women's Prison. But a hundred armed tribesmen journeyed to the capital, showed up at the prison gate, and forced her release. (The security men, nursing their grudge, spotted her at the airport a few months later, when she had slipped into town to see somebody off, and thrust her onto a plane bound for Cairo with just the clothes on her back.)

The dramatic small city of Sad'ah flourished at its peak about eight hundred years ago and must still be entered through thick wooden gates at a double-looped entry point passing through immense mud-brick walls looming fifty feet high—the double loop was first constructed to foil the use of a battering ram. Inside is a huge antique mosque, a good number of large residential tenements built of hand-slabbed, straw-strengthened mud, and the governor's lofty, imposing castle, as thick-walled as the city itself, with Yemen's red, black, and white flag flying over it, and looking more grand and awesome than the Tower of London because here it remains the seat of enormous power, including the possibility that one might be locked inside (which, I think, lends more pomp to a piece of architecture than anything else).

Sad'ah's pumphouse, thumpingly noisy, is fenced and surrounded by a lush, diminutive garden of weeds and trees watered by the trickling runoff. As in all Yemen's earthen towns, however, we saw houses that rather recently had collapsed and returned to a state approximating nature, four or five stories now reduced to a mound of brown sand. Others, still standing, glistened with sinister seeps and streaks. One of the plagues of development in a desert country is that the local authorities become so elated by the extravagant availability of deep-well water, such as they had never dreamed of before, that they arrange to pipe it into the buildings but do not spend much extra money to drain it out again. The result is that sewage and other exit pipes are skimped on, and running water leaks and leaches all through the structures, softens, soaks, and undermines everybody's walls, and brings a bunch of them down.

We walked a circuit atop Sad'ah's city walls, which also are crumbling, not from piped-in water but from the seasonal rains, because they haven't been replastered since the oil boom lured away the laborers who used to attend to such chores. Yemenis learned, anyhow, during the civil war—with casualties of two hundred thousand—that walls couldn't protect them anymore. But we were exuberant up there, shouting to children on both sides of the wall. A street-sweeping, garbage-picking outcast clan from Tihama lived in black tents on the outside, with a separate playground and tiny school. Inside, we watched a tumbledown house being rebuilt, a rapid, quite cheerful procedure of hand-shaped bricks thrown up from man to man to the mason straddling a scaffold, who slapped them into rows that curved slightly upward at each end for reinforcement. The householder meanwhile was pondering where he wanted his windows, not just the gothically narrow, arched, stained-glass jobs, but eccentric, oblong apertures out of which his wife and kids could poke their heads on a thousand mornings when the sun hit at a brief happy angle, or perhaps a screened and outcanted window ledge with perforations through which his womenfolk without revealing their presence could peer straight down at the street below.

Sad'ah was the refuge of the first Zaydis after they had been defeated by other Shiites in a holy war in Iraq and retreated to Yemen in about the year 870. Shiites—the word means "partisan"—believe Mohammad's son-in-law Ali was Mohammad's proper successor and had fought the rival Sunni Syrians over the question on the plain at Siffin near the Euphrates River in 657. (The Sunnis, whose name derives from the word for "tradition" and who now constitute ninety percent of Islam, believed in effect that the office of caliph or imam should be elective rather than hereditary.) The Zaydis' martyred leader, Zayd, was one of Ali's great-grandsons and was the focus of only this one of several early Shiite schisms. But Sad'ah had already emerged as a mining and trading center on the caravan route from Aden and Ma'rib toward Mecca and Gaza well before the arrival of this Bedouin band. Indeed, around the year A.D. 500, Sad'ah had been on the fringe of the short-lived Jewish kingdom in what is now extreme southwestern Saudi Arabia, which was an outgrowth of what may be the oldest Jewish community in the Diaspora.

Jews first came to Yemen around 1000 B.C., some possibly sent by King Solomon in the Queen of Sheba's train when she returned from her visit to him, others after the sack of Jerusalem in 922 B.C. More Jews followed after the destruction of the Temple in the sixth century B.C. and after the fall of Jerusalem to Titus in A.D. 70. Yemen's Jews remained a mysterious, isolated sector of the community until the state of Israel was established in 1948, and in the so-called Magic Carpet operation during the next two years, fifty thousand of them were airlifted out (with Alaska Airlines, curiously enough, doing a lot of the chartering). Only in the district surrounding Sad'ah is a remnant populace left, perhaps twelve hundred people, who by the force of tradition in this most conservative region have been afforded a measure of security even in the present climate of opinion in the Middle East. Though they aren't treated in a friendly fashion, their right of residence is recognized, and they aren't persecuted as much as might be the case where newer, more radical ideas hold sway. The Zaydi attitude is exemplified by Imam Ahmad, who, when San'a's Jews (who all departed in the exodus and had included the best handcraftsmen in his imamate) complained of being spit upon and struck in the streets, decreed that "one third of an ox" was to be paid by the perpetrator to the victim of such an insult, the other two thirds to go to the soldiery who enforced the edict. But no outsider can say whether the people still living near Sad'ah and working as carpenters, glassmakers, and jacks-of-all-trades chose to stay because, some forty years ago, most Jews there were anti-Zionist and believed that their ancient community should be maintained, or simply because they were the farthest from the British airfield at Aden, where the flights took off, a punishing walk of hundreds of miles through a succession of sheikhdoms and sultanates, each with its dangers, and a head tax of Maria Theresa thalers to be paid, if they—especially the elderly—survived.

In the town of Raydah we'd noticed a cobbler with sidelocks squatting by the sandal of an Arab who was chatting equably with him, though not so openly that we felt we could join them. Ali indicated he couldn't consider taking us off the main road to visit a Jewish settlement, but by dint of quietly pushing the issue, on our second day in Sad'ah we did manage to encounter two pairs of silent young men with sidelocks, seated cross-legged opposite each other in the souk with a modest but splendidly tooled display of silver set upon two blankets. Their faces, robes, and headcloths were not very different from those of the Arabs around them, but in manner they were aloof and gingerly, volunteering nothing by way of salesmanship, as a crowd immediately gathered and a plainclothes policeman materialized and began to question Ali and Bjorn aggressively as to why we were there and whether any information or leaflets had been passed. In the hubbub the four young men grew still more unbending and disdainful of the attention they were receiving, allowing their nervousness to show only by the way their straight-postured bodies tipped and swayed a bit like ninepins under the volleys of words going over their heads. For their sake and our own, Martha and I hurried to purchase half a dozen filigreed rings and biceps-sized bracelets that had been worked in time-honored patterns by the older women of the families they came from, Bjorn said; and having received our change in Maria Theresa thalers, and having purposely finished exploring Sad'ah beforehand, straightaway we left town.

Bjorn and his North African woman friend, while living adventurously in the Zone of Insolence, had not failed to pay a couple of visits to an off-road Jewish village, chewing qat and drinking the wine that the residents are permitted to brew, although the neighborhood sheikh had promptly showed up to check on them and had taken their supply of qat away with him. (Muslims in Yemen do not drink wine.) Bjorn added that, once, a strangely phlegmatic and yet vigorous sort of man had turned up in San'a, speaking a rudimentary but serviceable Arabic and telling people he was a

236

German who had lived in Cairo for two years and now was going to buy fine silverwork for an art gallery in Bern. He had come from accomplishing the same feat in war-racked Ethiopia, hiking with a backpack cross-country to remote Falasha settlements, though he said, when Bjorn mentioned Yemen's Jews, whose jewelry is renowned, that he hadn't known there were Jews in Yemen too. And so he started to go to the distant enclaves where Bjorn directed him, and beyond them on the mountain paths, carrying out packloads of museum-quality silver artifacts among the multitudes of poor Arab tribesmen armed with Kalashnikovs, spending the night in any farmhouse he happened to land at.

"They like guts like that. They didn't hurt him," Bjorn explained.

"Did he seem brave?" I asked.

"It's two different things, being fearless and being brave. He was fearless."

"Do you think he was doing a census for Mossad?" I asked.

Bjorn was surprised at the idea but agreed that a German backpacker from Cairo speaking bad Arabic and buying silver adornments for a gallery in Bern might be a clever cover; he himself had fallen under suspicion occasionally when traveling in Yemen because he spoke Arabic so well. But an Israeli agent, as he pointed out, would not have told people that he had just been on the same kind of shopping expedition in Ethiopia; nor would he have been so touched by the isolation of Yemen's Jews, after he'd met them, that he not only smuggled in some Hebrew religious texts on his next buying trip but confided to Bjorn that he had done so.

Yemen's foreigners, Bjorn said, were often people "hiding out, running away," or embarked upon odd, crazy, self-imposed missions, or hurling themselves into fantastical love affairs of a kind most piquantly pursued in San'a's stern warrens—though generally also, I found, waiting to hear news of jobs they had applied for elsewhere in the world, while whiling away the sunsets together over cups of mud-black coffee, leaning on the cushions of a *mafraj* with one leg bent and one stretched out, in the approved fashion, and listening to a dozen muezzins crying out in a holy bellow from the turrets of the capital, enhancing and harmonizing with one another as they exhorted the city to pray. In a sleepy provincial town, the muezzins will sometimes sound like frogs around a pond, or hounds baying at the moon, but in San'a there's the fervor of Islam alive, God in the air, life as a matter of life and death. Nowadays the newspaper prints the exact minute at which each call to prayer ought to be made, and the words are preordained, but even so there must be a first man to start the call and a last man to chime in, a high voice, a low voice, and a monotone, a musical voice that makes it into a song, a voice precise in diction, and a voice that attempts to sum it all up; and the politics or rivalry between individual mosques, the friendship or disaffection existing among six or a dozen muezzins who have been joining their voices five times a day above the city for many, many years, may well be imagined.

A discreetly glamorous Austrian woman with graying black hair, who was employed in the library of the Great Mosque, conserving and restoring manuscripts, had rented a small house with a romantic battlement and a widespread view, where we would loll in the chewing room talking of byzantine politics and desert hardship, British theater, and tenure denied at somebody's university back in the United States. The British Embassy Club, located in a tatty block-house adjoining the embassy tennis court and swimming pool, was another resort for Western "expats"—that whole semipermanent contingent of airline help, contractors' assistants, U.N. personnel posted here for medical or development projects, and low-rung diplomats. A good many I met seemed a little misshapen, strangely beefy or unusually gaunt, with puzzled foreheads or bombastic chins. Despair or baffled intransigence seemed to lie in back of the eyes of some of them, with a muddled, interrupted, huffing-and-puffing air. While they were talking at the horseshoe bar, their faces might go inattentive suddenly, as though yearning to be back at some previous stop-off or to leap fast-forward to their next date of departure and the bracing novelty of risk and difficulty they were anticipating at their next assignment. Many people live abroad partly in order to define themselves by where they are and where they've been, bolstering their sense of identity by standing against the relief of a foreign backdrop, an ancient hierarchy or rigid religiosity that has molded their surroundings so profoundly as to prop them up as well. And people postpone taking up the thread of their lives by traveling—the rush of airports, preoccupation with the new country, unpacking, settling in, learning the ropes, exploring, and *naturally* not being able to address any more lasting context in the meantime. Yet those of us who share their itchy feet, their rueful as well as gleeful addiction to being as far as possible from wherever they have lately been, making themselves special by the sights at hand, the rainbows, cliffs, and islands seen, the destinations they've achieved, instead of internal factors, believe this is partly what life is about: that it's the world that's special more than us. On alternate Sundays in San'a, fifty or a hundred of the expats run with the "Hashhouse Harriers," a British-centered institution of the Near and Far East by which lonely Europeans will slowly jog through scenery especially chosen for its loveliness, watching for tokens and clues—scarves tied to bushes, and such things—left by the "hares" they are pursuing, and crying, "On, on! On, on!" whenever they find one.

Emerson said, "Travelling is a fool's paradise. They who made England, Italy or Greece venerable in the imagination did so by sticking fast where they were, like an axis of the earth." And again: "I am not much an advocate for travelling, and I observe that men run away to other countries because they are not good in their own, and run back to their own because they pass for nothing in the new places." It's still an appealing argument, although the notion of any nation now becoming a proper axis for the earth, or of its intellectuals and industrialists struggling to make it so, seems funny. Rather, the fondest wish of many Western intellectuals and industrialists appears to be to retire and travel. With the crush of worldwide tourism, the search for authentic pockets of unspoiled exoticism by the more expensive outfitters has reached every redoubt—places such as this, which hadn't been exploited because of chronic civil war. And Islam has not been domesticated for Americans by homegrown faddist versions that correspond to Zen Buddhism or itinerant Hindu gurus expounding at weekend ashrams. On the contrary, decades of drumbeating bigotry on the subject of Islam have made that religion in itself a force for exoticism in the perceptions of the West; a Muslim country is always seen as alien, even dangerous.

Yemen is a miniature Afghanistan for connoisseurs of

the tourist circuit because of its mountain tribes (and you must have mountains now to have tribes). The very cisterns in which rainwater is collected are like gigantic bowls that have been artfully sculpted in the rock, into which the villagers descend by ledges that coil down. Towns like Kawkaban are set incredibly on pinnacles scarcely to be scaled. In an Italian walled hill town, surrounded by passionate architecture from an epoch of schism, with bands of partisans and neighborhood armies and a God of sword, fist, and martyrdom immanent everywhere, the traveler can try to imagine a life six hundred years ago that resembled Yemen's in the middle of our present century. But it's a decorous, sanitized experience, almost like visiting a large museum, whereas even close to his own home, Ali felt obliged to drive us way around the next village instead of chancing a trip straight through. There are famous scenic towns such as Shahara, with its giddy, rock-pieced bridge, where the local people simply take over the guidance of visitors, at gunpoint if necessary. At the imam's Palace on the Rock, a jumbled tall castle built of sandstone, bricks, and basalt atop a hundred-foot rock in Wadi Dhar, Martha and I spent our time closing windows and doors that were banging to bits in the wind—the walls were leaking, the fixtures falling off—so that its indoor curiosities might endure intact for a little longer.

Wadi Dhar is known as *the* wadi in Yemen and is used to illustrate to children what paradise perhaps is like, because of its green seethe of luscious trees—eucalyptus, sycamore, pines, palms, walnuts, apricots, cypresses, pepper trees, fig trees, mimosas, and huge oaklike *taluq* trees (*ficus vastus*)—its flocks of birds, and grape arbors growing black and yellow raisins in bountiful profusion, under the massif of Jebel an Nabi Shu'ayb, Yemen's highest mountain.

In Wadi Dhar we heard about the baboons, leopards, and hyenas that had lived here until the civil war brought in armies and firepower, and also about our first snake man, a tenant farmer who still caught snakes for part of his living when they appeared in other people's houses, or else would merely read the Koran to the snakes for about ten dollars. Though Ali wouldn't take us to meet him, we enjoyed asking after such individuals when we stopped to chat in other marketplaces or with women drying cakes of sheep dung for fuel or carrying green fodder on their heads, in tall villages built like hornets' nests with windows like knife punctures. In Yemen, musicians, barbers, butchers, and blacksmiths are regarded as of a debased caste; and so, it seemed, were snake men. Most towns did have one, and a hoot would go up when we asked for him. He was generally said to be dark-skinned, of slave origin, *Abadi*, but able to draw a snake out of its hole by repeatedly dangling a string down inside and slowly pulling it out again, communing with the snake in the meantime, so that eventually when it emerged it might follow him about the room for a while, until he picked it up and pocketed it. These men were said never to kill the snakes they caught, but rather to carry them off and let them go again, though they might draw out the fangs of a viper before doing so. Even under everyday circumstances, they liked going around with a snake concealed somewhere in their robes. It sounded like a good magician's business for a man born into a feudal system of landholding, where otherwise he would exist only to try to repay his father's debts.

In 1962, the yearly per capita income in Yemen was seventy dollars; there were a total of fifteen doctors, all foreign, and six hundred hospital beds. It's better now, but in the little fifty-six-bed facility near Sad'ah, where we stopped, the administrator, Wilfrid Hufton, from Saginaw, Michigan, told us that twenty babies a day were being turned away from "the triage room," too close to death to save. In the south, near Ta'izz, William Koehn, a Kansan who held a similar post at Jibla Baptist Hospital, with seventy-five beds to fill, said they were doing three thousand operations a year, charging twenty-eight dollars for the minor kind and a hundred thirty-five dollars for major surgery (a dollar seventy to see a doctor, four dollars to see him quickly). Relatives must give blood before an operation, a serious issue because many people believe blood, once given, is never replaced—a superstition that makes any fight in which blood is drawn a terribly grave matter.

When we got tired or nervous after an adventure, Martha would empty and repack her luggage, and I would try to find new hiding places for my money. Arabic is a breathy language, full of exhalation and expostulation, but in my ignorance it seemed to me not to contain quite enough breadth to encompass all the faces we saw—the disgruntled, haughty Egyptian pedagogues in pajama costumes restlessly roaming backwater villages; the stately, puzzled Sudanese; sleek, purposeful Saudis; Zaydis rich with wild-country hauteur; wary, mercantile Shafiis; and raffish-looking blacks engendering an élan of their own simply by being regarded as disreputable. San'a is a metropolis all eyes, and as unapologetic as the cities described by Marco Polo, which glances at stray Westerners as if to say, You burly, overanxious creature, or you skin-and-bones do-gooder, why are you so far from home? But there are many more Russians working in Yemen than Americans—fifty or sixty times as many military advisers, the American Embassy claimed—because in most Arab countries Russian military equipment is thought to be more durable and dependable than the Americans' faster, "smarter," elegant stuff. "The Egyptian Migs were as thick as mosquitoes over us. Our hair turned white defending our children," a retired royalist officer in Sad'ah had said fervently of that worst time in his life.

The soldiers in red berets looked straightforward enough when we met them at roadblocks, backed up by a light machine gun mounted on a jeep parked behind a piled-stone emplacement, but the security men, who maintained separate roadblocks, had older, subtler, more moody, sophisticated, amused, ominous faces. Schooled originally by Scotland Yard, they jockey with South Yemen's East German–trained security forces across "the" Yemen, as Arabists often call the whole region because the name translates in Arabic as "at the right hand" of Mecca (from the Red Sea). This passionate, endearing country of prickly-pear landscapes and hobbled camels, of tinkers, shawl sellers, snuff peddlers, and spice merchants, of Indian sweetmeats, brooms of palm leaves, see-through harem clothing, and pamphlet biographies of Abraham Lincoln sold in San'a's Souk of Salt, where men friends stroll about holding hands, each chewing a cud, in the afternoon; this country of impromptu houses striped with red clay and blue paint, decorated with stick-man figures or windows depicted as eyes by means of whitewash, where foreigners are sometimes called Kaffirs, and prisoners still must pay the salaries of the policemen who come to arrest them, depending on how far they have had to walk—the circuit judges used to employ a man to follow behind them counting their steps as they traveled between villages, and set their fees arithmetically—winds up being irresistible.

The incantations, ululations, invocations, the whistle blowing of San'a's watchmen signaling to each other all night; little girls in conical hats walking with fathers in skirts, jackets, and headcloths wrapped around pillbox hats; the bowls of *ful* (beans) eaten with "people's bread" and mango or guava juice drunk from a can, to the whack of dough being slapped against the round wall of a pot-shaped street oven with a white-gas flame hissing underneath: I would miss all of it. Bjorn had decided to stay longer than we'd planned, to check on a building project he had designed for the government, and he invited me to do the same. The bait he dangled before me was a rumor that had hit San'a's streets that the South Yemen army was going to invade "three days from tomorrow." Wouldn't a news hound like me want to witness that? Well, in truth, if I'd been fresh to the country I would have wanted to, though I doubted that the Russians, with their big naval base to protect in South Yemen—when they were expelled from Somalia in 1977, they had simply floated their drydock from Berbera to Aden—would actually allow the South Yemenis to invade anybody. They didn't, as it turned out. But I chose to fly back to London with Martha. Part of the purpose of travel is to slow down the incessantly accelerating velocity of one's life—not just to see new sights, but to experience unexpected resistance, encounter obstacles that give one pause, to stand at the brink of a civilization that may seem spiky or unfathomable and makes the clock stop. It's sometimes chilling, sometimes tiring for a visitor to feel ignorant, awed, or even fearful—America was undergoing one of its recurring convulsions of xenophobia at this point—when entering the heartland of a people, like the Arabs, who are distrusted or despised by many of one's countrymen, a place where God is still regarded as real and life as life-and-death, where the stones that a householder lifts to build his home may soon save his skin. I was tired.

The pilot for Yemenia Airways probably doubled as a fighter pilot, as many third-world pilots do. He lifted the Boeing very abruptly off the runway and into the sky, his voice on the intercom full of daring. And the stewardesses, who were refugees from the war in Eritrea and were willing to go unveiled, had about their pretty faces an air of glad desperation. Arabs have not forgotten that the Israeli air force deliberately shot down a civilian airliner that had wandered off course over the Sinai in early 1973, so we made calibrated adjustments that brought us from Saudi Arabian airspace directly over Cairo's defenses before reaching the Mediterranean. (This is the line that flies Yasir Arafat to San'a so often, the CIA station chief had told me, that his agency had stopped bothering to log him in and out of the airport; but *Fiddler on the Roof* was playing on the sound system.) I was watching two husky, hardened-looking expatriates sitting on the nearly empty plane who looked like mercenary soldiers, although perhaps they were only mining engineers. I'd supposed that they were British, but when we landed in Paris after more than seven hours, they stood up with sighs and broad smiles of relief and murmured in soft-spoken French, just as if they weren't tough guys at all.

I had flown into San'a at daybreak with the pyrotechnics of the sunrise promising me adventure. But we landed in London at nightfall; and night is a good time to arrive in London, when people are going out to plays, clubs, and restaurants, dressed to the nines. The electricity was blazing, and this infinite city devised for commerce, industry, and pleasure of every kind—designed, indeed, to rule the whole world, though it has become instead a favorite resort and refuge for all the world's exiles—laid out its evening charms. The lights were lovely, but the traffic was gridlocked.

Buckaroo Poets

I can ride the wildest bronco in the wild and woolly
* West,*
I can rake him, I can break him, let him do his level
* best.*
I can handle any cattle ever wore a coat of hair,
And I've had a lively tussle with a tarnal grizzly bear.
I can rope and throw a longhorn of the wildest Texas
* brand,*
And at Injun disagreements I can take a leading hand.
But I finally met my master, and he really made me
* squeal,*
When the boys got me astraddle of that gol-darned
* wheel. . . .*

The "wheel" in this famous cowboy poem, its author
now unknown, is on a bicycle, not a car, which may signify
how long ago the cowboys' West began its great decline. Yet
such poems are still being written, some of them nearly as
much fun to hear as the old ones are; and in Elko, in northeast Nevada, every midwinter for the past few years, a hul-
labaloo of poets has occurred, with thousands of spectators
cheering them on. Rimrock and slickrock and cool willow
draws, chuck wagons, pig irons, and sunfishing broncs, six-

horse hitches and batwing chaps, lariat loops and black stove-pipe hats—all of that good old stuff is involved. Robert W. Service's Sam McGee and Dan McGrew get their poems recited, as the edifice upon which such genre verse has been built, and perhaps Bill Simpson's recent epitome of what it's about:

> *An old drunk cowboy*
> *Stepped through the door,*
> *He staggered an' stumbled,*
> *Then fell on the floor. . . .*
>
> *Well, the crease in his hat*
> *It was crooked and worn*
> *An' the toes of his boots*
> *Was an old cow's horn. . . .*
>
> *He said, "I rumbled and rambled*
> *An' crashed through life.*
> *I never had the courage*
> *To take me a wife." . . .*
>
> *He told it so softly,*
> *With a tear in his eye,*
> *He said, "Son, life's a bitch*
> *An' then you just die."*

There's never a new idea in cowboy poetry. It's partly doggerel (or "ballad-style verse," as the folklorists say), and new ideas would go against the grain of reaffirming traditional sentiments and tall tales. Nor is its language juicy and original. Instead its virtues are frankness, starkness, humor, and the invariable yarn, as in Wally McRae's "Reincarnation," about a dead cowpoke who fertilizes a flower, which is eaten by a horse, whose droppings are recognized by the cowboy's pal: "You ain't changed all that much." Or Gail Gardner's "Dude Wrangler," who falls so low, wearing boots "green and red" and a shirt "loud enough to wake the dead," while boosting guests into their saddles and fixing their stirrups for them ("And they give me tips when I am through"), that his old pardner has to shoot him:

> *So I drawed my gun and throwed it on him,*
> *I had to turn my face away.*
> *I shot him squarely through the middle,*
> *And where he fell I left him lay.*

I shorely hated for to do it,
For things that's done you cain't recall.
But when a cowboy turns dude wrangler,
He ain't no good no more at all.

You might have thought a costume ball was going on at Elko's convention center, with dozens of fat hats and foot-long waxed handlebar mustaches, the blanket coats and calf-skin vests and "tough rags" (bandannas) decorating people's necks. Cowhands from a hotter, less windy country sported broad-brimmed, high-crowned lids, while those from a state such as Montana wore narrower, curlier brims, with a snugger crown, to keep the hat on in high winds and high brush. And they might prefer "packers' boots," which lace up, instead of the usual peg-heeled, narrow-soled, pointy-toed, slip-on buckaroo footwear, because of having to slide off their horses and walk a lot on bouldery mountain terrain. The clothes told a story; and the sun-pummeled, rain-stained physiognomies, the watchful, silent postures, the beards grown as fur against the cold, the lunging gait with which some of the poets strode across the stage to recite their poems, as if heading a bunch of horses toward the neck of a corral, all let you know that they were for real and this wasn't a dress-up party.

Find grass, make meat, drive the cattle to the killing house: it was as basic a business as that. Yet the truth is that Georgia produces more beef than Nevada does now, and that in the West cattle are often raised at enormous expense to such truer wilderness values as thriving wildlife populations and a healthy balance of vegetation on the public wildlands that every American owns, not just the local ranchers who lease and sometimes abuse chunks of wilderness for what in the past has amounted to a song. Even in its poetry, the cowboy ethic contains small provision for anything but abuse of the land, and there is a frequent subtheme of sadism—bullwhackers so cruel that their oxen moan in fear as they climb onto the wagon box at dawn with their whips already at work on the animals' backs; mule skinners and suffering stagecoach teams; "peelers" who make a point of breaking their horses in body as well as in spirit before they get through with them. "Man has injured every animal he has touched," the great conservationist John Muir wrote once (calling the sheep that ravaged California's mountain meadows "hoofed locusts," which could as easily describe cattle too), and Wallace Stegner and Edward Abbey, two of the West's leading literary lights, have expressed exasperation at the durable mule-headedness and mythic grotesqueries of the cowboy heritage, whose romanticized nihilism and destructive individualism have worked to speed, not resist, the countless developers' projects that are obliterating the same West that was host to cowboying in the first place.

But Elko, a town of twelve thousand souls almost a mile high in sagebrush terrain near the Ruby Mountains, and on Interstate 80, which runs from New York City to San Francisco, still does have, behind its highway clutter and three casinos with banks of slot machines and blackjack tables and play-money chips, a core of authenticity: old saloons and saddleries, creaky hotel buildings and "Basco" (Basque) boardinghouses, where sheepherders can winter for one hundred dollars a week, and five legal brothels between them and the railroad tracks. ("My name is Angel, but I've never been an angel," one of the prostitutes said, matching some cowboy verse we had heard: "Not much of a thinker, / He was more of a drinker.")

Cowboys don't really write poetry any better than lawyers play golf, but one can learn a good deal about lawyers by how they play golf, and in January, when most buckaroos (from the Spanish *vaqueros*) aren't doing much more than hauling hay to feed their "mother cows," maybe a talespinning and yodeling convention is a good spot to get a handle on them. One of my favorites who recited, Waddie Mitchell, had just split up with his wife and had lost thirty-five pounds in anguish over that, he said. Another, Wally McRae, was trying to organize opposition against strip mining in his ranching region, with little success. And a third, a gaunt, tall cowman of 1920s vintage, his skin mottled, his voice croaking now from having yelled at so many thousands of cattle for so many years, spoke of the cool shade and sweet drinking water of his Chino Valley in Arizona—where an acre is suddenly worth thirty-five thousand dollars, however, and he can't even go to the post office to pick up his mail without everybody falling silent and gawking at him as "a ghost out of the past. The last cowboy in town. It's plumb tough," Slim Kite said.

Poetry is engendered in solitude, so what better meter for it than the clip of a buckskin horse? "Anyway, it's better than talking to yourself," Slim remarked. We heard about moonlit stampedes; cowpokes dying of thirst with a broken leg, or shooting a wild horse that couldn't be caught; "cookies" (cooks) who drowned in fording a creek—"Had lived his life in one old shirt / But met his Maker clean"—and the branding, castrating, and earmarking of calves, then letting them go to grow again.

"Cowboys are so used to heat they aren't even allowed in hell," Slim said.

The contemporary life new poets described was as precarious, penurious, and lonesome as ever, and most had turned to other work—well digging, selling insurance, working for the government or at a gold mine—though celebrating past hardships, bad luck, practical jokes, and such. What the poetry is about is riding hard, punching cows, making a fool of oneself, and the ache of being poor in old age, when "memory replaces hope," in Bruce Kiskaddon's phrase.

Kiskaddon (1878–1950) was probably tops, and his life itself typified the ironies of the genre. He came from out East in Pennsylvania but by twenty was riding the range, until, nearing fifty, after adventures in Colorado, Arizona, and Australia, he went to Hollywood on a jaunt with some friends to take a pickup job driving a chariot in the 1926 silent-screen version of *Ben Hur*. There in Los Angeles he hired on as a bellhop at the Mayflower Hotel, married, had a daughter, and for the last third of his life carried luggage or operated the elevator. But he kept a pencil stub behind one ear to scribble with while waiting in the lobby, and once a month would walk down to the Union Stockyards with a ten-dollar poem for the auction catalogue, later to appear in *Western Livestock* magazine. Unknown, and wearing a bellboy's "monkey suit" in this era of Gene Autry, Roy Rogers, Hopalong Cassidy, and John Wayne, he was the real thing; and he wrote poems to a cow-camp oven, to a bunkhouse mirror, on the question of lice, on breaking a finger in a tangle of rope on the saddlehorn, and a longhorn's bafflement at a plump Hereford steer: "He ain't got no laigs and his body is big / I sort of suspicion he's crossed with a pig / Ain't fit for nothin' exceptin' to kill."

All told, Kiskaddon suggested, life was mostly fun. ("The biscuits she baked wasn't bad by no means / And she had the world cheated for cookin' up beans.") "As the long years come and go," he wrote, "You start with a swing that is free and strong / And finish up tired and slow." But his vigor and versatile sense of proportion—no false heroics, just matter-of-fact recollections set into couplets—deserve a revival that will outlive a good many tinseltown stars whose baggage he lugged.

A gloomier mood prevailed among the old men reciting their verses in Elko. Another longhorn died telling a herd of Holsteins, "Don't beller for me. I'm a diff'rent breed!" and mocking a circling coyote that expected a meal. And they quoted John Wesley's "Last Breathing Longhorn" like a tolling bell, sometimes with tears in their eyes:

> The cowboy's left the country,
> And the campfire's going out.

Abbey's Road

Edward Abbey, who died in March 1989, at sixty-two, seemed, at his best, like the nonparcil "nature writer" of recent decades. It was a term he came to detest, a term used to pigeonhole and marginalize some of the more intriguing American writers alive, who are dealing with matters central to us, yet it can be a ticket to oblivion in the review media. Joyce Carol Oates, for instance, in a slapdash though interesting essay called "Against Nature," speaks of nature writers' "painfully limited set of responses . . . REVERENCE, AWE, PIETY, MYSTICAL ONENESS." She must never have read Mr. Abbey; yet it was characteristic of him that for an hour or two, he might have agreed.

He wrote with exceptional exactitude and an uncommonly honest and logical understanding of causes and consequences, but he also loved argument, churlishness, and exaggeration. Personally, he was a labyrinth of anger and generosity, shy but arresting because of his mixture of hillbilly with cowboy qualities, and even when silent, appeared bigger than life. He had hitchhiked west from Appalachia for the first time at seventeen, for what became an immediate love match, and, I'm sure, slept out more nights under the stars than all of his current competitors combined. He was uneven, self-indulgent as a writer, and sometimes scanted his talent by working too fast. But he had about him an authenticity that springs from the page and is beloved by a rising generation of readers who have enabled his early collection of rambles, *Desert Solitaire* (1968), to run through eighteen printings in mass-market paperback and his fine comic novel, *The Monkey Wrench Gang* (1975), to sell half a million copies. Both books, indeed, have inspired a new eco-guerrilla environmental organization called Earth First!, whose other patron saint is Ned Ludd (from whom the Luddites took their name), though it's perhaps no more radical than John Muir's Sierra Club appeared to be in 1892, when that group was formed.

Like many good writers, Abbey dreamed of producing "The Fat Masterpiece," as he called the "nuvvle" he had worked on for the last dozen years, which was supposed to boil everything down to a thousand pages. When edited in half, it came out in 1988 as *The Fool's Progress*, an autobiographical yarn that lunges cross-country several times, full of apt descriptions and antic fun—*Ginger Man* stuff—though not with the coherence or poignancy he had hoped for. A couple of his other novels hold up fairly well too: *Black Sun* and *The Brave Cowboy*, which came out in movie form, starring Kirk Douglas and Walter Matthau, in 1962 (*Lonely Are the Brave*) and brought Abbey a munificent $7,500.

I do think he wrote masterpieces, but they were more slender: the essays in *Desert Solitaire* and an equivalent sampler that you might put together from subsequent collections like *Down the River, Beyond the Wall*, and *The Journey Home*. His rarest strength was in being concise, because he really knew what he thought and cared for. He loved the desert—"red mountains like mangled iron"—liked people in smallish clusters, and didn't mince words in saying that industrial rapine, glitz malls, and tract sprawl were an abomination heralding more devastating events. While writing as handsomely as others do, he never lost sight of the fact that much of Creation is rapidly being destroyed. "Growth for the sake of growth is the ideology of the cancer cell," he wrote. And he adopted for a motto Walt Whitman's line: "Resist much, obey little." Another was Thoreau's summary in *Walden*: "If I repent of anything, it is very likely to be my good behavior. What demon possessed me that I behaved so well?"

Abbey traveled less than some writers do, but it is not necessary to go dithering around our suffering planet, visiting the Amazon, Indonesia, Bhutan, and East Africa. The crisis is plain in anyone's neck of the woods, and the exoticism of globe-trotting may only blur one's vision. Nor do we need to become mystical Transcendentalists and commune with God. ("One Life at a Time, Please" is another of Abbey's titles. On his hundreds of camping trips he tended to observe and enjoy the wilds rather than submerge his soul.) What is needed is honesty, a pair of eyes, and a further dollop of fortitude to spit the truth out, not genuflecting to "Emersonian" optimism, or journalistic traditions of staying deadpan, or the saccharine pressures of magazine editors who want their readers to feel good. Emerson would be roaring with heartbreak and Thoreau would be raging with grief in these 1990s. *Where were you when the world burned? Get mad, for a change, for heaven's sake!* I believe they would say to milder colleagues.

Abbey didn't sell to the big book clubs or reach best-sellerdom or collect major prizes. When, at sixty, he was offered a smallish one by the American Academy of Arts and Letters, he rejected it with a fanfare of rhetoric, probably because it had come too late. War-horse that he was, he did not find a ready market in mainstream publications of any stripe and was relegated through most of his career by the publicity arm of publishing to the death trap of "naturalist" stuff. So the success, wholly word-of-mouth, of *The Monkey Wrench Gang* in paperback pleased him more than anything else, and he delighted in telling friends who the real-life counterparts were for its characters, Seldom Seen Smith, Bonnie Abbzug, and George Washington Hayduke. They, too, had torn down billboards, yanked up survey stakes, poured sand into bulldozer gas tanks, and sabotaged "certain monstrosities" in fragilely scenic regions that shouldn't need free-lance protection in the first place, as "Seldom Seen" says, still taciturn now, when you call him up.

"Abbzug" speaks of how Abbey in real life would go through three (used) cars a year, bouncing across the Sonoran desert on his pleasure jaunts, peeling the plates off of each as it died. And when they got fooling, he would laugh till he had to come up for air, then laugh some more, even once when they'd broken down a great many miles from water and thought they were doomed, with only a bottle of wine to live on. Most good writers are walkers, but Abbey was something different, ranging the Southwest afoot or river running with somewhat the scope of John Muir in the High Sierras. It was the building of Hetch Hetchy Dam in Yosemite National Park (now thought to have been unnecessary for San Francisco's water needs) that finally embittered Muir; and the unfinished business of "monkeywrenching" in *The Monkey Wrench Gang* is to blow up Glen Canyon Dam, a structure that, before Abbey's eyes, had drowned a whole stretch of the Colorado River's most pristine, precious canyons.

Robinson Jeffers, another regionalist of fluctuating popularity, who made of the close examination of his home country at Big Sur in California a prism to look at the rest of the world, concluded in several poems that mankind had turned into "a sick microbe," a "deformed ape," "a botched experiment that has run wild and ought to be stopped." In "The Broken Balance" (1929) he spoke for Abbey's anger as well:

> *The beautiful places killed like rabbits to make a*
> *   city,*
> *The spreading fungus, the slime-threads*
> *And spores . . . I remember the farther*
> *Future, and the last man dying*
> *Without succession under the confident eyes of the*
> *   stars.*

"Let's keep things the way they were," Abbey liked to say. Yet he was a bold, complex man who had had five wives and five children by the end of his life; and although he spilled too much energy into feuds with his allies and friends, he was often a jubilant writer, a regular gleeman, not just a threnodist, and wanted to be remembered as a writer of "that letter which is never finished"—literature—such as *Desert Solitaire* is.

We corresponded occasionally for twenty years, wanting to go for a lengthy sail on the Sea of Cortez or go camping somewhere in the hundred-mile Air Force gunnery range which for its isolation eventually became another favorite redoubt of his. I hoped we could drift down the Yukon River together and compile a dual diary. ("Is that dual or *duel?*" he asked once.) He had lived in Hoboken, New Jersey, for a couple of years while unhappily married, with the "Vampire State Building" on the skyline—also in Scotland and Italy—and responded to Manhattan's incomparably gaudy parade of faces as a cosmopolitan, though marked, himself, as an outlander by his uncut grayish beard, slow speech, earnest eyes, red-dog-road shuffle, raw height and build, and jean jacket or shabby brown tweed. On his way home to Oracle, Arizona, he'd usually stop in the Alleghenies, after conferring in New York City with editors, to visit his mother, Mildred, a Woman's Christian Temperance Union veteran, and his father, Paul Revere Abbey, a registered Socialist and old Wobbly organizer, who'd met Eugene V. Debs in his youth and has toured Cuba and still cuts hickory fence posts in the woods for a living.

Abbey was a writer who liked to play poker with cowboys, while continuing to ridicule the ranch owners who overgraze the West's ravaged grasslands. The memorial picnic for him in Saguaro National Monument outside Tucson went on for twelve hours; and besides readings performed with rock-bottom affection, there was beer drinking, lovemaking, gunfire, and music, much as he had hoped. The potluck stew was from two "slow elk," as he liked to call beef cattle poached from particularly greedy entrepreneurs on the public's wildlands. He was an "egalitarian," he said—by which he meant that all wildlife and the full panoply of natural vegetation have a right to live equal to man's—and these beeves had belonged to a cowman who specialized in hounding Arizona's scarce mountain lions.

Abbey died of internal bleeding from a circulatory disorder, with a few weeks' notice of how sick he was. Two days before the event, he decided to leave the hospital, wishing to die in the desert, and at sunup had himself disconnected from the tubes and machinery. His wife, Clarke, and three friends drove him out of town as far as his condition allowed. They built a campfire for him to look at, until, feeling death at hand, he crawled into his sleeping bag with Clarke. But by noon, finding he was still alive and possibly better, he asked to be taken home and placed on a mattress on the floor of his writing cabin. There he said his gentle goodbyes.

His written instructions were that he should be "transported in the bed of a pickup truck" deep into the desert and buried anonymously, wrapped in his sleeping bag, in a beautiful spot where his grave would never be found, with "lots of rocks" piled on top to keep the coyotes off. Abbey of course loved coyotes (and, for that matter, buzzards) and had played the flute to answer their howls during the many years he had earned his living watching for fires from government towers on the Grand Canyon's North Rim, on Aztec Peak in Tonto National Forest, and in Glacier National Park, before he finally won tenure as a "Fool Professor" at the University of Arizona. His friend who was the model for G. W. Hayduke in *The Monkey Wrench Gang* was squatting beside him on the floor as his life ebbed away—"Hayduke," under a real-life name, is a legend in his own right in parts of the West, a contemporary mountain man who returned to Tucson as to a "calving ground" several years ago when he wanted to have children—and the last smile that crossed Abbey's face was when "Hayduke" told him where he would be put.

The place is, inevitably, a location where mountain lions, antelope, bighorn sheep, deer, and javelinas leave tracks, where owls, poor-wills, and coyotes hoot, rattlesnakes crawl, and cacomistles scratch, with a range of stiff terrain overhead, and greasewood, rabbitbush, ocotillo, and noble old cactuses about. First seven, then ten buzzards gathered while the grave was being dug; but, as he had wished, it *was* a rocky spot. "Hayduke" jumped into the hole to be sure it felt O.K. before laying Abbey in, and afterward, in a kind of reprise of the antic spirit that animates *The Monkey Wrench Gang* (and that should make anybody but a developer laugh out loud), went around heaping up false rock piles at ideal grave sites throughout the Southwest, because this last peaceful act of outlawry on Abbey's part was the gesture of legend, and there will be seekers for years.

The stuff of legend: like Thoreau's serene passage from life muttering the words "moose" and "Indian," and Muir's thousand-mile walks to Georgia, or in the Sierras, "the Range of Light." Can he be compared to them? Muir, after all, bullied the Catskills naturalist John Burroughs from sheer orneriness, as Abbey, the controversialist, regularly blistered his colleagues with vitriol through the mails, and Thoreau—a

stark individual in his own way—orated vehemently on behalf of the reviled "terrorist" John Brown. (That Thoreau of
witticisms such as what a pearl was: "the hardened tear of a
diseased clam, murdered in its old age.") A magazine published Abbey's last account of a trip by horseback through
Utah's slick-rock canyons, and it's got a hop like a knuckle-
ball's on it, unmistakably Abbey, as briny with personality as
his heyday essays. Nor had twenty years changed him. Thoreau, by contrast, in a swift incandescent burst of work,
vaulted from the relatively conventional *Week on the Concord
and Merrimack Rivers* to the vision of *Walden*, but soon fell
back into dutiful natural science. And Muir went from being
a lone-wolf botanist and geologist to a passionate advocate,
skillfully lobbying Teddy Roosevelt and William Howard
Taft on behalf of Yosemite National Park, until, late in life,
when he was finished with localism, he wandered rather dis-
consolately to Africa, Asia, and South America in celebrity
guise.

Abbey was consistent but, unlike Thoreau, was not self-
contained; some compulsive agenda unknown to him
blunted his efforts to surpass himself. And his ambitions were
confined to truth telling, rhapsody, and the lambasting of
villains. As an essayist he did not aspire to the grandeur of
versatility, or try hard to turn into a man of letters either—
his novels can seem flat or foreshortened next to Peter Matthiessen's, for example, and his literary pronouncements
were scattershot, bilious, or cursory. Like most conservationists, he was a political radical but a social conservative, going
so far as to aver the old-fashioned idea that there are two
sexes, not simply one, which, expressed with his customary
crowing, abrasive overstatement, offended people. (Yet he
wrote in a love letter to a woman friend after a breakup, "If
you ever need me in any way I will cross continents and
oceans to help you," a sentiment that even his favorite *bête
noire*, Gloria Steinem, might have appreciated.) Speaking of
various sins of omission of his personal life, he would sometimes describe himself as a coward—as being a neglectful
father to his sons and a passive witness to his second wife's
death by cancer, in particular.

There's a saying that life gets better once you have outlived the bastards, which would certainly be true except that

257

as you do, you are also outliving your friends. I miss him. Sitting in silence in restaurants as our twinned melancholy groped for expression, or talking with him of hoodoo stone pillars and red-rock canyons, I've seldom felt closer to anybody. Honesty is a key to essay writing: not just "a room of one's own" but a view of one's own. The lack of it sinks more talented people into chatterbox hackwork than anything else. And Abbey aspired to speak for himself in all honesty—*X: His Mark*—and died telling friends he had done what he could and was ready. He didn't buzz off to Antarctica or the Galápagos Islands, yet no one will ever wonder what he really saw as the world burned. He said it; didn't sweeten it or blink at it or water it down or hope the web of catastrophes might just go away. He felt homesick for the desert when he went to Alaska, and turned back, yet if you travel much there, it is Abbey's words you will see tacked on the wall again and again in remote homestead cabins in the Brooks Range or in offices in Juneau, because he had already written of greed, of human brutality and howling despair, better than writers who write books on Alaska.

Last year a paean to Abbey's work in *National Review* finished with a quote from a passage in Faulkner: "*Oleh, Chief. Grandfather.*" To which we can add Amen. But instead let's close with a bit of Ed Abbey, from a minor book called *Appalachian Wilderness* (1970), which foretold why he chose that lost grave where he lies:

> How strange and wonderful is our home, our earth, with its swirling vaporous atmosphere, its flowing and frozen liquids, its trembling plants, its creeping, crawling, climbing creatures, the croaking things with wings that hang on rocks and soar through fog, the furry grass, the scaly seas . . . how utterly rich and wild. . . . Yet some among us have the nerve, the insolence, the brass, the gall to whine about the limitations of our earthbound fate and yearn for some more perfect world beyond the sky. We are none of us good enough for the world we have.

O Wyoming

S*aturday, September 3.* My nineteen-year-old daughter, Molly, and I have driven from Vermont to Dubois, Wyoming, to enjoy an eight-day pack trip along the southern edge of Yellowstone National Park. But smoke palls the town. Most of the customers at the Branding Iron Motel (which has a corral for people to park their horses in overnight) are Apache women from the San Carlos reserve in Arizona, who are here to earn $6.38 an hour on the fire lines—with yellow coats made of survival cloth, red backpacks, hard hats, kit bags, canteens, and other gear piled on the lawn. At the laundromat across the highway, the scent of smoke is everywhere—drawling, burly men in town for a couple of days are calling the Dakotas on the pay telephone and washing heaps of redolent clothes (redolent with memories for me, because I fought forest fires in California in 1953), between pit stops at the Outlaw Saloon or the Rustic Pine Bar, "The World's Most Unique." However, the conflagration burning what will wind up being a third of the park this very dry summer has crossed what was to have been our route, so we've changed our plans, with the idea of exploring part of the Absaroka range, a spur of the Rockies just outside Yellowstone's southeast boundary. (*Ab-*

saroka was the Crow Indian word for "Crow," and the range was a contested territory for the Crows and Shoshones.)

We've been riding for several days in Jakey's Fork and Torrey Canyon, two valleys of the Wind River Range, another core spur of the Rockies, which is also touched by the Continental Divide, for the extraordinary beauty there and to get our sea legs under us, in a manner of speaking, or to warp our legs into the weird-feeling shape horseback riders' have. Riding on a "lower" animal may fit very well with the human ego, but not with the human physique. All that personable meat and muscle moving under me—a whole butcher shop's worth, by the standards of the city—is terribly touching and comradely. I don't ride very well, but twenty or thirty years ago I did some riding and have happy memories and a feel for negotiating with horses. Besides, even though in this day and age he will be sold for forty cents a pound to make dog food when he slows down (yes, even here in the cowboys' "wild" West: specifically, he will be shipped to a vast abattoir in North Platte, Nebraska, to be knocked on the head), a horse is a quirkily sentient creature, like us, sometimes cheerful or conscientious, sometimes gloomy or rebellious or conniving.

Because it's the end of the dude ranching season and the horses are about to be driven some miles away to their winter range on the Shoshone Indians' reservation, where they'll go "barefoot" till spring, we had been put on a miscellany of horses who hadn't yet lost their shoes. But now, on our pack trip, led by Press Stephens, vice-president of the Wyoming Outfitters Association and a resident of Shell, Wyoming, a village of fifty people in the Big Horn Mountains northeasterly of where we are, I am on Buffalo. Buffalo is a strawberry roan with frost on his rump, only seven years old but until recently an actual wild horse, a young stallion roaming Nevada's Ruby Mountains until he was captured, castrated, branded, and shod. Though he carries people on his back just for about three months a year, he has adjusted quickly to domestication and has managed to take my measure in almost no time. In his case this revolves around the question of whether I will slacken my reins enough for him to snatch mouthfuls of food by the wayside as we travel along. I know that, on principle, a rider shouldn't, or his ride will become purely an occasion for the horse's eating, irregular in direction, all fits and starts. But on the other hand, in my middle age, I've turned more benign than I used to be, no stickler for rules, and more hopeful that people and animals will enjoy their lives.

Lars, a contemporary of mine, a patent lawyer from New York City, a large athletic man who eats, walks, and sometimes even talks prodigiously, and like me is a dude on this trip, seems to be the same way. He sits on his horse in the manner of Sancho Panza, with the reins in a nobly insouciant droop, and lets his beast eat so often on the narrow trails that I end up impatiently barging ahead and not letting Buffalo eat on the trail at all.

Lars, because of his size and crew-cut and half-hidden but overall competence, looks like an army colonel, but we have a real colonel along, Lars's friend Pat, an artillery officer from Arkansas and West Point—chairman of the English Department there, in fact—a smallish, red-faced, appealing man whose tales of Korea and Vietnam contrast with a present enthusiasm for teaching Virginia Woolf.

We packed out of a trailhead at Brooks Lake, above Dubois, and, after a few miles of climbing Brooks Lake Creek, went over the Continental Divide at Bear Cub Pass, from the Wind River (which is to say, the Missouri and Mississippi River) drainage to the Snake River (which is to say, the Columbia River) drainage. Wyoming is the classic state for basin-and-range, sagebrush-and-bunchgrass, parkland-and-forest scenery. It's the New England of the West in the sense that it's the founding fathers' West, haunt of the mountainmen and site of the early trappers' rendezvous on the Green River, not far from where we are, and then of quintessential cowboying.

Over the Divide, on the Pacific side, the stands of spruces get a little more serious about being spruces, and lovely sloping meadows alternate with them, and serious, speaking cliffs loom above the sidehills. After descending to Cub Creek, we went up it and camped by and by on a white sandy flat at eight thousand feet among lodgepole pines and knee-high willows, where a modest trickly brook comes in. The sky has stayed turquoise blue most of the time, except when the wind shifts Yellowstone way and carries smoke from the fires over us, acrid and propelling charred clouds, though, even so, we are somewhat sheltered from it. Molly and I unsaddled the horses and helped with the ten packhorses, while Lars and the literary colonel helped Press put up the tents, and their wives, Marit and Ann, helped his wife—my old friend Gretel—set up the part of the camp devoted to nourishment. Press and Jack Swenson, his horse wrangler, were talking about what they call "horse wrecks," which is just as it sounds: pack trains derailed on a mountainside.

This high country was too snowy for Indians to live in regularly, but they hunted elk, moose, and bighorn sheep here, as whites do now. Press, our leader, is mid-thirties, a converted Easterner or self-created cowboy from Atlanta (his father a Coca-Cola executive), by way of South Kent School in Connecticut (where at sixteen he started chewing tobacco, he says), Bowdoin College in Maine, and a year playing rugby and studying art history at the University of Madrid. He has been doing this sort of thing for the past eighteen summers, though he also rodeoed off and on for about the first ten years after he got here. He compares that sport to fast downhill skiing in the rhythmic techniques and physical prowess required, having quit both (and chewing tobacco, "another stupid thing") at about the same time. He is strong, tall, and—as this is his last tourist trip of a strenuous season— thin, with a twisty grin, a fin of a nose, and a gusty voice, slurring his words in a tenor monotone that sounds like the wind. He's a gentle man—Gretel met him at a John Wayne movie festival in midwinter, where they'd each gone to alleviate bouts of cabin fever, and she noticed him because he had tears in his eyes—who loves these mountains and reels off the names of dozens of creeks, trails, routes and passes, aspects of mountains, and private hideouts for camping whenever he can possibly bring them into the conversation. He wears red suspenders, which he likes to pluck when introducing himself and launching into a little peroration, almost as if he were a tall-tale spinner, but otherwise is modest about everything except his dislikes. As is the case with so many people who make their living outdoors, serving as hosts in the wilderness, he has by now had a bellyful of guiding sport hunters, is sick of the butchery of the hunting season (this week beginning again); is sick of gun blasts, elk "murdered," black bears, antelope, and moose knocked over, not for food anymore but for stranger motives.

Because of our inexperience and despite Press's deft assistance, it takes us about four hours to set up or strike camp, which in this era of backpacking seems like a turn-of-the-century way to go about traveling, but on the other hand, somebody in my kind of shape couldn't go far anymore in this tall terrain except on the back of a horse. We eat well too—no freeze-dried food—and the conversation has more spaciousness, I suspect, more elevation, more of a frame of reference, animal, vegetable, mineral, than if we were walking. Press used to teach history-of-civilization night courses at Central Wyoming College (or "Country-and-Western College," as they called it), while wintering on an Indian reservation, watching an outfitter's herd of horses, and intriguing juxtapositions come naturally to him. And Gretel Ehrlich, with *The Solace of Open Spaces,* has emerged lately as a star writer of this region. She has just won a Guggenheim Fellowship, whose first check she spent on a new refrigerator and on bailing a friend out of jail. Over the ten years I've known her, she has added gravity to her beauty and other substantial virtues and sits her horse at the rear of our caravan with the look of a matriarchal squaw (or Georgia O'Keeffe)—solid and still, observant and straight. Her small dog, Rusty, a Kelpie–Blue Heeler cross, trots inseparably a few paces behind her.

Though we're both animal lovers, we irritate each other by "spoiling," respectively, Rusty and Buffalo. I don't think she should encourage Rusty to eat off her plate; she doesn't approve of my feeding Buffalo my orange peels while taming him down. Besides, as a wild horse, won't he get a belly-ache? Press and she ask. Where could he ever have digested such tastes before? I laugh, being a native New Yorker talking to Wyoming ranchers: "Don't think you know all the tastes of the wilderness just because you live here! Any spirited horse that lives wild will have tasted dead fish in a stream and carrion killed by a snowslide for the sake of the salts they have." Gretel laughs in return and tells me that Rusty is her psychiatrist and deserves to eat off her plate. He does indeed listen whenever she speaks, cocking his head like the RCA Victrola dog.

Jack, the wrangler, who sings Jimmy Buffett songs to the little horse herd as he rounds them up near dawn, is five years younger than Press, ten years younger than Gretel, and twenty-five years younger than me. He's a likably knockabout ornithological field assistant, wildlife photographer, and adventure guide, who has recently studied shearwaters in Hawaii and has counted the catch on Russian trawlers for the U.S. government. He plans, not long after our trip is over, to go to the Himalayas in search of a yeti to take pictures of. Says he will look for one at between eight and twelve thousand feet, just the sort of altitude conducive to such a creature's good health but where climbers from Europe and America, ambitious for K^2 or Everest, don't bother to stop.

Sunday, September 4. Today we rode to the head of Cub Creek, at a level of ten thousand feet. Saw a sharp-shinned hawk, a Swainson's hawk, a raven family stunting, magpies, several sets of elk tracks, some bear-bashed logs, some dashingly black-and-white Clark's nutcrackers flying overhead, heard gray jays whistling, and saw a goldeneye duck on a pond. It has rained in these mountains only twice all summer, and every form of plant life has retrenched to its survival mode, but high up here, the melting snowfields have kept the creeks flowing and the water table close under the soil.

I should mention that the lenses inside my eyes are clouding over with cataracts—this seemed like a good way to spend the time waiting for an eye operation, taking my daughter for her first trip out West. So when I say that we've seen a sharp-shinned hawk, I mean that my friend Jack did. I, too, am interested in hawks and yetis, but I see most inaccurately at this point. The big old silvery blowdowns in the forest look like silver horsemen to me. The packhorses standing together look like mounted Indians. Masses of trees spread over a sidehill look like Paul Bunyan and Babe, his legendary blue ox. But I do see the smoke crimson the sun or block the passes on both sides of us periodically, like a windborne narrative of the conflagration in Yellowstone, which is two or three dozen miles from us at its leading edge. But the fire doesn't preoccupy me, as it does Press and Gretel, because this isn't my home and I long ago removed my heart's strings from Wyoming (I, too, was here in my teens, when a first visit counts) to Alaska, where there is more space and time. I wrote Yellowstone off. What I really care about are the evolving tragedies of bureaucratic mismanagement in Alaska's wildlands.

Cub Creek heads at a flat pretty pass, and we rode over that to the head of the south branch of the South Fork of the Buffalo River, one of the Snake's largest tributaries, eating our luncheon sandwiches next to a collection of tiny black springs that popped from the raw tundra soil, where we were squeaked at by voles while Press described the vicissitudes of doing an oral history of your hometown, each family complaining about the "play" it received, or absence thereof.

Sticker, our strongest, most independent-minded packhorse, who Buffalo pals with, was "Indian-broke," as they say, and also was a bucking horse for a while, till one day he simply stopped bucking: realized it wasn't necessary. He is head shy and won't tolerate being examined or stared at, but will stand still to be loaded or unloaded as long as nobody looks at him. All of these horses are leased from a man who owns nine hundred and fifty, picking them up wholesale roundabout by the semi-rig load and looking them over when he gets home, walking through his corrals, figuring out which can be used to carry dudes, which for cowboys, which for packing, which for rodeos, and which should go straight to North Platte for Fido to eat. Buffalo, being a "government horse," from federal land, with whitish numbers that were freeze-dried into his neck when he was caught, cost the man only a $125 adoption fee.

These high-altitude trees "feed" by straightening up, not spreading out to catch the sun, probably in order to offer the heavy snows a slimmer target, but just below timberline they're grouped talkily enough, in clusters. We saw a moose with its dinglebell swinging and a hatrack perched on its head, augering fast up into the timber from a willow swale. The avalanches here architecture the timber into ribs along the side ridges, cutting chutes that determine where anything lives; because we're in steep country now. We've followed new forks off of forks, the trail dipping down, then scrabbling up through scree and brush, to a "nameless drainage," as Press puts it, at the head of the north branch of the

South Fork of the Buffalo River, a little ways from the shoulder of Wall Mountain (11,600 feet), and near one head of the Yellowstone River too. Yellowstone water, however, eventually reaches the Gulf of Mexico through the Mississippi, but Buffalo water reaches the coast of Oregon, so we are camping on a slant of ground by a frigid swift mini-watercourse among stubby chest-high spruces a few hundred feet below the Continental Divide.

Press says he loves these wild camps: "The wild specter to it. There's a magic about timberline, a mystery to why the trees grow just exactly to here and not ten yards further." This is the highest and roughest place he's ever stayed with a party, and for the latrine he has dug a "four-day hole," choosing a noble outlook for the throne. Besides canvas and food, his essential kit is an ax, a shovel, a bow saw, and a pistol. At this altitude the snows of the fall could begin falling anytime now. That's what Press, Jack, and Gretel joke about, whereas we tourists joke about bears, specifically a "timberline bear," a grizzly you can't climb a tree from. Jack had seen the tracks of a grizzly making its way along this creek as we rode up, and for a while, with field glasses, thought he might have spotted a bighorn or a bear among boulders or clumps of vegetation on the far ridge, thrown into relief against the backdrop of the blue sky, but after two hours it still hasn't moved.

Labor Day, September 5. Molly is a pretty good rider and is of course delighted to have nineteen horses to watch and get her hands on. But her deeper pleasure in what we are doing has transformed her face: more glee than sophistication, and as "boyish" as "girlish." Presumably it has transformed mine too. Lars, only thirty-six hours out of Newark Airport, is an astonishing athlete, climbing our ridge, up and over, leading the "assault" on Wall Mountain. And Jack, still more light-legged and in training for his pursuit of the yeti of myth, did the same climb in only a T-shirt and shorts. As the group's senior member, I was glad to stop partway up, once we had crossed the Divide, and laze on the bank of a lovely green tarn with a single duck floating on it and the tracks of an itinerant coyote and a couple of elk discernible in the moss at the outlet, where Bliss Creek starts.

Bliss Creek (or "Crick," as they say) is named not for ecstatic emotions but for a horse rustler who made his home in its meadows, two thousand feet lower than we are, and used to steal horses in the vicinity of Cody, Wyoming, east of the Divide, and bring them up here and over to the settlement of Jackson, on the Pacific side, then steal a few Jackson horses and drive them up and over through here and sell them in Cody. It worked for a time, till in 1896 he was hanged at the creek's mouth.

Bliss, which goes into the Shoshone River, then the Bighorn River, the Yellowstone, the Missouri, the Mississippi, and the Gulf of Mexico, finally—like the nameless mini-creek that rushes past our camp, a mile away, and that flows instead to the Buffalo River, the Snake River, the Columbia, and the Pacific—starts just as upwellings of black water from thimble-sized springs seeping underground from the white remnants of the winter's snowfields. But Bliss immediately slices into a series of corkscrew clefts, sharply dropping, which I enjoy staring down into through my binocs, when I'm not following Lars's hiking feats above me on Wall Mountain. He's such an enthusiast that, discovering a hundred-dollar bill in one of his pockets this morning, he wanted to fling it away. "What use is money!" He's asking Press about buying a ranch somewhere around here, "to preserve this way of life," and is thinking about digging a latrine as admirable as Press's in his own hundred acres of woods on the Hudson when he gets home. Speaking of permanences, we're finding chunks of petrified wood amid about ten thousand years' worth of volcanic ash. But along most every ridgeline, summits or spurs of rock poke up like turtle or camel or bobcat heads, or ancestral otters, bears, vultures, and other totems. Our horses—which are brought in to lick salt and remember their provenance every morning, even when we don't plan to use them—were found this morning under a giant statue of Lenin at timberline on another creek.

I had a friendly dream last night: a friendly woman, encountered by chance, who wanted to make love with me. Breakfast was Cream of the West cereal and Western Family creamer in our coffee. Small throngs of rosy finches are larking about, and we've seen water ouzels, water pipits, and three red-tailed hawks chasing a Swainson's hawk. Fireweed fluff is blowing, and there are harebells and asters. The ground is honeycombed with voles' holes, and pikas live here, storing small hay piles. Yesterday's "timberline bear" is still stationary, but our hay-colored gulch leads up to the rim of the world with only a backing of sky. That's where the tarn is, and the black wall of Wall Mountain, and the plunge down toward life-giving forests again, a place where people can live. At the inlet of the black-and-green tarn, thirty acres of water surrounded by spongy tundra and a litter of lichen-decorated (green and red) rocks, we saw three migrating Baird's sandpipers—Arctic nesters that winter high up in the Andes—picking up tiny crustaceans or nymphs. I drank Mississippi-destined water, thinking of Pilottown, the ultimate village that stands by a boardwalk on stilts at the very mouth of that river, where I've visited, a hundred-plus miles below New Orleans, and all the turbid life these snow waters are going to pass between here and there. Then I followed the record of horse shit back to camp, till I heard the neck bells.

Ordinarily one looks from a cold aerie like this toward the forest as a refuge where one could build a campfire in an emergency, or climb a tree. (I remember an Eskimo telling me that that was the difference between his race and mine: Mine couldn't bear living long without trees.) And except for the human face and form, no sight is more precious and tender to a person undergoing the sensations of dimming eyesight than the incredible shapes of trees. Yet nevertheless, with the sky turning charred, the air smelling barbecued whenever the wind blows news of the fires our way, we get chatty and gay for a moment, realizing the one zone that's safe is where we are. No fire can trap and incinerate us above timberline.

Tuesday, September 6. The wind buffeted our tent all night with boisterous, mean gusts, though fortunately from the south, blowing sand and not snow. Molly talked to her mother in her sleep, saying, "I'm all right. I'm not hungry. I'm not cold." Reassuring words, but I wake up abruptly with anxiety if she coughs or talks. Her posture when riding is sort of great, and she looks golden-faced when the sun hits the frames of her glasses, but at least since the age of eight she has been worrying me by choosing in macho fashion (origins unknown: certainly not me) to underdress when possible against chilly winds.

Another personage I've worried about subliminally is Buffalo, whose gait has become a bit humpety or wobbly. I should have called for a consultation (to be truthful, I'm such a tyro at riding that I've never saddled a horse unassisted). But finally Press noticed and found that a nail from his left hind shoe was scratching the frog of his foot, and—calling him "Son" to soothe him—has reshod that hoof.

The stream is bruisingly cold when we wash (to the eye, like seething pewter), and lighting the little steel stove becomes life's focus, while we hear the wind hiss, and wait for the sunshine on the rimrock of the west ridge to slide slowly down nearer us, and for the dwarf willows to collect yellows, and for the short spruces on the east slope to invent individual long shadows. It's another uncannily cloudless day with no hint of the fire, if the wind stays southeasterly. We leave our camp where it is for another night and ride up on the whaleback ridges west of Wall Mountain, seeing a prairie falcon sailing over the bare alpine heath, and a ferruginous hawk, and rosy finches tumultuously flocking, perhaps after snow fleas, and a migrating goshawk crossing the Continental Divide and then diving down toward the squirrely spruce woods again, where it belongs. We come to the head of Wallace Creek and then to the head of Turner's Fork, which is named for Press's old boss, so he jumps down to have a taste of its water; and we go up onto an ultimate knob of rock at 11,300 feet—Jack Swenson all the time afoot, bare-armed and in shorts, though the temperature is in the forties, in training for his pursuit in a couple of months of the Abominable Snowman in Nepal.

From this knob of the Divide, above the Buffalo Plateau of the Teton National Forest, we look down at Simpson Meadow, and at Jack Davis Peak, which is named for the "last old-time cowboy in the Jackson region," says Press, who knew him, and at the south fork of the Marston Fork of the Shoshone River. Also across at Yount's Peak, farther off, at the headwaters of the North and South forks of the Yellowstone River (and named for Yellowstone's first game warden), and at Thorofare Mountain, which separates Yellowstone water from the Thorofare River. Beyond them we cannot see because of the vast gulf of smoke being churned up by the so-called Mink Fire, a little way down the Yellowstone. The scope of this fire (like the halving of Yellowstone Park's grizzly population recently) seems to be a result of bureaucratic meddling, however well-intentioned, in a wilderness of terribly limited area, an area insufficient to absorb misguided planning. So as I see what's going on, I'm glad that after loving Wyoming in my teens, I tied my heart's strings to Alaska, with wildlands a hundred times larger, postponing being utterly heartsick over something like this.

Riding about, we see springs that are the very sources of the Snake and Shoshone rivers. See ridges like animals' heads, and ridges like rows of molars, and the wonderful amplitude of the saddles swinging in between, with, a bit lower, convivial-looking trees placed talkatively, where the grim avalanche chutes haven't imposed an implacable order. Through glasses we pick out the minute and tentative figures of three sheep on a stratified hump above Simpson Meadow and Lost Creek, our only "game" for these days at timberline; and in the opposite direction see Smokehouse Mountain, Coffin Butte, Crescent Mountain, and Ramshorn Peak, above Frozen Lake Creek. Then the hysterical smoke swallows everything, glowing red from the sun as if from ubiquitous fires that foreshadow the end of the world.

The terrain is like tussocky or mossy moor, interspersed with spindles of shallow soil that supports sedge grass and bluestem hay, or else barrens covered with blackish slag broken into scree. Except on the latter stretches, Buffalo likes loping uphill to overtake any horse that may have gotten ahead of him (particularly if I click my tongue), but then he may suddenly try to rush to one side of our progress, where good grass grows—playfully, as if to convince me that he and I are just on a grazing expedition. Lars, the lawyer, meanwhile is exclaiming to his very dear wife, Marit, a weaver and helpmeet type, how full of possibilities life is. But Pat, our literary artillery colonel (his wife, a fourth-grade schoolteacher, is a fellow Arkansan), is the opposite in the sense that he stays in character even more than he wants to. In these V-cut, ramparted valleys that mount toward the edge of the world, he finds himself irrelevantly figuring where he would place 105- and 155-millimeter howitzers to defend our position, as if this were Korea or Vietnam—both campaigns, he says, having scarred him.

Wednesday, September 7. One is tired of a tent site by the fourth day, having slept at the same head-to-heels slant, on top of the same stones, voles, and willow stubs, for three nights running. This is a harsh, scrabbly environment anyway, with only a veneer of dirt on the basic rocks, and thin stingy air with the imminence of winter on it, up where mammalian life gets difficult. But at the same time all these conditions are exhilarating on a summer day, even if you just walk off somewhere by yourself and lie down spread-eagled, gazing at the convex sky. The closer you are, the bigger it swells.

Jack left to catch the horses at 7:00 A.M. but didn't bring them all in till half-past eleven. Buffalo hangs out with Grump, Arlene, and Sticker, the tough, brown, "Indian-broke" former bucking-bronc packhorse, and they move lots at night; but when faced with a mare named Irene, he lays back his ears. Every horse has nip scars. By talking, feeding him cookies and orange peels, and lingering with him, I've gotten Buffalo willing to hang around camp sometimes when let loose in the evening, until the others are well under way. The cusps of his teeth still mark him as young at age seven. A horse isn't "smooth" in the mouth until ten, Press says.

We have F-15 interceptors accelerating overhead, inflicting sonic booms on this pocket of wilderness because it is marked on the pilots' maps as "uninhabited." Gretel and Molly mutter ironic comments about "men" as they wash the camp dishes (though maybe more at my loafing than at the airplanes).

We rode down a couple of thousand feet in altitude and a distance of three or four miles to camp in a gentler terrain of fine meadowland by a slow piece of stream under big old spruce copses in ground-squirrel and red-squirrel country, choosing a spot where the sunrise will hit us and warm us by eight in the morning, if the smoke keeps blowing toward Oregon instead of toward us. Today was splendid, though we saw no game. What's also remarkable is the absence of wildlife such as elk, sheep, and moose when you glass far-distant slopes out of rifle range.

I've been astonished at the scarcity of animal tracks, because if they should be anywhere, they ought to be here in Wyoming's grass mountains, designated as a national showplace, with prime summer feed, and the drought and fires elsewhere should have funneled them in all the more. It seems to confirm what I'd heard in Dubois about how badly overgrazed and overhunted Wyoming is. This beautiful alpine fodder—sedge grass that's fourteen percent protein—goes untouched because the fall and winter and spring ranges that the animals must depend on during the year's hard seasons are overused. In the Big Horn Mountains, where Press himself lives, he says there is no place that you can go on a wilderness trip without meeting cattle and sheep. It's one reason why he brings his summertime customers here. Wyoming's Fish and Game Department is funded by hunting and fishing license sales, not general state revenues, so there is a maximum emphasis upon kill or "harvest" figures, on game earning cash by being killed, not the attention to conservation matters that occupy fish and game departments whose funding attunes them to other concerns. And much of the old winter range has been carved up for summer homes (called "ranchettes") or grows sugar beets and beer barley, besides the miles devoted to cattle. It's important that the cowboy heritage be maintained in this setting of its heyday, but in this age of cheap instant travel, when these last roadless paradises like Yellowstone *do* really belong to everybody, the question is even more urgent whether beef should be the emphasis here, in competition with rare, dwindling collections of wildlife, instead of in states like Georgia, which are already more efficient producers of beef than any part of the Old West. Georgia can't preserve for the rest of us herds of elk, abundant moose, healthy scatterings of bighorn sheep and grizzly bears, wilderness meadows, creeks, and forests, and a sense of what the Wild was.

Thursday, September 8. Before sunrise the valley was misty, though the billowy-looking mountains and frog-headed ridges at the far end rose out of the pretty white haze (not, I think, smoke)—raw land that is "holding the world together," as a farmer I know back in Vermont says of his own patch of undeveloped acreage. I walked with the light-legged Jack up to a trail on the slope opposite our camp to look at some bear tracks. I'd thought I'd seen grizzly tracks yesterday along a creek bank but foolishly hadn't jumped off my horse to check for sure, presuming somebody coming along behind me, with better eyesight, would confirm them. We see bear tracks because grizzlies are protected here, unlike other game. These new ones were fresh and clear, and from the precision of the claw marks we assumed they were a small grizzly's. Anyway, they went in both directions, as if he or she had made a round trip, so I followed them—"Follow the toes," I kept saying to myself—toward the bear's first destination, to find out what he'd been after. They led me a couple of miles through a lovely wide saddle between Crescent Mountain and Coffin Butte, a spacious high pass, which itself crossed the Continental Divide, with two patchy glaciers above me on my right. At the head of Du Noir Creek, which flows sixty miles southeastward to the town of Dubois, then into the Wind River, the Bighorn River, and eventually the Mississippi, I found a cluster of white-barked pine trees, whose nuts are a principal food for bears fattening for hibernation at these altitudes. The creek cuts a humpy but precipitous slot in the crumbly conglomerate rock, and I sat looking down into that and across up at the streaks of silver meltwater running down the pitch of Coffin Butte from remnant snow and the shrinking little glaciers. "Hold out a week or two more, and there'll be new snow!" I told them loudly. It was an impeccably balmy day, as happy for me as when I'd sat by the green glacial tarn at the head of Bliss Creek, gazing down at the corkscrew slit of that water's course toward the Shoshone River, except that today, in effect, I had the bear's company.

Starting back, I followed his or her returning tracks to a shallow turquoise lake immediately east of the Divide, where a sheep had incised half a dozen footprints in the bank when it had come down to drink. I lay there in the veldt-tan grass of the watershed saddle a long while, picturing myself as bear bait, both hoping and fearing that Toes would return, and so still that a hawk stooped over me and buzzed me repeatedly to see what my condition was. My condition under that turquoise sky by that turquoise lake was happy! And at suppertime I headed home. In up-and-down country, the country is everywhere, and the wind was all wrong for stealth now, alerting any wild animals that might be ahead of me, but I got glad about that.

Friday, September 9. Press and Jack like to joke that their outfit runs "on diamond hitches and duct tape," everything is so thoroughly taped up. I'm the same. Yesterday I lost my binoculars from not being able to see where I had put them, and today a crown on my back tooth fell out. I was nauseous at first, expecting pain, but when the pain didn't come I stopped feeling nauseous. I remind myself that sometimes a dude is doing his share just by keeping up, filling his belly.

"A horse that farts will never tire./A man who farts is the man to hire," says Press. He is "on a See-Food diet. If I see food I eat it." He's reading the fine writer Jim Harrison and slinging the "bear box" up and down from a tall tree limb night and morning. He speaks of the people in Wyoming who don't live by tourism—and for whom the satellite dish isn't "the state flower"—living "like coyotes," by scavenging elk horns that have been shed in the winter, for China's horn-as-an-aphrodisiac market, by gold panning, trapping, cutting firewood. Maybe the best sheep rancher he knows is working as a jailer in Riverton because of the effects of this summer's drought. Press's previous trip was with a psychiatrist from the East and seven of the man's patients. That was fine, but some of the hunters he takes out bug him. One almost shot him, aiming through a scope sight that shut off the hunter's side vision. He talks about rodeoing: A Nez Percé Indian named Jackson Sundown, who is in a class by himself in rodeo history because he rode every horse he ever got on to a standstill, was never observed being bucked off. Nowadays the cowboy has to stay on for only eight seconds. The heart of rodeoing is in Henrietta, Oklahoma, he says, but he likes the big Canadian broncs best. More northerly horses are bigger.

I should mention that he came within possibly a day of dying on the trip a couple of weeks ago. He'd developed an abscess on his butt, which he thought was a boil and ignored; developed blood poisoning; a raging fever; couldn't ride; walked alone ten miles out to a road; got himself to a hospital and located a competent doctor and underwent surgery just in time. He got out of bed for this special outing and has been riding by means of a child's round air-filled life pre-server, which he fastens to his saddle each day to keep his weight off the wound. Gretel, too, in bronc mishaps and two lightning strikes, has nearly died.

Last night I dreamed of traveling on a passenger ship, and a shoot-'em-up there. We're camped by a purling stretch of what might be described as the south fork of the South Fork of the Buffalo River, which flows to the Snake by and by. But our tents, underneath very nobly old-looking, hardy, sizable spruces that, with this short growing season, probably predate the white man here, are pitched between two steep creeks, which, plunging down six or eight hundred feet from the stubborn snowfields above, are doing the work of the world and producing a wonderful, perpetual ruckus, a noise to induce dreams of the sea. In the outdoors, water is where the action is. It contains all sounds when it runs and, in the sunlight, wrinkling like an elephant's skin, all colors too. It speaks in tongues.

A flock of geese labors south with a beat like heat shim-mering, Molly says. Blundering blindly around in my sun-glasses, I remind her of Ray Charles, she says. It's odd to think about, but we communicate with our horses by tucking our fingers into their lips. Regardless, Buffalo spooks at light-and-shadow configurations sometimes and needs more than the reins, needs talk then. This complex valley with rimrock and headlands and red and green meadows, up and away from the population centers, is "holding the world together," says Press, like my farmer friend. And we agree it shouldn't have to be "used," can just be looked at occasionally, or *not* be looked at, just exist by itself.

There's a bitter quarrel between the Indians on the Wind River reservation—the only Indian reserve in the state, but almost as large as Yellowstone Park—and the many whites with inholdings or on nearby ranches about water rights, always a cruel issue in the West. The Indians have won a substantial water allotment, based on their treaties, in a re-cent court fight but are driving their white neighbors into a fury by not *using* it all, letting some of the water stay in the river and flow right by, just listening to it and looking at it as it goes.

We rode up on the high flanks of Crescent Mountain

(11,375 feet) today. It's one of the mountains where hunters shoot sheep, like Whiskey Mountain of the Wind River Range, under which, in Torrey Canyon, I saw a good number of petroglyphs last week. Torrey has a valley with three or four lakes and an exploding brawny creek that twists in its rocky bed with the force of an omen, in otherwise very dry country. With monoliths and burial sites, a fertile floor and nesting ospreys and eloquent cliffs, it's a place full of the ancient presence of man. We saw representations of owls, eagles, and what looked like "airplanes," and what looked like sprites. Also thick-bodied, sinister figures, and armless hands and legless feet stuck onto trident shapes. Bow-and-arrow men; mountain sheep. Skulls; death's-heads; thunderbirds; crowned, toothed "masks" complete with illustrated "brains." A horned dancer with one arm up and one arm down; and various skeletal frames, some of which looked to be inspired not so much by a human or animal array of bones as by the fossils that occur side by side with these cryptic scratchings in the sedimentary beds.

But we're too high here for such evidence of habitation. The snow may get twenty feet deep, and the cold intolerable. And Crescent Mountain is volcanic in origin, scattered at the top with blackish slag or tuff that is speckled with bilious-colored lichens and tinkles like broken slate when dropped, though some of the mountain's shoulders are undulantly grassy or comfortably dark with timber. We rode close to the summit and climbed a bit, then descended over a shelving ledge of compacted snow to a miniature crater lake that was chocolate at first, later purple, as the sun's angle shifted. There are elegant ramparts and turrets to gaze at, and abrupt, intimate cliffs to peer down, reminding me of some of the dioramas at the Museum of Natural History in New York that engraved themselves upon my enthusiasms when I was a child. You can see why this has become a final hideout for sheep, but on the other hand, two were shot here a week ago. We met their heads strapped to the back of a packhorse going down to Dubois on our second day out and, probably as a result, saw none today.

Borrowing my colonel friend's field glasses, I went off alone and studied the several levels of the view. In such a spot I like to scare myself by imagining I'm in some giddy fix, on some ultimate knoll, where nothing is higher, and must climb off. Except for the line of smoke, the sky was cerulean blue and soundless, spreading over the world. In this crazy-hot summer, ice in the Du Noir Glacier on Coffin Butte must be melting that fell as snow hundreds of years ago. It was a sailing view, a vulture's view. And Lars was catching California golden trout that the Fisheries biologists (with their zany ideas for the "wilderness") had helicoptered in. Californian indeed, with their spotted tails, fluorescent red bellies, and longitudinal red stripes on olive sides, and with spawn in them.

Climbing out of the crater (perhaps a volcanic vent?) that the lake is in, I frightened myself while slipping on the steep scree by suddenly visualizing the pitch as becoming nearly perpendicular. You can do that: have your eyes play tricks, turn a sixty-degree slope to eighty-five degrees, and nothing for you to hold on to but pebbles and gravel. Scrambling and sliding, I gave myself a cardiologists' stress test. It told me I should have a normal life span.

Saturday, September 10. Last day. In the wee hours I heard taps on the tent and thought it was rain. Went outside. There, thought it was only the spruces shedding their needles. The roar of water from the two tumbling creeks was so pervasive it seemed to be floating the tent, and I thought the taps might be an illusion produced by that. Still, the smell of the sky did have rain in it. And sure enough, rain came in earnest by breakfast time. Hallelujah. Third rain of the summer. Not yet snow. The temperature stayed in the forties, as we whirligigged slowly down toward home through tall rain-forest-looking woods of Douglas fir, Engelmann spruce, lodgepole pine, with dank-looking ponds and swamps alongside, past finger meadows and willow breaks now springing rib-high. The aspens have yellowed too. At lunch my chapped lips burst blood into my sandwich once again. ("Put horse shit on them. That'll keep you from licking them," Jack joked.) The switchbacks got like a merry-go-round as we went lower in the cold rain—the wind "strong enough to blow Christ off the Cross," as a wrangler said when we met him.

It's not that one does anything so very different in these alpine valleys with a vista of runneled headlands and mauled ridgelines, lens-shaped glaciers and snowslide chutes, and the Continental Divide, at the top of the world. One sits (or *I* do) picking at loose flakes of skin, biting one's nails, thinking of the politics of one's marriage, friendships, or career, replaying in one's tediously repetitive mind old conversations or correspondence from weeks or months before and two or three thousand miles away (or that never took place at all). In other words, one remains human; one doesn't calcify into rock. But fitfully there's a feeling of peace, which comes not just from the beauty spread out everywhere, but from a far-flung frame of reference.

We got back to the world of pickup trucks with collie-huskies bounding around in the back—where Gretel heard that a skunk had killed one of Rusty's new puppies at their ranch and that alfalfa was heading for one hundred dollars a ton. At the laundromat across the highway from the Branding Iron Motel, a poignantly lonely firefighter from Chicago, not black from the fire but black, was at the pay phone, calling home.

Learning
to Eat Soup

Learning to eat soup: Like
little boats that go out to sea, I push my spoon ahead of me.

At my parents' wedding in Michigan, one of Mother's
uncles leaned over before the cake cutting and whispered to
her, "Feed the brute and flatter the ass." The uncles threw
rice at them as they jumped into their car, and Dad, after
going a mile down the road, stopped and silently swept it out.
That night, before deflowering each other (both over thirty),
they knelt by the bed to consecrate the experience.

To strike a balance is everything. If a person sings quietly to himself on the street, people smile with approval; but
if he talks, it's not all right; they think he's crazy. The singer
is presumed to be happy and the talker unhappy, which
counts heavily against him. . . . To strike a balance: If, for
example, walking in the woods, we flake off a bit of hangnail
skin and an ant drags this bonanza away, we might say that
the ants were feasting on human flesh, but probably
wouldn't. On the other hand, if a man suffers a heart attack
there and festers undiscovered, then we would.

•

Baby inside M.'s stomach feels like the popping and sim-
mering of oatmeal cooking, as I lay my hand across. Pain, "a
revelation to me like fireworks, those comets that whirl," she
says in the labor room. She lies like a boy under stress in the
canoe-shaped cot, the nurses gathering gravely, listening to
the baby's heartbeat through the stethoscope between contractions—heart like a drumbeat sounded a block away. Baby,
with bent monkey feet, is born still in its sac. Doctor is unlo-
catable. The interns gather. A nurse picks up both phones
simultaneously and calls him with urgency. The crowd, the
rooting and cheering in the delivery room—as if the whole
world were gathered there—after the solitary labor room.

Very old people age somewhat as bananas do.

Two Vietcong prisoners: An American drew crosses on
their foreheads, one guy's cross red, other guy's green, to
distinguish which was the target and which the decoy to be
thrown out of the helicopter to make the target talk.

Winter travel: Snowbanks on river ice means thin ice
because snow layers shield the ice from the cold. And water
is always wearing it away from underneath; therefore keep
on the *inside* of curves and away from all cutbanks, where the
current is fast. Travel on barest ice and avoid obstacles like
rocks and drift piles sticking through, which also result in a
thinning of the cover. Gravel bars may dam the river, causing
overflows, which "smoke" in cold weather like a fire, giving
some warning before you sink through the slush on top and
into the overflow itself. Overflows also can occur in slow sections of the river where the ice is thick and grinds against
itself. A special danger area is the junction of incoming creeks
whose whirlpools have kept the water open under a conceal-
ment of snow. If the water level falls abruptly, sometimes you
can walk on the dry edges of the riverbed under solid ice
which remains on top as though you were in a tunnel, but
that can be dangerous because bears enjoy following such a
route too.

You butter a cat's paws when moving it to a new home,
so it can find its way back after going out exploring the first
time.

•

My friend Danny Chapman, the Ringling Bros. clown, had a sliding, circus sort of face, like the eternal survivor, marked by the sun, wind, pain, bad luck, and bad dealings, the standard lusts and equivocations, like a stone that the water has slid over for sixty years. Face was much squarer when not in august-clown blackface, its seams smudged by reacting to all he'd seen, and holding so many expressions in readiness that none could be recognized as characteristic of him.

Success in writing, versus painting, means that your work becomes *cheaper*, purchasable by anybody.

The New York Times is a vast democratic souk in which every essayist can find a place to publish his or her voice. But otherwise, for a native New Yorker with proud and lengthy ties to the city, it's not so easy. The *New York Review of Books* is published by a group of sensibilities that give the impression of having been born in this metropolis but of wishing they were Londoners instead. And *The New Yorker* traditionally has been the home of writers and editors born in Columbus, Ohio—who yearned so much to seem like real New Yorkers that their city personalities in print had an artificial, overeager sophistication and snobbery.

I ride my stutter, posting over its jolts, swerving with it, guiding it, if never "mastering" it.

At the annual sports show at the New York Coliseum: "Stay straight with sports," says a poster, a picture of a girl wearing a T-shirt with that slogan over her breasts. An exhibitor tells me he just saw two men fondling each other in the men's room—"It just turns your stomach." A woman wearing a huge odd-looking hat made of dried pheasants' heads is cooing affectionately at a cageful of pheasants. A skinning contest is held in which three taxidermists go to work on the carcasses of three Russian boars.

"If two people are in love they can sleep on the blade of a knife."

•

Karl Wheeler used a baby bottle until he was five years old, whereupon his mother said to him, "That's your last bottle, Karl. When you break that one you'll never get another one!" and he began to toss it idly in the air to catch it, but missed.

First white men in British Columbia sold some of the Indians their names: $10 for a fine name like O'Shaughnessy, $5 for the more modest Harris.

At 6:00 A.M. I shoot a porcupine in the garage (knew about it from seeing Bimbo vomit from a fear reaction after his many tangles with porcupines). It goes under the building to die but not too far for a rake to reach. I take it to Paul Brooks's house. In his freezer he has woodchucks, beaver, bear, deer, bobcat, and porcupine meat (he is a man living only on Social Security), and he cleans it for me. We see it's a mama with milk in her breasts. His mouth fills with saliva as he works; he's also preparing a venison roast for lunch, with garlic salt, Worcestershire sauce, pepper, onions, etc. Says this time of year, first of June, the woodchucks are light as your hat, the winter has been so long for them; you can feel their thin legs. Porcupine liver is a delicacy, the rest not so much. The porcupine had been chewing at my garage for the salts; I eat the porcupine; therefore I'm eating my garage—dark drumsticks that night by kerosene lamp. Game tastes herby even without herbs—best is bobcat and muskrat, in my experience, not counting big meats like moose. One countryman we know had his ashes scattered on his muskrat pond. The porcupine had chattered its teeth and rattled its poor quiver of quills as I approached with my gun. Was so waddly it could not even limp properly when badly wounded. Lay on its side gurgling, choking, and sighing like a man dying.

At the Freifields' one-room cabin, with snowshoes hung under steep roof, I read Larry's father's hectic journal, written in Austro-English, of desperate orphanhood on the Austrian-Russian front in WWI. He, adopted by the rival armies as they overran the town, living in the trenches with them, living off stolen crusts otherwise, surviving the bombardments, dodging the peasants who hated Jews, but cherished by Austrian soldiers, who then were killed—saw one's legs blown off just after he'd changed places with him. That night peed in his pants in the trench and froze himself to the ground.

"Old Bet," the first circus elephant in America, was bought by Hachaliah Bailey from an English ship captain in 1815 but was shot eventually by religious fanatics in Connecticut as resembling the biblical Behemoth of the Book of Job (as indeed she did).

My first overtly sexual memory is of me on my knees in the hallway outside our fifth-grade classroom cleaning the floor, and Lucy Smith in a white blouse and black skirt standing above me, watching me.

My first memory is of being on a train which derailed in a rainstorm in Dakota one night when I was two—and of hearing, as we rode in a hay wagon toward the distant weak lights of a little station, that a boy my age had just choked to death from breathing mud. But maybe my first real memory emerged when my father was dying. I was thirty-five and I dreamed so incredibly vividly of being dandled and rocked and hugged by him, being only a few months old, giggling helplessly and happily.

Had supper at a local commune where they have a fast turnover and have made life hard. They buy $20 used cars instead of spending $200, use kerosene instead of the electricity they have, and a team of horses to plow. They got 180 gallons of maple syrup out of their trees, but they washed 1,400 sugaring pails in the bathtub in cold water, never having put in a hot-water heater. Much husky embracing, like wrestlers; and before they eat their supper they have Grace, where twenty-some people clasp hands around the table, meditating and squeezing fingers. Bread bakes on a puffy wood stove. Rose hips and chili peppers hang from the ceiling on strings, other herbs everywhere and pomegranates and jars of basic grains. The toilet is a car on blocks up the hill. Supper is a soup bowl full of rice and chard and potato pancakes with two sour sauces and apple butter, yogurt for dessert; and we drink from mason jars of water passed around. And the final "course" is dental floss, which everybody solemnly uses. A dulcimer is played with the quill of a feather, accompanied by bongo drums. The women ended the public festivities by each announcing where she was going to sleep that night, which bedroom or which hayloft, in case anyone wished to join her. Clothing is heaped in a feed bin near the bottom of the stairs, and everybody is supposed to reach in in the morning and remove the first items that fit them and come to hand, without regard for which particular sex the clothes were originally made for. The saddest moment of the evening for me was when a little girl came around to her mother carrying a hairbrush in her hand and asking to be put to bed. The mother lost her temper. "Why run to me?" she said. "Everybody in this room is your parent. Anybody can brush your hair and tell you a story and put you to bed."

Manhattan, now 14,310 acres, was 9,800.

Bernard Malamud speaks of writing as a battle: "go to paper" with a novel. At age sixty-one is trying to "write wise," a new aim, and hard. Being between books, I say I'm in a period of withdrawal and inaction like that of a snake that is shedding its skin.

On the crest of Moose Mountain is an old birch growing low and twisty out of the ruins of a still older, bigger bole, surrounded by ferns, and it's there that the deer that feed in my field bed down during the day.

There is a whole literary genre that consists, first, of foolish writing and then later capitalizing upon the foolishness by beating one's breast and crying *mea culpa*. Why *was* I a white Black Panther, a drug swallower, a jackbooted feminist, a jet-set-climbing novelist, a 1940s Communist? How interesting and archetypal of me to have shared my generation's extremes.

Busybodies are called in Yiddish *kochleffl*, "cooking spoon," because they stir people up.

•

The hollow in the center of the upper lip is where "the angel touched you and told you to forget what you had seen in heaven."

Wife of F.'s uncle, to prevent him from going to work one morning when she preferred he stay home, set the alarm so that it seemed it was too late for him to make the train when he woke. But he did rush so terribly he got to the station, and there collapsed and died, and she, only twenty-seven, never remarried.

Joyce consulted Jung, who diagnosed his poor daughter as incurably schizophrenic partly on the evidence of her brilliant, obsessive punning. Joyce remarked that he, too, was a punner. "You are a deep-sea diver," said Jung. "She is drowning."

The cure for stuttering of holding stones in ⌐⌐⌐ ⌐ ⌐⌐⌐⌐⌐⌐ works because of the discomfort of them rattling against one's teeth. Stones from a crocodile's stomach were thought to be best.

Amerigo Vespucci said that Indian women enlarged their lovers' sexual parts by applying venomous insects to them.

After losing her virginity at seventeen, she felt unstoppered on the street, like a hollow tube, as though the wind could blow right through her.

The sea, at the village of Soya on Hokkaido island in 1792, was so fertile that twelve quarts of dry rice could be bartered for 1,200 herring, 100 salmon, 300 trout, or 3 sealskins.

How Davy Crockett kept warm when lost in the woods one night: climbing thirty feet up a smooth tree trunk and sliding down.

•

Am drunk from a soft-shell-crab lunch with Random House's Joe Fox, but stutter so vigorously with William Shawn as to obscure both from him and myself my drunkenness—stutter through it and give myself time to recall names like Numeiry and Assad, necessary to win Shawn's backing for the trip to Africa. He, as reported, is excessively solicitous of my comfort and state of mind; insulated and jittery; heated by electric heater (in August), yet fanned by electric fan; in his shirtsleeves, and immediately suggests I remove my coat. He has an agonized, bulging baby's head with swallowed-up eyes, like that of the tormented child in Francis Bacon's painting *The Scream*. Questions me effectively, however, on my knowledge of the Sudan and the prospects for a salable article there. Says O.K. I go to 42nd St. and watch screwing to relax—crazily enough, less is charged to see live souls (25 cents) than for a porno flick—then walk home. Lunch the next day with Alfred Kazin, my old teacher (and the day after that with Barthelme, who has just broken through a writing block, he says, and is therefore more cheerful and sober than I have seen him in a considerable while; says women's movement will produce changes as profound as the abolition of slavery). Kazin as always is a veritable tumult of impressions, like H. S. Commager and other busy intellectuals I have liked, but in Kazin's case it is enormously in earnest and felt. Expresses hurt at Bellow's recent inexplicable anger. Otherwise an outpouring of talk about his new book on the forties, when he published his first book and met the literary figures of the day. Played violin with drunken Alan Tate. Advances the idea that William James, a hero of his, is a better direct heir of Emerson than Thoreau; also the view that students now resent the fact that a professor knows more than they do, want him to learn along with them in class, as in group therapy, and when caught out on homework facts, get offended instead of trying to fake through, as in the old days. On Ph.D. orals, the candidates seem to have no favorite poem, no poem they can quote from, when he asks them for one at the end.

I like Easterners more than Westerners but Western geography more than Eastern geography; and I like the country more than the city, but I like city people more than country people.

•

Essays, the most conversational form, have naturally drawn me, who have a hard time speaking with my actual mouth.

Tail end of hurricane rains buckets, flooding Barton River. Then the sky clears with nearly full moon, and I hear the deer whickering and whanging to one another gleefully, the mountain behind them gigantic and white.

Bellow says in Jerusalem journal that "light may be the outer garment of God."

Oil spills seem to attract aquatic birds; the sheen may resemble schooling fish. Also, oil slicks calm the surface, look like a landing area.

Roth speaks of his debt to both Jean Genet and the Fugs for *Portnoy*. Roth a man who wears his heart on his sleeve, thus rather vulnerable to insult and injury; part of his exceptional generosity. Tells story of man bleeding in front of God but trying to hide blood from His sight apologetically.

William Gaddis: jockeylike, narrow-boned, fastidious Irishman, clever and civilized, with none of the usual hangdog bitterness of the neglected writer.

Warhol: keen, Pan face with tight manipulated skin that makes it ageless except for his eyes. Bleached hair hanging to his leather collar. Fame based upon being immobile.

Pete Hamill, bursting personality, does columns in half an hour, movie script in three weeks, discipline based upon not drinking till day's stint is through. Fewer bar brawls now, more empathetic, though still lives from a suitcase. "Irish Ben Hecht," he laughs.

Malamud: not at all the "Jewish businessman's face" I'd heard about, but a sensitive, gentle face, often silent or dreamy at Podhoretz's, disagreeing with the host and Midge, but holds his tongue and hugs him at the end with professional gratitude to an editor who once published him. When he speaks, his voice is young, light, and quick, an enthusiast's, idealist's. Hurt by attacks on him in *Jerusalem Post*, for dovishness. Extremely solicitous of me, as kind in his way as Bellow, though style of it is modulated lower. Both of us distressed by Israeli's grinning description of Arab prisoners being beaten up. William Phillips says he thinks the Palestinians probably have a point but that he's not interested in hearing what it is. Podhoretz mentions Israel's "Samson option," pulling everything down, and makes fun of Malamud's "ego" when he's left.

Grace Paley: short, stocky woman who at first sight on the Sarah Lawrence campus I mistook for the cleaning woman; asked her where the men's room was. We rode rubbing knees throughout that semester in the back seat of a car pool. She'd been marching in protests since high school (Ethiopia and Spanish civil war), but her exhilaration at being arrested in Washington peace march in midterm reminded me of my own exuberance at completing the hard spells of army basic training. Yes, we were good enough!

Heard MacLeish at YMHA. Afterward unrecovered yet from defeat of his play *Scratch* on B'way. Sweetness and bounce of his voice, however, is unchanged in twenty years; sounds forty, a matinee tenor, and the old lilt to his rhetoric. Face like a sachem's, too wise, too heroic, with a public man's nose. Talks of friendships with Joyce and Hemingway and imitates Sandburg's *O* very well. Talks of Saturday Club in Boston where monthly Harlow Shapley debated Robert Frost. Reminisces of artillery lieutenant days in World War I, "making the world safe for democracy," where his brother was killed. Five years later he and other nondead *did* die a bit when they realized it had been a "commercial" war and they had been lied to. He is a man of Hector-type heroes. Says Andrew Marvell poem was written while going home from Persia after his father's death.

Berryman given $5,000 prize at the Guggenheim reading, wearing a graybeard's beard which hides tieless collar. Reads best "Dream Songs," plus two sonnets and Rilke, Ralph Hodgson, and eighteenth-century Japanese poet. Emphatically, spoutingly drunk, reads with frail man's grotesqueries, contortions, and his own memorable concoction of earnestness, coyness, staginess, name dropping, and absolutely forceful, rock-bottom directness. Becomes louder and louder at the end of this floodlighted moment after long years of obscurity and hardship. Here was the current Wild Man, people thought, successor to Pound, there being one to a generation, though many others may have been reminded of Dylan Thomas as he fell into the arms of Robert Lowell, punching him affectionately, when he finished. His whole life was thereupon paraded before him, when old mistresses and chums and students like me came up, expecting recognition, and one of his old wives, presenting him with a son whom obviously he hadn't laid eyes on for a long while. He boomed with love and guilt, with repeated thanks for letters informing him that So-and-so had had a child or remarried, till one was wearied of watching. One felt guilty too, as though competing for his attention with the neglected son. I felt Berryman had not long to live and I ought to be content with my memories of him and lessons learned and not join in the hounding of him. Nevertheless, I did go next afternoon to the Chelsea Hotel, with bronze plaques outside memorializing other tragic figures, like Thomas and Brendan Behan. He'd said the son would be there, so I was afraid that, like my last visit with Bellow, I would be taking time away from a son who needed to see him much more. But the son had left—all that remained was a note in Ann B.'s handwriting. Instead a *Life* photographer and reporter were talking with him, plying him with drinks, though he was holding back dignifiedly, talking of fame, of Frost, and his own dog Rufus. Frost was a shit who tried to hurt him, but he quoted the wonderful couplet about God forgiving our little faux pas if we forgive Him His great big joke on us. Is bombastic in his total commitment to words. Legs look very small, but chest inflates with importance of uttering snatches of poems, till he collapses in coughs. Rubs beard and hair exhaustedly, recklessly spendthrift with his strength, and begins harder drinking; leads me to bar, where waiter, thinking from his red face and thin clothing that he is a bum, won't serve him till he lays a ten-dollar bill on the table. I soon leave, but he was hospitalized within a couple of days. "Twinkle" was his favorite word at this time. He used it for commentary, by itself, and irony, or expostulation, quoting an enemy like Oscar Williams, then merely adding a somber "Twinkle."

Turgenev's brain was the heaviest ever recorded, 4.7 pounds; three is average.

Child's tale about a man who suffered from shortness of breath. Afraid he would run out, he blew up a bunch of ' balloons as an extra supply for emergencies. Blew up so many that he floated away holding on to them.

Updike comes to U. of Iowa for first workshop session in three years (hasn't really taught for sixteen years) but handles himself in a classy manner nevertheless, and very well prepared with students' manuscripts beforehand, and in the exhilaration of reading his own work in front of 1,000 people in McBride Hall (which we call Mammal Hall because it's part of Nat'l Hist. Museum), freely sheds his private-person role that had made him a bit stiff before, when he'd refused even a newspaper interview. Signs autograph cards for eleven-year-old boys and physics texts for Japanese students and mimeo forms for students with nothing better to offer him. Wife is ample, attractive woman with large, intense face, obviously both loving and sexy, a relaxed, close companion—he is wearing a wedding ring and ignoring the ambitious students who show up for his morning class wearing cocktail dresses. We talk of Africa—both finishing Africa books—and classmates and lit. hierarchies. He mentions Cheever's drunkenness—once he had to dress him after a party like dressing a father. Our mothers are same age. "Poor Johnny," his said, watching a TV program about senility with him recently.

Updike says he quit teaching years ago because he "felt stupid," seeing only one way to write a given story properly, not the endless alternatives students proposed in discussions.

Indians used to scratch small children with mouse teeth fastened to a stick as a punishment for crying in front of white men. (White man, of course, a "skinned" man.)

290

•

Short stories tend to be boat-shaped, with a lift at each end, to float.

Richard Yates says art is a result of a quarrel with oneself, not others.

Five toes to a track means it's wild, four toes means cat or dog.

Writers customarily write in the morning and try to make news, make love, or make friends in the afternoon. But alas, I write all day.

Bellow says he spent the first third of his life absorbing material, the second third trying to make himself famous, and the last third trying to evade fame.

"A woman without a man is like a fish without a bicycle": T-shirt.

People say they'll take a dip in the sea as if it were like dipping into a book, but I nearly drowned in surf's riptide off Martha's Vineyard's South Beach. Repeatedly changed swimming strokes to rest myself as I struggled in the water, surf too loud to shout over, and I'm too nearsighted to see where to shout to. Reaching beach, I sprawled for an hour before moving further. Spent next day in bed, next week aching.

New England is "pot-bound," says Charlton Ogburn; thus superfertile.

Petrarch, climbing Mount Ventoux in 1336, began the Renaissance by being the first learned man ever to climb a mountain only for the view.

Rahv told Roth, "You can't be both Scott Fitzgerald and Franz Kafka."

•

People who marry their great loves sometimes wish they'd married their best friends; and vice versa.

Trapeze artists some days complain "there's too much gravity," when a change of the weather or the magnetic field affects their bodies. Elvin Bale bought his heel-hook act from Geraldine Soules, who after a fall started doing a dog act instead. Soules had, in turn, bought it from Vander Barbette, who, walking funny after *his* fall, had become a female impersonator and trainer of circus showgirls.

In old-time Georgia you ate mockingbird eggs for a stutter; boiled an egg for jaundice and went and sat beside a red-ant anthill and ate the white and fed the yolk to the ants. For warts, you bled them, put the blood on grains of corn, and fed that to a chicken. Fiddlers liked to put a rattlesnake rattle inside their fiddles.

The fifties are an interim decade of life, like the thirties. In the thirties one still has the energy of one's twenties, combined with the judgment (sometimes) of the forties. In the fifties one still has the energy of one's forties, combined with the composure of the sixties.

The forties are the old age of youth and the fifties the youth of old age.

Adage: "God sends meat, the Devil sends cooks."

Carnival stuntman whom Byron Burford banged the drum for used to swallow live rats and Ping-Pong balls, upchucking whichever ones the crowd asked for first. Stunned the rats with cigar smoke before he swallowed them.

> *The intellect of man is forced to choose*
> *Perfection of the life, or of the work,*
> *And if it take the second must refuse*
> *A heavenly mansion, raging in the dark.*
> Yeats, "Choice."

Lying to my lieutenant as a private at Fort Sam Houston as to whether I'd shaved that morning before inspection, or only the night before—he reaching out and rubbing his hand down my face.

Glenn Gould liked to practice with the vacuum cleaner on, to hear "the skeleton of the music."

Nature writers, I sometimes think, are second only to cookbook writers in being screwed up.

Deer follow moose in these woods, says Toad. I say maybe they look like father (mother) figures to them.

At Academy-Institute ceremonial, the big scandal is Ellison's lengthy introduction of Malamud for a prize and Barbara Tuchman's brutal interruption of it. Stegner very youthful, as befits an outdoorsman. Cowley very food-hungry as always, as befits a 1930s survivor. Commager tells my wife that his daughter loved me and so he loved me. Lots of cold-faced ambitious poets cluster around each other and Northrop Frye; Galway seems likably unaffected and truthful next to them. Ditto Raymond Carver. Ellison had tried to speak of blacks and Jews.

Joe Flaherty's line for the Brooklyn Bridge: "the Irish gangplank."

Whale mother's milk would stain the sea after she was harpooned, and the calf would circle the ship forlornly. "I do not say that John or Jonathan will realize all this," said Thoreau, in finishing *Walden*; and that's the central and tragic dilemma as the environmental movement fights its rearguard battles.

In starving midwinter, foxes catch cats by rolling on their backs like a kitten ready to play.

Warblers average 8,000 or 10,000 songs a day in spring; vireo 20,000. Woodchucks wag their tails like a dog. Blue jays like to scare other birds by imitating a red-shouldered hawk.

My bifocals are like a horse's halter, binding the lower half of my eyes to the day's work.

•

At my frog pond a blue heron circles low overhead while
a brown-muzzled black bear clasps chokecherry bushes and
eats off them thirty yards away from me.

Only six hours old, a red calf stumbles toward the barn,
as mother is herded in by Hugh Stevens on ATV vehicle, and
is eventually tied to its mother's stanchion with hay twine,
while a six-inch red tab of its previous cord hangs from its
belly. It's as shiny as a new pair of shoes, its deerlike hooves
perfectly formed, including the dew claws. Mother and calf
had had a brief wild idyll under the summer sky before they
were discovered by Hugh—the last sky this vealer will ever
see.

Crocodiles yawn to cool themselves in hot weather, but
coyotes yawn as an agonistic device. Mice yawn from sleepi-
ness, as people do, but we also yawn from boredom, which is
to say contempt—agonistic again.

Old people seem wise because they have grown resigned
and because they remember the axioms, even if they've forgotten the data.

"When you come to the end of your life, make sure
you're used up."

I trust love more than friendship, which is why I trust
women more than men.

"All hat and no cows." Or, "Big hat, no cattle": Texas
saying.

"Eat with the rich, laugh with the poor."

Buying a new car after thirteen years, I discover why
country people like to keep the old one about the yard. First,
it makes the house look occupied. Second, it's a nesting site
for ducks and geese and a shelter for chickens during the
day. Third, it reminds you of *you*.

Incomparable Land

What I liked best as a boy was my bike, my closest friends (who didn't live particularly close), a couple of ponds and streams on spare patches of land that had big spruces to climb, or think of climbing anyhow, the company of my goat and dog, and how tumultuous and hot the sky grew in the summer, when the Yankees games played on the radio. I liked having two parents, who could correct each other's excesses, and the fact that women and men were rather different in temper and emphasis, life therefore becoming a two-party democracy for adults, not a one-party state.

Of course, it took the women's movement until long after my childhood to make two-gender democracy real; but now it seems that the swing toward interchangeability or unisex may gradually flatten those two parties into one again, soon after we have gotten accustomed to enjoying the give-and-take of men and women who, without being completely alike, are coequals. Children, too, lose out. The surge in divorces and day-care improvisations has limited the benefit of growing up with parents who live together on new terms of equality.

Velocity is rife—pell-mell airplanes, job change, social

rejuggling. Speed burns up the old values. Although life is perhaps more mystifying in its entirety than in its details, I have spells of being surprised enough wherever I am, puzzled to be going lickety-split on a superhighway toward Roanoke, Virginia, where I may have business but have no family or friends, or to be chatting at a New York cocktail party with people who have clothed themselves by the labor of silkworms and the fish mink eat. Centrifugal forces begin to operate that spin us out. Sometimes it's less unsettling to stand at the rim of the world—hiking with African spearmen to a grass-hut village or gingerly treading the Arctic Ocean's ice—than to mill around in a milieu of "support groups" and feel-good "product centers." Minor rumbles shake us, as if a fault line lies underneath, with major earthquakes imminent, whereas a definitive experience, instead of pushing us over the edge, is likely to identify our true location and root us.

And yet two of the most stirring innovations of the past thirty years—the moon shots and our sense that, to a decent degree, racial bigotry could be abolished—have bogged down into the semblance of no change. The space program mired itself in cold war theatrics and profitmongering, and bigotry has so much of the shamefaced but chop-licking sensualism of lechery that it may never be eradicated. There are other throwbacks. A revivalist's "Tent of Miracles" set up shop in a vacant lot next to a vast Price Chopper supermarket in my Vermont town the other day, and in no time people were speaking in tongues, holding their hands up to be healed. *Ohmonamonamonadeedadeedadeedahish!* I preferred it at least to the regimentation of televised religion, where you forfeit the comfort of worshiping shoulder-to-shoulder with other parishioners, seeing their anxiety or serenity brought near the altar. It's a comradely experience when you see the reach that families can attain, from the wobbliness of infants fresh out of the mysteries of the birth canal to the loss or crescendo of dignity that people may display as the staggers afflict them eighty-some years later.

Religion is also private and idiosyncratic—though watching TV preachers in the "privacy of one's home" is no more privacy than opening a can of soup is really cooking. Obsessed with private ownership, we Americans forget that amassing property does not ensure privacy and can even be inimical to it. Genuine privacy—space to walk about, unwind, daydream, and think—is going to depend more and more upon property held by the public, such as greenbelts, parkland, wildlands. An early principle of this nation was that a person wasn't judged merely by his bank account. At Ellis Island they checked for tuberculosis, not for business acumen. Nor had we noblemen or Chosen People here (once the Puritans had discredited the latter idea with witchcraft trials).

I have a CB radio, on which I hear hobbyists chat, ambulances dispatched, and robbers caught. But what is notable is how like an old-time barbershop this electronic marvel remains. It drawls with humdrum talk, laconic next-door coziness, dismissing the notion that miles and regions of the earth and sky may count for anything. The banality is reassuring at the same time that the homogeneity of town and state distresses me. People used to try to cross the tracks of their hometown—wrong side to the right side—if they could. Then, instead, the effort was to get from a small town to a big city and never go back. Now, however, buying a country place has acquired a cachet for those with extra money, and as they reach a level of affluence, they can be found there for long weekends, eventually perhaps retiring to the country. An interesting reversal, but complicated for many busy people because their lives are becoming continental or international. Born near Chicago, they go to college in New England, marry in Houston, raise their children during stints of work in London and Seattle, vacation abroad or at a cabin purchased in Montana, but retire to Tucson's climate.

So which is home? Home used to be where the last turn in the road made you unsteel your heart; where you heard rain on the roof without feeling lonely. And whether you were fiddling with a large or a small dab of ground, you could point out flower beds that you'd put in and peas so fresh that they bit back. The scarecrow wore your cast-off clothes. Hummingbirds had perched at the top of the same apple tree for dozens of years, darting to sip from the lilacs; and after pushing the lawn mower, you sat on your front steps with a mouth organ, come July, and listened to a train hoot at dusk and watched the fireflies. These deep pleasures hadn't threatened to turn into a question of prosperity (the house I love cost me five thousand dollars in the year of the first moon shot) but of stability.

Indeed, going farther back, people used to recognize the individual taste of their own mountain's water. A certain valley, you might hear, had "sweet water. Nobody's water is better." And they knew how the hay was doing even if they didn't farm. They had a feel for sunshine, humidity, inches of soil, inches of rain, first frosts, wind speed. Without knowing birds' bird-book names, they'd learned the calls and recognized which whistles marked dry fields or swamplands. The local names told firsthand tales: Rice-bird, Road-bird, Toad-head, Tip-up, Meadow-chicken, Teacher-bird, Preacher-bird, Swamp-angel, Speckle-belly, Teeter-peep, White-face, Whip-tail. They knew a Quail Hawk from a Frog Hawk, a Skunk Duck from a Dipper Duck—and snakes too. Bull snakes made bovine grunts. Corn snakes and chicken snakes were named for where they prowled; the hognose snake for its schnozzola. King snakes ate other snakes. Fox snakes smelled like a fox.

Nostalgia is our anchor. It helps to keep us in one piece. For plenty of us, slick streets, snow in the face, and starlings' twitters are all the outdoor nature there is—although the sky is left after every environmental mistake, roiling in perpetuity. We can squint up at that. Can't chain-saw or bulldoze it, or buy and sell the clouds, pave them over or dig them up. To live well, one needs to be unafraid to die; but this is a matter of peace of mind, not daredevilry, and being at peace depends upon an acquaintance with broader perspectives.

Many of us have suffered through a foggy approach to a chancy landing, the pilot's voice a bit trembly on the intercom. The upper sky was clear; then stormy castled clouds. Most passengers hardly look out an airplane's windows anymore, don't see "the heavens," as the sky used to be called. They pull the shades for the movie or choose an aisle seat for legroom and a quick exit. But this is a landing to sweat through. Like converts, they peer outside, murmur jokes or prayers, possibly clutch hands, as the wheels clunk hopefully into landing position. The blind plane banks and turns. At last, they cheer the jounce of touching down. Yet without ever laying eyes on the man who, holding their lives in his hands, had piloted them back to the ground, and averting their eyes from each other, they scurry through the maw of the ramp to anonymity again.

It is hobbling how we have zip-locked ourselves into one-class suburbs, some of them devoid of toddlers because the neighborhood is so expensive that only older people can afford the tab. A meager manner of living, I think, though co-ops, apartment hodgepodges, and tract housing do have their charms as long as your marriage is a happy one. But primacy of property must leave space to turn around in, a place with no leash laws, where the trees creak and frogs sing from prehistory and, walking, one can still wonder what's beyond the bend, or listen to an utter silence.

I love the rootlessness of America, too, which was innate to a raw democracy. When I was younger I exulted in non-stop, nightlong drives across the Texas Panhandle or the Dakota Badlands, or grabbing trains and buses, slipping into towns where I knew not a soul, and roosting marginally to see if I could make enough friends to survive. But that stayed fun because I had a home in the East to go back to, a room of my own to burrow into, and a refrigerator waiting for me that would be full. I don't believe that so-called quality time makes up for a shortage of time spent being a parent, establishing in the child a confident sense of home, or that any particular zing in the "workplace" can replace for most people the pleasure of watching their kids grow. And I'm suspicious of the chameleon fluency friendship acquires when people on an upcurve keep moving along, abandoning previous friends who are traveling a different economic or geographic arc, estranged as well from aging parents by bleak stretches of distance. But this is how great numbers of us live, in interchangeable towns, with interchangeable friends.

Among the detritus of flood-tide change, some of the best stuff does keep bobbing up. Radio, for instance, is managing to stay afloat in competition with the Box, and baseball has more than survived the commercial challenge of faster, harsher sports. Amtrak hasn't been killed off. The age-old tinkering impulse of carpentry maintains as much appeal as computer hacking. Rodeos and canoeing still hold their own against motorized pastimes, though only about a dozen tented circuses are left in the U.S.; we mustn't lose these. I don't see loads of people turning into couch potatoes. On

Labor Day, when so many of us stroll out, you'll notice that the fattest Americans are generally the poor. No one should envy our poor, but our hospitality to the wretched abroad, legendary to the rest of the world, has not dried up. Certain traditions ballast us—our wilderness frontier, our mongrel vigor, our statue representing freedom in New York harbor, our eye for merit in almost any knack at doing something well. The point over here has been that Irish marry Italians and Jews marry Anglo-Saxons and mix it up. And we applaud, in any case, when somebody born into tough circumstances wriggles free and goes for broke like a quarterback scrambling. We're slow to call it greed.

Greed *is* a problem when it conflicts with our revolutionary concept of equal opportunity, or our special affinity for wild places, drawn from that wilderness frontier. Over and over, the first explorers were impelled to rhapsodize about "this incomperable lande," as the French Huguenot sailor Jean Ribaut wrote while coasting *Terra Florida* in 1562. Ours is a national rapport with nature, not the parochial concern of environmentalists. We were a land of jubilance to start with, and jubilation repeatedly—a land not foisted on its people; a land its people had sailed to see. We forget what's integral lately—the jubilance, the value of our oldest allegiances and rolling lands.

The Job Is
to Pour
Your Heart Out

I wrote my first poem when I was nine, visiting my grandparents in a rented beach house in La Jolla, California. It was Christmas 1941, and we regularly woke up to the sight of a thousand marines with black grease slicked on their faces storming ashore alongside tanks, jeeps, and howitzers from landing barges in front of the house. My mother, the maid, and I would carry out a pitcher of coffee and a plate of doughnuts, and about a dozen of the marines nearest us, after a glance at their sergeant, politely swallowed what they could before heading into the sandy hills—then, within months, no doubt, overseas to the horrific casualties of the amphibious campaign. But my poem was about a frog that lived in the brook behind the house, whose man shape and thin skin in a dangerous, adventurous world had touched my heart in ways that a nine-year-old could comprehend.

John Steinbeck and Saul Bellow became my special heroes a little later, as I decided I wanted to be a writer, and each (I notice now) chose to write a slapstick tour de force about a slaughter of the innocents in which the innocents were frogs. I shared Steinbeck's affection for dogs as well, and Bellow's for lions and bears (brown Smolak, with teeth like date pits, riding the terrifying roller coaster, clasping the teenaged Henderson). Like Henderson the Rain King, I worked in a circus early on, and at times laid my life between the paws of lions in order to learn from them whatever I could. Bears now leave their sign within a hundred feet of my house in Vermont, and when I've written about them, I've first gone to one of my hunter friends for a chunk of bear meat from his freezer (though I'm pained by hunting), which I put in a stew pot over a wood fire until the house is full of bear smell, and live on that for the first draft. Though this might not be Bellow's method, a bear that set off on a comparable effort of transubstantiation would probably begin like me.

I believe, incidentally, that those of us who care about bears and frogs haven't much time left to write about them, not just because—among the world's other emergencies—a twilight is settling upon them, but because people are losing their capacity to fathom any form of nature except, in a more immediate sense, their own. We ski or pilot boats and planes, and to reach "deeper" rhythms and ramifications in ourselves seem to prefer sidetracks such as drugs. Even when we speak of a literature that plumbs deep, we tend to mean that it examines narcissism, inertia, random murder, and other modern deadnesses or griefs, which are as recent as they are "deep."

However, very soon, I found the world scarier than I am pleased to admit. Visiting my old prep school in Massachusetts on the thirtieth anniversary of my graduation, I didn't tour the wooden dormitories with nostalgia, as I'd expected to, but tiptoed through like Ulysses revisiting Cyclops' cave. Though I'd spoken condescendingly of the school as a place where attendance was taken seventeen times a day and where for my bookishness I'd been assigned to a corridor called The Zoo, I'd always claimed to have been happy there. Virtue lay in being happy, I'd thought, but my recollections were rancid.

In those years, Steinbeck had been my favorite living writer. At his best he wrote with likable clarity, picturing in shorter works like *The Red Pony* and *Cannery Row* boys and men such as I wanted to be. His friendship with the biologist Ed Ricketts, which lay behind the appeal of *Cannery Row* and is described directly in *The Log of the Sea of Cortez,* corresponded to some dream of mine of what friendship between men could be. I hoped for a writer-zoologist's career, so Ricketts—living with a series of girlfriends in a laboratory on the oceanfront in Monterey, across the street from a whorehouse, whose inhabitants dropped in on him for advice, and half a dozen chummy bums, who slept in a row of rusty steam pipes—seemed enviable. A natural man, he sniffed the food on his fork before he ate and yet worked hard, wading in the tidal pools to collect specimens with a feeling of citizenship in a vaster, time-stunned concord of sea and sky, which most writers have never attempted to convey.

Steinbeck was the first writer I met. It came about because my "Zoo" roommate, Eddy Mumford, had an uncle who was designing the Broadway sets for Steinbeck's ill-fated play *Burning Bright* and kindly took the two of us to lunch with him at Sardi's. (My friend would have preferred to talk to Thomas Wolfe, but Wolfe was dead.) Steinbeck turned out to be a thick-shouldered man with a becoming ease and modesty. Neither a bully nor a toady to the headwaiter, he was staying at the Biltmore Hotel, and although edgy about his play's title, the late rewrite job he was attempting, and what the critics might say, he had remained enough of a man who cultivated cronies that the afternoon before, he and his secretary had been interrupted by the hotel detective, who'd been tipped off by a prankster to the possibility that he was entertaining a prostitute. He spoke with choosy fondness of New York City and his miserable first visit, when, fresh from several years of roaming the curriculum at Stanford, he'd worked as a hod carrier on the construction of Madison Square Garden. His upbringing had been middle-class—his father the treasurer of Monterey County—so as he glanced at the two of us in our white shirts and ties and sport jackets, such as would pass muster at the door of the dining hall at Deerfield Academy, but obviously wanting the wider experiences he and Thomas Wolfe had sought, he may have seen himself thirty years earlier.

Forty years after that lunch, I find that my closer friends tend to be women rather than men and that the whores who haunt the waterfront in New York, where I winter, are mostly transvestites, not ladies of the night. I know Steinbeck sentimentalized his perceptions and that he couldn't account for the fact that the bouncer in Ed Ricketts's whorehouse killed himself with an ice pick, for instance. By long acquaintance with animal lovers and champions of human underdogs, I know, too, that these enthusiasms that Steinbeck and I shared may hide substantial kinks of character (if never so many as those of people who harbor no sympathy at all for animals and underdogs). But Steinbeck's liberal spirit had its roots in a feeling that everybody should have a fair start—a revolutionary American perception, which has kept his liberalism fresh.

There is a peculiarly American tradition that families swing "from shirtsleeves to shirtsleeves in three generations." Radicals make conservatives make radicals again. I've seen the process in dozens of friends. Probably the American dream is so riven with paradoxes (free speech versus free enterprise, money-making versus "the best things in life are free") that its incongruities can be accommodated in no other way. "I must study politics and war so that my sons may . . . study mathematics . . . in order to give their children a right to study painting, poetry, music, architecture," as John Adams wrote to his wife, Abigail. The entrepreneur's children, hedged in by the special privileges he has won for them, want instead "a better world." Or, moving in the opposite direction, the cry has been: "The working class can kiss my ass. I've got the boss's job at last," as generations of new or neo-conservatives have said.

Saul Bellow captured my attention in college. It was not that I pored over his novels with an intensity Cervantes and Tolstoy deserved—not that I learned as much of writing about nature from Steinbeck as from Turgenev, or about solitude from Bellow as from Chekhov. But one needs a ladderlike array of models, from Shakespeare to Erskine Caldwell; and Bellow, who was warier than Steinbeck yet somehow readier to blurt out every intimacy, who was unable to write well at length about women but appeared to like women better than men, reached me in a way that mattered. It's important to have living exemplars, not just dead masters—and also fellow countrymen. That Faulkner, an adornment to world literature, was walking about at the same time we were made an enormous difference to writers who started out in the 1950s. People met him on the stairs at Random House and never afterward could take writing for the movies any more seriously than he did; or wealth and fame. Though a young American novelist can gawk at Günter Grass, V. S. Naipaul, and Gabriel García Márquez and be astonished at their talent, even in the event that one of them eventually develops into a fiery, tenacious genius on the scale of Faulkner, they do not share the nuts-and-bolts hardware of being countrymen.

If Bellow was no Faulkner, he excelled at making the most of what he had. Nothing went to waste; and being a teacher by profession, he was more at ease with cub writers, less intimidating to me, though less superbly self-possessed, than Faulkner. I never quite considered that he had the intellectual hardware sometimes ascribed to him, but he caught the temper of his time with marvelous particularity. Also, I felt like him when I read him, and, in person, still more akin. Thirty years ago he had not yet flowered into fashionability. One took a little ribbing on the Upper West Side of New York, in Greenwich Village, and from the East Side *Paris Review* crowd if one did not prefer Mailer to Bellow. *Time* magazine regarded him as "a smart Jew," he said, and he sounded as though *The New Yorker* could have been Heartbreak House for him, if he had let it be. Though he hadn't cut himself loose from his roots, as Steinbeck did in finally moving east, Bellow from his citadel in Chicago in 1964 smelled the poisons of New York's literary scene and, more than Californians like Steinbeck and Saroyan, was pained. ("We made you and we can break you," a New York critic was to tell him during a political disagreement at a White House reception several years later.)

Like Steinbeck in 1950, Bellow was ambitious to branch out to the theater, and he had written a similarly static play, *The Last Analysis,* which starred Sam Levene (not, as he had hoped, Zero Mostel, who had had the bad taste to strut the boards in a new presentation called *Fiddler on the Roof* instead). An air of despair pervaded the rehearsals, and on the spiderwebby stage set, the desperate actors launched their lines as if still trying to understand them. Bellow's Reynard face had lost its shape and grown irregular in coloring. In his posture he resembled a man awaiting an announced punishment. Indeed, on the night after the opening, the Belasco Theater was already one fourth empty, though some soldiers and sailors had gotten free tickets from the USO and stood about during intermission looking bewildered. But Bellow had just had a splendid pair of front-page reviews for *Herzog* in the *New York Times* and the *Herald Tribune* book sections to comfort him; and when, cublike, I asked which spread he'd liked best, he shrugged, like the writer I wanted him to be. He inveighed against the "professionalism" of American writing, by which he meant drawing from literary, not street-smart, sources, and said there was "a line of succession," already fearing that he might become an institution and lose his anonymity, as his friend Arthur Miller had done, for different reasons, after marrying Marilyn Monroe. Gingerly and elusive, with his sharp, shy smile, he said that writers were by nature eccentrics, and to accept that, be honest with oneself, and then not worry about one's personal reputation.

Cublike, I followed him another time across Central Park from a meeting we had had at the Metropolitan Museum of Art, stutteringly telling him that he reminded me of Nathanael West, a flattering comparison that he said he hadn't heard before. But at the far edge of the park he stopped and said goodbye so I wouldn't see where he was going—again, just as, in my secretive way, I imagined I would have.

Like Bellow, I lived as though life were precarious, as though the roof might fall in. I lived as if I didn't entirely know where next week's meals were coming from, and this not only because I admired Joyce Cary's caricature of the artist's life in *The Horse's Mouth*. My childhood had been teetery, and generally I'd kept a cache of cash around in case I felt a need to hit the road—as would have happened if the threat had been fulfilled that I might be required to put in an extra, postgraduate year at that prep school. With the bad stutter I suffered from, I suspected, too, that later I would not be able to depend upon the professorships and public-reading income with which other writers supplemented whatever their books earned. Nor did I necessarily expect to sell better than the American writers I admired most, Melville and Thoreau.

I had arrived in New York from humble origins. That is, I was a WASP with an Ivy League education and a lawyer for a father at a time (a decade or more after Bellow's debut) when it was important for a young writer in the city to be an "ethnic" whose father was a milkman or a bartender and to have gone to City College. My prep-school mate John McPhee and college classmate John Updike both needed to write twice as many books twice as well to gather an acclaim at all equivalent to what they would have won much more quickly if they had not been WASPs from the Ivy League.

Yet, of course, we'd benefited from our sumptuous educations. I'd enjoyed an uncannily balancing pair of writing teachers—Archibald MacLeish, who taught me how to be usefully sane, and John Berryman, who taught me how to be healthfully crazy. And though my father, lawyerlike, wrote to my first publisher's lawyer to try to stop my first novel from coming out, earlier he had traveled with me on a privileged vacation to western Canada, where in the mountains I experienced one of those visions of the work one hopes to do for years ahead such as Willa Cather described in *The Professor's House*. Young Professor St. Peter, "from the rose of dawn to the gold of sunset," lay on his back in a little boat skirting the south coast of Spain and saw the ranges of the Sierra Nevada, "snow peak after snow peak, high beyond the flight of fancy, gleaming like crystal and topaz . . . and the design of his book unfolded in the air above him," just as did the mountain ranges. Fourteen years later, I returned to Canada to write *Notes from the Century Before*, my first and favorite travel book, and more than thirty years later published *Seven Rivers West*, my best novel.

My father grew up in Missouri with a paper route, a neighbor who kept pet coyotes, and the rest of it, working his way east in cattle cars and to Europe on a cattle boat. He was the first person of whom I endlessly asked the question that has been my stock-in-trade ever since: "What was it like back then?" Though he became an elegant citizen who seldom wanted to remove his tie even on weekends, he retained that capacity to pile in the car and go and buy a couple of goats, stuff them in the back seat and bring them home, into the house, to show me, when I was sick in bed. He gave me my first oysters at the University Club on Fifth Avenue when I was seven, and I've always liked revisiting it or similar places because of my secret sense of still belonging there. The money stopped when I was twenty-one, and for the next fifteen years I lived on an average of three thousand dollars annually; yet these memories of fancy clubs and summer resorts and suburban lawns manicured by gardeners named Alfonso or Brooks lent me a precious freedom from conflicting ambitions later on. Fame I did want as a writer, but money beyond financing the necessities meant much less to me. Choosing to be a writer from my background had involved surrendering the idea of money to begin with, and when I saw my colleagues standing around shooting their cuffs at publishing parties, yearning for somebody to advance them the wherewithal to buy a house like the one I had grown up in, I felt lucky.

My father was not a mover and shaker. He considered that a good lawyer never got his name in the papers. If a client ignored his advice and got into trouble, a gamecock-peacock attorney should be hired, whose delight it was to wrangle out the matter in front of a judge. He was interested not in power for himself but in the smooth exercise of other people's power in an insulated world of adept phone calls and quiet meetings in high-up offices and on the golf course, where the arcane disciplines of the game—better than the pert procedures of a business lunch—prevented a prospective partner from concealing the full gamut of his emotions beneath the surface of his face.

My father taught me, however, to betray less information and fewer opinions than I really had in asking questions, and to cut my losses and not argue unduly if I made a mistake in a business arrangement, because most people are a mixed bag of honesty, dishonesty, charity, and meanness. They may turn around, if they have done you dirt, and do you a favor to make up for it. He taught me that the choice of whom to work with, more than the words in a contract, is what lubricates a professional agreement and that the chief considerations may never even be stated. All good advice for an interviewer; but though he knew how to flatter individuals he wanted to talk to, I think he was too innocent to practice the ultimate flattery of putting himself at their mercy, as I have frequently done when far afield. He avoided confrontations but as a lawyer shared the interest that lawyers and essayists have in figuring out how to go against the grain of received opinion and attack "honorable men" occasionally. He would have approved of my going to school to Shakespeare's Antony for the purpose and beginning nearly any controversial essay with some variety of "I come to bury Caesar, not to praise him."

My first long walks as a boy were with my father on the golf course, and if he teed off before the crowd arrived, we might see a fawn and doe, or a mink, mobbed by red-winged blackbirds, crossing the fairway with a nestling in its teeth. I could talk easily to dogs and goats, though not to people, and so to the extent that stuttering directed my course as a writer, the choice for me all along may have been whether to become an essayist or to write about animals. After my first book, a circus novel called *Cat Man*, was published, several readers asked whether I didn't want to simplify things for myself and capitalize on my rapport with animals by setting out to wind up as Ernest Thompson Seton. Emphatically I didn't. My heroes were literary, and besides, I wanted to pour my heart out, which Ernest Thompson Seton never had done. The work of an essayist is, precisely, to pour his heart out. In fact, I recognized that one couldn't get to be as good a writer by writing about animals: first, because of the limits placed upon what a human being can observe of them; second, because to escape those limits and imagine one's way too deeply into the existence of an animal would remove the very itch that causes people to write books; and third, because of the limitations inherent in animals.

I was impatient, nevertheless, and remain so, at being patronized for writing about a primitive, eclipsed world, a child's world of folk figures. Somebody who writes much about animals now must deal with the death of whole constellations of creatures, perhaps half of creation in a single lifetime. And thus it turns out that the naturalist's path has converged with the novelist's or essayist's in the great, ungraspable, unspeakable (even fashionable) subject of the death of the earth, which has lately seized so many people's imaginations.

Still, I believe that we are here to thrive, not to die or to "die" prematurely from timidity and discouragement. The evidence is everywhere, in the gaiety and speed of nature during the intense pursuits of getting food and lovemaking, and in our own sense of peace and ebullience when we feel attuned to where we are—reaching back again within ourselves for that natural man who smells the food on his fork before eating. A writer's job is to pour his heart out, and whether his immediate concern is the death of whales and rhinos or the death of civilization, there will be plenty of chances for him to do so.

In Okefenokee

O kefenokee Swamp in south-
eastern Georgia comprises about six hundred square miles.
It's home to perhaps twelve thousand alligators, a hundred
fifty black bears, six hundred otters, eighteen thousand white
ibises at the peak of the summer, nine hundred great blue herons, a hundred fifty sandhill cranes, twenty-five ospreys,
forty-five hundred egrets of three species, four thousand
wood ducks, and assorted populations of pileated woodpeckers, wood storks, barred owls, red-shouldered hawks, parula
and prothonotary warblers, and numerous more commonplace songbirds. All told, there are forty kinds of mammals
and forty of fish, thirty-five species of snakes, fourteen of turtles, eleven of lizards, twenty-two of frogs or toads, within the
national wildlife refuge, which is by far the largest in the eastern U.S. And yet it's not really such a swatch of swamp—
thirty-five by twenty-seven miles at its longest and widest—
considering the ecological and even mythological freight that
it must carry for all of the uncountable wild wetlands that have
been drained, plowed, and subdivided.

Okefenokee is much smaller than Florida's Everglades
(which is a national park), but because of its isolated location
it has been less injured by the pressure of development at its

boundaries. The soil at surrounding drier elevations is the color of a supermarket shopping bag, and indeed the principal industry roundabout is raising and cutting twenty-year-old slash pines for pulpwood that goes to manufacture paper bags. The swamp lies in the shallow dish of an old seabed, forty-five miles west of Georgia's present lush coastline and about the same distance east of the rich pecan-, peanut-, tobacco-, and cotton-growing country that begins near the prosperous city of Valdosta. It forms the headwaters of the Suwanee and Saint Marys rivers, and for the local Indian tribes, too, it was a region of mystery and legend, a hunting ground more than a home, until the Seminoles, the last of the tribes in the area, hid there as white settlers spread across the South after the War of 1812, raided the whites who were encircling them, then finally were driven out by army troops in 1838, escaping toward the deeper fastnesses of the Everglades.

Okefenokee was the last haunt of the panther and wolf in Georgia. They and its mosquitoes and reptiles—as well as the raffish reputation of its "swampers," the families who lived on its islands and hunted and trapped its hammocks and watery "prairies" by poling themselves in dugouts or trudging knee-deep through the peat bogs—kept most other people out. Some swampers were said to be descended from Civil War draft dodgers. At dawn and dusk they would let out ululating two-mile "hollers" that went on for a minute or two from their feeling of pride and primacy, and they were serious moonshiners, distilling corn whiskey from the sugarcane and white corn that they grew in locations no federal agent was likely to reach on his own or alive. In towns like Fargo, at the southwest corner of the swamp, a bootlegger could park his high-springed truck loaded with jugs in front of the post office and chat for an hour and nobody thought twice about it.

However, the whole swamp was logged for its cypresses and crisscrossed by a network of tramways in the first quarter of this century. Earlier, during the 1890s, a brief but concerted attempt had been made to drain it to create agricultural land with a canal, which remains to this day the principal pathway inside. Because wildlife refuges differ from national parks in that their first purpose is supposed to be the preservation of habitat, off this canal one travels into Okefenokee only by canoe and only by precut water trails through the sea of floating lilies and other vegetation to wooden camping platforms set out on the prairies five or ten miles apart, each trail and platform being reserved for a single party of canoers by arrangements made with the refuge manager beforehand.

In my capacity as a chronicler of other people's vacations, I paddled about forty miles on a four-day trip last spring that wound through the more familiar passages of the swamp from refuge headquarters near the town of Folkston, on the east side, to the Suwanee River at Fargo on the western edge, as part of a group of eighteen people, including two guides provided by an outfitting company called Wilderness Southeast. Except for our guides, who were women of thirty-four and twenty-two, and two teenagers on spring vacation, we were mostly in our fifties—a marine engineer from California, a career IBM man, an army defoliant chemist, a closemouthed, wise-looking country lawyer from Kentucky, a folksy, rawboned radiologist from Valdosta, a hospital head-of-pharmacy, a Cincinnati schoolteacher, and the wives of the IBM man, the defoliant chemist, the lawyer, and the radiologist. Although, except for the teacher, these women were housewives, our guides were enthusiastically liberated women who immediately asked us men whether we were wondering where the real, *male* guides were. To distinguish us and help us remember each other, they had us attach animal names to ourselves, such as Art Aardvark, Beetle Bob, Betty Bee, Bear Bill, Betsy Beaver, Bobcat Bob, Evelyn Eagle, Polly Parrot, Jackass Jason, Ouzel Ottway, Possum Pollard, Ted Turtle, Lynn Lynx, Mary Mouse, and so on. I thought it a vaguely humiliating procedure, but it did furnish us food for thought about each other. Jason, the radiologist, was anything but a jackass, for instance, and his wife, "Polly Parrot," besides being a regent of the Daughters of the American Revolution, whose grandfather had been toted about in his infancy on the back of a male slave, had recently gone through an Outward Bound program, rappeling down cliffsides, and had soloed in an airplane. "Mary Mouse," the teacher, wore a sweatshirt saying "It's sporty to be forty" and said she made a habit of spending summer vacations in places

313

like New Guinea or Newfoundland, when she wasn't picking up pocket money delivering vans nationwide from a factory in South Bend. "Bobcat Bob," on the other hand, did look like a likely hunter, and "Evelyn Eagle" gave the impression of being an outdoorswoman who probably did truly aspire to wings. "Possum Pollard" looked as if he could play dead in court and then wake up and surprise the opposition, and "Ouzel Ottway," a bachelor pharmacist, was a passionate Sierra Club devotee and was signaling as much, because John Muir, the founder of the Sierra Club a century ago, often wrote of the water ouzel as his favorite bird.

We had compulsory campfire gatherings for group-think purposes in the evening, our leader Viva!—she spelled it with an exclamation point—having worked previously as a counselor in juvenile-delinquent prerelease programs. She encouraged us to explore our behavior patterns and do things differently from what we were used to (indeed, on the application forms, the fee for the trip had been labeled "Tuition"), but this was a rather unnecessary suggestion, because although the self-employed people—lawyer, doctor, marine engineer—didn't much change their personalities, which at home and on the job were approximately the same, the men who worked as cogs in large organizations had turned zany by the second day. The IBM man became bombastic and mock lecherous and the army chemist "fuzzy," eccentric, bewildered, "unstrung." Viva!—who paddled with me for most of the trip—spoke of her "listening skills" and "confrontation skills" in Reality therapy and Gestalt therapy, but I got quite fond of her even as she tried to tinker with my motivations, because she was so sympathetic, affectionate, vulnerable, and earnest, and her own personality seemed so contradictory. She had a skinny straight nose, a string-bean frame, and a frenetic metabolism that grew desperately hungry at frequent intervals, so that she would stop paddling in the midst of a downpour to gobble nuts and dried fruits almost in sight of our tent frames. She confessed that she had been disillusioned by the "fail rate" among her contingents of delinquents but that she believed everyone had control of his own destiny; and for all the intensity with which she tried to mold us into a unique, "bonded" group, permanently enriched by the experience of crossing this swamp, she said she herself "burned out" quickly in groups. Ours was the only one she had scheduled herself to guide that spring. She usually preferred to stay in the office or else went out for extended sojourns alone in a cabin in the woods.

It's a phenomenon nowadays that youngish retired people, or prosperous couples on the verge of retirement, venture in increasing numbers into outdoor group adventures led by young ideologues from what is left of the counterculture, who pay themselves almost nothing (Wilderness Southeast's partners got $8,500 a year) but who believe in a special agenda of education, activism, and behavior modification, often incongruously at odds with the beliefs and careers of their customers. What they all do have in common is the modern conviction that life is lived in modest niches—whether one occupies a slot at a huge corporation or mildly does one's own thing, protectively colored by a graduate degree—that our aspirations are complexly and dauntingly circumscribed, and that life must be selective and specialized.

We had spent the first night in a small piney graveyard in Folkston and next morning left solid land at the entrance to the Suwanee Canal near Chesser Island, paddling ten miles on this twenty-yard-wide relic of Harry Jackson's 1889–95 attempt to drain Okefenokee, while listening to cricket frogs gick-gicking, carpenter frogs calling with a sound like a hammer tapping, pig frogs grunting like impatient hogs. These species are not musically the prettiest of amphibians—not like toads or spring peepers—but here in their confident legions they reminded us that their race probably fathered all of the vertebrate music on earth. We stopped to watch two warblers weaving a nest of Spanish moss and several fishing spiders poised to grab insect larvae on the rims of the lily pads. Viva said she was "heavily into snakes and spiders. It's like a secret, looking for spiders, because nobody else is."

Fish crows flew about uttering *uh-uh*, and *uh-uh* again, for which reason they are known as virgin birds, our younger guide, Nancy, told us, while paddling in her black bathing suit in the stern of the *National Geographic* photographer's canoe. He, "Bear Bill," was a former quarterback and "monster back" for Arizona State, and she was a sharp, smart naturalist, just out of the University of Vermont, who, with her chipmunk cheeks and sorority hairdo, looked collegiate when paired with him, though neither in fact was unduly so. Viva and I raced ineffectually with them, when we had a chance, though mostly our job was to harry poor Pollard, the Kentucky lawyer, who was casting for bass at the rear of our procession of nine canoes, quite competent with his rod and possessed of an eye that loved currents. But he was supposed to keep up.

Under the warm sun, the alligators lying on both banks seemed more assured in the presence of humans than they would have been in chilly weather, when they have to make allowances for the sluggishness of their own bodies by sliding into hiding underwater much sooner. Their heads were flat-looking and grimacey because of the long mask of their mouths—a grin that is two hundred million years old. Swimming alligators have horsey heads, however; the eyes and high nostrils are emphasized, instead of their fixed somber smiles. They look more like a sea horse than a sea horse does (though the inches between their nostrils and eyes denote their total length as measured in feet).

When they bellowed, the gators sounded like motors starting up, not like horses whinnying, and, besides answering each other, felt obligated to answer the airplanes that crossed the swamp. Such an outlandish challenge from high above may sometimes conceal from them the triumph of their position at the top of the food chain here (since people in a wildlife refuge don't kill them for their skins or to eat their tasty tails). A baby alligator's first meal is likely to be a crayfish, but the adults eat an occasional bear cub whose mother was forced to cross deep water between islands; and they will camp under the nursery trees where colonies of ibises, herons, and egrets nest, to devour not only the nestlings that have the misfortune to fall but also the raccoons that otherwise would decimate the baby birds ensconced in the branches above. Alligators create new water trails through the matted plant life during their nocturnal wanderings and dig essential water holes used by many other creatures during a drought.

One twelve-footer we met, after we had left Suwanee Canal and entered the narrow passageways of Chase Prairie, hissed and blew itself up formidably when it felt surrounded, but then let us slide by in a gingerly file, without flailing its muscular tail. The tail is both a chief weapon and the alligator's main means of travel; but they have a variety of sounds, including the primeval roar of conquest that a great one will utter when it charges and seizes a deer mired in mud and lifts it bodily out and swaggers back to its pool with the deer gripped crosswise in its jaws—a roar that sounds more Triassic than contemporary, more like a titanic burp than a lion's intellectual roar, and therefore more nightmarish and terrifying, which surely helps to stun and immobilize deer. On the other hand, a male in courtship hums *umphs* underwater in such a way that the water vibrates deliciously around the female, until she closes her eyes, puts her chin on his head, and twists her body around his. And this is the sound the alligator hunters of Okefenokee used to imitate, groaning softly while mouthing the end of a punting pole thrust into the water near where they knew a gator was lurking.

On Chase Prairie we heard an osprey mewing as it hovered above a fishing stretch, and two hawks crying to each other connubially, two owls barking back and forth informatively, two cranes garrooing as they beat by in uxorious, coordinated majesty, a woodpecker cukcukking loudly from a line of cypress trees, and a bellowing alligator in full rut—all at once. Chase Prairie is named for the chases the swampers used to conduct, one man driving game animals off the hammocks and islands, another poling fast after them in his dugout or jonboat as they waded and swam to escape.

We were in the midst of pond lilies and bonnet lilies, bladderworts and pipeworts, neverwet and maiden cane, pitcher plants and pickerelweed, wampee and hardhead grass—all that mob of plant life that defines the swamp. The leaves and stalks, dying off in the winter, settle on the decomposing layers of peat on the bottom, ten or fifteen feet thick from the centuries of vegetation that have rioted on the surface in the sultry sun and died and rained down on the impermeable clay understrata. Their constant decomposition produces gases that now and again push up whole mats of this peat, called "blow-ups," which, if they float for long, catch seeds of sedges and grasses and, as they get larger and larger, twenty yards across and more, are called "batteries," so solidly bound together that they can support a person, though often swaying under his feet because they may be floating on six feet of water. ("Okefenokee" comes from an Indian name meaning "land of the trembling earth.") Then cypresses, buttonbush, titi and gallberry shrubs and bay tree seedlings grow and send down roots that eventually stabilize the battery, until, when enough of a patch of dry soil has formed that finally the old swampers could have camped there on their alligator hunts, the battery is called a "house." "Hammocks" are large "houses" where hardwood trees like water oaks, laurel oaks, swamp maples, black gum and sweet gum trees have gotten a foothold. Also, there are as many as seventy regular islands in Okefenokee Swamp, most of them former sandbars left from half a million years ago, when, probably, this area was part of the sea. On the islands are forests of loblolly and slash pine, as well as large cypresses, magnolias, and other glories. But the swamp is gradually, over the millennia, filling in; the actual open prairies that are most "swampy" constitute only fifteen percent of it today.

At lunch we'd talked of trips down the Snake River and the Grand Canyon, into the Smokies, the Sierras, and the Wind River Range, all taken under the tutelage of America's drifting populace of "wilderness guides"; and as we paddled along in wildlife-refuge-type silence, I doubt that many of us failed to think intermittently of retirement strategies and financial stratagems, of midlife crises, romantic tangles, children-at-a-standstill, or whatever middle-age hex happened to be enlivening our existence at the time, while my austere, frenetic friend Viva—who would certainly have risked her own life in a flash to rescue a stranger—sat ready to help us or save us.

Nancy was as enthusiastic a naturalist as Viva was an educator. At her urging we stopped to look at larval dragonflies preying on other larvae under the lily pads. After a year or two of doing that, the nymphs metamorphose and crawl onto a stalk, to dry in the sun and pump blood into their wings for some still more dramatic hunting activities performed in the air. We stopped to watch this occurring too. And there were predatory diving beetles, known as "water tigers" in their larval stage, and hunting-diving grasshoppers, as well as the fishing spiders waiting on the water lilies. Cormorants flew over, black, agile diving birds, which old fishermen across the South still like to call "nigger geese" because they're dark and fly like geese, although they live on fish, not plants, as geese mostly do. The many turkey vultures soared with a dihedral cock to their wings; and the few ospreys with a flat, boomerang-type crook to theirs. In this cost-effective era, no spectacular bird such as an osprey can expect to be allotted enough space to nest and feed its brood unless it pays for its acreage by being ogled by hundreds of human beings. The pair nesting along our route were magnificently wild-looking, nevertheless, with their brown capes and backs, white heads and underbodies, their handsome straight postures when they clasped a branch, and utter mastery of the air, oddly combined with a repertoire of chirps, cheeps, kiweeks, and kyews.

We used yellow fiberglass Mohawk canoes and green Eureka tents, and when we reached our camping platform, which measured twenty by twenty-eight feet in the midst of a mile-square parcel of water, Viva had us stand in a circle and massage one another's shoulders. The sunset was only a rip in the clouds, but ruby, carmine, and puce all the same, and ibises, egrets, herons, and storks flew home in discrete flocks to their several roosts and rookeries after the long day's frogging and fishing. Being bird buffs, we didn't mind feeling caged in their garden spot, but, after a supper of salami and cheese, went out again in our canoes to see more alligators by shining our flashlights into their eyes, which reflect like coal embers. Nighttime is when alligators come alive and hunt, so we located a number of them, their eyes that prodigally passionate color. The raccoons' shone bright white, by contrast, as they foraged the house and hammock margins; and the spiders on the lily pads had eyes that glittered emerald green. Frogs had white eyes, and besides the cricket, carpenter, and pig frogs, bullfrogs were croaking, and pickerel frogs that sounded like two balloons being rubbed together. Bear Bill, Violet Viva, and I (Ted Turtle) slid close to a raccoon that was feeling for frogs in the shallows under the silhouettes of tall trees. He was silvery and ghostly in our flashlight beams, displaying a stand-up, tiptoe curiosity elaborately tempered with fear. Up on his hind legs and down he went, ears pricked, fluid with tremulous life, until, still undecided about us, he finally fled.

The white-eyed frogs would gobble the emerald-eyed spiders, and the white-eyed raccoons ate the frogs when they could, but the coal-eyed alligators would devour the raccoons eventually. For each, it was a case of waiting and traveling, waiting and traveling, and by quiet paddling toward a coal-colored pair of eyes we got close enough to a middling gator to have killed it as the old gator hunters would have done, with a .22 bullet shot into one of the red coals, for twenty cents a foot for its belly skin.

Sunrise next morning was another blaze of reds glimpsed through the clouds. A ten-foot alligator cruised close to our platform, belatedly waiting for the couple of coons who had swum over during the night to climb the posts and scavenge our leftovers. So much of nature's picturesqueness is really a series of relentless tests of stamina. This Jurassic beast, like hundreds of its toothy fellows in the Okefenokee that are just as big, floated unobtrusively or lounged on the bank night and day, waiting for hunger to operate irresistibly on the possums, coons, rabbits, deer, and bobcats living on various dabs of land surrounding this wet prairie so that they'd enter the water to swim from one to another to feed. (Overpopulation alone would force most of the year's crop of young to do this, but wise veteran animals wait for autumn, when temperatures fall, to relocate or range about much.) And the herons, watchfully statuesque in shallow water, waited by the minute or hour for some frantic frog, hidden in the mud but smothering for air, to make a desperate dash for breath.

Large birds, with the freedom of the skies, swept toward their hunting grounds to the west—the egrets flapping and sailing, the herons with a rocking slow down-beating flight—while we sat and gazed at their grandeur over our Sierra Club cups of scrambled eggs. The Sierra Club, like any other significant institution, combines bits of the sublime with the ridiculous. What's ridiculous are these smallish metal cups from which its wilderness votaries are supposed to eat all manner of meals, from steaks to soup, with a single spoon, which our particular outfitter provided on a red cord to be worn around the neck betweentimes, along with a hand lens for looking at plants and a whistle for emergencies. All good fun, perhaps—like our leaders' "teachable moments" and "solo time" or "private space"—except that my tentmate, Bill, from *National Geographic,* and I were out of temper because, in order to discipline us for what they claimed was his snoring, they had made us take our tent down that morning, although after canoeing a circuit we would be coming back to the same platform in the afternoon. And sure enough, three miles out, the clouds burst with the first of what would add up to five inches of rain. The wind ribbed the water; everybody was drenched and chilled, though the tree swallows swooped down festively to grab disoriented insects, and wading birds rushed in hasty uncharacteristic glee to grab subsurface creatures that the wild water forced out. Viva and I in the last canoe watched the black paddles of the eight craft ahead of us rising and falling, like fish crows descending to feed and rising swiftly to descend again. She teased me, but then assuaged Bill's and my chagrin by installing him with Nancy and her in her own tent and me in Mary Mouse's, to shiver, be comforted, and sleep.

It was a rough storm, testing everybody's cheeriness. Our IBM man performed a comedy routine that had worked well, he said, during bad thunderstorms on dude-ranch rides in the Rockies. He seemed to be the most Thoreauvian of us all and most objected to the regimented parts of the trip, but everyone who signs up for wilderness trips has a soft spot somewhere, a feeling for wild things—which is to say for the underdog, nowadays—underneath a frequently quirky, abrasive, or camouflaged exterior. We all had in common a respect for privacy, individualism, and self-sufficiency, a love of birds, plants, and animals, and because we were, in the manner of the eighties, a "single-issue constituency," we had no political arguments, being content to ignore everything else. Gone with the 1970s was the unanimity of the old alliance on civil rights, a dovish foreign policy, and the "ecology movement." When one of our number said she believed in shooting any robber you caught in your gunsights, somehow none of the rest of us objected, because she'd also said that she believed in "protecting God's creatures."

Next day the sun smiled, and the flocks of ibises arrived again, with their splendid red bills. We paddled to Floyd's Island, past blooming iris, pipewort flowers like upright hatpins, and the flowers that the bladderworts send up like innocuous buttercups while the voracious bulk of the plant beneath the surface consumes minute crustaceans and water larvae. Everywhere there was neverwet, its spadix shaped like a thick pencil, white with a golden tip. And when the bottom lifted under us and scraped our canoes, we entered into effusions of greenbrier, wild grape, pepperbush ("poor man's soap"), yaupon, holly, titi and gallberry (both favorites of the honeybees), and, especially, thickets of the "hurrah bush" (a relative of fetterbush and staggerbush), as the swampers called it because it is so dense that anyone struggling through might wish to yell "Hurrah!" at the end.

We saw and heard an otter chirping to its mate; saw the personable kind of lizard known as a skink on a loblolly bay tree; heard yellow-throated and prothonotary warblers—the latter golden orange—and mockingbirds, catbirds, red-winged blackbirds, and one painted bunting, which was blue, green, red, and brown. On the island were some magnificent live oak trees that the loggers had spared, one with resurrection ferns spreading high from a crotch and another with a beehive inside. Floyd's Island was the site of the Seminoles' last encampment in Okefenokee. Under their resident chief, Bolek, called "Billy Bowlegs" by the whites, they raided a settler family on Cowhouse Island, on the northeastern edge of the swamp, killed seven people, and then retreated most of its width and much of its length to Billy's Island, pursued by troops under General Floyd, who chased them on here, whence they escaped unscathed.

On Billy's Island, a little later, we encountered a diamondback rattlesnake and saw where the "Good Black" and "Bad Black" cypress loggers had been quartered (the latter were prisoners who'd been bailed out of jail), as well as the site of the "juke" where Good Blacks danced, or "juked," on Saturday nights.

The sun seethed on the currents in myriad popping points of light or lay like a platter of gold where the water was still. Because of the peat's tannic acid, Okefenokee's water itself is the color of dark tea and a perfect reflecting medium, so that on the narrower waterways, lined with gum and bay trees and cypresses festooned with Spanish moss, a photograph not only is arrestingly beautiful but may look the same upside down. When a wind blows, however, the resplendent image of the trees on the water is broken into zebra zigzags.

We finished crossing the swamp at Stephen Foster State Park, on the Fargo side, where the Suwanee River starts flowing in earnest, and paddled six miles downstream past many Ogeechee lime trees, whose fruit makes good pies and preserves, and water tupelo and black tupelo gum trees, whose blossoms are a nearly peerless honey-making source for the bees, and then camped at the fishing camp of a famous old-time bootlegger and guide named Lem Griffis, now an apiary and campground run by Arden, his gentler, law-abiding son. The river was at its highest level in ten years—the people on Wilderness Southeast's previous trip had eaten a canebrake rattlesnake that had been flooded out of its usual holes—and we built big bonfires for our final two evening confabs, with mosquitoes whining near us of a size that swampers say "will dress out at a pound."

We had white stubble beards and white-and-black beards, and the women were as sturdy as those with the beards. Our lawyer said that when the bull alligators in rut were bellowing, it was just what he'd heard the hippos in Kenya say: "*I want some!*" Our doctor repeated to us several times that he'd "promised my wife's daddy thirty-seven years ago that I was going to take care of her, and he would kill me now if he saw her in this swamp." But she was the one who had rappeled down cliffs and soloed in an airplane. Our Thoreauvian IBM man—whom my heart went out to because he kept trying to pretend that there weren't eighteen people on this trip—grew quickly impatient when the sociable moments veered at Viva's urging toward a conventional group-grope session. He would grab his wife's hand and say this was their wedding anniversary, for God's sake, and they had to get to their tent—which really did have the desired effect the first night.

By the time we quit paddling, my shoulders were getting stronger and my back felt delightfully limber, as though I could push on to California if only some of the populace between Fargo and there would clear out of the way. Both Viva and I were heading for solitary spells in isolated portions of the Appalachians. Bill, the photographer, on the other hand, was returning to Miami, the base from which he often goes to crisis assignments in Central America. Nancy, equally a modernist—her mother a socialite, her father an airline pilot, and she a Miamian who had chosen to go to the University of Vermont—was on her way to a career in wildlife management. More and more women are entering the environmental fields and gradually transforming the predatory bent of those vocations. The wardens used to be hunters who preyed on lesser hunters—who poached the poachers— but now the swing will be to a more protective, even "maternal" approach, which will be necessary if wildlife is to survive at all. And this is going to be how the wilderness will be experienced in the next century: in groups of twenty people, by prearrangement, led by specialists in group dynamics to preselected birding or bear-viewing sites, and efficiently out. Otherwise there won't be any wilderness.

I poked around Fargo a little and looked up Barney Cone, aged sixty-six, who has retired after many years as the refuge's patrol officer and has the likably boiled look of W. C. Fields. As we talked, riding around in his pickup truck, he would raise two fingers from the wheel every time that we met another vehicle. Before his day, he said with a lawman's aplomb, plume hunters had combed the swamp after egrets, and when plume sales had been outlawed, the swampers went after gators. When the refuge was established, in 1937, that had to be stopped. He'd paddled its water trails with a partner by night for thirty-five dollars a week, watching for the gas lamps that the poachers mesmerized the animals with. "At first, if you made a case against a poacher, the judge would just about run you out of court. But gradually it got to where they were sending them off for a year and a day," he said.

The local sheriffs wouldn't help him, but the state game wardens sometimes did, and the sheriffs at least didn't interfere with him the way they warned the moonshiners about the revenuers' raids. Not until "nineteen and thirty-eight" had a paved road reached Fargo, so before then the moonshiners had pretty much run everything during the rainy season, when the roads were mud, and the dry season, when the sand was a trap. "Shine" sold for $4.50 for a five-gallon jug. A hundred-pound sack of sugar cost that (if you didn't raise your own), but you made two jugs of shine with that hundred pounds, soaking it for three days with a mash consisting of fifty pounds of cornmeal and fifty pounds of whole-grained rye that had already soaked together for three days to get good and sour, then "running it off" (distilling it).

"How else did people make money?" I asked him.

"Oh, dipping turpentine, or at the sawmills," he said. "They cut cypress for crossties for the railroad, they cut black gum trees and water oaks for plywood and boxes. Sold peat moss. Raised those backwoods cows that you didn't have to feed, or the hogs too. Ate wild meat and huckleberries," he added with a laugh, though he'd stopped eating bear meat after a plague of screwworms reached Georgia in the 1930s and bored into the bears—burrowed into the cattle too, till the cattle got so sick the bears started catching up with them, and of course that sent the swampers out after the bears with their dogs. "That hurt the bears a whole hell of a lot. The beekeepers were already after them."

The price for alligator skins had risen from twenty cents a foot at the turn of the century to fifteen dollars a foot in the 1960s, but in 1955, during a drought, the swamp suffered four major fires, the gators each time going into their holes underwater to try to survive. Even so, he found many of them whose tails had been scorched because they hadn't been able to get all of themselves inside. Without law enforcement the population would have plunged. The hunters used a "pig pole" with a barbed spear or hook on the end for fishing up the animals that sank after they had "shined" them with the lamp and shot them from real close. "They'd fill the boat and pile them out, kill some more and pile them out, four or five at once, and go on ahead and next day come back to all of the piles and skin them out. Or in a dry spell, they walked the swamp looking for holes in the mat where a gator was and haul him out and ax him in the head.

"You know what a redneck was?" Barney continued with a chuckle. "A redneck didn't just mean somebody who got himself sunburned out in the fields. It meant a man who only buttoned his shirt collar to go to church, so his neck looked chafed on Monday morning."

I went back to Folkston, on the east side of Okefenokee, and talked with Ralph Davis, who's seventy-three and mostly

Irish but one-eighth Cherokee. He says he helped survey the refuge's boundaries. Claims jokingly that, after that, the government men chased him for forty years in airboats and motorboats because of his poaching, until finally they had sense enough to save themselves some money by hiring him. He says by then he knew the swamp so well at night he could hardly find his way around in it during the day. He'd killed maybe a thousand gators, though tried to limit his kill to bulls by leaving the pools alone where he saw babies. He got a dollar a foot for skins in the Depression, and since he could kill twenty-five or thirty in a four- or five-day excursion, it was very good money.

Mr. Davis seems quite "Cherokee" in his sentiments, bad-mouthing the Seminoles, saying that the seven-footers of an unknown tribe buried in mounds before history began were probably "a better class of Indian" and joking about "hundred-and-fifty-pound coons" coming as tourists to the swamp "to look at the coons." In a kinder tone, he speaks of how he loves the smell of "spirits of turpentine," which is best from a green young tree—you can put either crude pine gum or its spirits directly onto a cut or pour the liquid on the dressing after bandaging it. And a few drops on a lump of sugar will defeat a cold. From March to October was the gathering season. The pine trees were precisely scarred, about chest-high, and a two-quart can was hung on a nail underneath to catch the drippings, emptied once a month. They got paid from thirty to fifty dollars for a fifty-gallon barrel, and the resin left after the spirits were boiled off was used to caulk their boats with. (More famously, by pitchers in baseball.)

Davis, a chair-loving fellow but vociferously folksy, claims his father named Bugaboo Island—the wildest island left in the swamp—once when the wind caused two trees to rub together all night, moaning above his campsite. Honey Island had bee trees, and Blackjack Island blackjack oaks. John's Negro Island was where a slave stolen from a man named John was secreted. The Chesser family arrived in "eighteen and fifty-eight," and their homestead on Chesser Island, now watched over by him, has been restored by the refuge management, with its cane-boiling syrup equipment, its "hog gallows" and toothed otter traps, its gourds hanging

up for purple martins to nest in and clear the air of mosquitoes and flies, the whole yard scraped bare so wandering
snakes or scorpions would have no place to hide. While he
was growing up, the Chessers cultivated melons, corn, peas,
beans, and sweet potatoes, and ran loose livestock in the
swamp, and grew about thirty acres of sugarcane, which
made a clear, sweet syrup of renown. A bobcat skin was worth
only fifty cents and a fox three dollars, but in the winter he
and his friends would go out after fur for a week or so in a
twelve-foot dugout, carrying their traps, their bacon and
sweet potatoes, pushing themselves with an eight-foot pole
with a Civil War bayonet strapped to the top end to fight off
alligators, planning to meet other kids who were trapping at
a certain "house" in the middle of the swamp and camp
there, drink and swap stories, butchering a deer or a "piney-
woods rooter"—one of the bristly, gray, big-headed, big-
tusked, wild-running hogs. At dawn they'd let out a couple of
old-time Okefenokee two-mile, one-minute hollers to wake
up the sun and wake up the swamp.

Okefenokee is sometimes called the Yellowstone among
wildlife refuges, it's so important. Yet as I drove around its
perimeter it seemed awfully small and fragile, like a drop in
a dynamo, when I knew what encircled it. In the town of
Waycross I met Johnny Hickox, a round-faced, mellow-
looking gentleman of fifty-nine in gold-rimmed glasses, with
a straight short smile, a farmer's sloping shoulders, and bib
overalls. Though neither a retired lawman nor a reformed
outlaw, he grew up on Cowhouse Island, "dipping turpentine" from the collection pails for sixty-five cents a day in his
first job, then hunting alligator belly skins, until, after World
War II, you could make fifty cents an hour at the sawmill.
The steers his father raised in the swamp grass sold for only
ten dollars, and bearskins had no better use than being cut
into wads to stuff in the holes the pigs dug under the fences,
to scare them back inside. ("Most pitiful thing, to hear them
holler for mercy if a bear caught them!") His grandfather at
the turn of the century had earned only ten cents a day,
logging cypresses, including the services of his horse. But in
that era you could buy swampland for eleven cents an acre.

A guy and he would spend two weeks "pushing a pole,"
wandering a whimsical course from Waycross to Fargo with

a load of traps, and sell whatever furs they'd caught, then enjoy another two weeks poling back, with many stops. No swamper ever starved in the swamp. There were so many fish to catch that "you had to hide from them to put your bait on," Johnny says. Four-pound pickerel, two-pound "mud-cats," and the smaller "buttercats," which are catfish with yellow on their bellies. Twelve-pound bass, swarms of perch, and delicious soft-shell turtles. His great-great-grandfather had fathered twenty-one children, by only one wife—which is one reason nearly everybody around this patch of swamp seems to be related to him—but nobody went hungry.

There is no lawman-outlaw edge to Johnny Hickox; and from the tourist park where he works, he took me out along the "Wagon Road," a water trail that logs used to be floated over, to "Sapling Prairie" for a picnic in a jonboat with a light motor on it—though he paused to demonstrate his push-poling for fun, telling me it was a skill that, like riding a bike, you never lose the hang of. He said these old water trails "tuckered out" if not cleared by a government cutter boat or a big alligator swimming through occasionally, and he pointed out a few other trails leading off through the wet maze of sedges, lilies, swamp grass, and bushes to former haunts where he had camped and earned a living with his ax and fish lines and traps. A gator was eating bonnet lily roots, while a "Florida cooter" turtle steered well clear of it. He pointed out swamp iris, and wampee, with an arrow-shaped leaf and hot roots that the Indians seasoned meat with, and Virginia chain fern, and "soap bush," whose leaves make suds when scrubbed, and "hen-and-biddies" pitcher plants, named for the lineup of their bloom and leaves, and pipe-worts, also called "ladies' hatpins."

"I was married to this swamp," he said happily, though he has four grandchildren already and his wife still pampers him. He showed me what bears like to eat—black gum ber-ries, greenbrier berries, highbush blueberries, live oak acorns, wild-hive honey, and palmetto fruit—as if to indicate how much abundance they also found here.

We ate our sandwiches on a "house" on Dinner Pond, ten miles out, facing one of only two virgin stands of cypress trees left in Okefenokee, and listened to a Carolina wren sing *tea-kettle, tea-kettle, TEA-kettle.* Two paired cranes flew overhead as if they were married. The trees' strange "knees" sticking out of the water and the hanging Spanish moss (which old-timers burned in smudge fires to keep the mosquitoes off) gave us the pleasure of their company, not to be encountered widely in the South anymore because cypress fetches so much as a log and air pollution kills the moss. Eight or nine days' traveling in the jonboat would bring us to the Gulf of Mexico, a happy trip, he said.

Southerners, like New Englanders, whom I know better, are survivors by temperament. But they use talk instead of taciturnity, zaniness instead of stoicism, as their method of getting by, and that's more fun. We agreed, over our tea at Dinner Pond, that neither of us would ever see a wilderness that was as pristine as what we had loved before. But wildernesses have a special value, apart from sheltering so many primeval creatures that elsewhere are nearly gone. The South is becoming homogenized into the rest of America because so many Northerners are moving there. And it may be that regionalism will survive best in wild places such as Okefenokee, where the South is not the "Sunbelt" but remains the South to eye and ear. Cypresses and ibises, wood storks, snowy egrets, timeless turtles, hordes of frogs, hurrah bushes, and Ogeechee lime trees can preserve alive our sense of human as well as natural history.

Revolution

In 1775, the year the American Revolution got started, Jane Austen was born. And William Blake's *Songs of Innocence* was published in 1789, when the French Revolution began. Russia was convulsed by its Red Revolution in 1917, the same year as T. S. Eliot's first book of poems, *Prufrock and Other Observations*, came out. I've been looking up these odd details rather hopefully in a book called *The Timetables of History*, for the obvious reason that 1989 and 1990 were comparably dramatic, and we readers may discover in retrospect that a literary event, momentous but presently unknown to us, coincided with them. We don't know if a new Austen has just been born or a Blake or an Eliot quietly launched, but the surface of contemporary literature has seemed as unruffled by the knifing fin of a genius writing at full tilt as it may have in 1775, 1789, and 1917.

I am oversimplifying (Goethe and Samuel Johnson were active around 1775), but literature does need a period of gestation after seminal events. In 1848, when major revolts broke out in Vienna, Paris, Rome, Berlin, Venice, and other European centers, the best bookish events were James Russell Lowell's *Biglow Papers* and volumes by Elizabeth Gaskell and Dumas fils. Then, however, an eruption occurred—the mid-nineteenth-century glory of *David Copperfield, Moby-Dick,* the young Turgenev and Tolstoy, Flaubert, *Les Misérables,* Whitman, Thoreau, and so on. And in about the same rhythm, a burst of enduring work appeared in the 1920s, a sort of silver age in literature and the arts following the Red Revolution and the First World War.

It's not that the revolution must be a good one; wars, too, in a very few years provoke books. Like a kick in the butt, the force of events wakes slumberous talents up. But many American writers have been operating under the assumption that nothing good *could* happen. The world was careening toward blowing itself to kingdom come, and meanwhile life was in shards and splinters and smithereens. Be absurdist or minimalist or miniaturist or Dada, but don't be "judgmental." Similarly, a hortatory impulse was to be squelched. It was not only that TV sound bites allowed no time for eloquence in politics; the prose of a Jefferson, a Lincoln, or an Emerson would be unstylish from top to bottom.

Those of our fictioneers who weren't deconstructing the novel were disassembling publishing houses by negotiating six- and seven-figure book contracts if they could—you cannot overestimate how important making really big bucks has become to many respected writers—or else, if they couldn't do that, were "networking" and trading off "readings" and visiting appointments with one another on the road to a tenured chair at a university, in whose shallow soil, at sixty thousand dollars a year, they could slowly grow into ornate, small shapes, like a bonsai tree.

Now, I like what money buys, though I think a whole lot of it tends to cut writers off from their material. And I like teaching and regard the extraordinary profusion of writing programs as the latter-day equivalent of Latin: the means by which many adolescents explore the roots and construction of language and learn to organize and elucidate their thoughts. Furthermore, teaching or mentoring (or parenting) at its best is like the she-wolf who patiently, over time, licked and suckled Romulus and Remus into becoming the City of Rome. But the number of earnestly gifted writers engaged in this one occupation has reached preposterous proportions. Maybe the number who have been divorced is also ridiculous, but unlike lifetime job tenure, divorce is at least a state or statement they share with the general populace.

We see in Czechoslovakia and Poland, mirabile dictu, writers who are heads of state—can you imagine? so trusted!—the Czech quoting Jefferson and Lincoln to our Congress, having previously spent years in prison. Is it easy to picture one of our expensive writers, a Tom Wolfe or William Styron, voluntarily leaving his dacha and going to prison under any circumstances for his beliefs (if, for the sake of the argument, one could discern Wolfe's beliefs: he is of the I-am-a-camera school)? I should confess that my bias is toward the idea that establishment writers in one place would be establishment writers in another and that the apparatchiki who speed up or slow down careers in a totalitarian system would hold the same position here. But this is nonsense in certain cases. Norman Mailer, alongside Robert Lowell at the Pentagon in 1967, has already proved he would go to jail. So would Philip Roth, I should think, because of his heartfelt championing of Eastern European writers over a considerable span when scarcely anyone else was paying any attention to them, and the vicarious courage he must have absorbed.

Yet the question is silly, you may respond. After our revolution we did not have czars or dictators, and our writers, from Henry Adams to Saul Bellow, have usually danced at the White House when asked, no matter how witty they waxed at the occupant's expense afterward. Even Thoreau, in inventing civil disobedience in America, only chose to go to jail for one night in 1846, versus Dostoyevsky's compulsory, frightening confinement from 1849 to 1854 for dissident activities. We have a mordant tradition of verbal dissent instead, notable in Mark Twain and his various pups like Kurt Vonnegut and Joseph Heller of these postwar years. And our Lost Generations—both of the much-romanticized F. Scott Fitzgerald ilk, who larked off to Paris, and the Donald Barthelme bunch fifty years later, who believed, like Chicken Little, that the sky was falling and that words on the page should break like a mirror—mainly just wanted to throw up their hands and get away. Nor did anybody sensibly believe Allen Ginsberg's complaint in "Howl" that "I saw the best minds of my generation destroyed by madness, starving hysterical naked,/dragging themselves through the negro streets at dawn looking for an angry fix . . ." We knew such people, but they weren't "the best minds," and it was not necessary that they self-destruct.

Of course, "the negro streets" were a genuine issue. By *Mr. Sammler's Planet* (1970), even so centrist and humane a writer as Bellow, who had declined to slide into the fashionable despair of literary "postmodernism," seemed to have turned peevish in contemplating America, like the returning and disillusioned Henry James, in the spring of 1905, in a New York that "rushed and shrieked," walking out of a Yiddish comedy at a theater on the Lower East Side because "it was a scent, literally, not further to be followed." Bellow and other suddenly neoconservative Jews likewise wanted to pull up the gangplank, or else felt perhaps that their roots on the continent did not go back far enough to encompass blacks as fellow Americans. (Cynthia Ozick wrote in *The New York Times* that American literature doesn't begin for her until Theodore Dreiser. That leaves out *Huckleberry Finn, Moby-Dick,* and whatnot.)

Bellow, the centrist, the Whitman spirit of *The Adventures of Augie March* (1953), had formulated for me the postwar novel: "I am an American, Chicago-born Chicago, that somber city—and go at things as I have taught myself, freestyle, and will make the record in my own way: first to knock, first admitted; sometimes an innocent knock, sometimes a not so innocent. . . ." Remember? Or the Bellow of *Henderson the Rain King,* six years later, in which the heart's ceaseless voice reiterates, "*I want, I want, I want, oh, I want—yes, go on,* I said to myself, *Strike, strike, strike, strike!*" I suppose it presaged the greed of the eighties.

Who's centrist now? Well, E. L. Doctorow and Anne Tyler are humane, accomplished, prolific, and calm in demeanor. But novelists in America have lost a good deal of their moral force, and we ought to cast about a bit, wondering why. Woody Allen's movies appear to have more ethical influence. I asked two college students, and they said that books are "a higher art" than movies because they are the product of single minds, not collaborative, just as the paintings in a museum, also solo creations, are "a higher art," but that you visit great books for pleasure, unassigned, about as often as you visit the oils in a museum. It's kind of a sideways explanation, but it does not convince me that if one of our gifted city writers grew angry enough at the sufferings of the homeless people camped in the streets, he or she couldn't galvanize a huge readership, as John Steinbeck did for *The Grapes of Wrath.* Or that if Mailer had ever gotten his act together after *The Naked and the Dead,* instead of floundering awash in the breadth of his own talent . . . Or that if John Barth had held on to and pyramided upon the zest of *The Sot-Weed Factor* in his succeeding novels . . . Or that if Philip Roth or John Updike had figured out the larger context, within nature, of the antic sex animating their respective oeuvres, which would place it in an explicating relief . . .

There is a steadiness to Updike and a suppleness to Roth bespeaking amplitude and integrity. Neither seems hobbled by the lucre-brutal climate of money-making that has afflicted younger writers who clamber toward brand-name status and that may partly explain why no writer of a more youthful vim (Steinbeck was thirty-six when he did *The Grapes of Wrath*) has hit those mean streets with a spellbinding anger. Updike, in fact, has applied time and vigor to the unmercenary aim of becoming our foremost book critic and man of letters. But this strange dichotomy we accept nowadays of certain authors, like Roth and Updike, writing best about nature indoors, and others, like Peter Matthiessen and Annie Dillard, ghettoized as "nature writers," being masters outdoors, is not inevitable; it didn't use to pertain at all. Turgenev, Melville, Thomas Hardy, Joseph Conrad, William Faulkner, wrote better about both people and the outdoors than any writer now living.

Nature itself has been ghettoized as it shrinks, and writers who do well by it are almost presumed to be gimpy, misshapen in some way—to have spent a year of their childhood in bed, or to stutter, or to "like animals better than people"—to be compensating with bulging muscles in one avenue of the art for a wizened, concealed limb somewhere else. And it's true that Matthiessen's, Barry Lopez's, and Edward Abbey's finest books are rudimentary in their depiction of human beings.

Yet what is happening in America is too complicated to catch vast gobs of in a single book. The million-footed ambitions of John Dos Passos (*U.S.A.*) and Thomas Wolfe (*Look*

Homeward, Angel), which I loved in my teens (like the ideo-
logically impacted tales of Hemingway, as poignantly impec-
cable in style as these seem), have not maintained the same
honest force with which they were created. The fanciful coherence of Faulkner, or of Isaac Bashevis Singer, holds up
better; and who cares whether Mississippi, or corners of Poland, are still "like that"? Bernard Malamud's city fiction had
a comparable cohesiveness (if he didn't match Singer's, it
may have been that he taught too much); and I was amused
one time to hear him blurt out the reason why he thought his
marriage had lasted, while so many other writers' marriages
were falling apart: "I guess it's character," he muttered,
mostly to himself. Character comes in different cloaks, such
as Joan Didion's admirable rage in El Salvador, or the furnace underlying a Toni Morrison novel. Few writers are truly
"nonjudgmental," even the modish ones who tell you how to
snort coke and perform fellatio.

Literature is the study of life: Tom Jones's, Anna Kareni-
na's, Madame Bovary's. To major in English in college should
be as basic a choice as to major in biology, and although
savoring James Joyce or Vladimir Nabokov shades into questions of verbal elegance more than conduct, these have the
rigor of conduct if you carry them far. Did you once read
books in order to learn how to live? And do you still? Don
Quixote's epic issues and gambits, Balzac's kaleidoscope of
vitality, Henry James's cat's cradle of nuances, Defoe's brisk
versatility, Dickens's bravura colorations of evil and good?
Did you want to pack your bags with B. Traven, confront
African wonders with Joyce Cary's humor and Mary Kings-
ley's equanimity, examine the basic enigmas with Dante's panache, be magisterial like George Eliot or as wise as Willa
Cather, or just go for broke like Jay Gatsby? Morality was
inherent in *Gulliver's Travels, Pride and Prejudice, Barchester
Towers, Dead Souls, The House of Mirth, An American Tragedy,
The Magic Mountain*; but maybe it wasn't exactly ethics that
you were after. You longed to live with a whoosh like Jack
London, be loopy like William Saroyan, be lean like Stephen
Crane, though as thoughtful as Virginia Woolf, or go along
with a fine flourish like D. H. Lawrence.

The velocity of celebrity, however, is such that artists are
whisked offstage after fifteen minutes of limelight. New "ma-

jor" books will bring them briefly back, but we no longer have much encouragement to grasp the continuity of any writer's work, and in this age of the bellying ego, virtually no critics to help. The money and spotlight for critics are in huffing and puffing about the movies, a soft punching bag, not books, and the handful of old-line stalwarts like Updike, reviewing in his spare time, and Alfred Kazin, heir to Edmund Wilson but now seventy-five, can't keep up. The end result is this farcical situation where, for instance, no reviewers know how good they think Joyce Carol Oates is, because she has written more books than any critic I know of has bothered to read and thus is always reviewed piecemeal. Imagine the astonished contempt that Wilson, who died twenty years ago, would feel at this lazy state of affairs—or Malcolm Cowley, who single-handedly, by a series of detailed essays, rescued Faulkner from the out-of-print obscurity to which he had sunk by midcentury because nobody had ever painstakingly troubled to fathom the reach of his work.

We needn't cry "That's me!" in literature, but—Flem Snopes, Carrie Meeber—we do need to remember the people in a book. And historically, it's been rare for novelists to write so continually about themselves; until 1940 it would have seemed quite absurd. Is life more difficult and bewildering now? The point can be argued that, flooded with novelty, we have no polestars and, as in a second childhood, have been reorienting ourselves by blindly feeling around our own psyches and bodies. But if we did have that stringent, no-nonsense eye watching the literary carousel (I think a more apt analogy is the Eugene Ionesco play *Rhinoceros,* in which everybody grows a brutalizing and corrupting horn on his face), wouldn't this observer finally break in and say: Hey, you fat cats, and you other guys, who write "experimental" prose but cautiously cling in real life to your professorships, hasn't the group grope gone on long enough? Hasn't the day dawned to let some fresh air in?

Cynicism has become so commonplace that no vocabulary, no mind-set existed for digesting the gleeful events in Eastern Europe. "Glee"—who even remembered the word "glee" anymore—and "gaiety" meant a more complicated condition. Besides the incongruous spectacle of Václev Havel knowing more Lincoln and Jefferson than they do, most

American intellectuals have been further surprised by history because they are unfamiliar of late with *War and Peace*: namely, that masterpiece's Mikhail Gorbachev-like character, Kutuzov, who saves his country by go-slow withdrawals, as well as its epilogue, in which Tolstoy seems to predict or explain events of 1989.

We are a provincial nation, never much concerned with what goes on abroad, a nation of immigrants intent upon getting a foothold first, then conquering a westward frontier, not interested in crossing the ocean again except as a badge of genteel status. So we have hatched remarkably few travel writers and—unless the U.S. military invades a place—need lots of prodding to pay attention to anything overseas. One can scarcely believe, when attending an "A-list" New York literary party, how few of the worthies and luminaries rocking on their heels like pouter pigeons with drinks in their hands, prosperous enough to twinkle back and forth across the Atlantic on magazine junkets or vacation jaunts, have ever been to a southern continent, or wanted to go. There would be no money or creature comfort in it. What they know is Edinburgh, Florence, Salzburg—*you* know the round.

O.K.: Africa, South America, Asia—the curiosity of most of our main-stem writers does not extend so far. (It took an Australian, Thomas Keneally, to come back with a first-rate novel, *To Asmara*, from Africa's twenty-eight-year Red Sea war in Eritrea.) But what's at home? Well, we have a drug crisis, a regular plague. And how has drug popping been treated by writers for the past thirty years? Playfully, as a rule; sort of like John O'Hara on the subject of speakeasies. And in numerous circles, if you yourself didn't smoke or sniff you were regarded as not very promising material. Drugs were supposed to be work-enhancing as well as life-enhancing to many a literary figure. We're talking about not just William Burroughs, Paul Bowles, Tennessee Williams, Truman Capote, and jet-set or avant-garde-mag types, but Mailer and so on.

And crime? Crime, which leaches city life of its fabric and fun like an acid, was romanticized and made morally "relative." Murderers were kissable to Capote. Mailer, as well, had a tropism toward murderers (even stabbed his wife); and

337

a variety of more effete, "existential" admirers of the modern French novel took a parallel though intellectualized view of cruel, grubby crimes.

And racism, our special American blight? Racism expressed in print against blacks and Jews has been out of bounds since perhaps Mencken's day, but a casual racism referring to Arabs has been endemic among a great many of our best, brightest writers for the past generation or two.

Common sense, you might think, would have divined that expecting drugs to enhance your life was pathetic; that crime was about as romantic as cancer; that racism directed at Arabs was corrupting, would kick like a rifle and end with a backlash; but we are dealing with voguishness here. How about AIDS? AIDS is as complex in its origins and victimization as in its medical effects (I wrote about its sister retrovirus, "green monkey disease," in Africa in 1977), but it spread with a faxlike speed, as Randy Shilts recounts in his bravely frank book, *And the Band Played On*, because of a gale of often icy promiscuity. The extremes were outré, such as fist fucking or marathon ejaculatory frenzies performed through a row of "glory holes" bored in a barroom wall; but milder modes, too, employed the excretory orifice in a manner that mammals had all but stopped using seventy to a hundred million years ago and that tore lesions in the rectal lining, through which the strange, savage virus entered. Writers in numbers witnessed all this (I lived in Greenwich Village these twenty-plus years), but forbore to comment for fear of becoming unpopular.

Some novelists *were*, however, in the meantime chronicling a delirium of change—Walker Percy, Robert Coover, Louise Erdrich, Robert Stone, Don DeLillo—as others produced more affectionate, less alarmist portraits of the nation's state—John Irving, John Nichols, Bobbie Ann Mason. Maybe unfairly, though, so much else seemed small-bore, miniaturized, "minimal," that fans of the form kept waiting for a talent to fledge that would grab for a great gaudy tale—a lift like *Portnoy* wedded to John Barth's scope, or Bellow's judgment combined with Mailer's daring. I. B. Singer gradually came to seem like the only American writer of genius alive. Which was nobody's fault; we were in a trough. But Singer wrote God-filled work. That was a help to him: that and possibly his lengthy daily walks and avoidance of constant money hustles or windbag teaching.

But can you imagine? God-filled work, and from an author who didn't eat chicken, not in order to protect his arteries but "for the sake of the chicken." American and British writers were flabbergasted that educated Muslims (leaving Ayatollah Khomeini out of it) were offended by Salman Rushdie's ridicule of God and "Mahound" in *The Satanic Verses*. In the beginning their sympathy for the author was aroused because he wouldn't be able to flog his book, *do his tour!* The idea that religion could be a life-or-death matter at this fin de millennium floored people. Surely he could hide out, as dithering writers do from angry creditors, the tax man, crazed fans, or libeled former friends, until the whole fuss blew over? Most of them had never seen a mosque unless maybe under Israeli police supervision in Jerusalem, and if God wasn't dead, then He just inhabited *Memories of a Catholic Girlhood*. I hold no brief for Islam, but this fleering assumption that God is either dead or a plaything helps explain why my reductive colleagues—and they are legion—both in their work and their public personae have shown no anguish at the holocaust that is quickly consuming the natural world, and thereby have countenanced it.

The arts of self-advertisement have saturated our credulity until books of genuine legerdemain lose punch. Can't we be modern, instead of "postmodern," again, even specifying that life of itself is good? From Hawthorne to Nathanael West, we have masterpieces of private vision, if you don't like crusaders' books. But there has been a feeling lately that to be thought ethical would be an embarrassment. If not the horn of success, people wear on their faces Pinocchio's nose. Hyperventilating, posing for *People,* they have lost that instinct for self-effacement which is a writer's talisman, at least in his salad days, and that precious fluidity—turning scatterbrained, yet bloating and stiffening.

You remember the old saw that a writer's career should be like a ballplayer's. First the high hard barn-burning fastball that no one can hit. Then, as that loses its edge, the big jughandle or "yellowhammer" curve (from the flight of a "yellowhammer," or flicker, a bird). Then, when both curveball and fastball fade, the huge blooping change-up and spitball and knuckler, to carry the pitcher on for a few more years. Our literature, at this fin de siècle, lacks repertoire.

The twin elements of a life lived intelligently are fidelity and spontaneity, and if it turns out that life isn't absurd, that we're probably not going to blow ourselves up, that God may be alive, these are the virtues we need. How sad that our literature rather lacks both.

Revolution II: The Sequel

Academic politics, which are so often a mess of razor cuts and rabbit punches, have become a tank trap lately. For the past year I had been watching people flunk the litmus tests of political correctness with a bystander's detachment, being, I thought, a standard sort of liberal. I had watched Martin Luther King deliver his I-have-a-dream speech at the Lincoln Memorial in 1963, and tore my draft card in half and sent it to Lyndon Johnson to protest the Vietnam War, a year later. But at my fifty-eighth birthday party, my insouciance dissolved. A fellow English teacher with champagne glass in hand offered me his mordant congratulations "on being the first person ever fired from Bennington College for opposing sodomy."

I was startled; just four days earlier, the department had voted to rehire me. He in turn was surprised I hadn't been notified of the reversal. After that vote, several students from the Lesbian/Gay/Bisexual Alliance on campus had suddenly charged me with "homophobia," not on the basis of my teaching or any personal acquaintance with me but solely because of two or three sentences I had pub-

lished in *Esquire* six months before. This essay, which ran
with no fuss in the *Manchester Guardian* afterward, had crit-
icized the greed, talking-head ego-slavering, provincialism,
racism, and romanticism of drugs and crime I saw in much
of the current literary scene. About the AIDS epidemic, I
briefly said that the disease had spread with faxlike speed
because of a gale of often icy promiscuity enjoyed through
an orifice that mammals had all but stopped using sexually
when the cloaca was abandoned seventy to a hundred million years ago. As a nature writer, I argued that anal sex is
dangerous because it's not provided for physiologically, not
because it is morally wrong. I'd lived in various neighborhoods in Greenwich Village for a quarter of a century, witnessing the Gay Revolution in both good aspects and bad,
had tried promiscuity and anal intercourse myself, and
thought I'd earned the right to a few feisty words on the
subject.

For a while after my firing, I settled into the paralysis
one reads about in memoirs by writers blacklisted during the
1950s for advancing unfashionable ideas. My own college
years had coincided with McCarthyism, and my teachers'
mood at Harvard had been darkened by the twelve-story
leap of the famous critic F. O. Matthiessen when he was
under fire for being a Communist dupe. Then, in a couple of
months, as my spirits picked up, I sought out and talked with
two of the "LGB" students, telling them that my free speech
was theirs and that academic freedom is based on the notion
that if everybody's ideas are the same, we don't need univer-
sities or magazines. I said I'd been called a "queer" and a
"Commie" in prep school for listening to classical music with
close friends on football afternoons. At college, much of
Dartmouth's student body had marched by my window one
Saturday on their way to the Harvard stadium, shouting
"fairy" at me because I was indoors, "grinding" at my homework.

The Bennington students told me their protest had not
been spontaneous but had been instigated by a professor
who showed them the offending article after the faculty
vote to rehire me. He is a man who says he started writing
at the age of eight (as I did) and has amassed a forty-
thousand-page unpublished diary, but our only quarrel that

I can remember was over hiring as a teacher of Chinese a Confucian scholar whom the Beijing authorities had imprisoned for twenty-one years. He'd dug out river mud to spread on the labor-camp fields—"Les Misérables," as he calls the experience—for political incorrectness, indeed.

Academia begs for a C. P. Snow novel. Another figure in this contretemps wrote his thesis on Eros and *Tristam Shandy*, teaches a course on "The Sadeian Woman," and says he is "writing a book about Lying." But one of an essayist's jobs is to push on the seesaw of public opinion, reconsider eclipsed orthodoxies, and air bottom-drawer ideas. My teaching career began at the New School for Social Research in New York in 1963, yet our 1950s generation, besides watching McCarthyism on campus, had been abuzz with quips about Freudian slips ("*Sigmund Freud is overjoyed*"), which seemed a fresh concept, and other ambiguities. We joked about "H.D.," by which, being bisexual at heart, like most young men, we meant "Homosexual Dread." So if the young gays at Bennington, with their edgy charm and French-movie glasses, had come to me after the *Esquire* polemic had been handed to them and said, "You're an old fart and you're suffering from B.O. and H.D.," I would hardly have minded. Then we could have shaken hands, gotten acquainted, and they might not have wanted to have me fired. But I still would have needed to explain to them some of the rudiments of freedom of speech and exchanging ideas. That's where my colleagues failed them and me.

The vote switch occurred as *Newsweek* was running a cover story on political correctness, "The Thought Police," and it was part of a nationwide surge of hysteria on campuses, yet within our department ejecting me seemed quite original and "unexpected," as the chairwoman later told me. She, like the preceding chairman, is struggling to complete her Ph.D. thesis after many years and is not a confident leader. Our department is fractured, and the college is a bit jittery because enrollment is down and the faculty and administration are at loggerheads and three students in a year and a half, male and female, have sought legal or procedural redress after alleged sexual incidents with faculty members. I have appealed my case to the Personnel Review Committee.*

At any rate, we Americans seem not to be good with dissent. Even the tolerant are intolerant of unorthodoxy. Minorities are catching the hectoring tone of majoritarians toward heterodox opinions, and our colleges are turning inhospitable to diversity.

---

*The Personnel Review Committee decided that an "injustice" had been done, and at the suggestion of the president of the college, the board of trustees voted to rehire me, six months after the original, reversed vote on the charge of "homophobia." The novelist Robert Stone, for the Freedom-to-Write Committee of PEN, a writers' organization, later wrote to Bennington's president on this matter: "A writer's freedom to imagine on paper is essential to the process of literature. The writer requires scope to speculate, to reduce, to draw paradox and explore irony, to conduct a dialectic examination of ideas and notions. Words cast shadows; they have primary and subsidiary meanings and a vast array of associations. The best and most memorable writing does not always reinforce our rightmindedness, nor should it. The best writers often catch us off guard and make us uneasy. In doing so, they serve our inner life. Because we value art and reason we permit them their reflections, suitable and unsuitable. This is the essence of artistic freedom. . . ."

On a wider scale, Stone's statement sums up as well the Salman Rushdie affair, which at first had seemed so much to revolve around a famous author's right to hawk his wares and appeared to feed into well-grooved Western bigotries, but then became, not an issue of talk-show appearances and book sales, but real free expression and life and death. It left behind the hucksterism of the eighties and served to sober the West's literati.

Reunion

hat does life mean? Or how, at least, can one make a difference? More modestly, how does one go about keeping one's footing? We go to college partly to learn these things, and recently I returned to my thirty-fifth reunion for another go at a lifelong project. My classmates, privileged people with the head start that Harvard had given them, had worked hard to feather their nests, but I couldn't see how we offered much of a lesson at making a difference. Perhaps that's why the world stays so much the same.

I like reunions for their lion-lies-down-with-the-lamb aspect, however—the momentary illusion of a Peaceable Kingdom. A navy war planner chats with a flute teacher. But people seemed more subdued than at the twenty-fifth, because they knew by now that they had had their best run. To my question of what that was, a stockbroker mentioned self-deprecatingly that he had once "bought at two, sold at six hundred." Lawyers had slowed down. A surgeon had come a cropper and was "doing paperwork triage" in a salaried position at an insurance company. Our children were at the forefront of many discussions, it being acknowledged that if we hadn't made a difference, maybe they would.

My daughter is growing up well, and in four decades of work I have written the particular books I wanted to write in the daydreams of my youth, plus others I didn't imagine then. I can foresee dying, therefore, with a certain sense of fulfillment. Yet I don't dream well—I have nightmares. My mother, on the other hand, who is eighty-seven, does dream quite happily. She has "sweet dreams," she says, and from her manner when she wakes up, I believe her. But she is of a generation of women whose career dreams were stifled. Hers were. Thus my daydreams versus her night dreams are at issue. She tells me disingenuously that she has a "clear conscience" and dreams just of her friends—no divorces, and so on—while my nights are gnawed.

You may recall when you first heard the term "missionary position," referring a bit jeeringly to sex performed in a way conducive to having children. It was about the same time you last heard the phrase "God's green earth" and was meant to imply at a minimum that straightforward sex was boring (though the missionaries I've known have been Catholic celibates and not boring). I don't view the efflorescence of sexual excess of our era as being more extreme than the naked excesses of greed on concurrent display. But neither could go on forever. Stress makes even greed become carcinogenic after a while, or wrings us dry. Of course, the nature of life is that good behavior becomes carcinogenic too. Drinking milk eventually gives you heart attacks, and sunshine, cataracts.

I don't speak as someone who stood comfortably apart from the excessive eighties, yet lately I have been serving on grand juries, which in the court system of the state of New York means you are fingerprinted and interviewed to make sure you are a solid citizen of presentable appearance and middling age. (Petit-jury pools, from which final justice is dispensed, are not so intended to represent the established order and are drawn from voting lists by lot, instead.) Sitting on a grand jury, you may hear a hundred crimes testified to, in skeleton form, and besides all of this having the salubrious effect of turning you off mystery stories—crime has no pain, no *commitment*, in mystery stories, and from the vantage point of a jury room they soon come to seem like a whorish genre—the weeks of testimony give food for thought.

Reunions, grand juries: What else do I do when I have time? Well, when I was young, drafted into the U.S. Army, I got myself into the medical corps, for the reverberations of the experience. Once there, in search of privacy to write a novel, I became partly a diener, an arcane word from the German for "servant," which pathologists use for the assistant who helps them perform a postmortem. I sawed open skulls and sewed up cadavers, my reward being the solitude of the morgue to write in at night when other privates were in barracks. Cancers, fractures, quiescence—delving into the body's secrets, I looked death in the face, so to speak. Like looking at these bank robbers and murderers in a New York court.

Do I still hope to find the meaning of life? No, it's footing I'm after and food for thought, if curiosity deserves such a dignified title. Being often employed as a "nature writer," I've seen a lot of the greener earth: big trees, spacious rivers, and what in scientific circles is called "megafauna." True solitude is a din of bird song, seething leaves, whirling colors, or a clamor of tracks in the snow. Though many people go to the country to "get away," anybody who makes a living from nature faces it as a mob of details, a thousand spiral-notebook pages of details, such as how throaty and peppy crows grow when the temperature rises from zero to thirty degrees. The question of whether it's God's green earth is not center stage, except in the sense that if so, one is reminded with some regularity that He may be dying.

But I was outside last night at 3:00 A.M. with insomnia— this not in the city—and heard three painless screamings. This was Vermont; they were discrete, distant sounds, from as many directions, and I sat down in the cold moonlit grass to figure them out. One was from the little steel fabricating mill located in the valley, which must have added an extra shift to fill a rush order. The second was from a car, probably a drunk's, cornering on the highway. And the third was a coyote family, parents and progeny, rallying each other.

The coyotes' high tremolo howls sounded sweet to me because I am not a rabbit, but all three, even the drunk's tire squeals, were welcome company in the absence of airplanes, chain saws, eighteen-wheel trucks, and the cacophony of other noises that echo in daylight on this same hill. I go to the country for peace, not silence—peace being three painless screamings, one of them a coyote family collecting its wits for a hunt, after the forty simultaneous shrieks and rumbling roars of a great city. Peace is relative.

Then a pair of owls caught the spirit and made a fourth voice. That was perfect. That was just right. What more could one ask? That was enough to quiet my nerves and put me to sleep.

Acknowledgments

These essays originally appeared in various publications:

"West on the Zephyr" as "Passing Views" in *Harper's Magazine*. Copyright © January 1991 by Edward Hoagland.

"From Canada, by Land" as "Three Trains Across Canada" in *Travel and Leisure* magazine. Copyright © March 1987 by Edward Hoagland.

"Up the Black to Chalkyitsik" excerpted in *House and Garden*. Copyright © June 1984 by Edward Hoagland; in *The Manchester Guardian*. Copyright © March 31, 1991, by Edward Hoagland; in *Outside* magazine. Copyright © May 1992 by Edward Hoagland.

"In Praise of John Muir" in *Anteaus*. Copyright © 1984/1986 by Edward Hoagland.

"Holy Fools" in *The Nation*. Copyright © September 16, 1991 by Edward Hoagland.

"Maximize" as "On the Literary Congress" in *The New York Times Book Review*. Copyright © January 11, 1986, by The New York Times Company. Reprinted by permission.

"Balancing Act" Copyright © 1991 by Edward Hoagland. Originally appeared in *Bad Trips* by Keith Fraser. Published by Vintage Books; in *The Manchester Guardian*. Copyright © 1991 by Edward Hoagland.